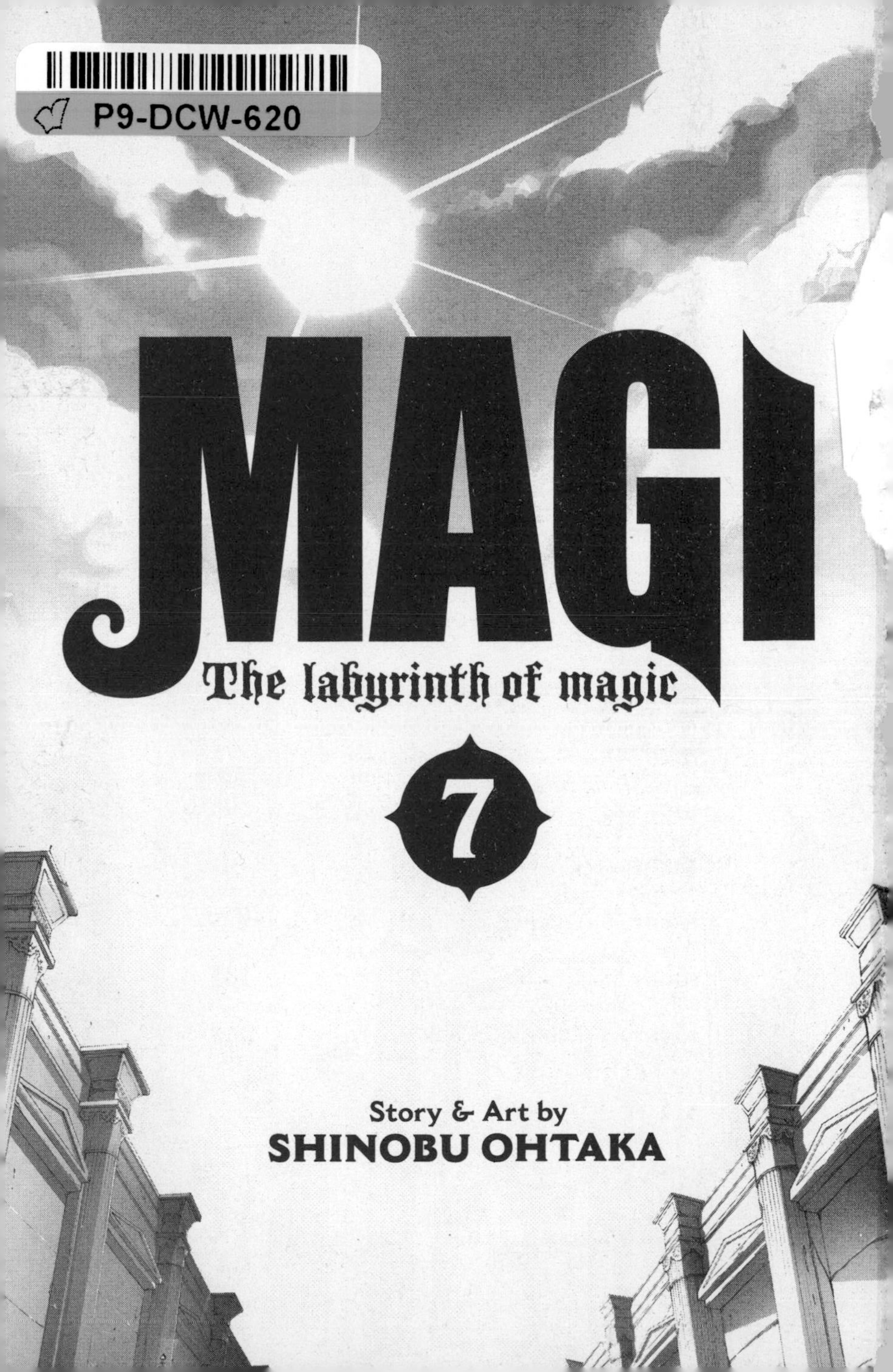

MAGI
The labyrinth of magic

7

Story & Art by
SHINOBU OHTAKA

MAGI
The labyrinth of magic

7

CONTENTS

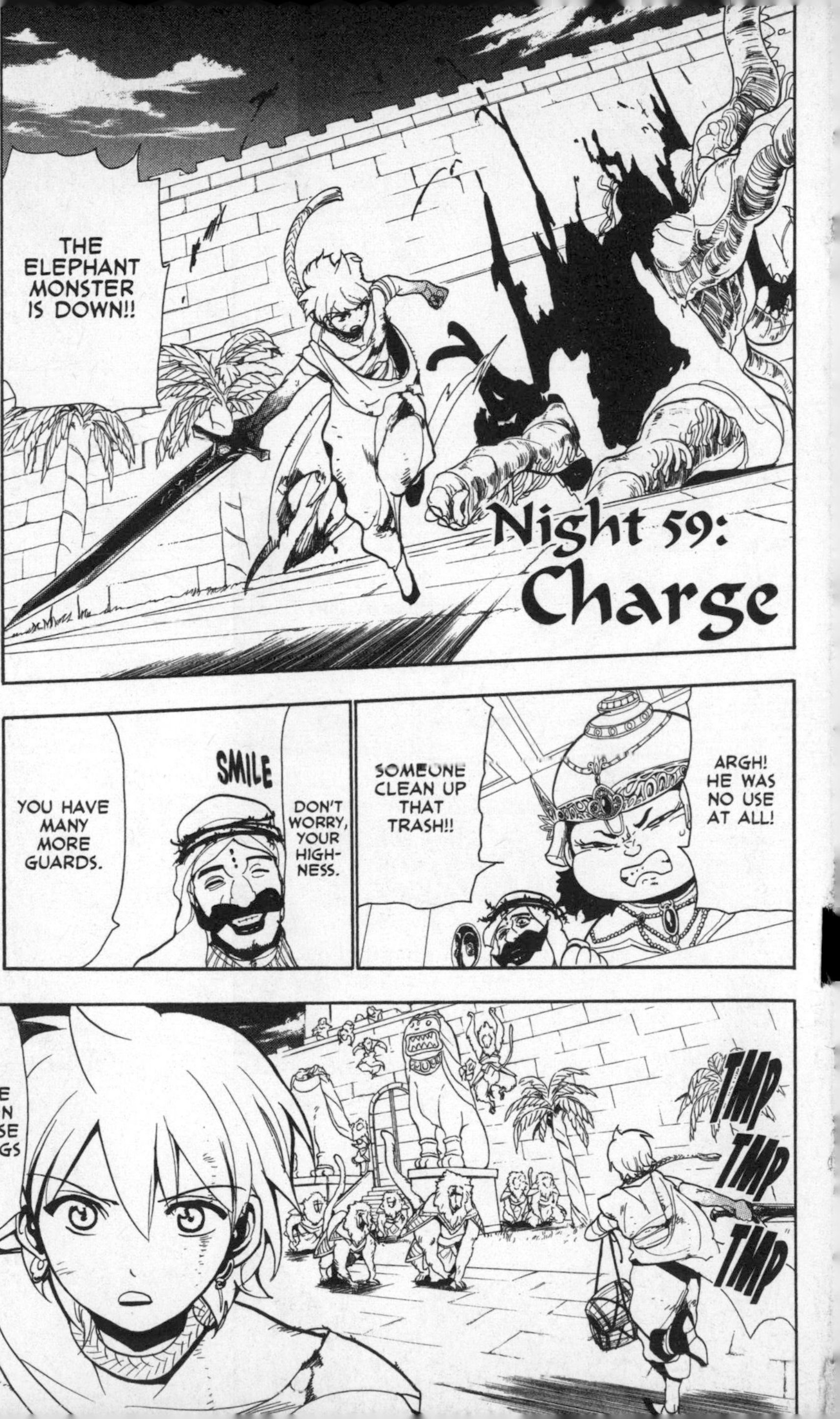
THE ELEPHANT MONSTER IS DOWN!!
Night 59: Charge
ARGH! HE WAS NO USE AT ALL!
SOMEONE CLEAN UP THAT TRASH!!
SMILE
DON'T WORRY, YOUR HIGH-NESS.
YOU HAVE MANY MORE GUARDS.
TMP TMP TMP
I'VE SEEN THOSE THINGS ...

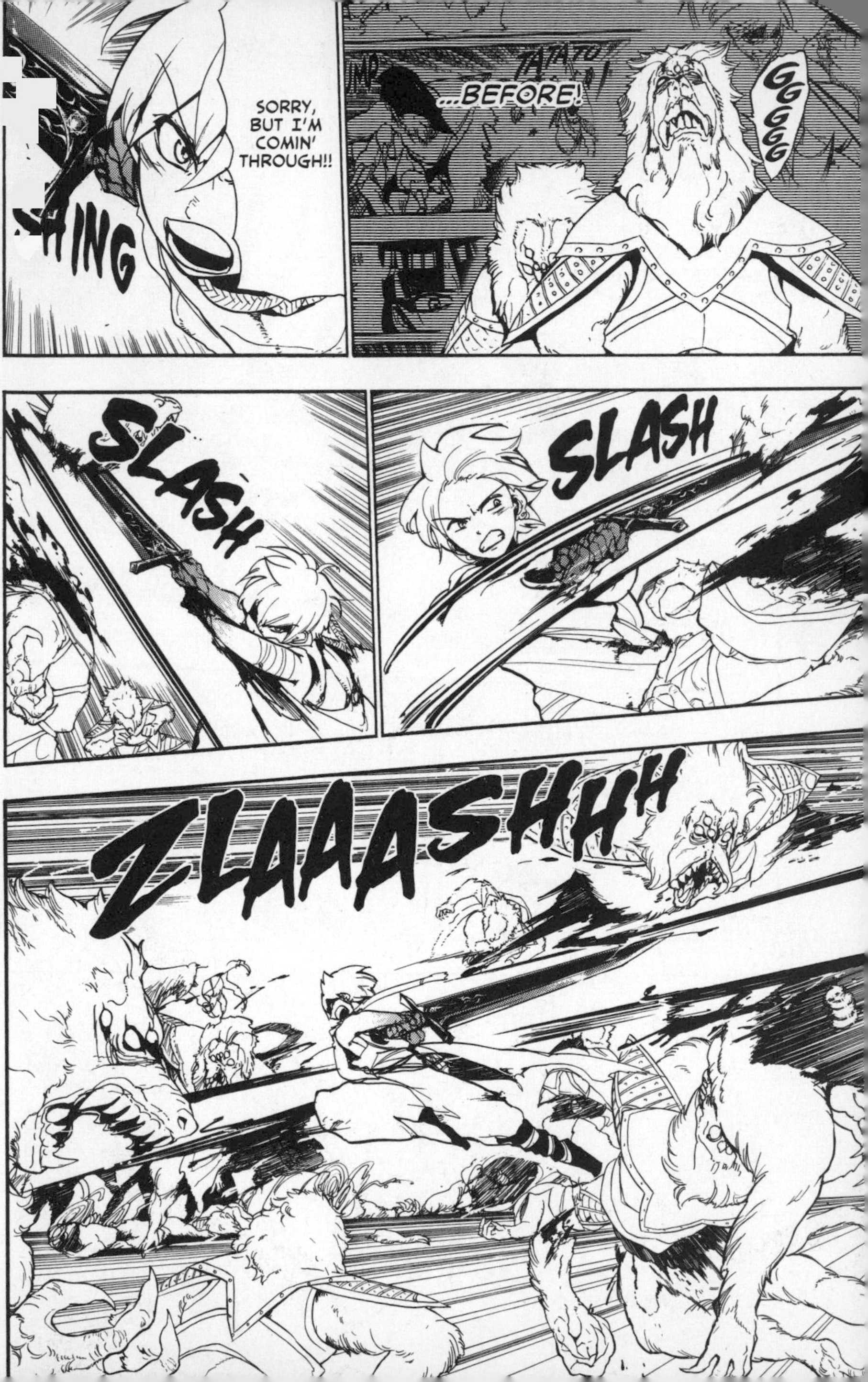
TATATU
...BEFORE!
GGGGG
SORRY, BUT I'M COMIN' THROUGH!!
SLASH
SLASH
ZLAAASHHH

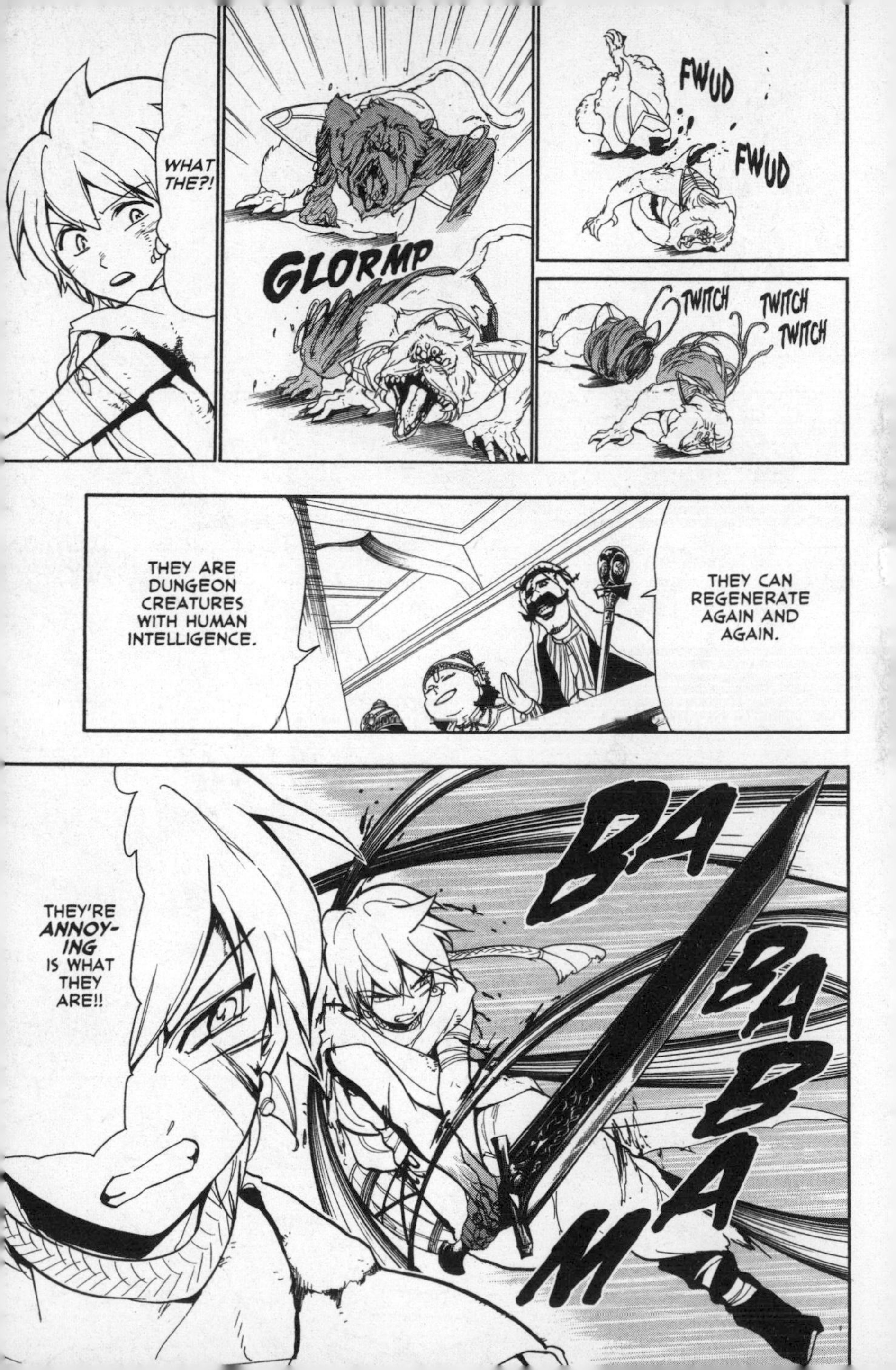
FWUD
FWUD
TWITCH
TWITCH
TWITCH
GLORMP
WHAT THE?!
THEY CAN REGENERATE AGAIN AND AGAIN.
THEY ARE DUNGEON CREATURES WITH HUMAN INTELLIGENCE.
BA BABAM
THEY'RE *ANNOYING* IS WHAT THEY ARE!!

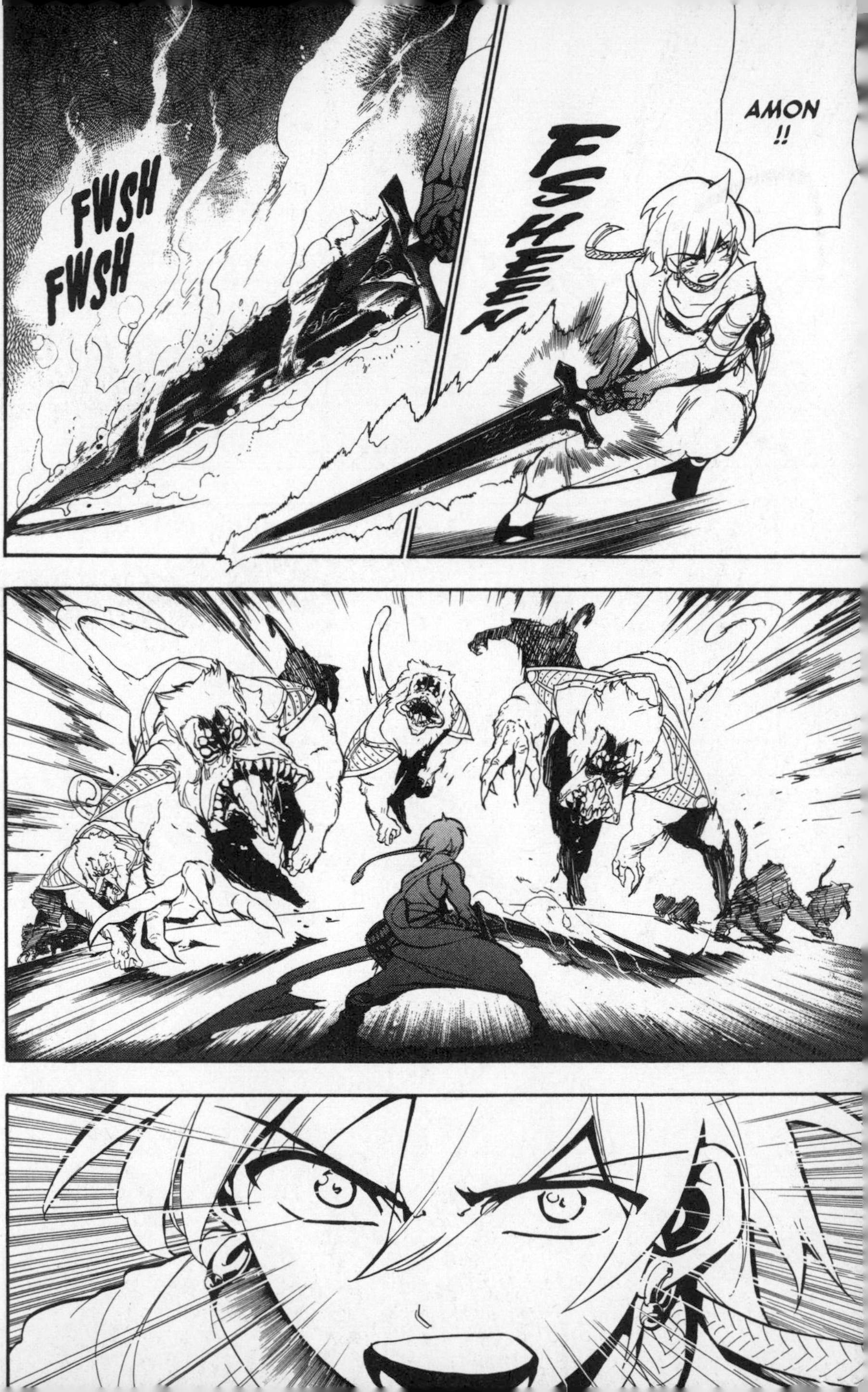
AMON !!
FSHEEN
FWSH FWSH

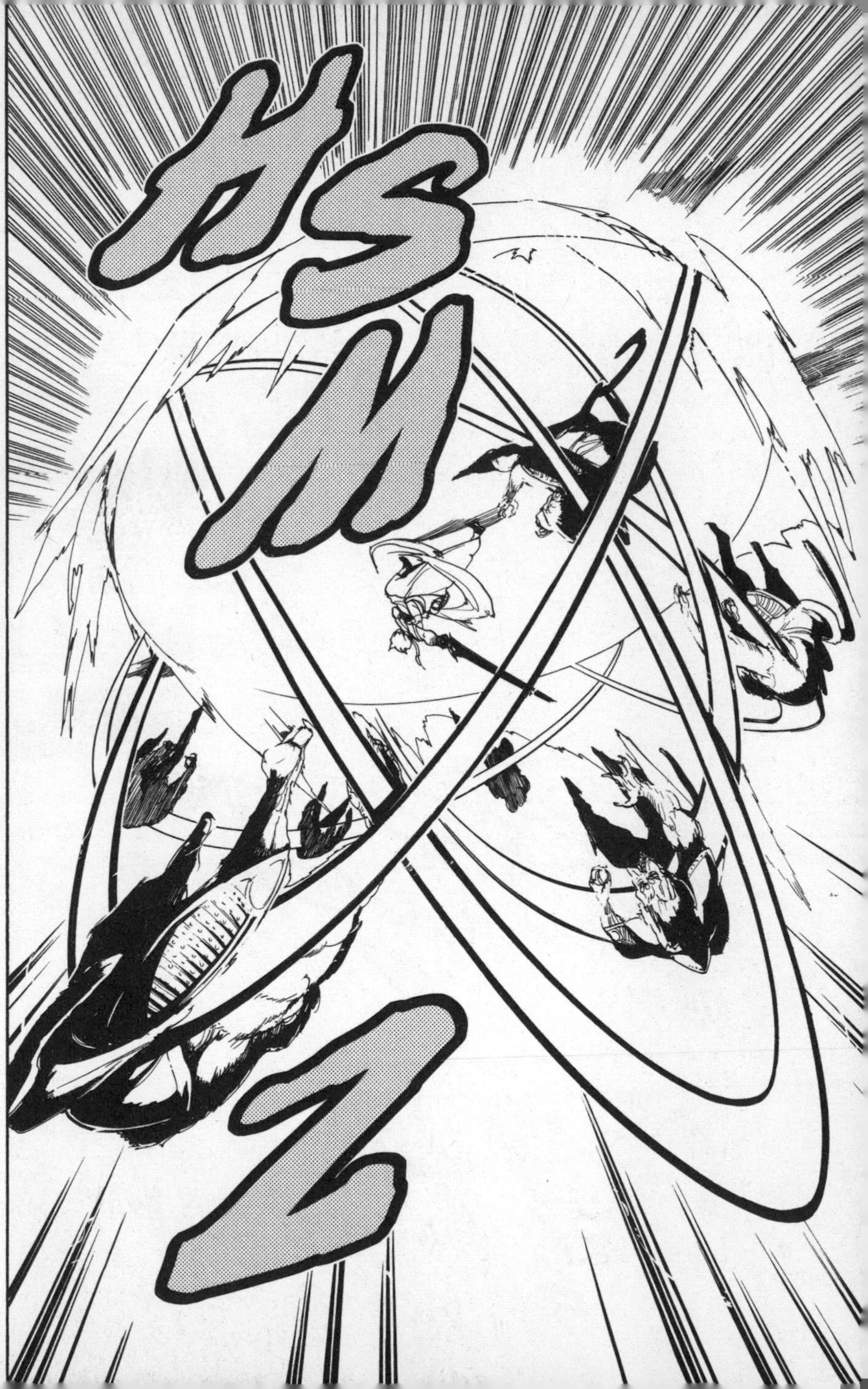

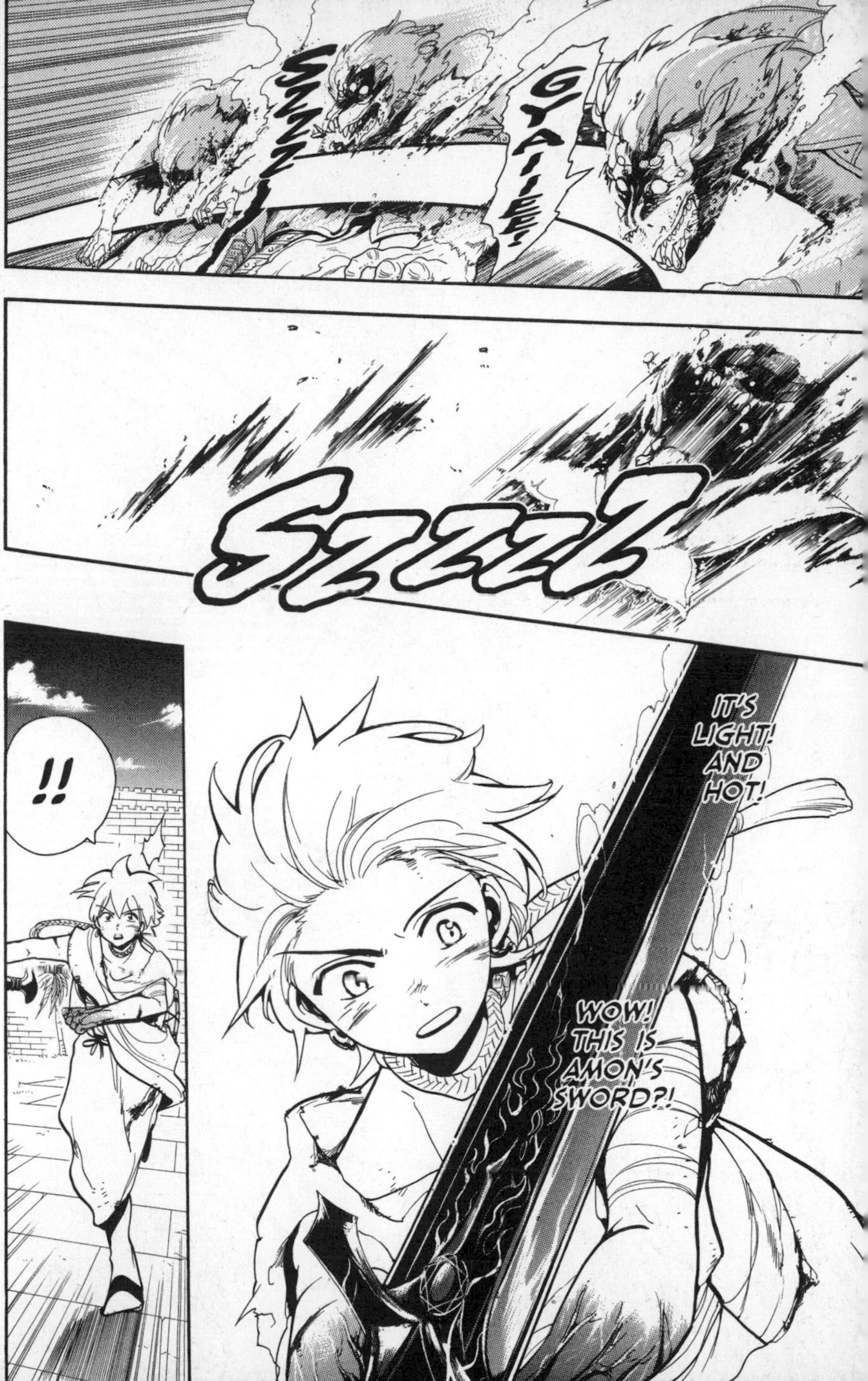
GYAIIEEE!
SIZZZ
SZZZ
IT'S LIGHT! AND HOT!
WOW! THIS IS AMON'S SWORD?!
!!

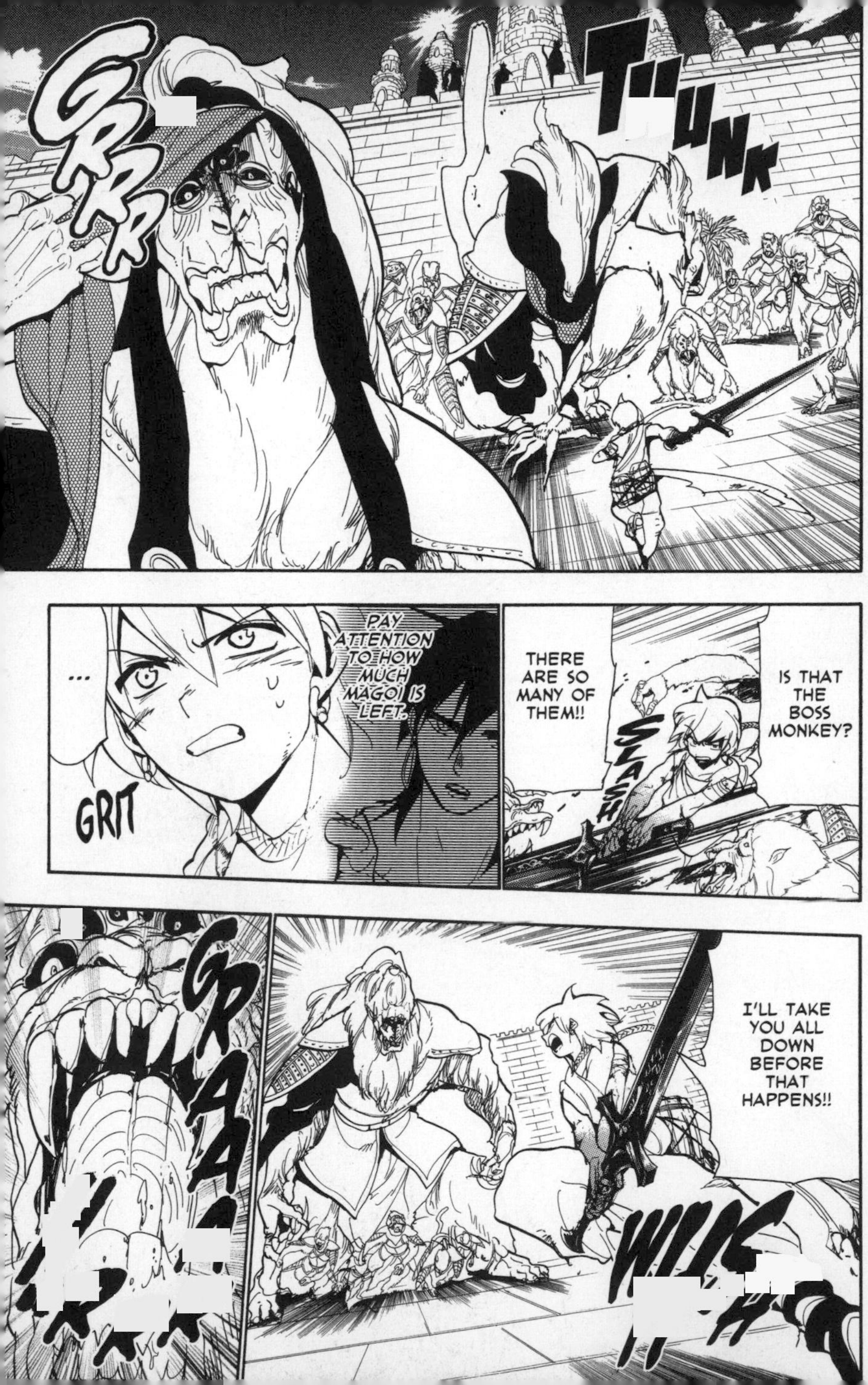
GRRR
IS THAT THE BOSS MONKEY?
SLASH
THERE ARE SO MANY OF THEM!!
PAY ATTENTION TO HOW MUCH MAGOI IS LEFT.
...
GRIT
I'LL TAKE YOU ALL DOWN BEFORE THAT HAPPENS!!

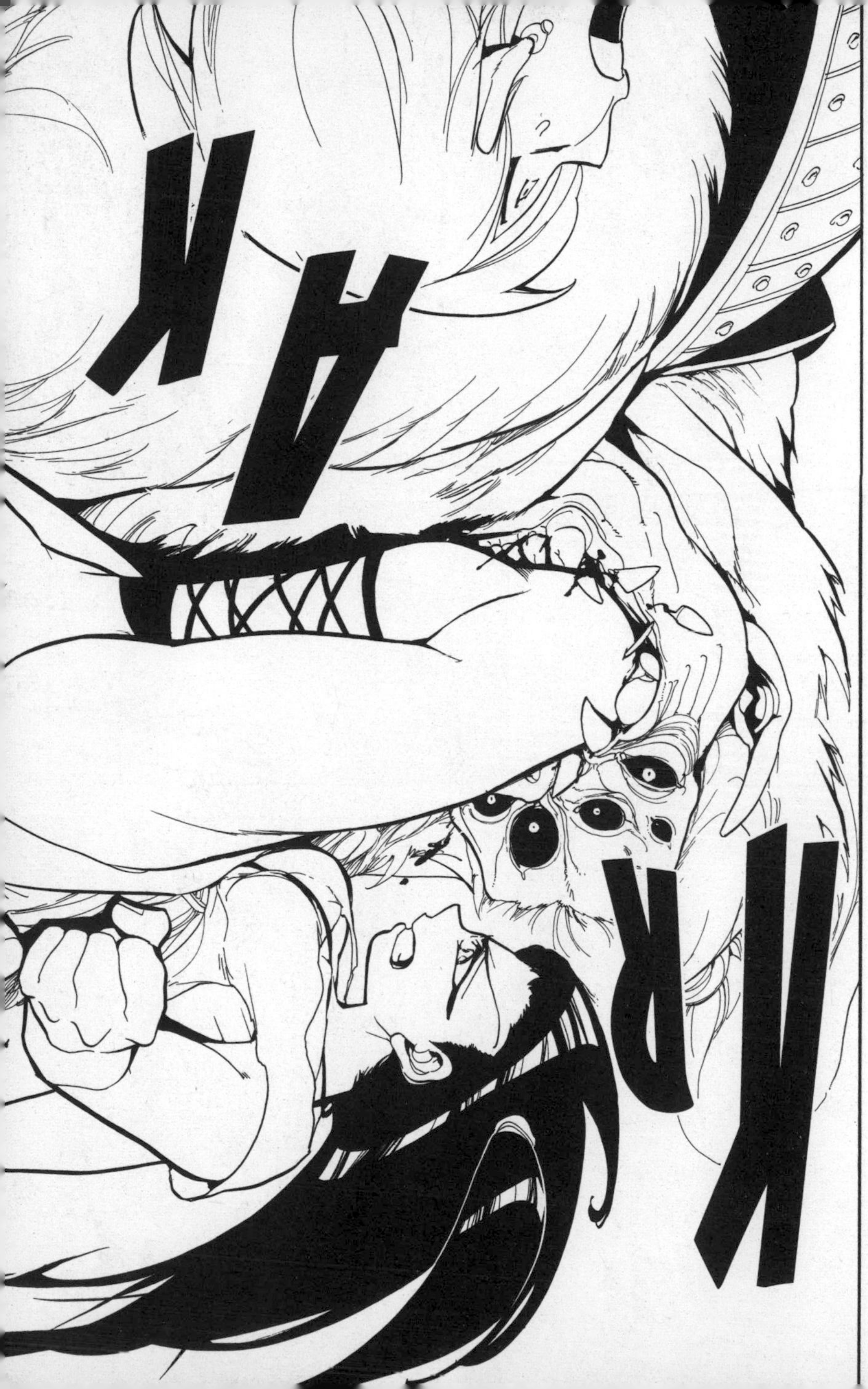
KRAK

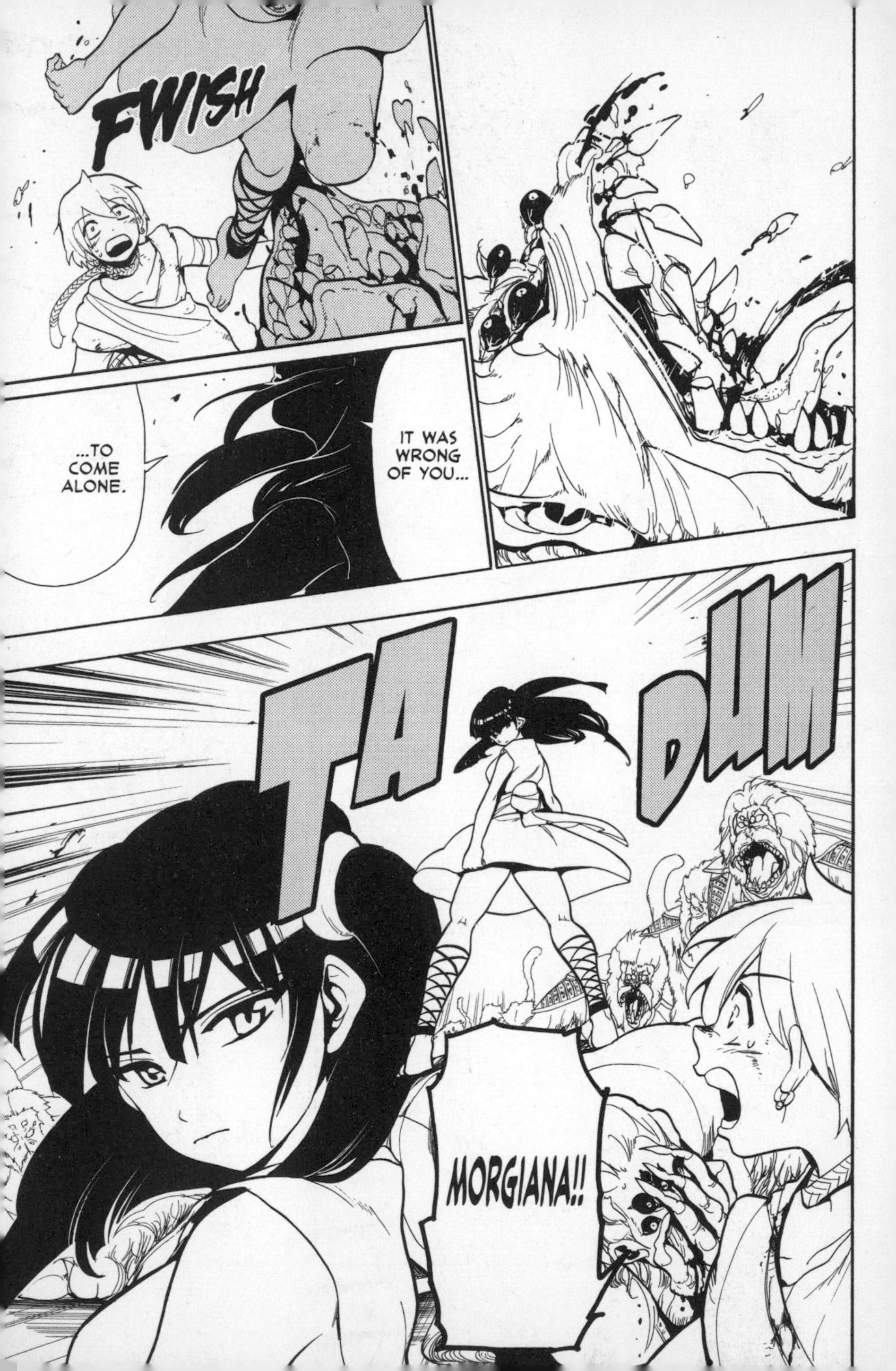
FWISH
IT WAS WRONG OF YOU...
...TO COME ALONE.
TA
DHM
MORGIANA!!

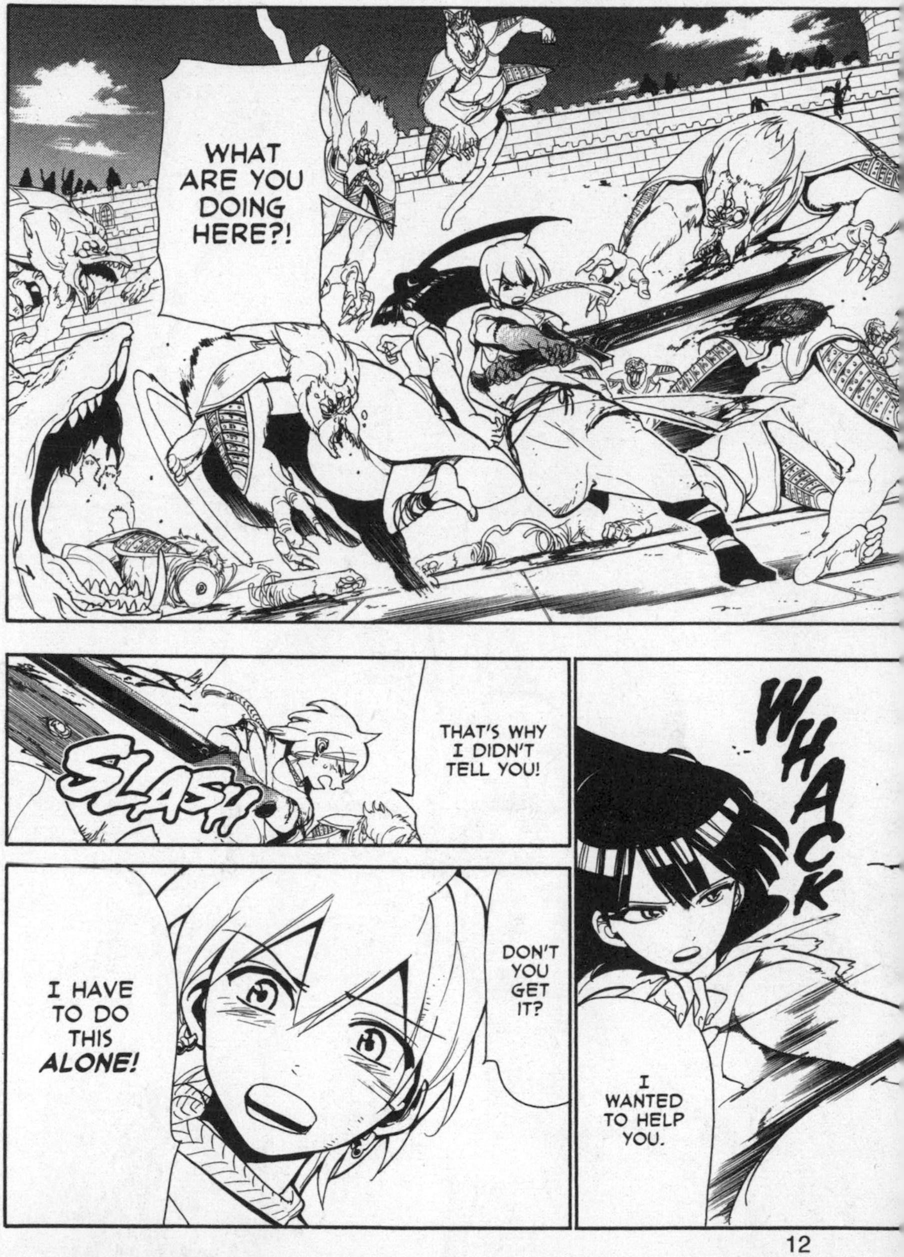
WHAT ARE YOU DOING HERE?!
WHACK
I WANTED TO HELP YOU.
THAT'S WHY I DIDN'T TELL YOU!
SLASH
DON'T YOU GET IT?
I HAVE TO DO THIS ALONE!

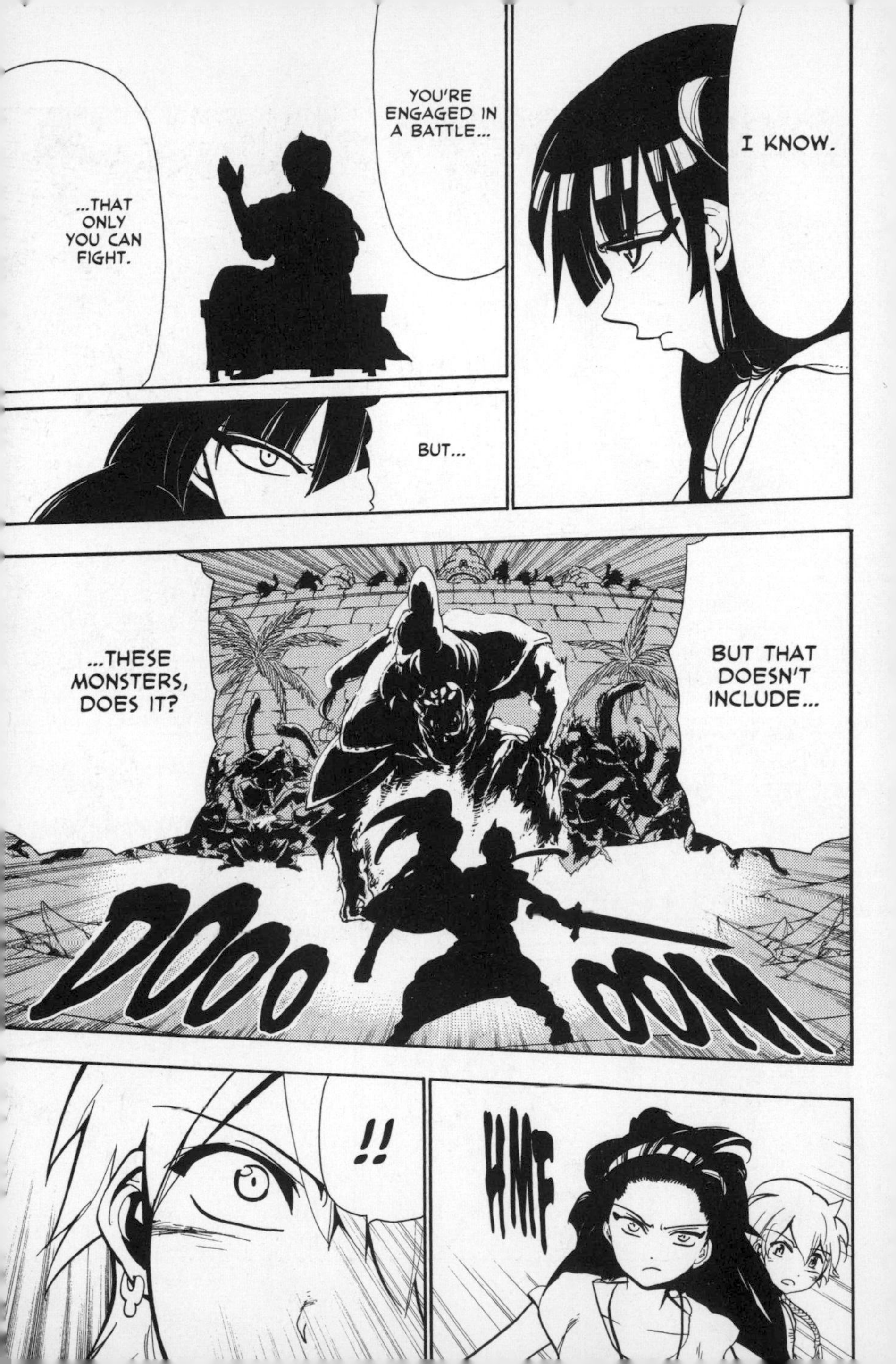
I KNOW.
YOU'RE ENGAGED IN A BATTLE...
...THAT ONLY YOU CAN FIGHT.
BUT...
BUT THAT DOESN'T INCLUDE...
...THESE MONSTERS, DOES IT?
DOOOO OOM
HMF
!!

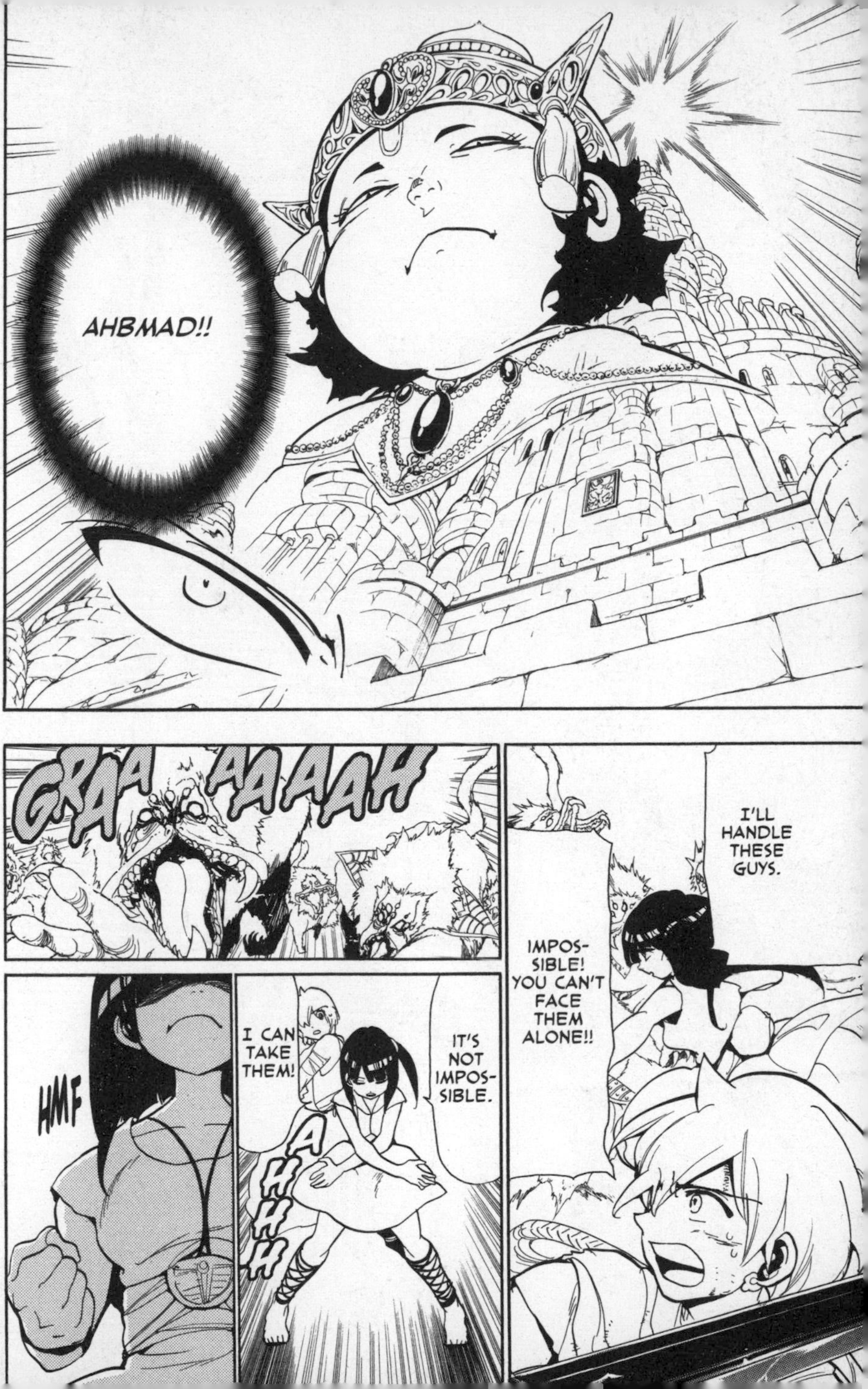
AHBMAD!!
I'LL HANDLE THESE GUYS.
IMPOS-SIBLE! YOU CAN'T FACE THEM ALONE!!
GRAA AAAAH
IT'S NOT IMPOS-SIBLE.
I CAN TAKE THEM!
AHHHH
HMF

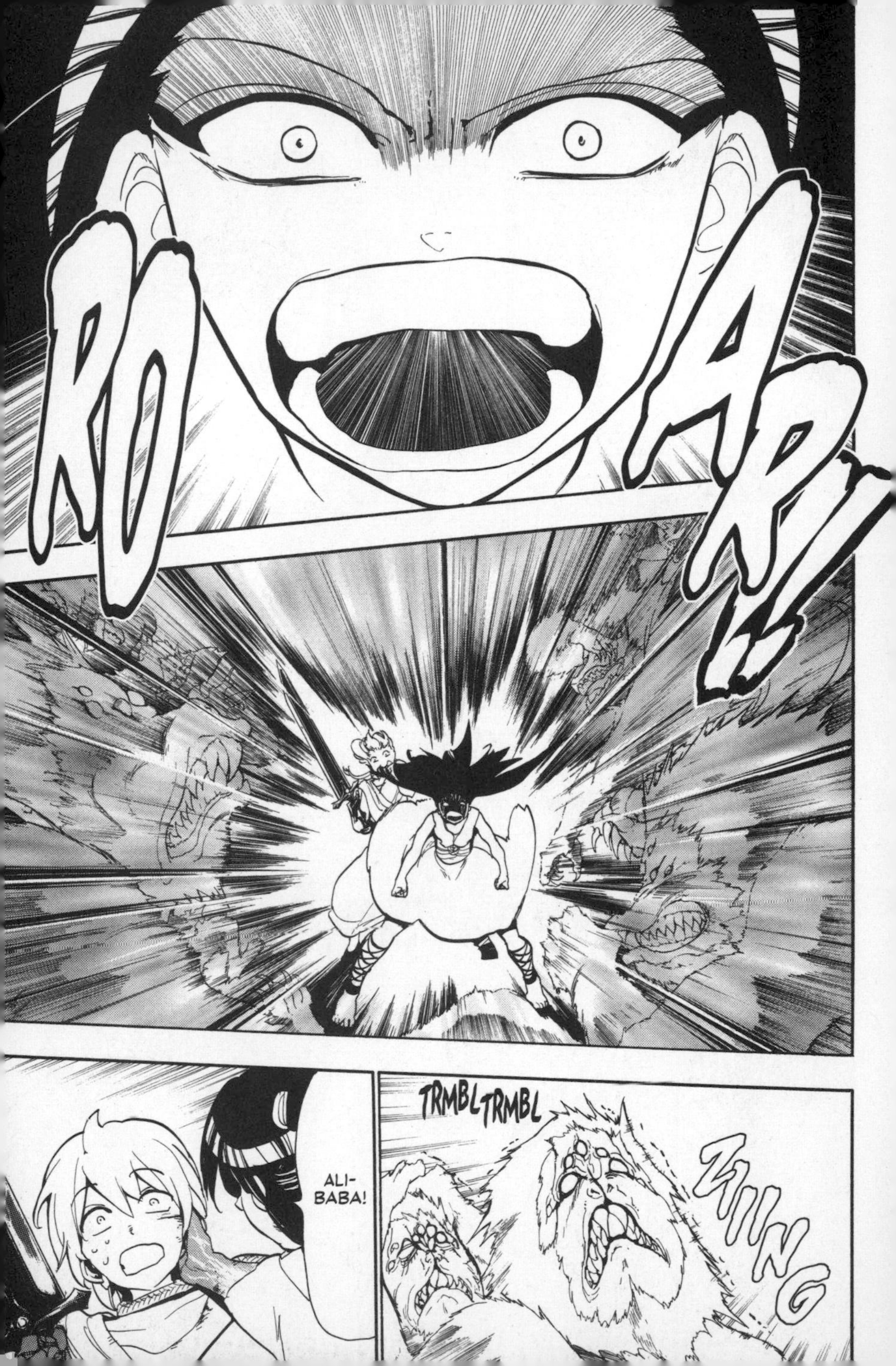
ROAR!!
TRMBL TRMBL
ZIIING
ALI-BABA!

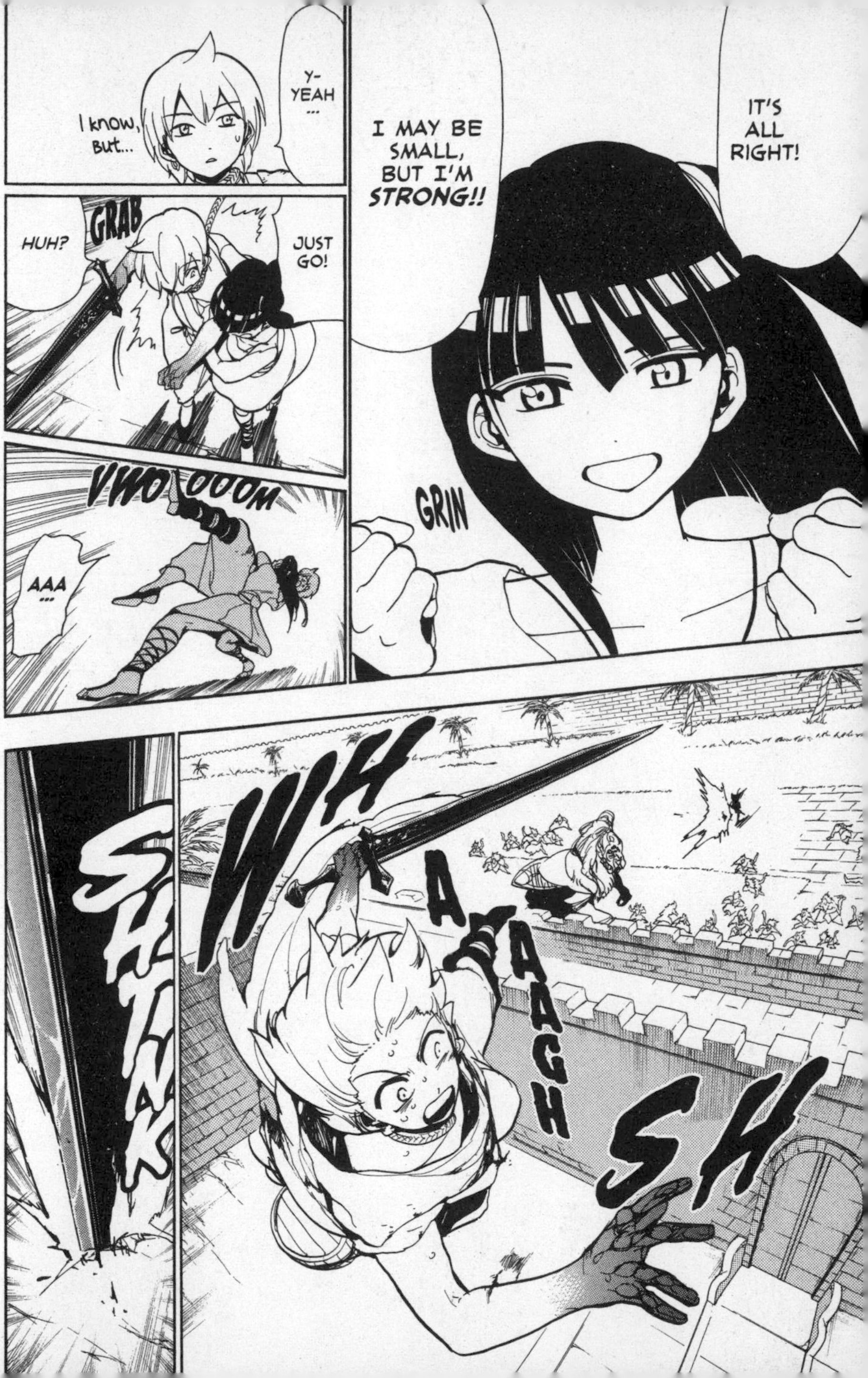
IT'S ALL RIGHT!
I MAY BE SMALL, BUT I'M STRONG!!
GRIN
Y-YEAH...
I know, but...
JUST GO!
HUH?
GRAB
VWOOOOM
AAA...
SH
WHAAAGH

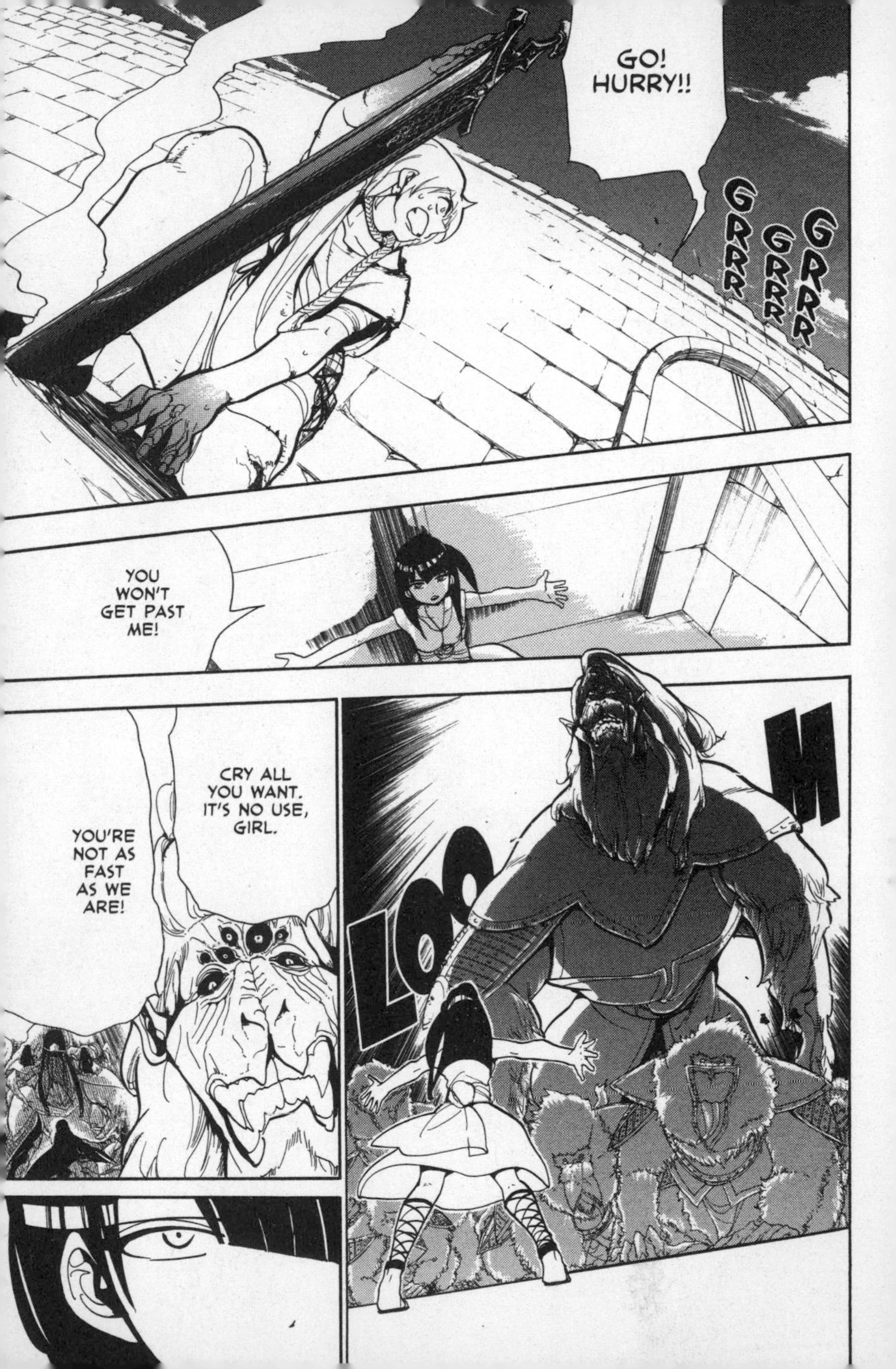
GO! HURRY!!
GRRR GRRR GRRR
YOU WON'T GET PAST ME!
LOOM
CRY ALL YOU WANT. IT'S NO USE, GIRL.
YOU'RE NOT AS FAST AS WE ARE!

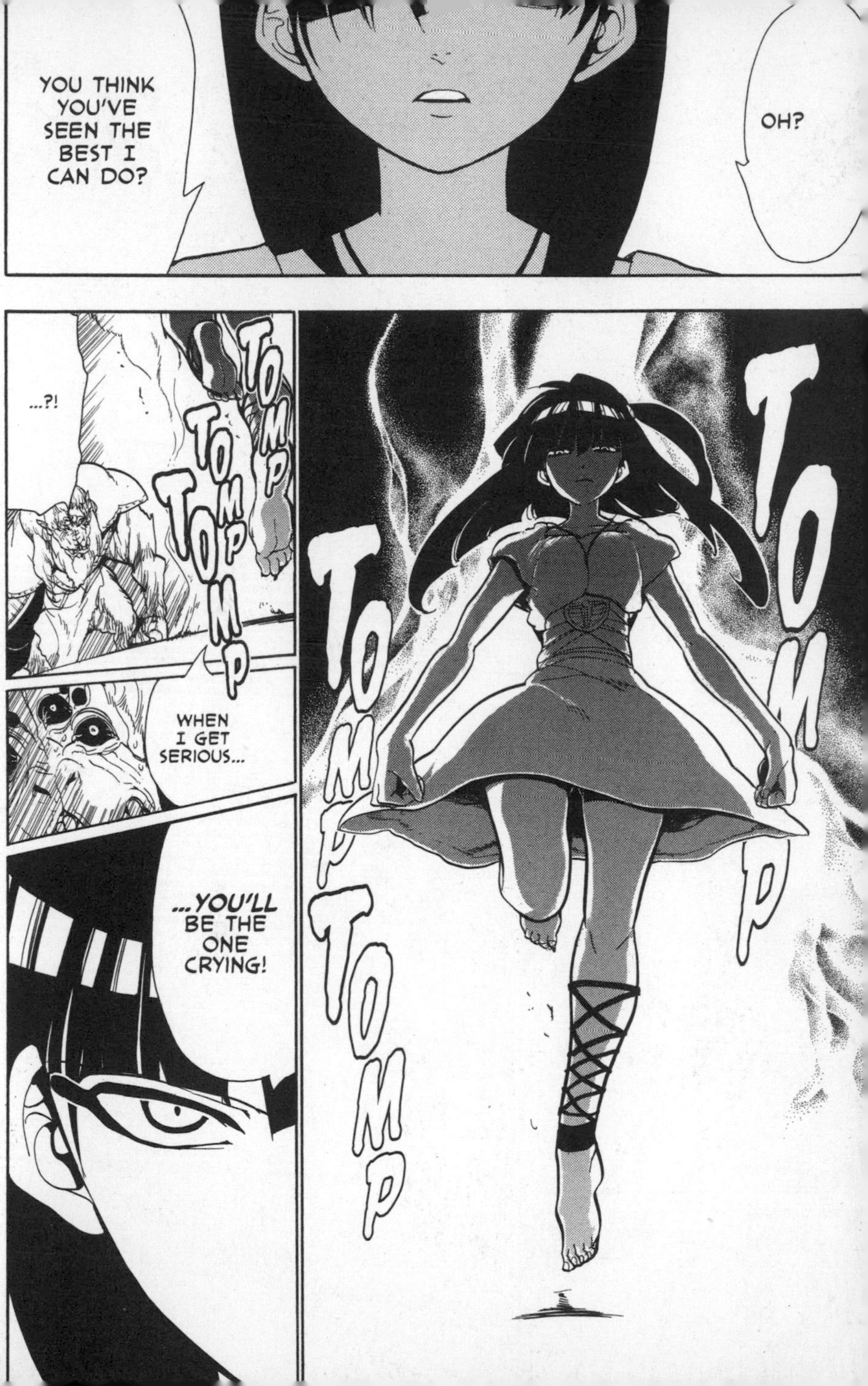
OH?
YOU THINK YOU'VE SEEN THE BEST I CAN DO?
TOMP
TOMP TOMP
...?!
TOMP
TOMP
TOMP
WHEN I GET SERIOUS...
...YOU'LL BE THE ONE CRYING!

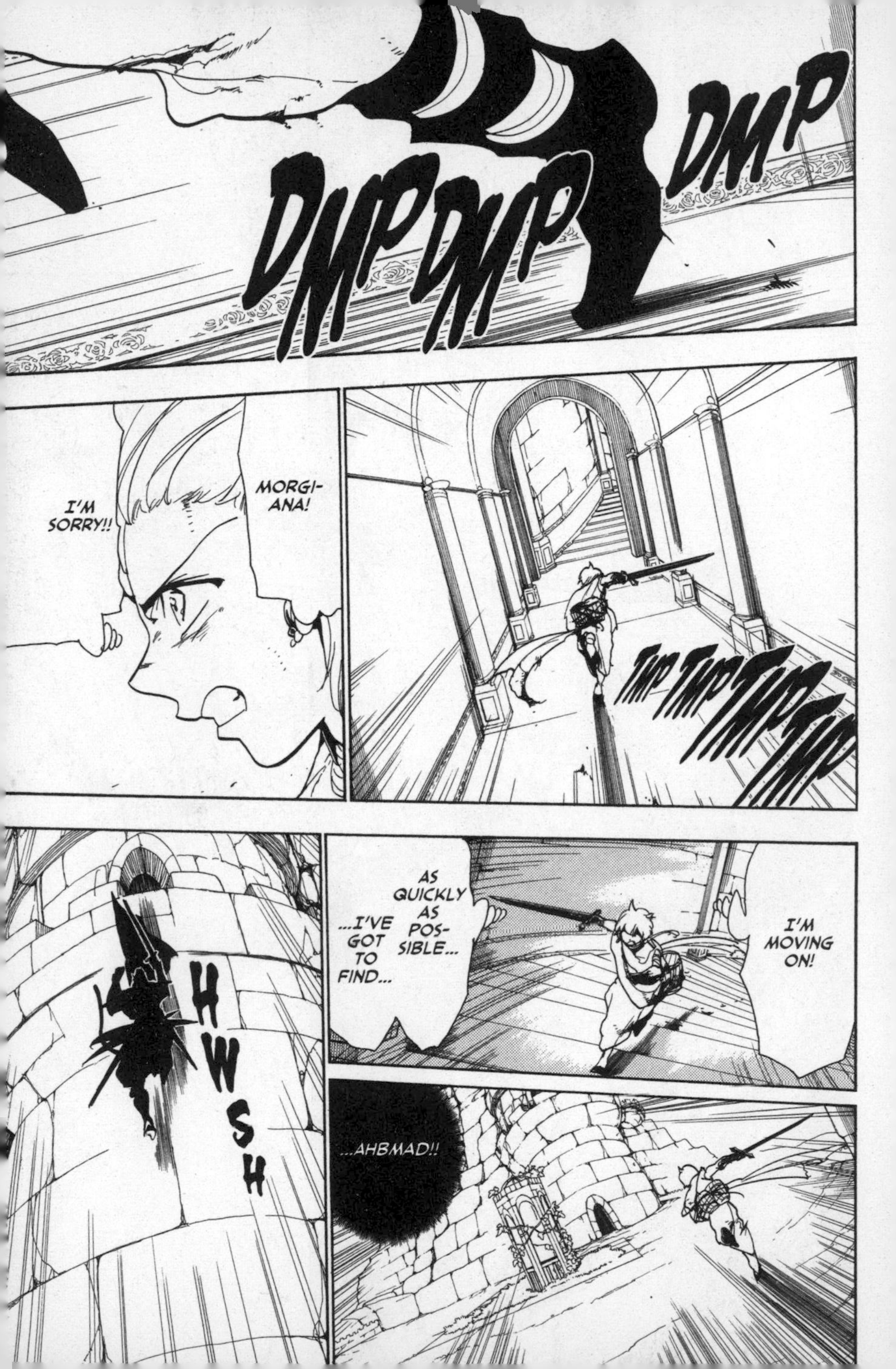
DMP
DMP DMP
TMP TMP TMP TMP
MORGI-ANA!
I'M SORRY!!
I'M MOVING ON!
AS QUICKLY AS POS-SIBLE...
...I'VE GOT TO FIND...
...AHBMAD!!
HWSH

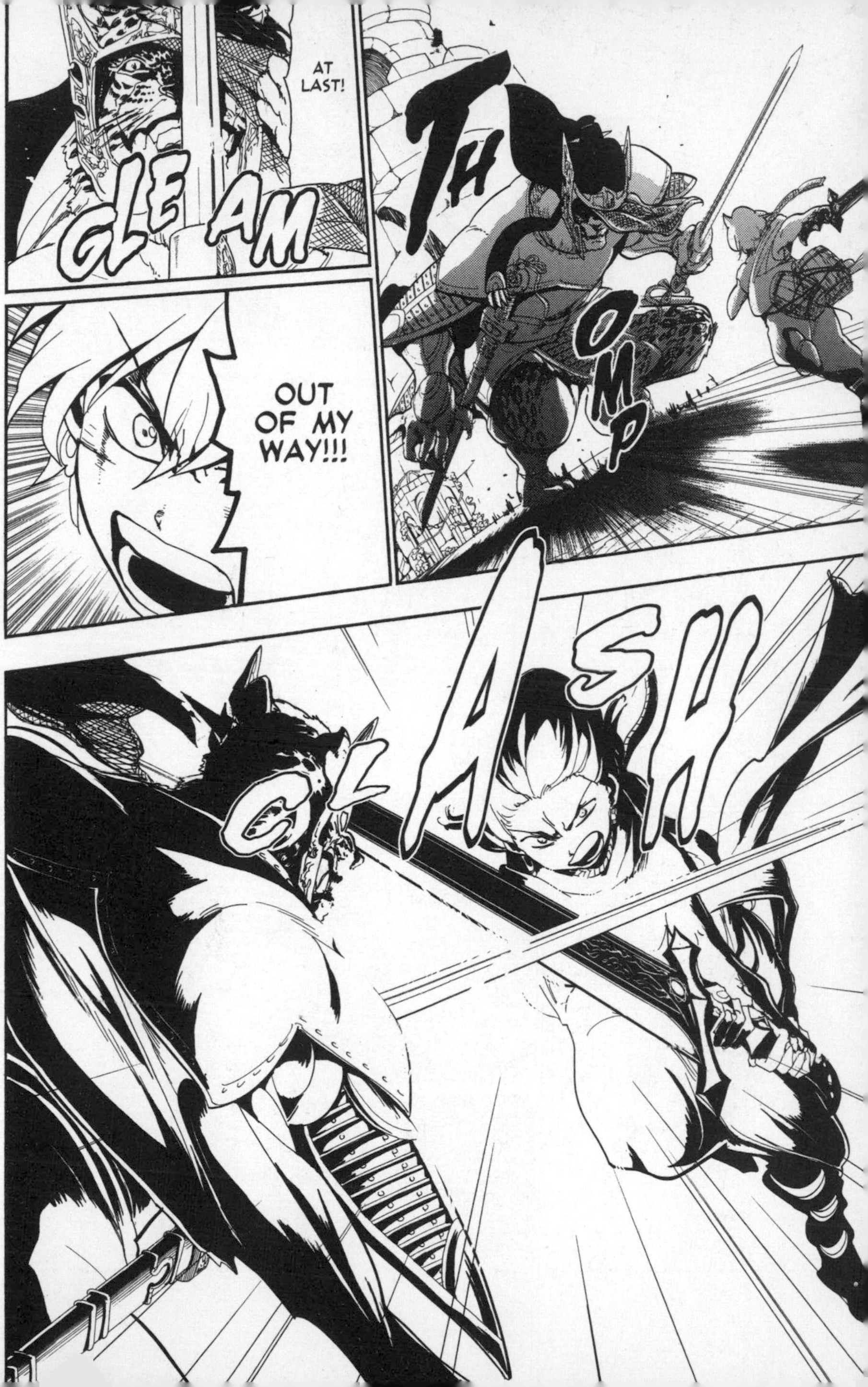
THOMP
AT LAST!
GLEAM
OUT OF MY WAY!!!
CLASH

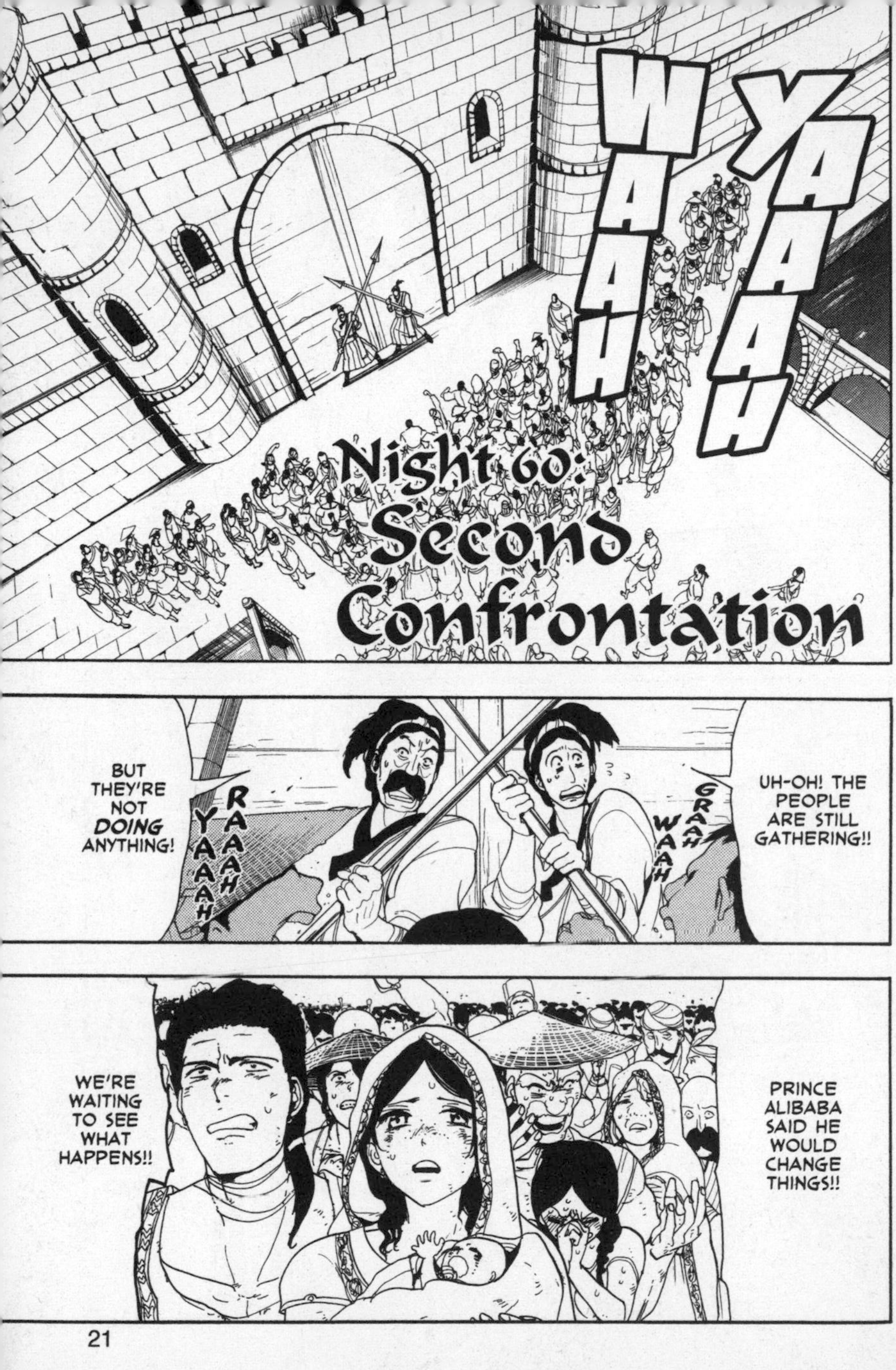
YAAAH
WAAAH
Night 60: Second Confrontation
UH-OH! THE PEOPLE ARE STILL GATHERING!!
GRAAH
WAAH
BUT THEY'RE NOT DOING ANYTHING!
RAAAH
YAAAAH
PRINCE ALIBABA SAID HE WOULD CHANGE THINGS!!
WE'RE WAITING TO SEE WHAT HAPPENS!!

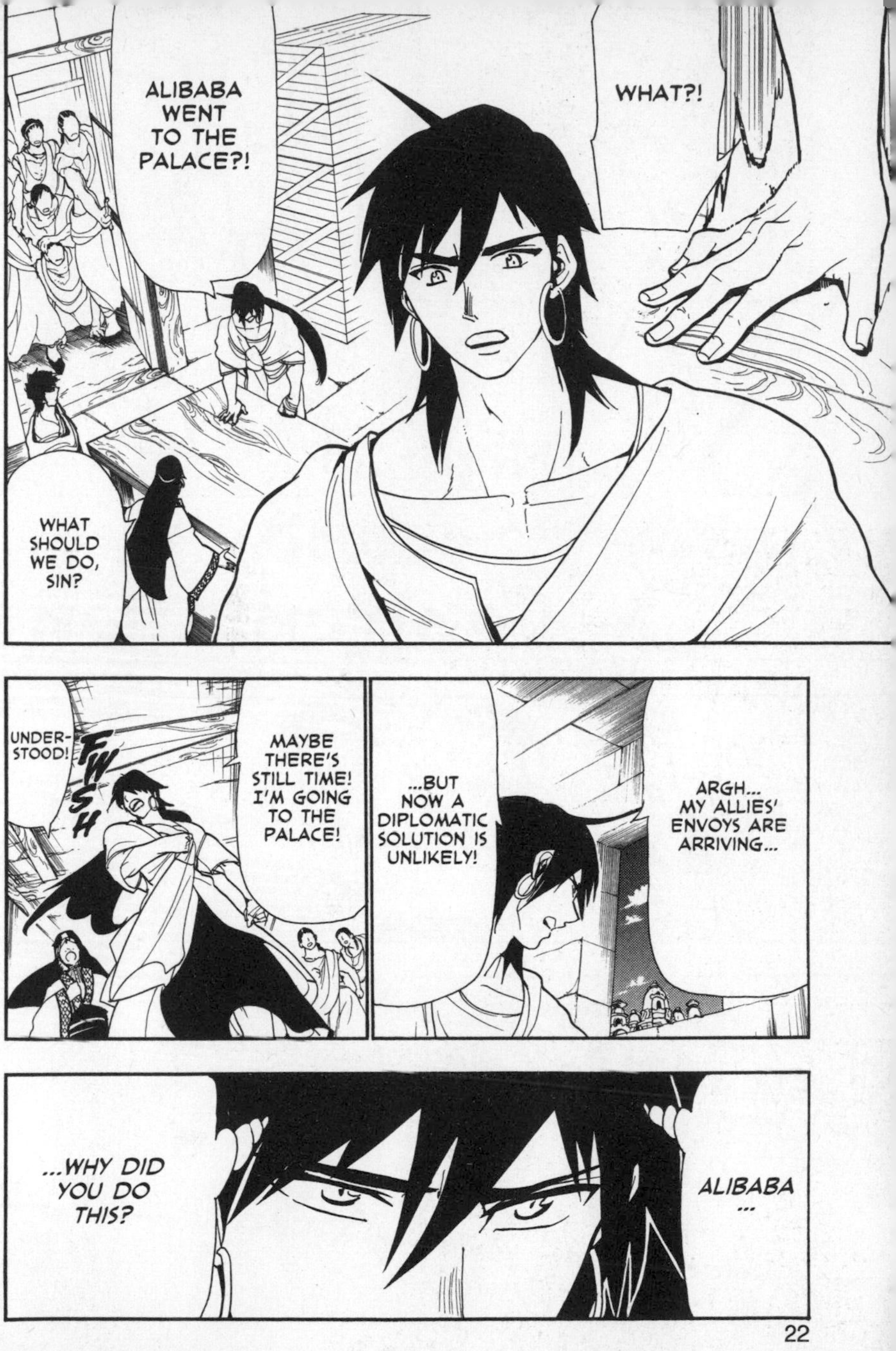
WHAT?!
ALIBABA WENT TO THE PALACE?!
WHAT SHOULD WE DO, SIN?
ARGH... MY ALLIES' ENVOYS ARE ARRIVING...
...BUT NOW A DIPLOMATIC SOLUTION IS UNLIKELY!
MAYBE THERE'S STILL TIME! I'M GOING TO THE PALACE!
UNDER-STOOD!
FWSH
ALIBABA ...
...WHY DID YOU DO THIS?

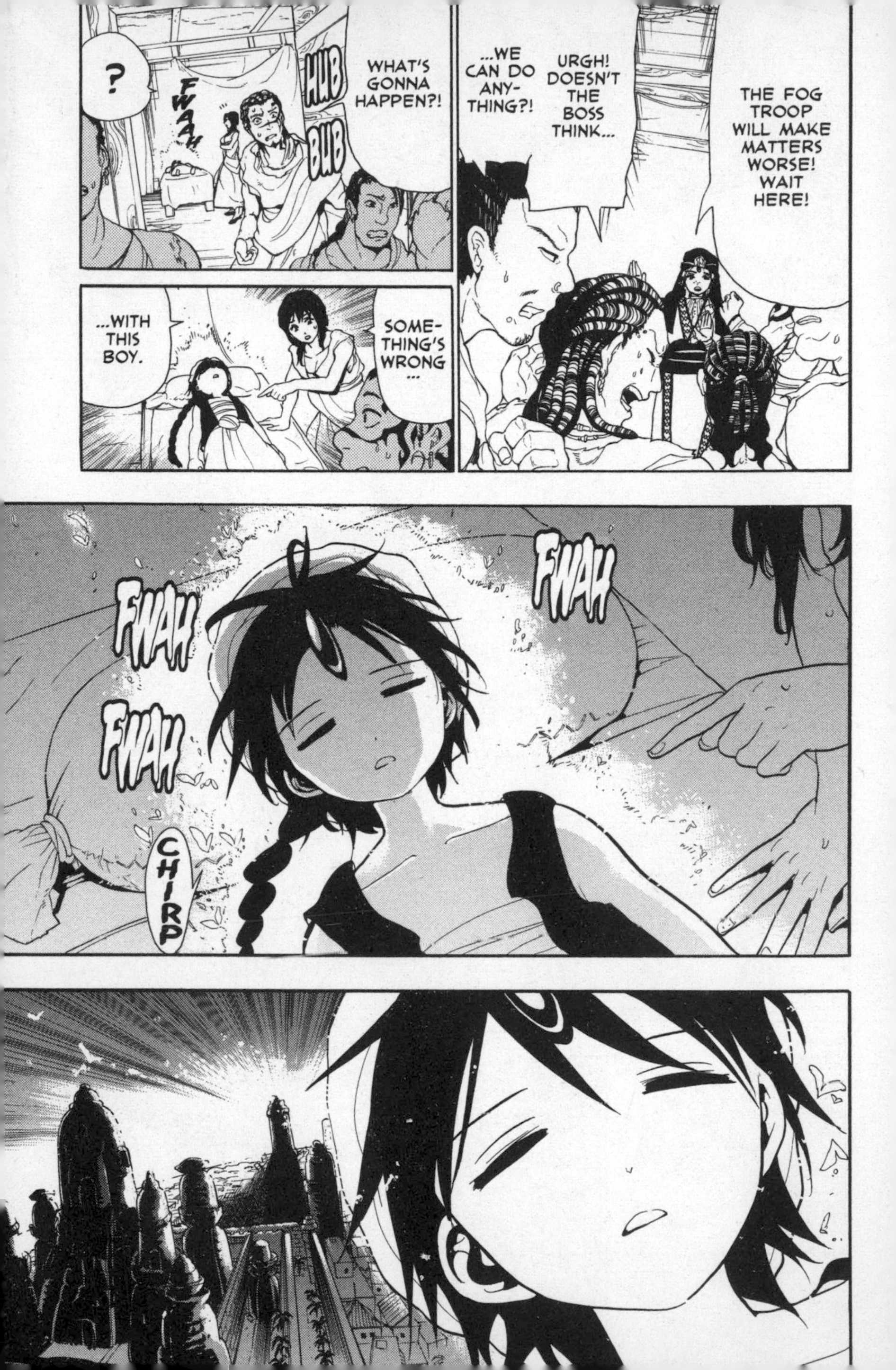
THE FOG TROOP WILL MAKE MATTERS WORSE! WAIT HERE!
URGH! DOESN'T THE BOSS THINK...
...WE CAN DO ANYTHING?!
WHAT'S GONNA HAPPEN?!
HUB
BUB
FWAAH
?
SOME-THING'S WRONG...
...WITH THIS BOY.
FWAH
FWAH
FWAH
CHIRP

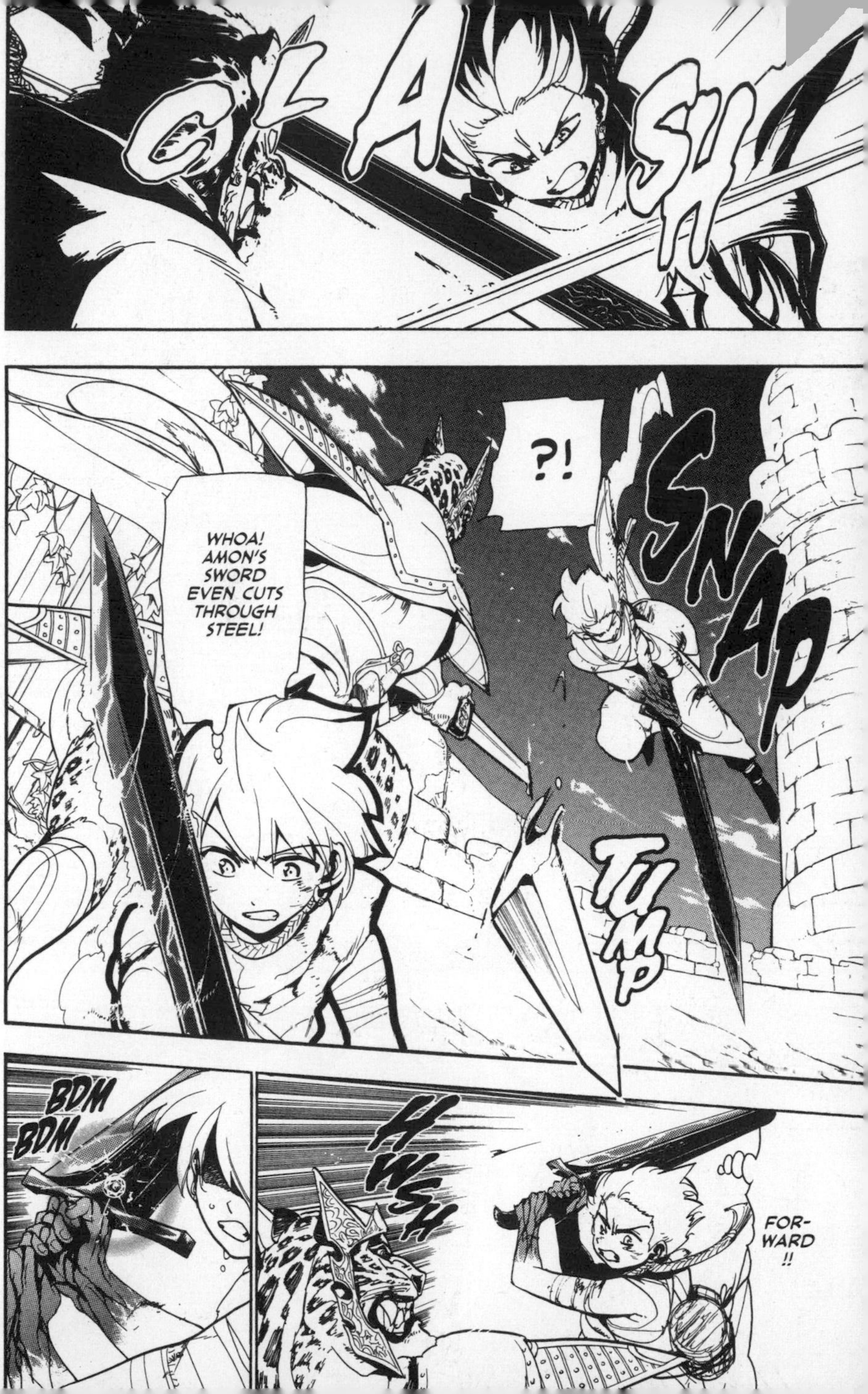
CLASH
SNAP
?!
WHOA! AMON'S SWORD EVEN CUTS THROUGH STEEL!
TUMP
FOR-WARD!!
HWSH
BDM BDM

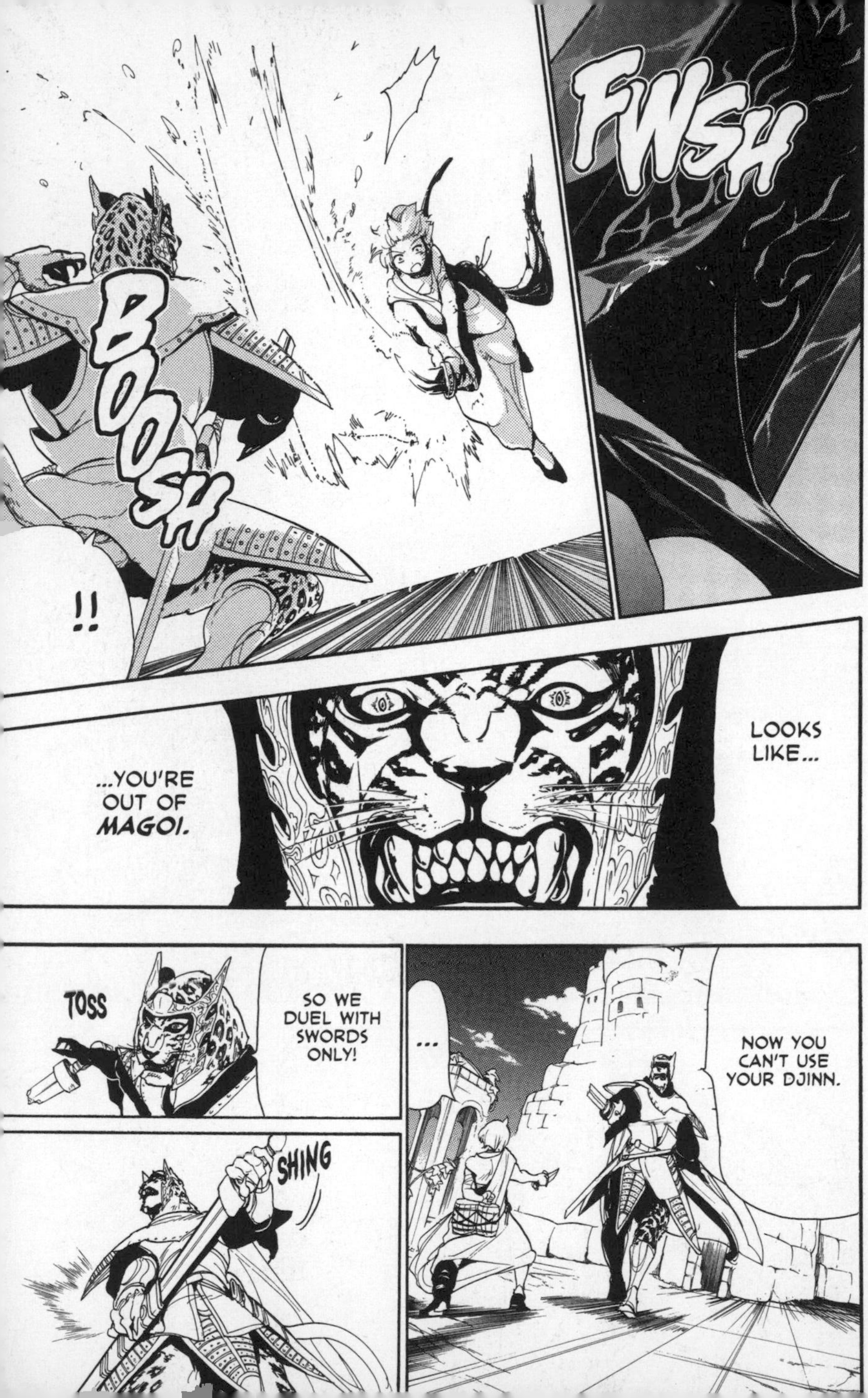
FWSH
BOOSH
!!
LOOKS LIKE...
...YOU'RE OUT OF MAGOI.
NOW YOU CAN'T USE YOUR DJINN.
...
SO WE DUEL WITH SWORDS ONLY!
TOSS
SHING

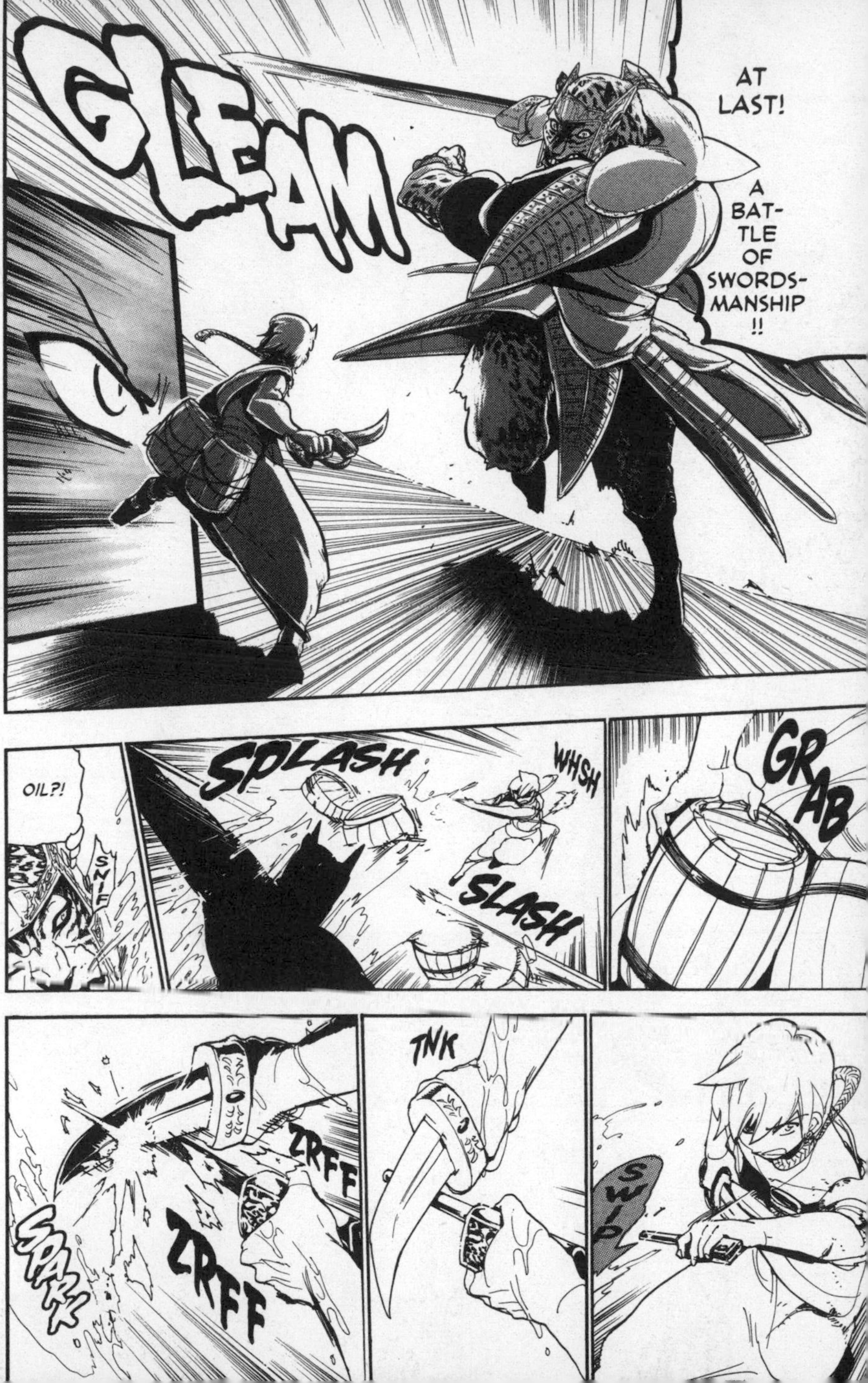
AT LAST!
A BATTLE OF SWORDSMANSHIP!!
GLEAM
GRAB
WHSH
SPLASH
SLASH
OIL?!
SNIF
SWIP
TNK
ZRFF
ZRFF
SPARK

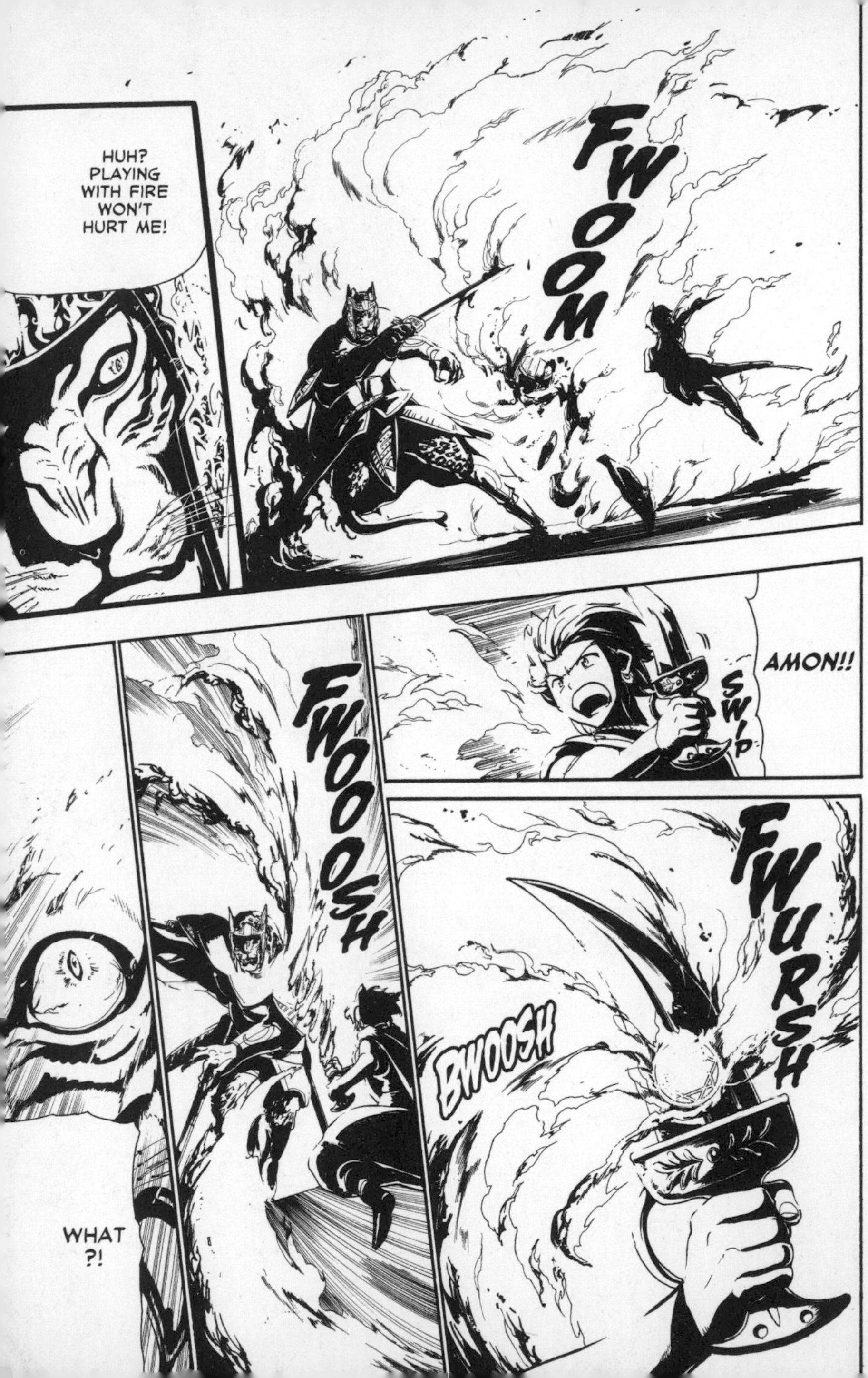
FWOOM
HUH? PLAYING WITH FIRE WON'T HURT ME!
AMON!!
SWIP
FWURSH
BWOOSH
FWOOOOSH
WHAT ?!

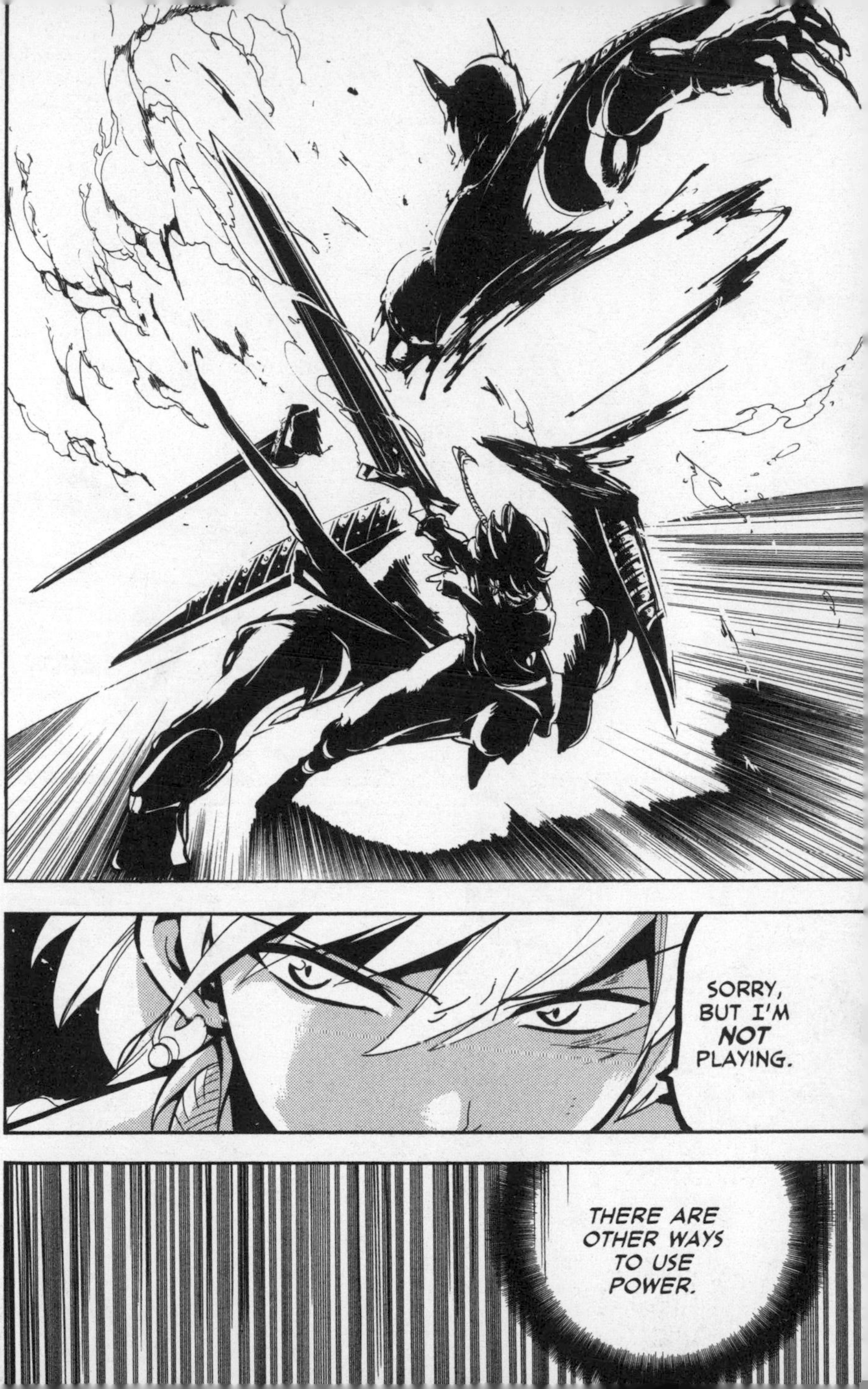
SORRY, BUT I'M NOT PLAYING.
THERE ARE OTHER WAYS TO USE POWER.

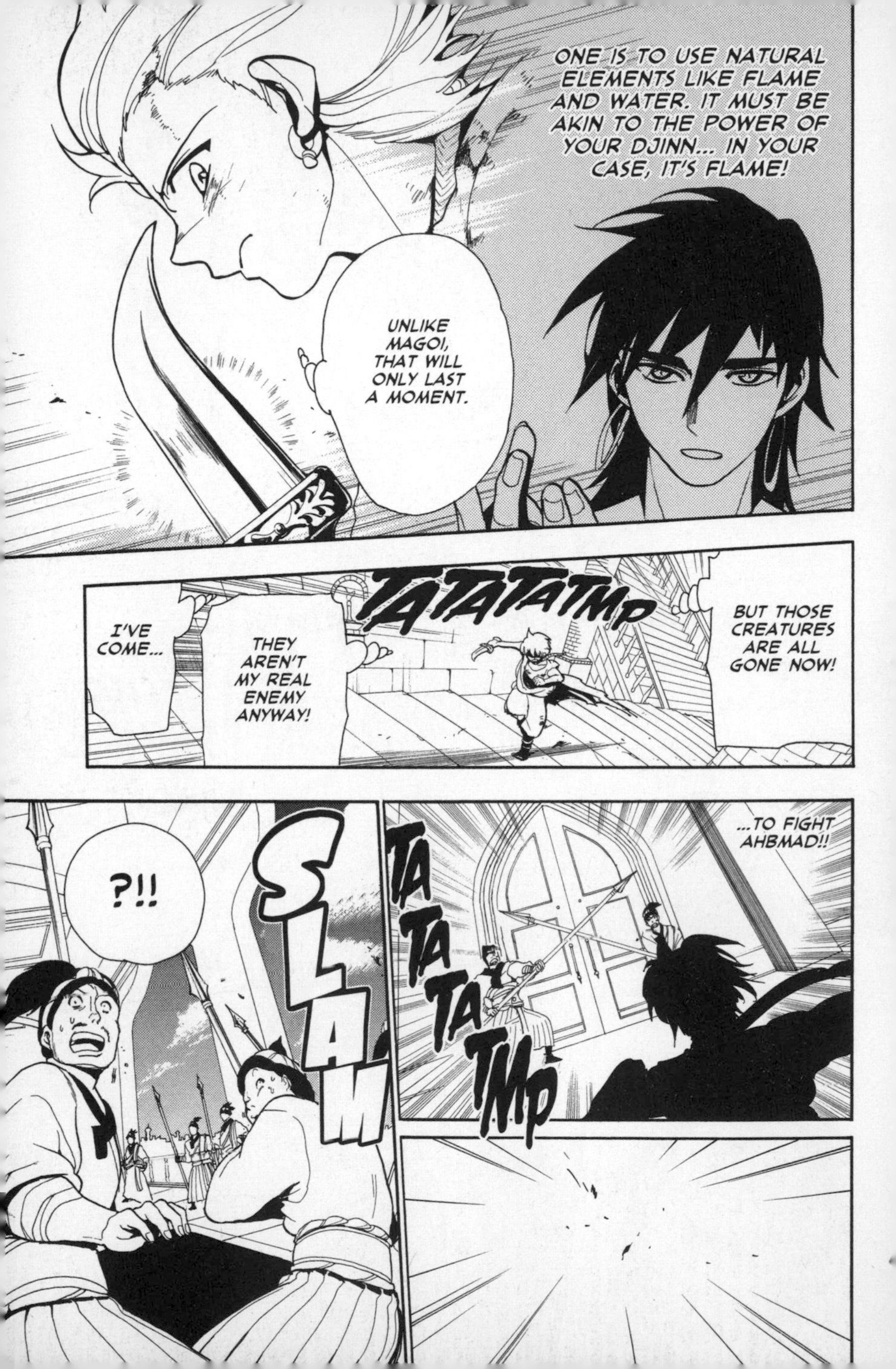
ONE IS TO USE NATURAL ELEMENTS LIKE FLAME AND WATER. IT MUST BE AKIN TO THE POWER OF YOUR DJINN... IN YOUR CASE, IT'S FLAME!
UNLIKE MAGOI, THAT WILL ONLY LAST A MOMENT.
BUT THOSE CREATURES ARE ALL GONE NOW!
TATATATMP
THEY AREN'T MY REAL ENEMY ANYWAY!
I'VE COME...
...TO FIGHT AHBMAD!!
TA TA TA TA TMP
SLAM
?!!

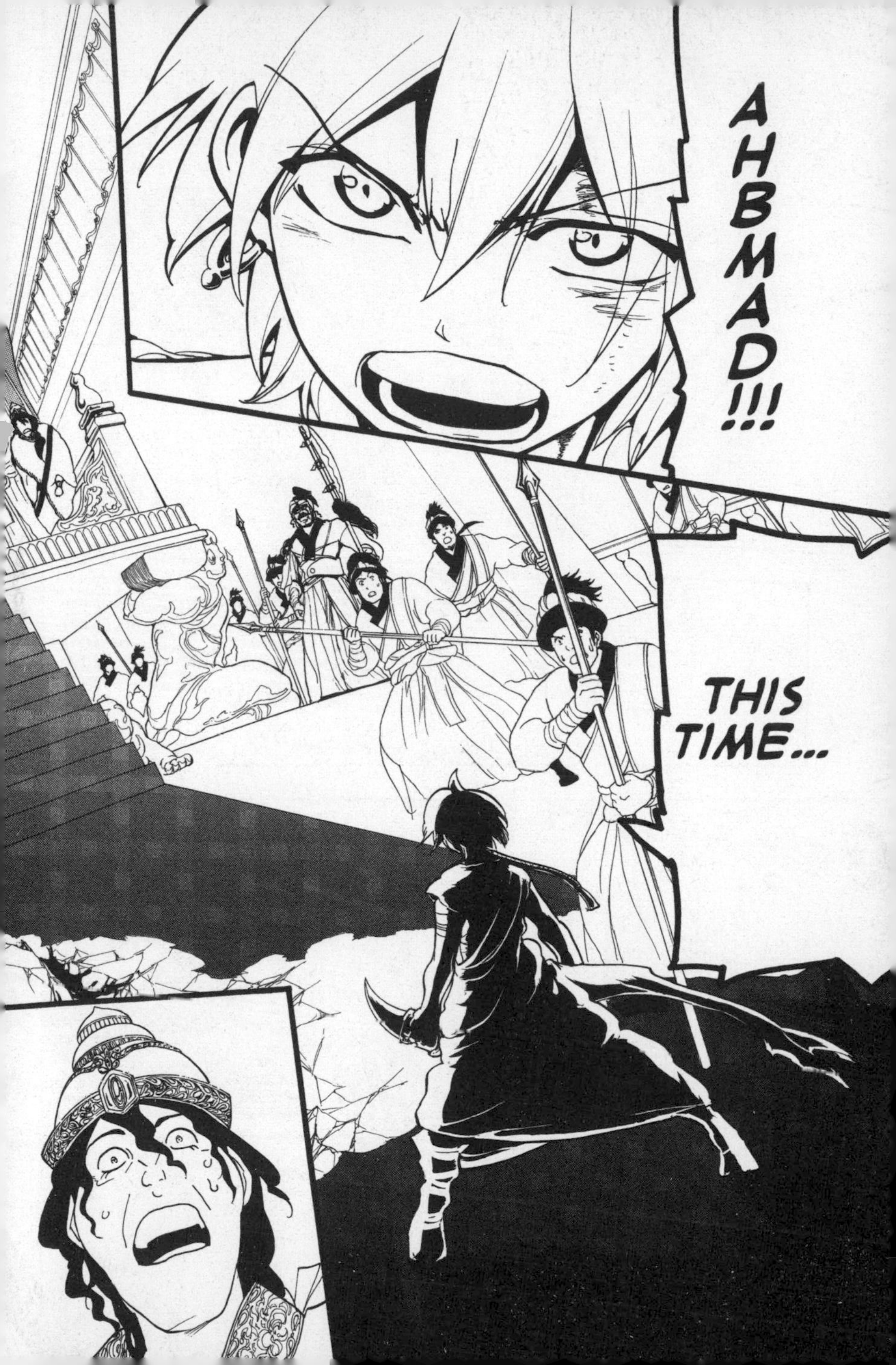
AHBMAD!!!
THIS TIME...

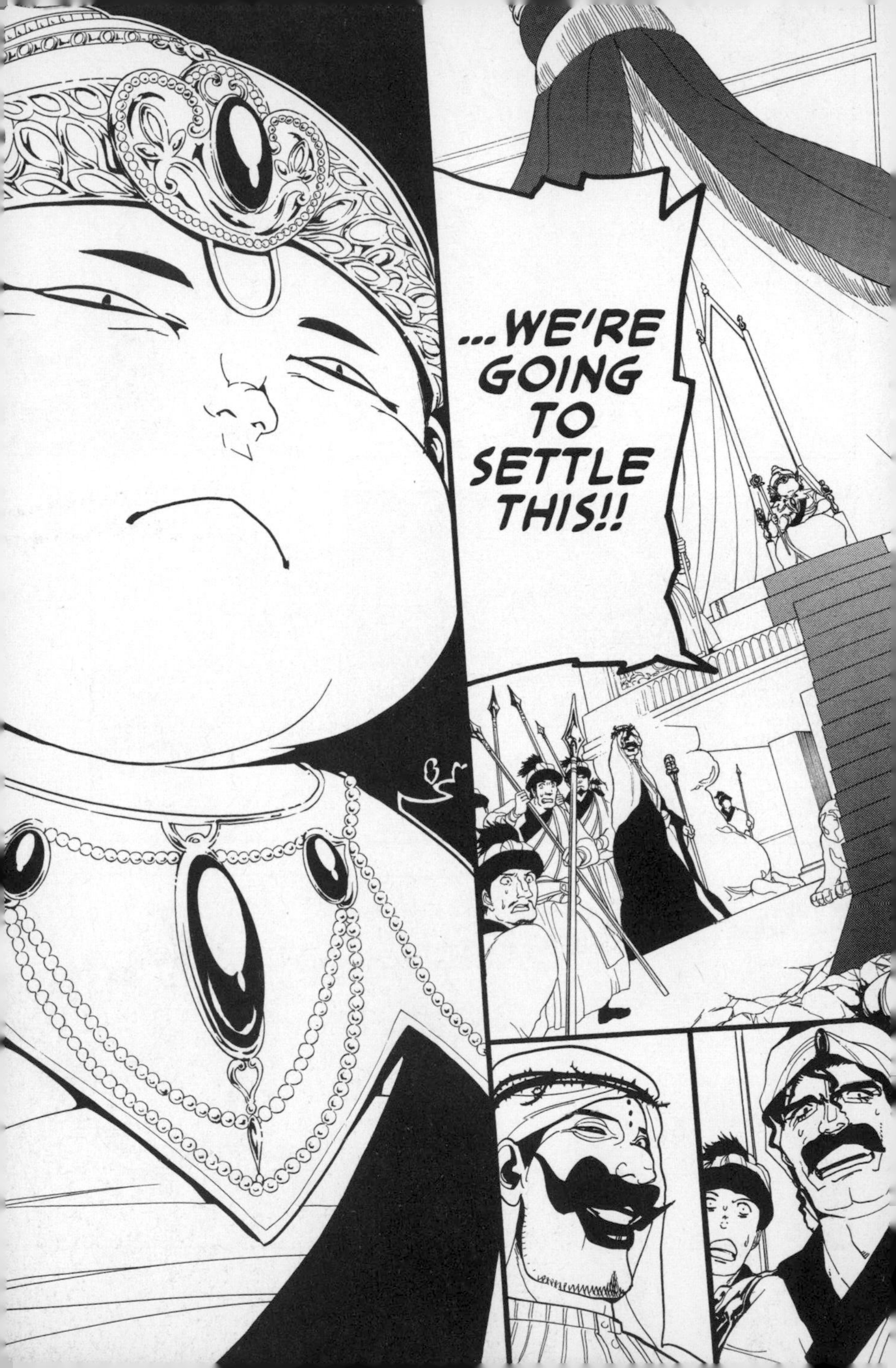
...WE'RE GOING TO SETTLE THIS!!

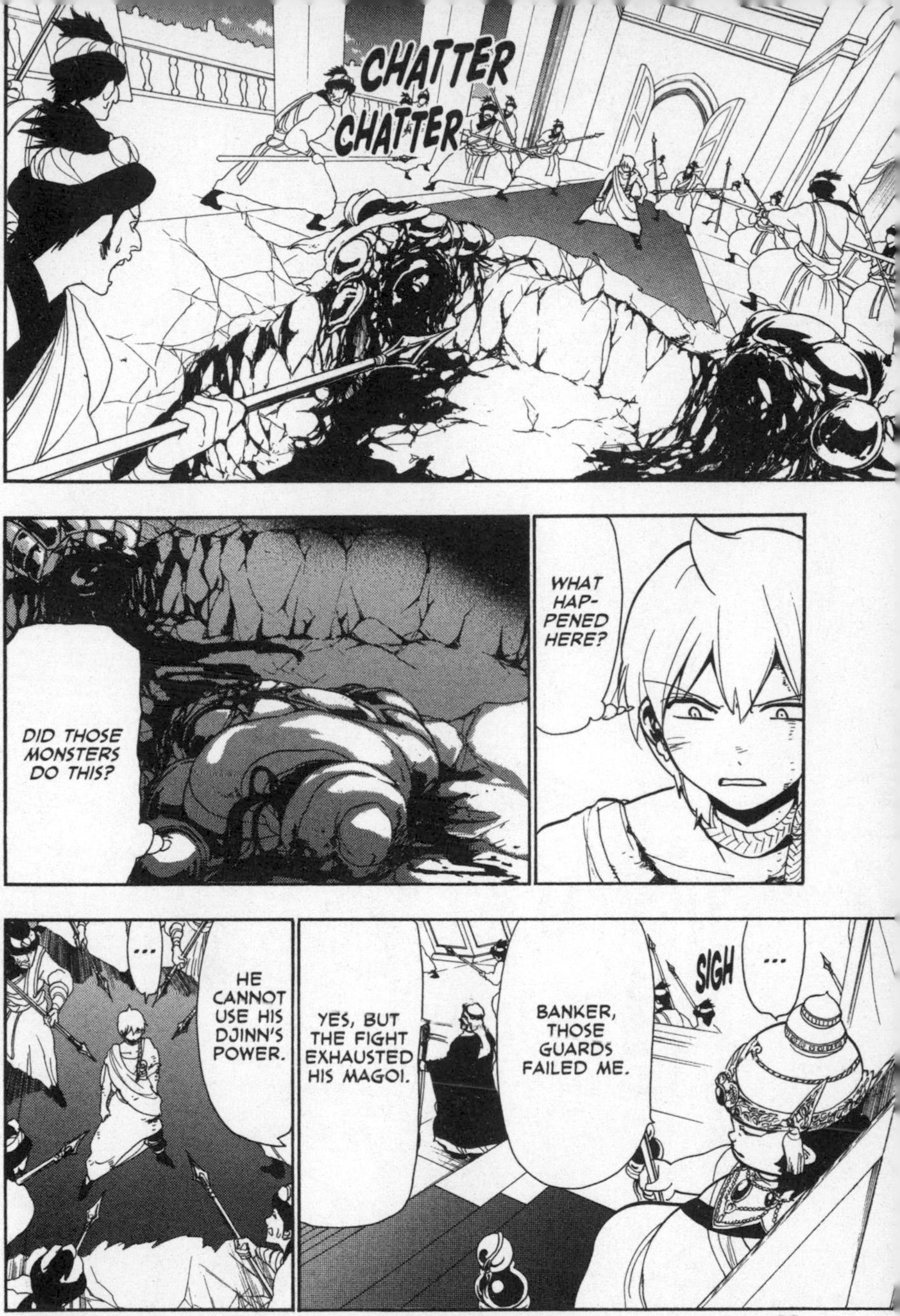
CHATTER
CHATTER
WHAT HAP-PENED HERE?
DID THOSE MONSTERS DO THIS?
...
SIGH
BANKER, THOSE GUARDS FAILED ME.
YES, BUT THE FIGHT EXHAUSTED HIS MAGOI.
HE CANNOT USE HIS DJINN'S POWER.
...

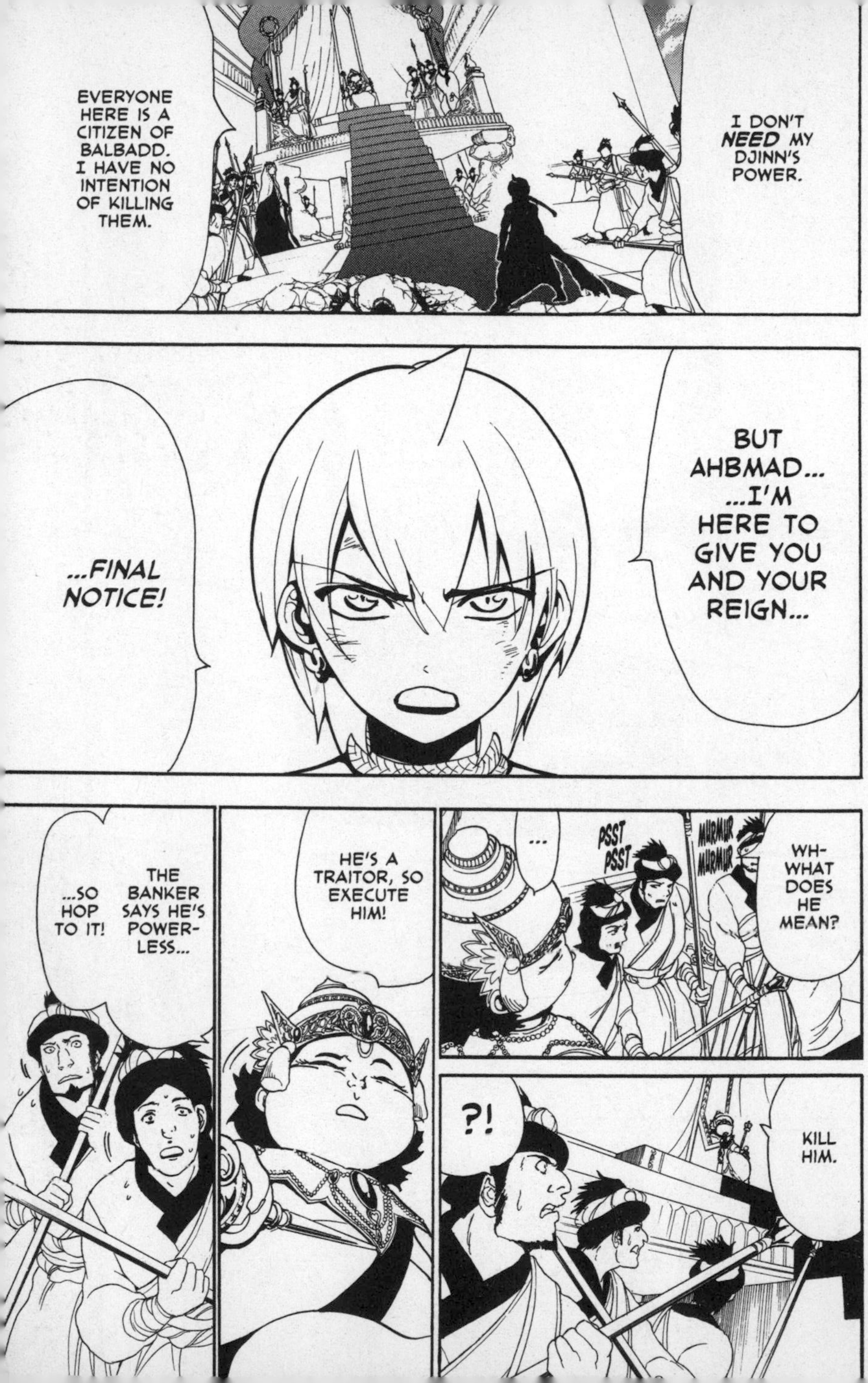
I DON'T NEED MY DJINN'S POWER.
EVERYONE HERE IS A CITIZEN OF BALBADD. I HAVE NO INTENTION OF KILLING THEM.
BUT AHBMAD... ...I'M HERE TO GIVE YOU AND YOUR REIGN...
...FINAL NOTICE!
WH-WHAT DOES HE MEAN?
MURMUR MURMUR
PSST PSST
...
KILL HIM.
?!
HE'S A TRAITOR, SO EXECUTE HIM!
THE BANKER SAYS HE'S POWERLESS...
...SO HOP TO IT!

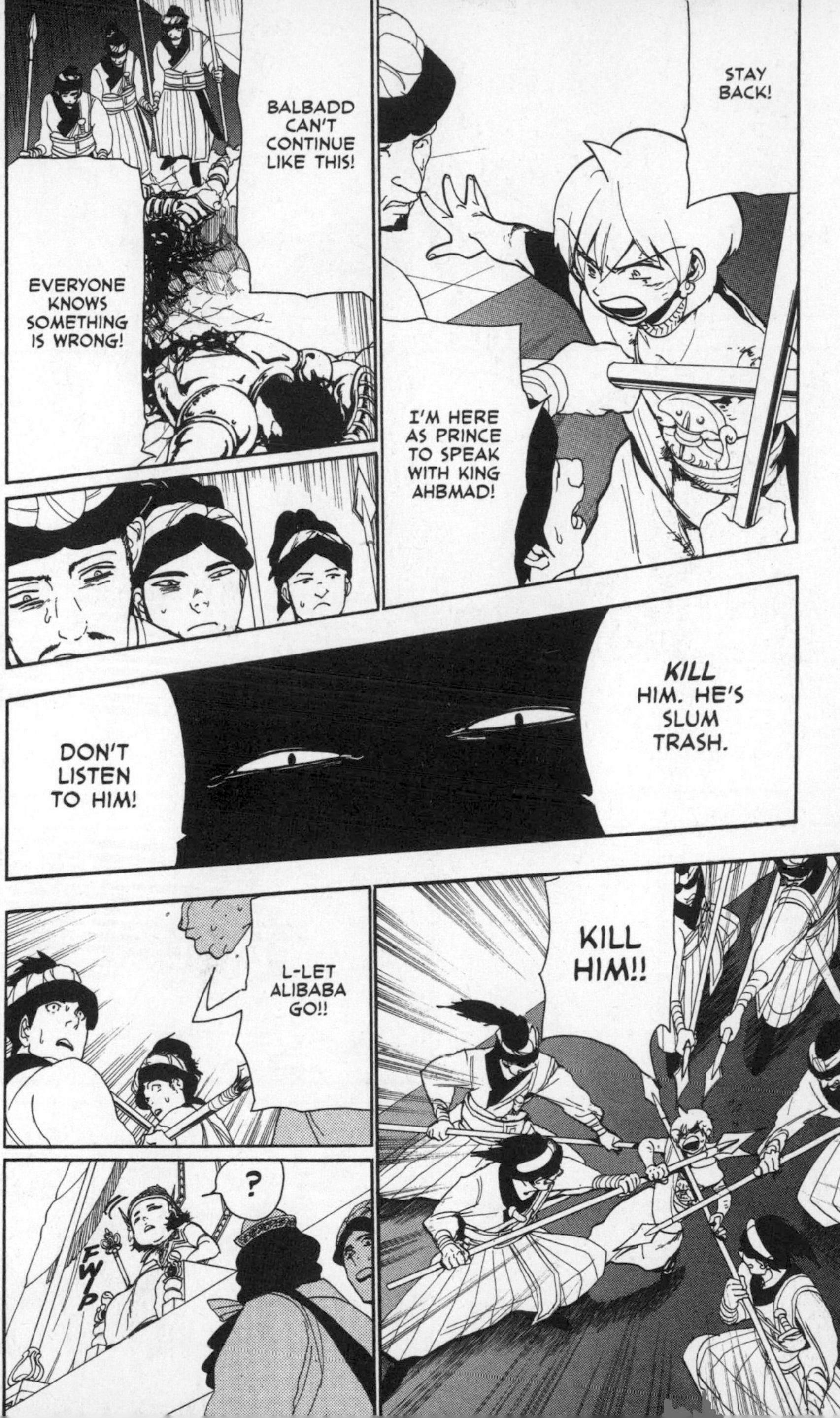
STAY BACK!
I'M HERE AS PRINCE TO SPEAK WITH KING AHBMAD!
BALBADD CAN'T CONTINUE LIKE THIS!
EVERYONE KNOWS SOMETHING IS WRONG!
KILL HIM. HE'S SLUM TRASH.
DON'T LISTEN TO HIM!
KILL HIM!!
L-LET ALIBABA GO!!
?
FWP

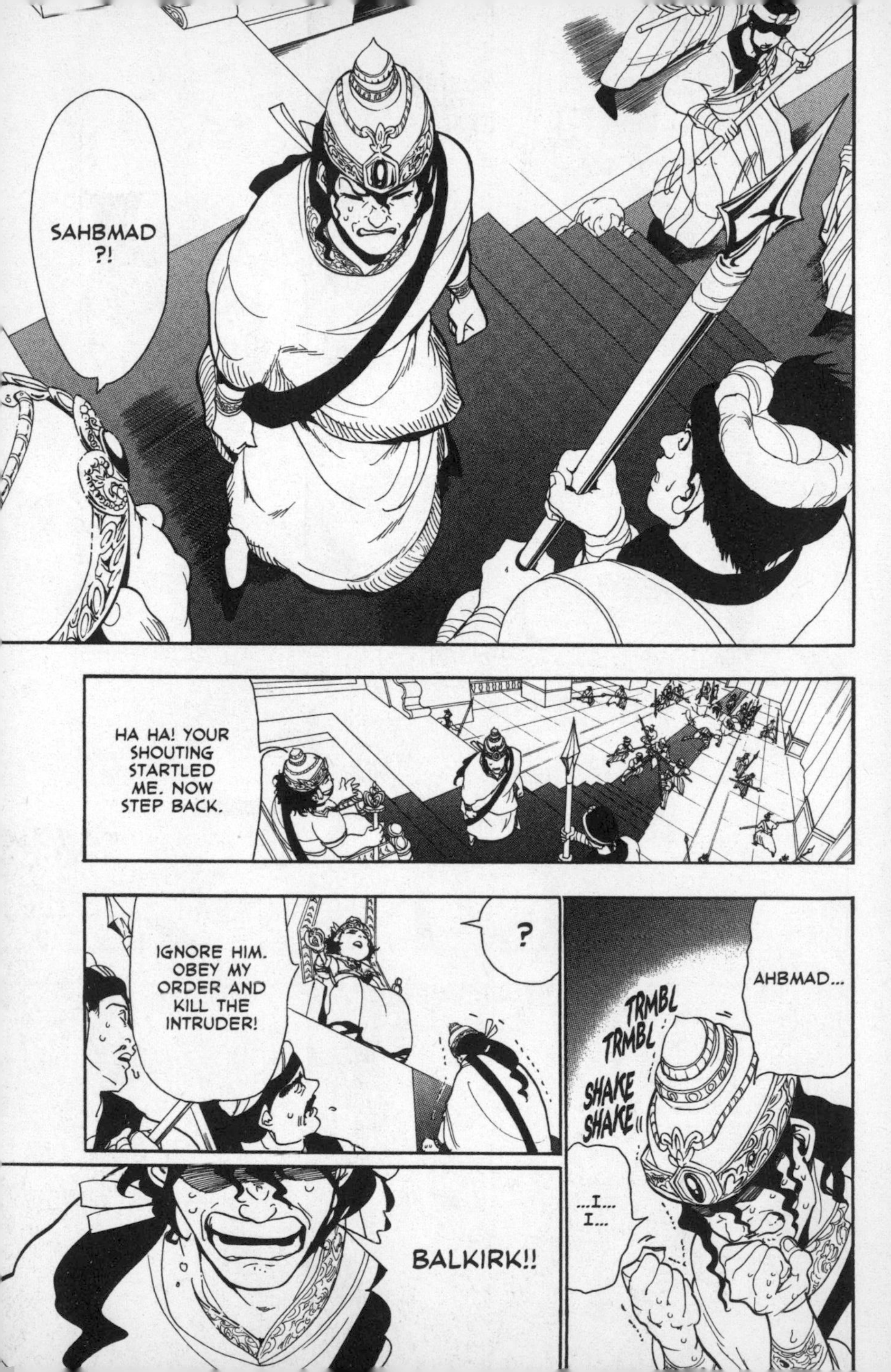
SAHBMAD ?!
HA HA! YOUR SHOUTING STARTLED ME. NOW STEP BACK.
AHBMAD...
TRMBL TRMBL
SHAKE SHAKE
...I... I...
?
IGNORE HIM. OBEY MY ORDER AND KILL THE INTRUDER!
BALKIRK!!

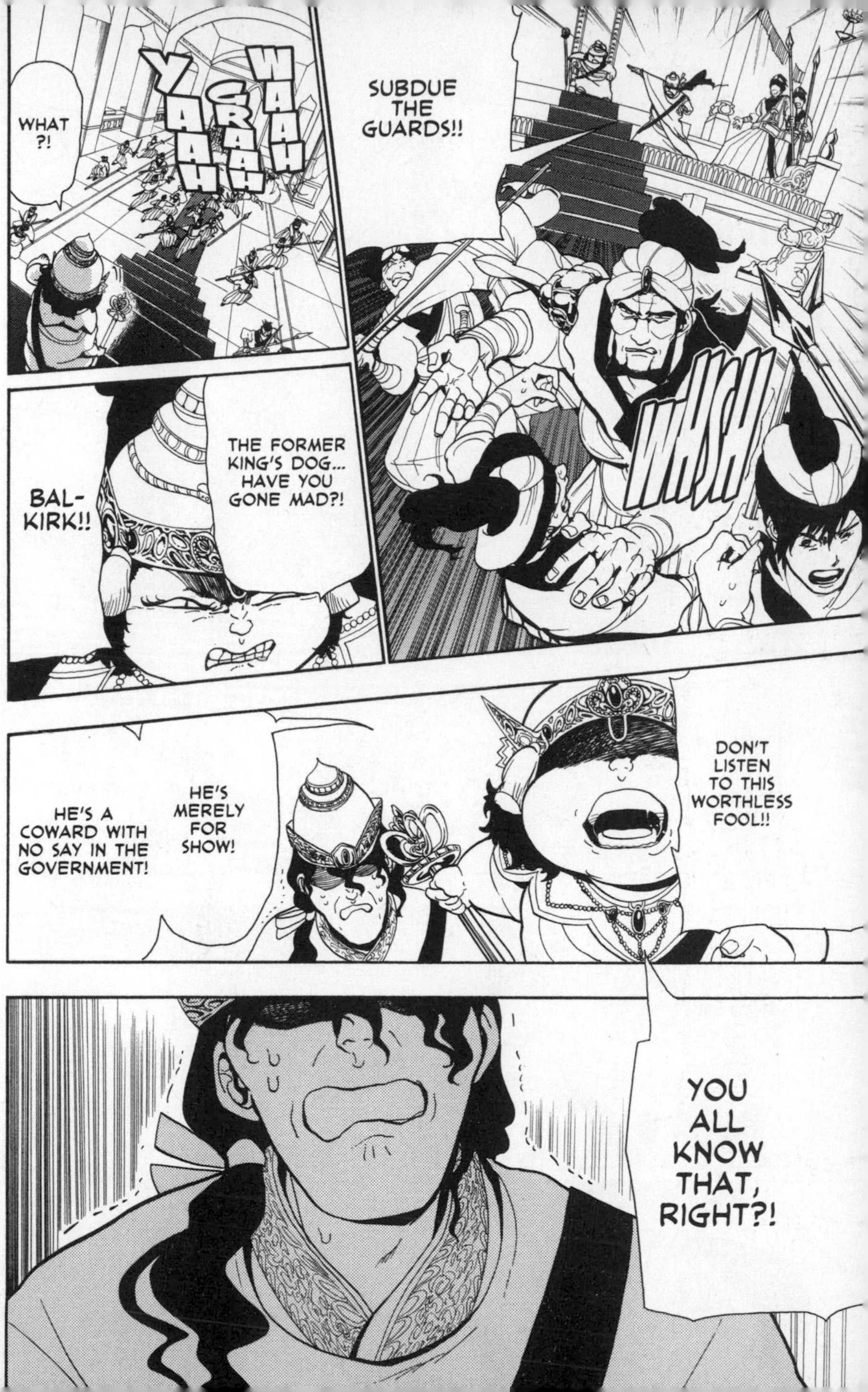
SUBDUE THE GUARDS!!
WHSH
WAAH
GRAAH
YAAAH
WHAT?!
THE FORMER KING'S DOG... HAVE YOU GONE MAD?!
BAL-KIRK!!
DON'T LISTEN TO THIS WORTHLESS FOOL!!
HE'S MERELY FOR SHOW!
HE'S A COWARD WITH NO SAY IN THE GOVERNMENT!
YOU ALL KNOW THAT, RIGHT?!

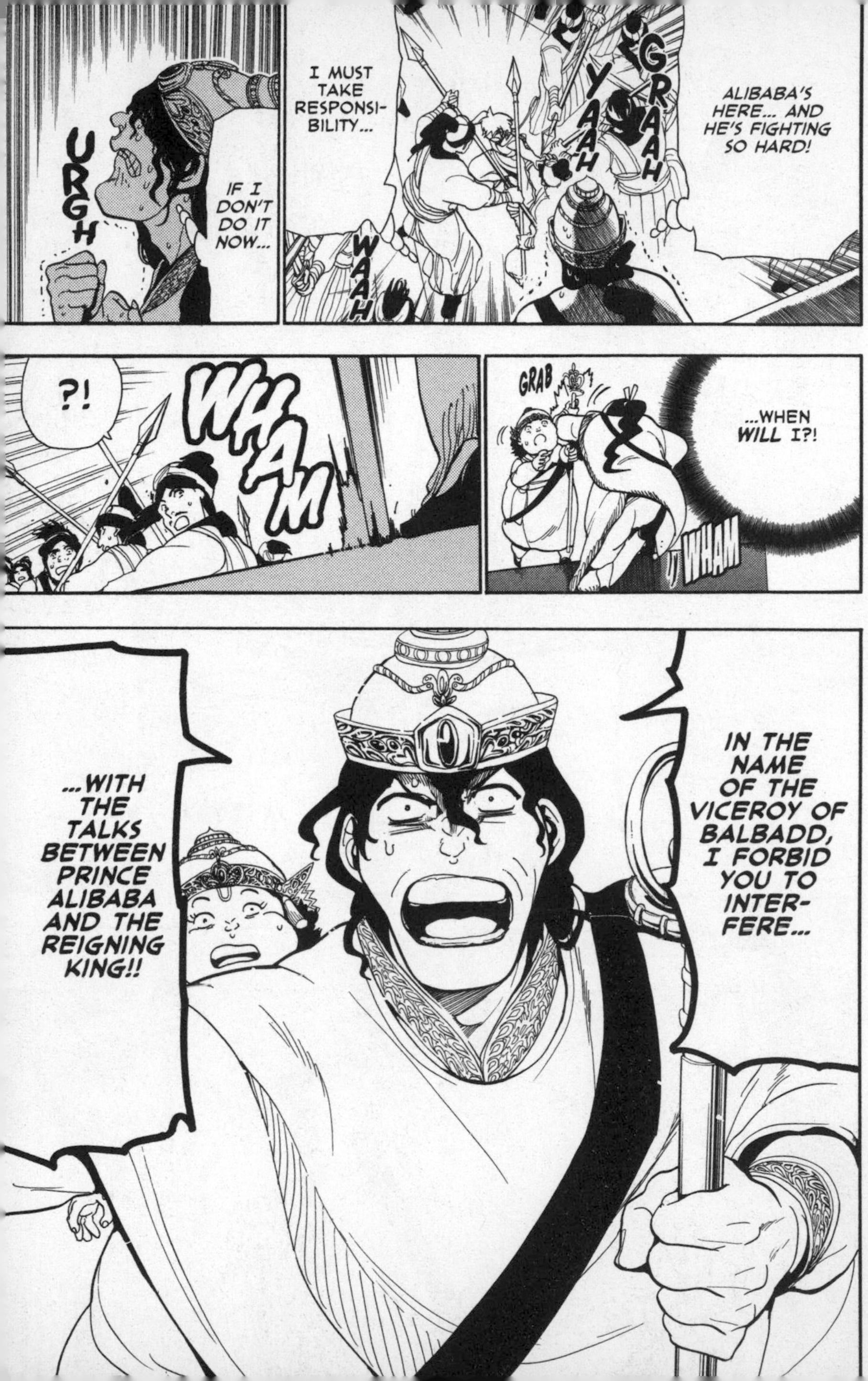
ALIBABA'S HERE... AND HE'S FIGHTING SO HARD!
GRAAAH
YAAAH
WAAH
I MUST TAKE RESPONSI-BILITY...
IF I DON'T DO IT NOW...
URGH
...WHEN WILL I?!
GRAB
WHAM
WHAM
?!
IN THE NAME OF THE VICEROY OF BALBADD, I FORBID YOU TO INTER-FERE...
...WITH THE TALKS BETWEEN PRINCE ALIBABA AND THE REIGNING KING!!

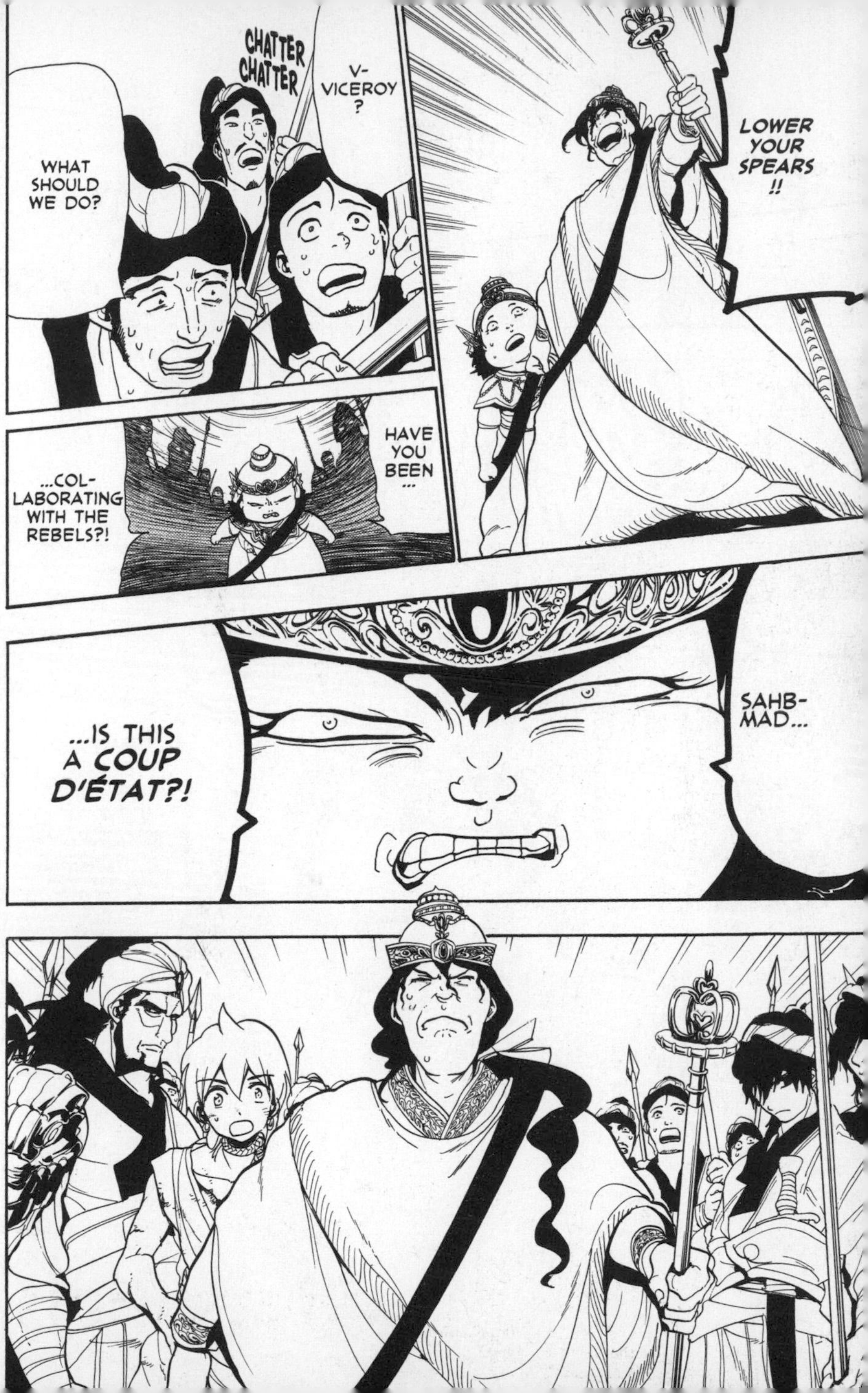
LOWER YOUR SPEARS !!
V-VICEROY ?
CHATTER CHATTER
WHAT SHOULD WE DO?
HAVE YOU BEEN ...
...COL-LABORATING WITH THE REBELS?!
SAHB-MAD...
...IS THIS A COUP D'ÉTAT?!

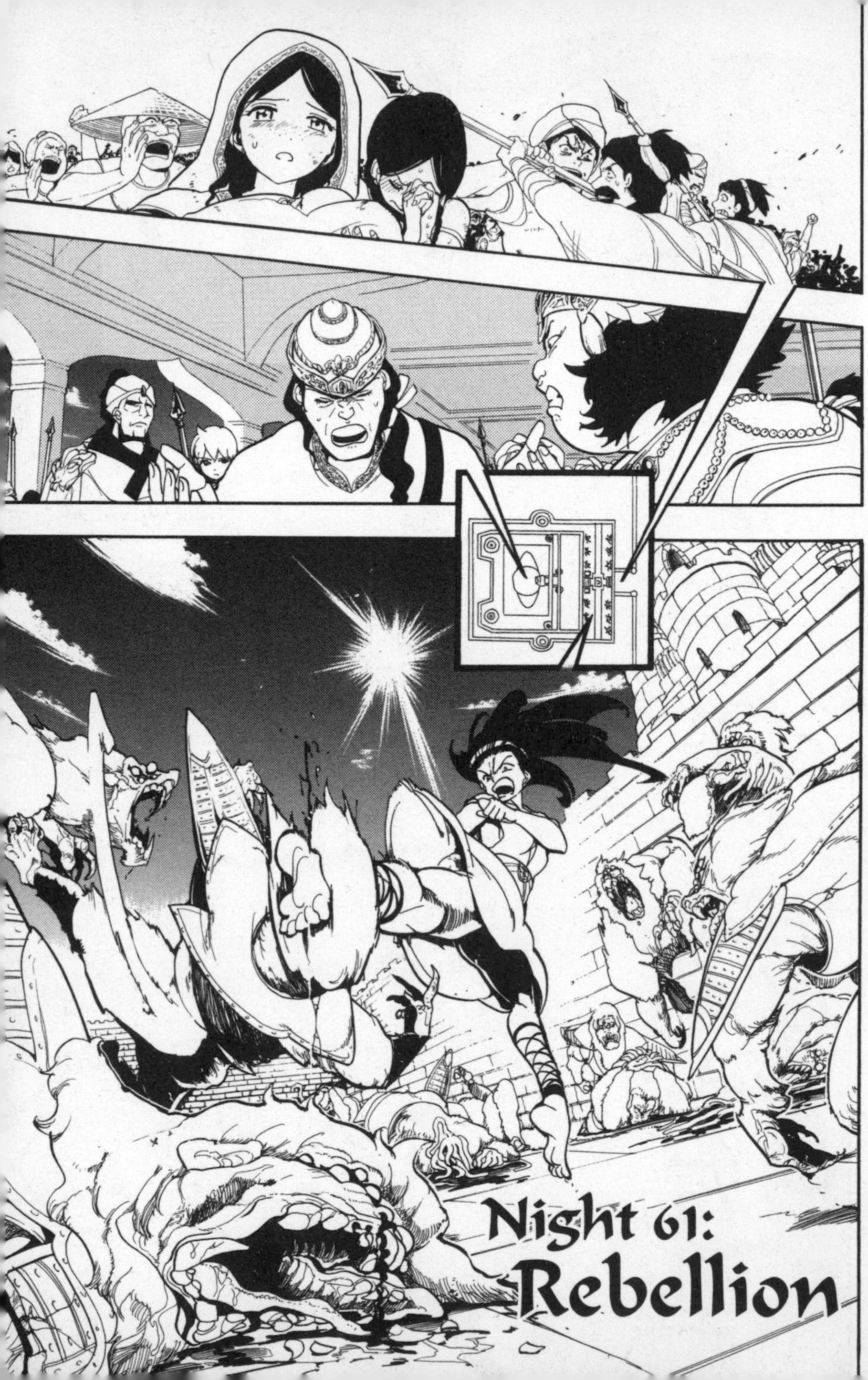
Night 61:
Rebellion

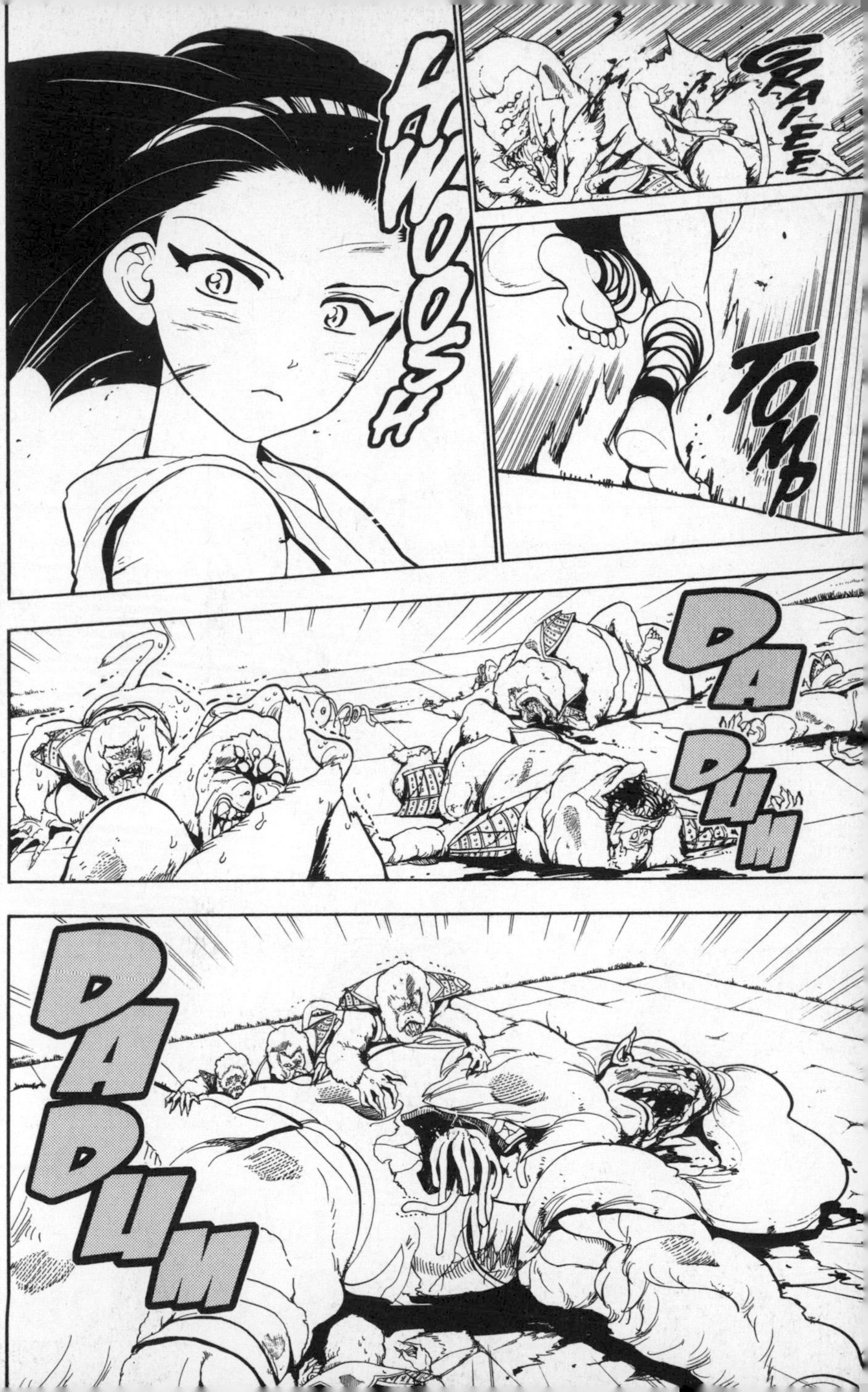
GRAIEEE
TOMP
WHOOOSH
DA DUM
DA DUM

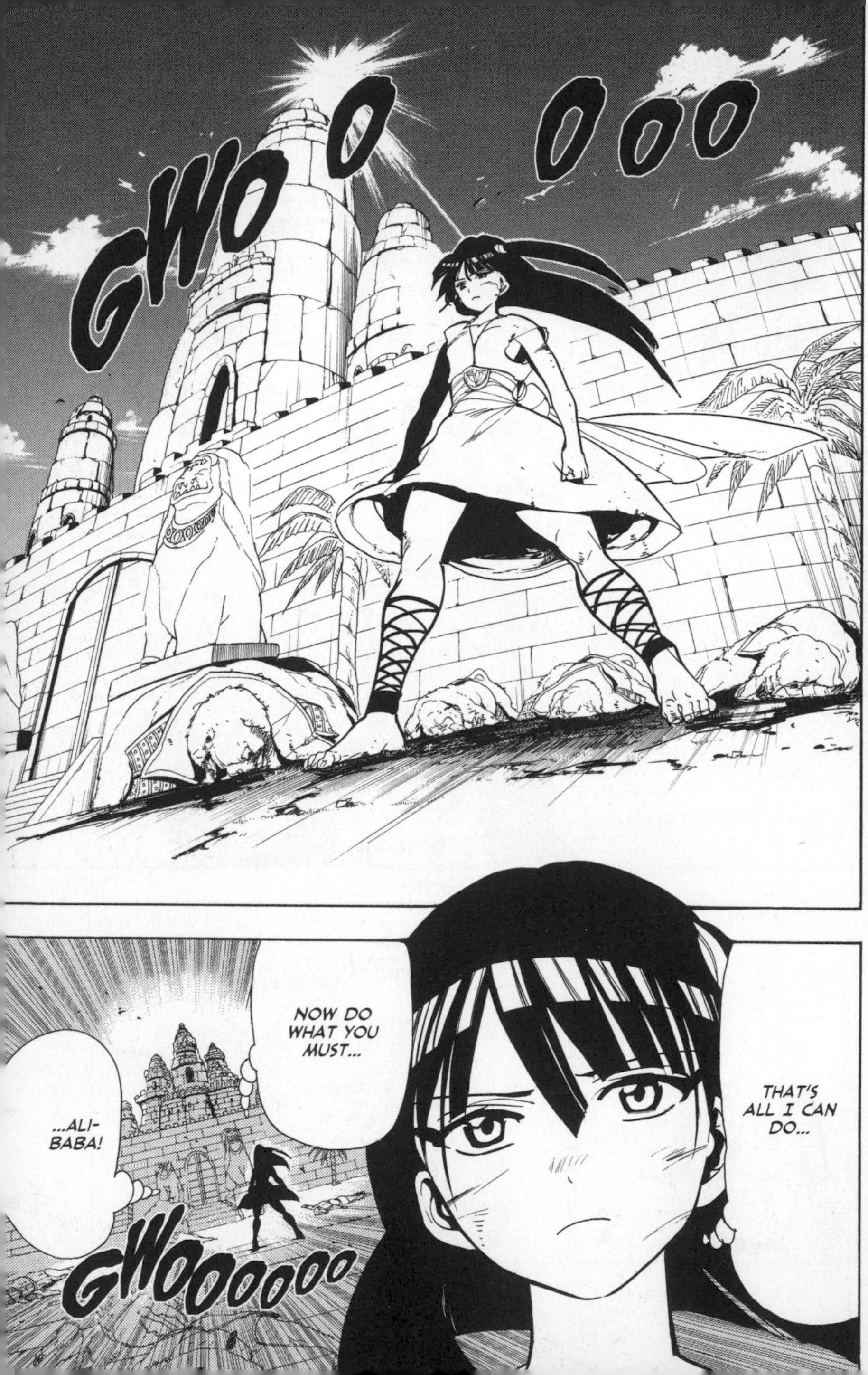
GWO O O O O
THAT'S ALL I CAN DO...
NOW DO WHAT YOU MUST...
...ALI-BABA!
GWOOOOOOO

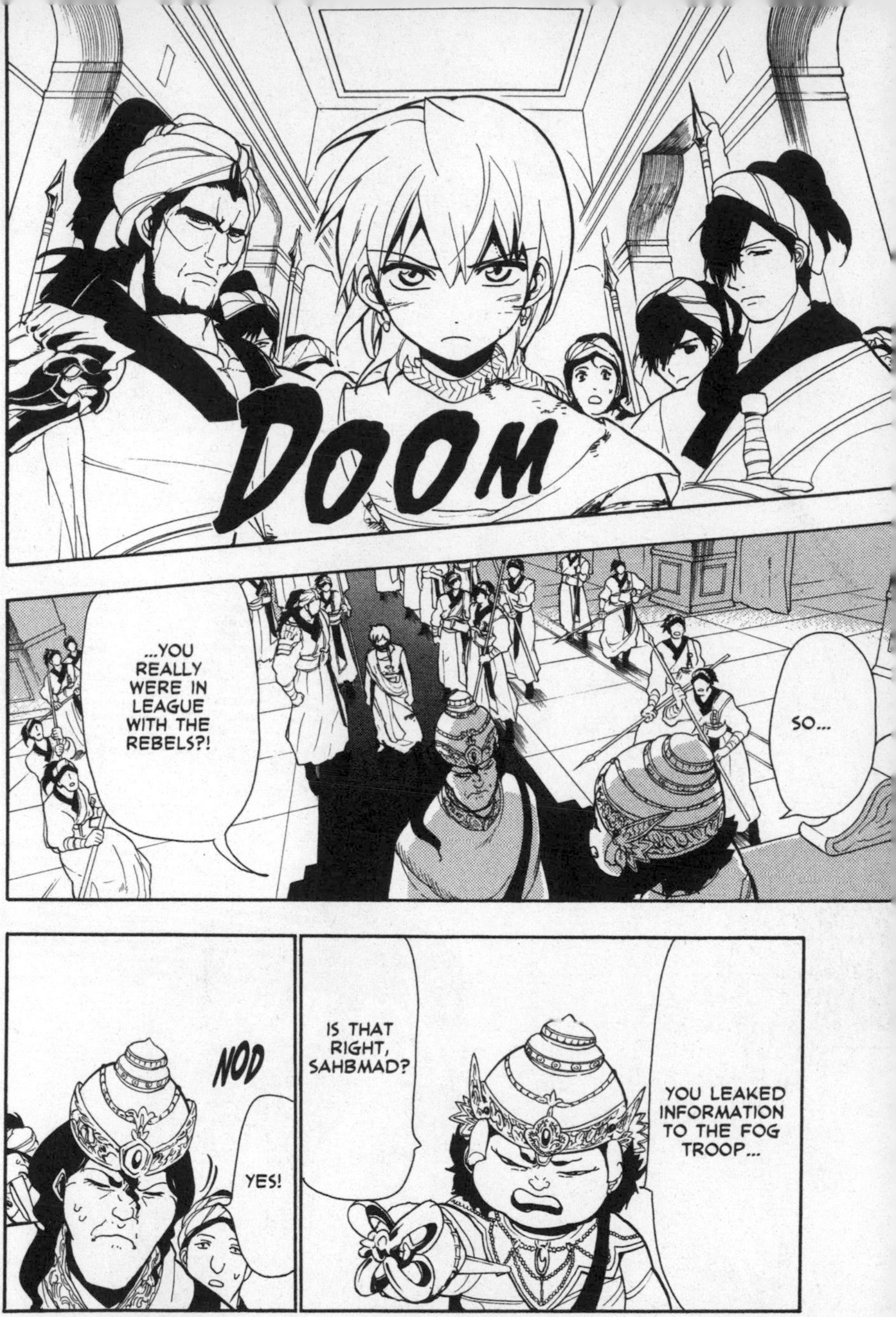
DOOM
SO...
...YOU REALLY WERE IN LEAGUE WITH THE REBELS?!
YOU LEAKED INFORMATION TO THE FOG TROOP...
IS THAT RIGHT, SAHBMAD?
NOD
YES!

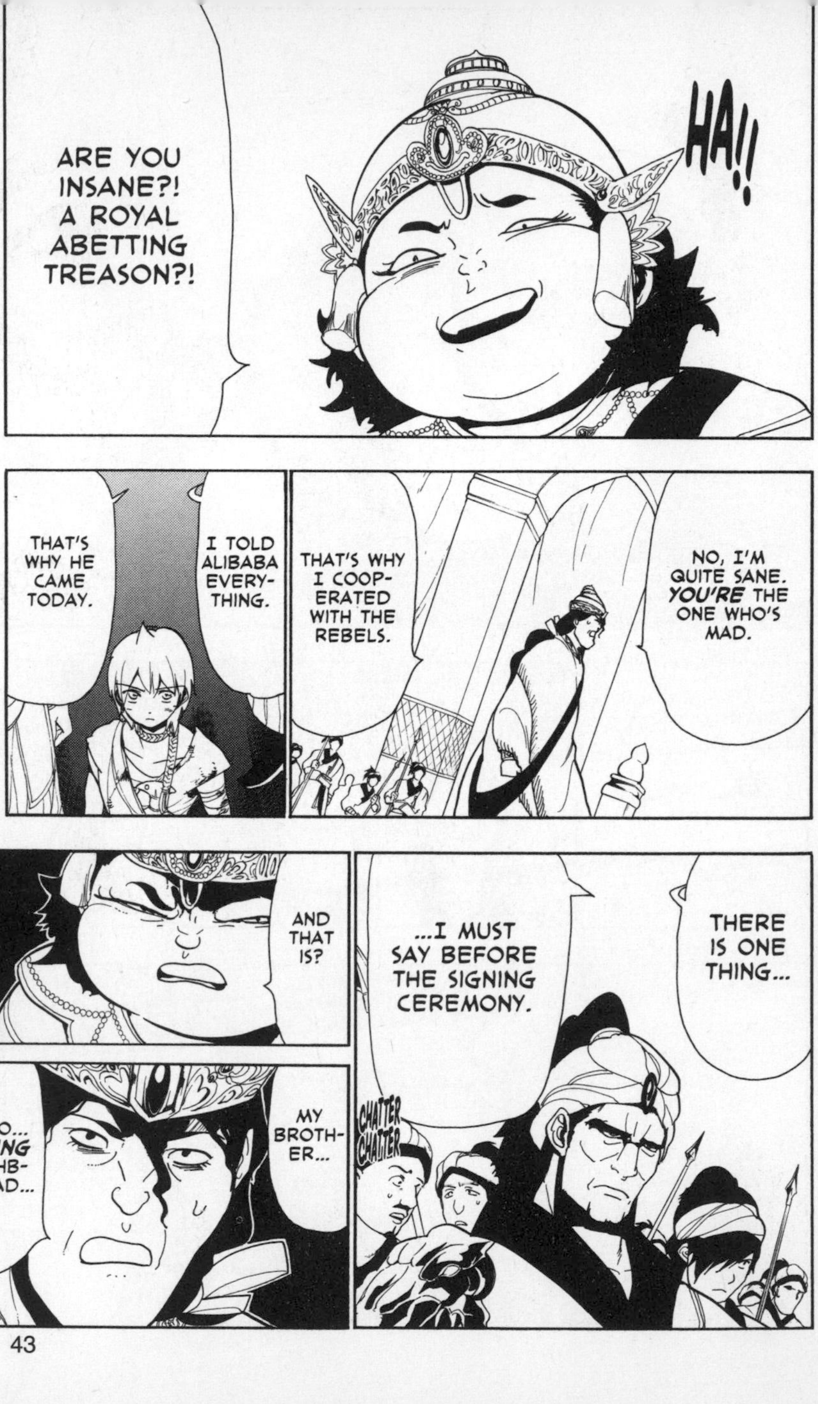
HA!!
ARE YOU INSANE?! A ROYAL ABETTING TREASON?!
NO, I'M QUITE SANE. YOU'RE THE ONE WHO'S MAD.
THAT'S WHY I COOPERATED WITH THE REBELS.
I TOLD ALIBABA EVERYTHING.
THAT'S WHY HE CAME TODAY.
THERE IS ONE THING...
...I MUST SAY BEFORE THE SIGNING CEREMONY.
CHATTER CHATTER
AND THAT IS?
MY BROTHER...
NO... KING AHBMAD...
...

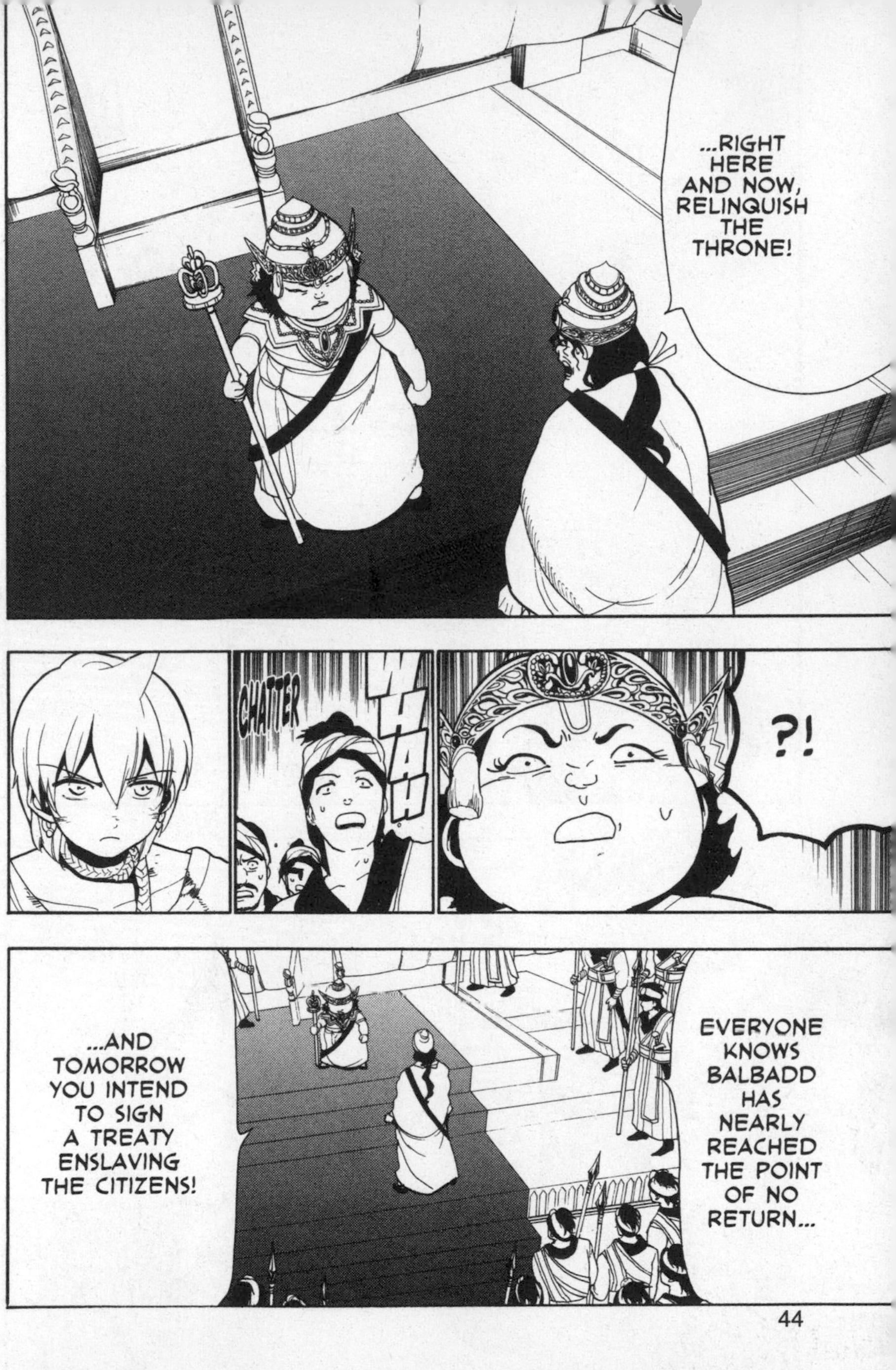
...RIGHT HERE AND NOW, RELINQUISH THE THRONE!
?!
WHAH
CHATTER
EVERYONE KNOWS BALBADD HAS NEARLY REACHED THE POINT OF NO RETURN...
...AND TOMORROW YOU INTEND TO SIGN A TREATY ENSLAVING THE CITIZENS!

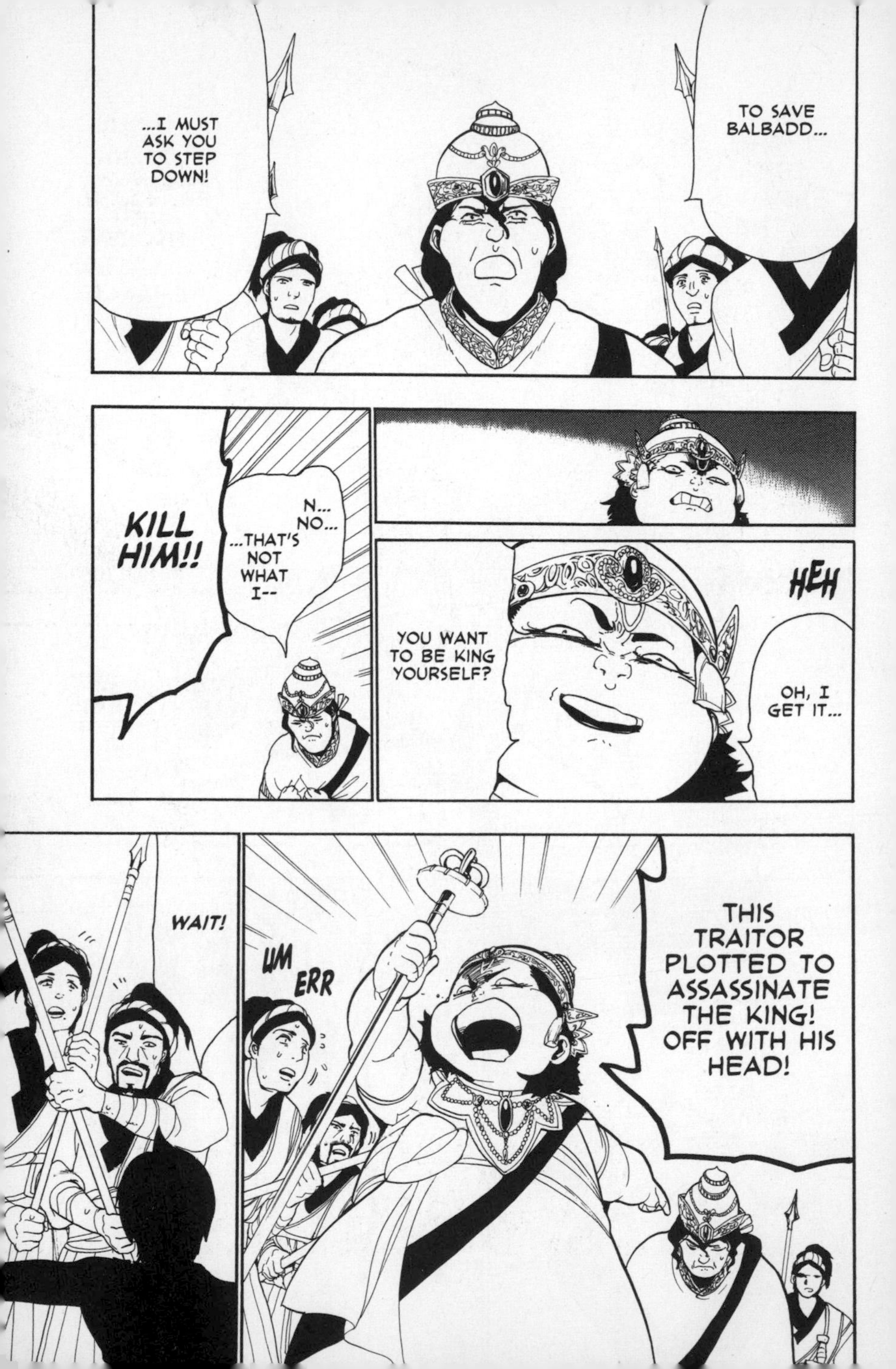
TO SAVE BALBADD...
...I MUST ASK YOU TO STEP DOWN!
OH, I GET IT...
HEH
YOU WANT TO BE KING YOURSELF?
N... NO... ...THAT'S NOT WHAT I--
KILL HIM!!
THIS TRAITOR PLOTTED TO ASSASSINATE THE KING! OFF WITH HIS HEAD!
UM
ERR
WAIT!

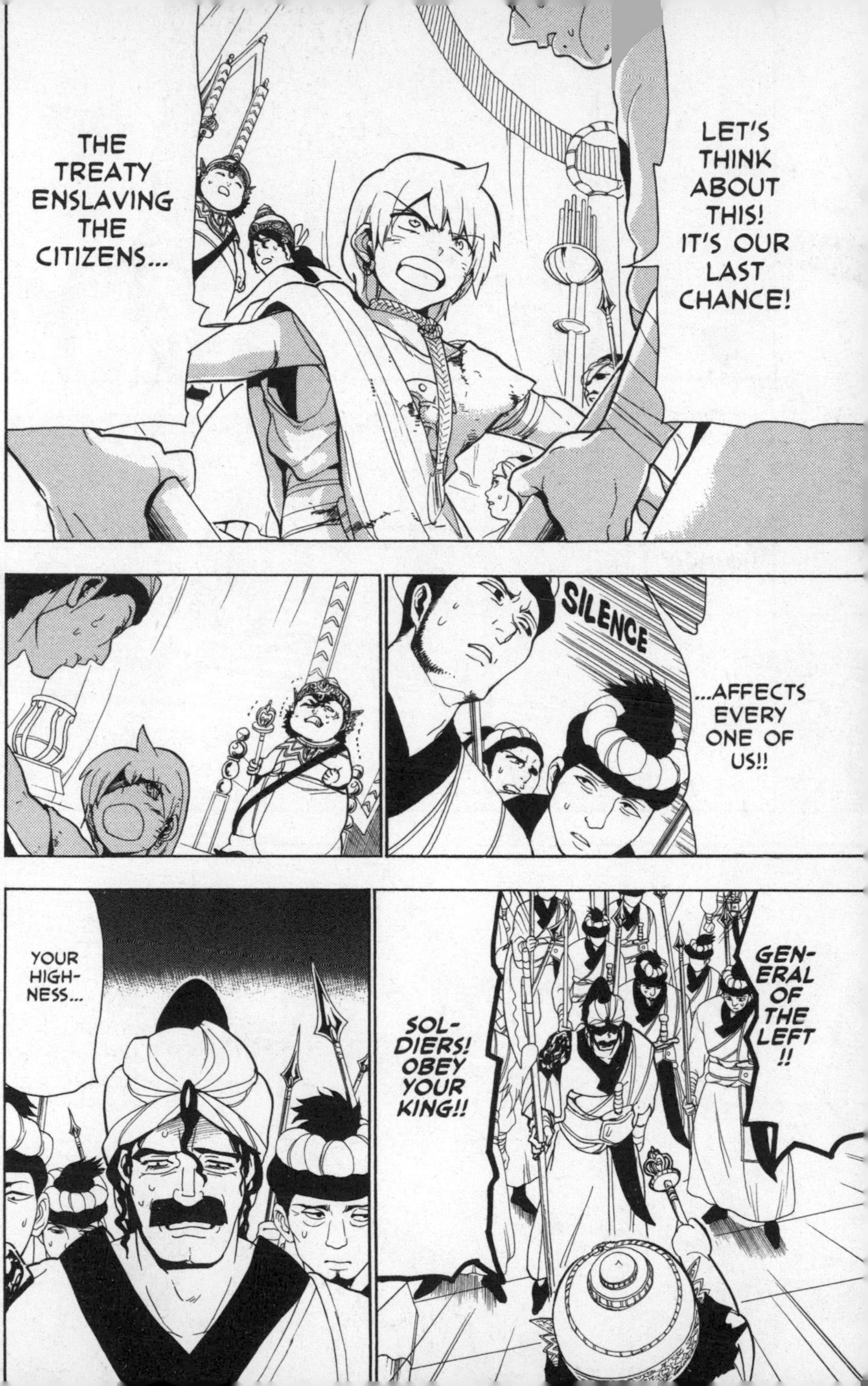
LET'S THINK ABOUT THIS! IT'S OUR LAST CHANCE!
THE TREATY ENSLAVING THE CITIZENS...
SILENCE
...AFFECTS EVERY ONE OF US!!
GEN-ERAL OF THE LEFT !!
SOL-DIERS! OBEY YOUR KING!!
YOUR HIGH-NESS...

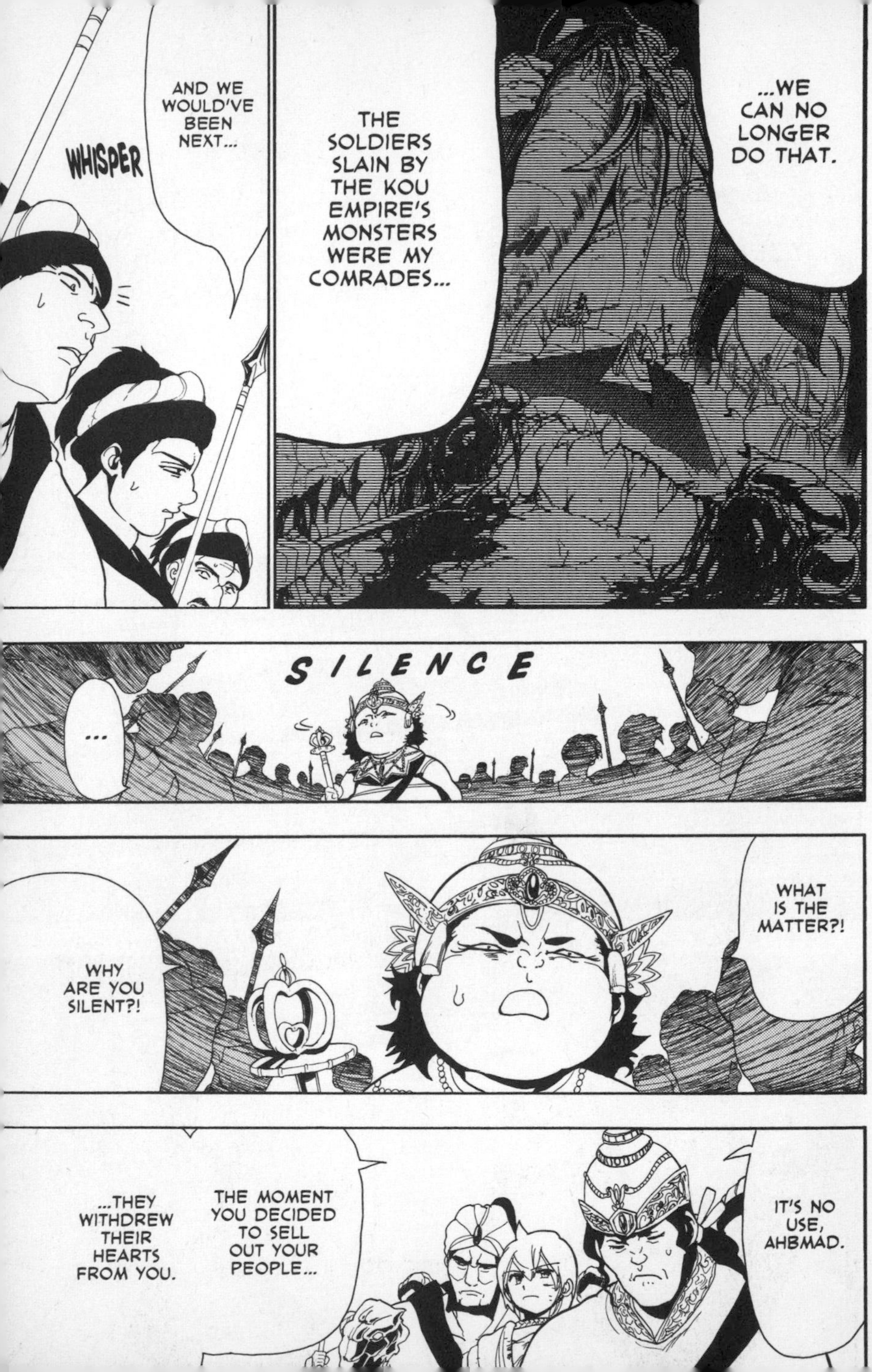
...WE CAN NO LONGER DO THAT.
THE SOLDIERS SLAIN BY THE KOU EMPIRE'S MONSTERS WERE MY COMRADES...
AND WE WOULD'VE BEEN NEXT...
WHISPER
SILENCE
...
WHAT IS THE MATTER?!
WHY ARE YOU SILENT?!
IT'S NO USE, AHBMAD.
THE MOMENT YOU DECIDED TO SELL OUT YOUR PEOPLE...
...THEY WITHDREW THEIR HEARTS FROM YOU.

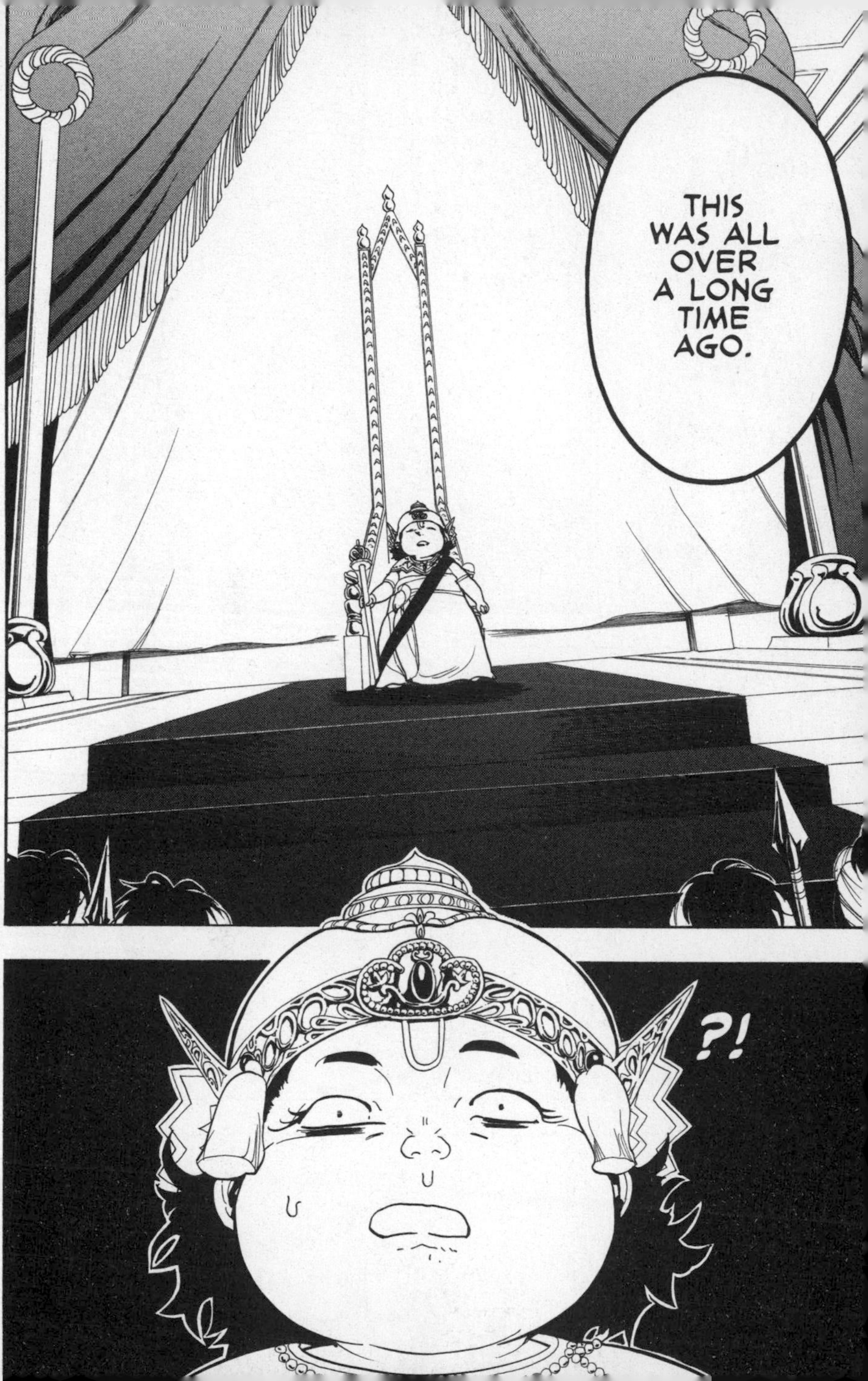
THIS WAS ALL OVER A LONG TIME AGO.
?!

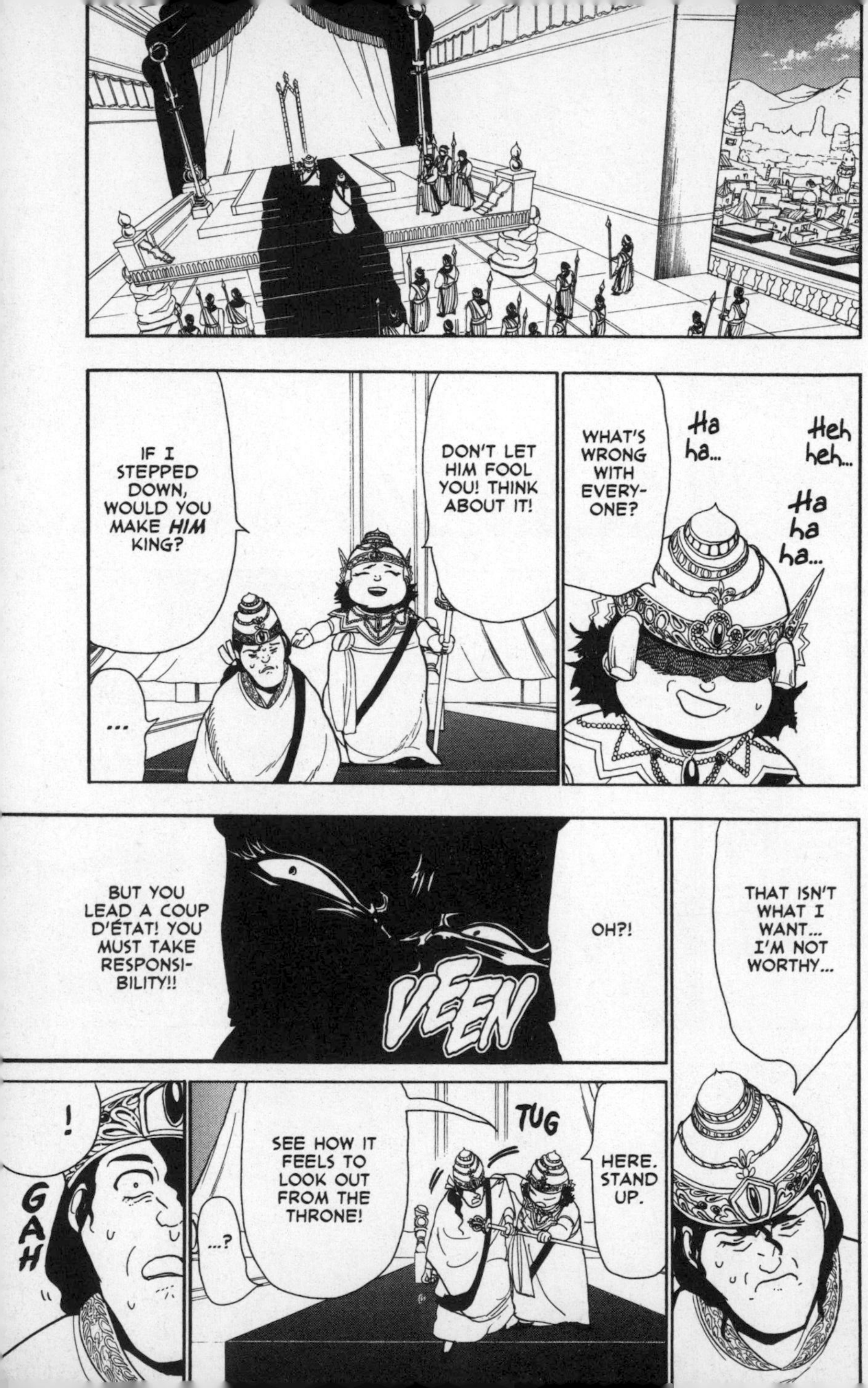
Heh heh...
Ha ha...
WHAT'S WRONG WITH EVERY-ONE?
Ha ha ha...
DON'T LET HIM FOOL YOU! THINK ABOUT IT!
IF I STEPPED DOWN, WOULD YOU MAKE *HIM* KING?
...
THAT ISN'T WHAT I WANT... I'M NOT WORTHY...
OH?!
BUT YOU LEAD A COUP D'ÉTAT! YOU MUST TAKE RESPONSI-BILITY!!
VEEN
HERE. STAND UP.
TUG
SEE HOW IT FEELS TO LOOK OUT FROM THE THRONE!
...?
!
GAH

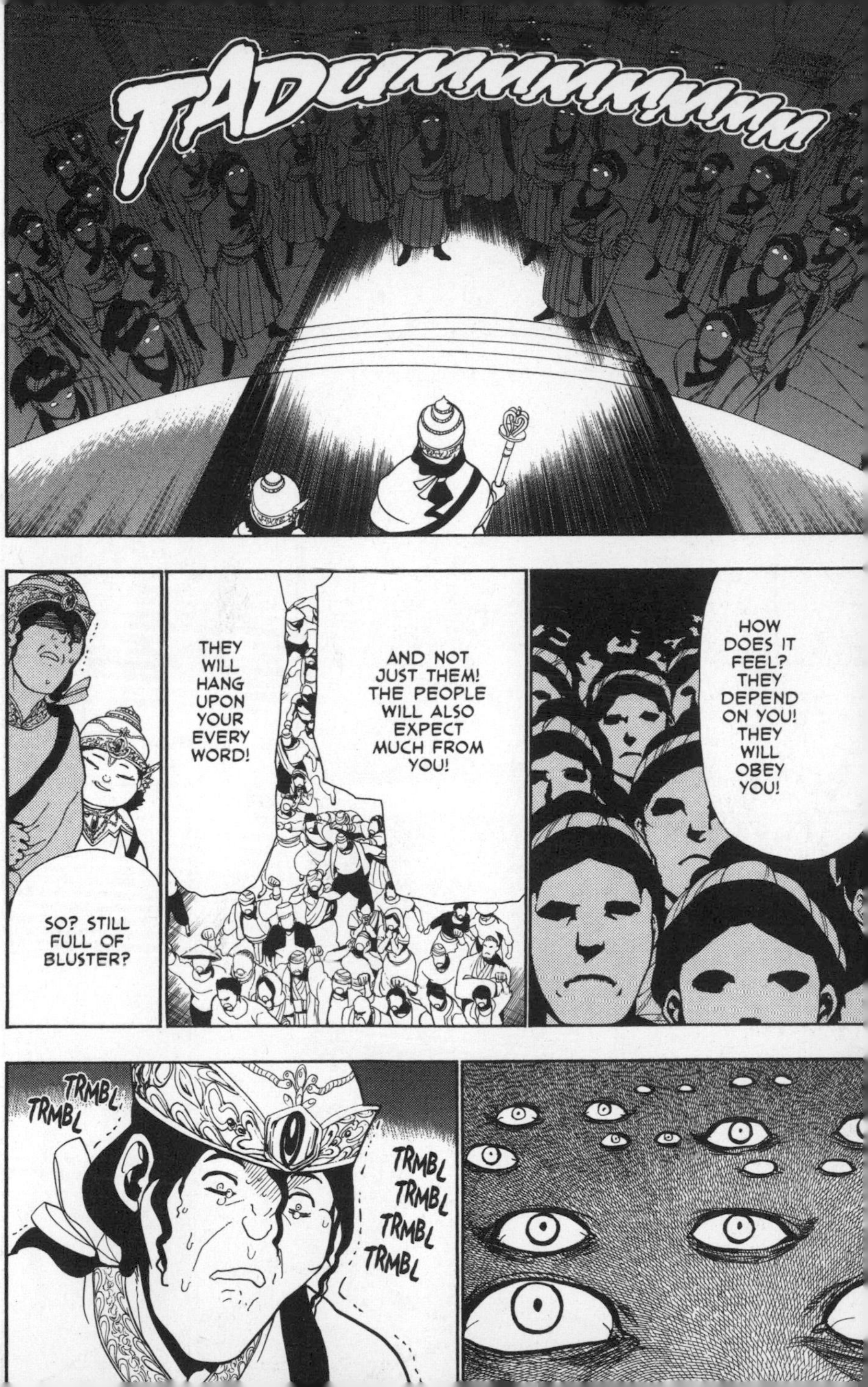
TADUMMMMMMMM
HOW DOES IT FEEL? THEY DEPEND ON YOU! THEY WILL OBEY YOU!
AND NOT JUST THEM! THE PEOPLE WILL ALSO EXPECT MUCH FROM YOU!
THEY WILL HANG UPON YOUR EVERY WORD!
SO? STILL FULL OF BLUSTER?
TRMBL TRMBL TRMBL TRMBL
TRMBL TRMBL

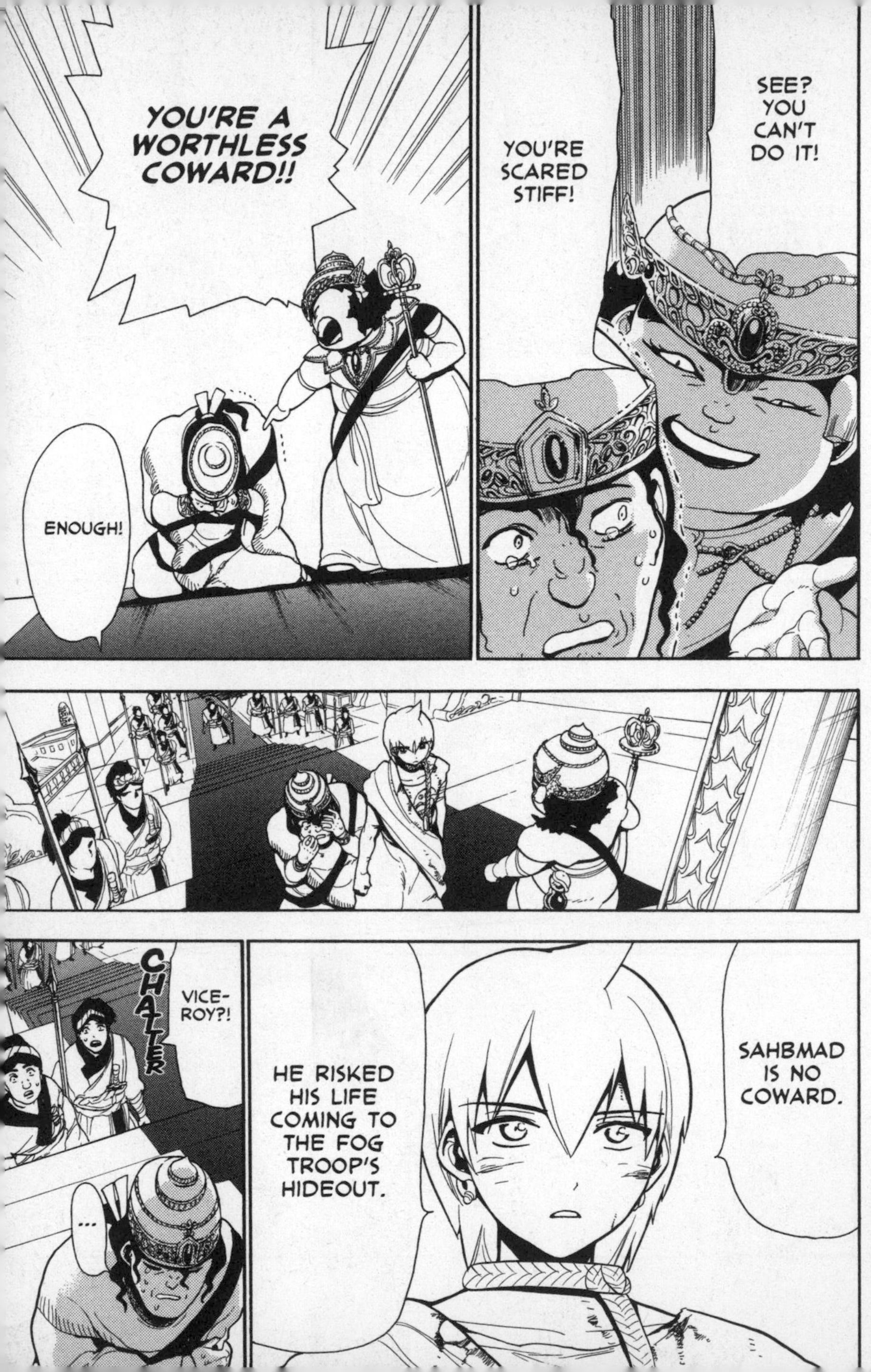
SEE? YOU CAN'T DO IT!
YOU'RE SCARED STIFF!
YOU'RE A WORTHLESS COWARD!!
ENOUGH!
SAHBMAD IS NO COWARD.
HE RISKED HIS LIFE COMING TO THE FOG TROOP'S HIDEOUT.
VICE-ROY?!
CHATTER
...

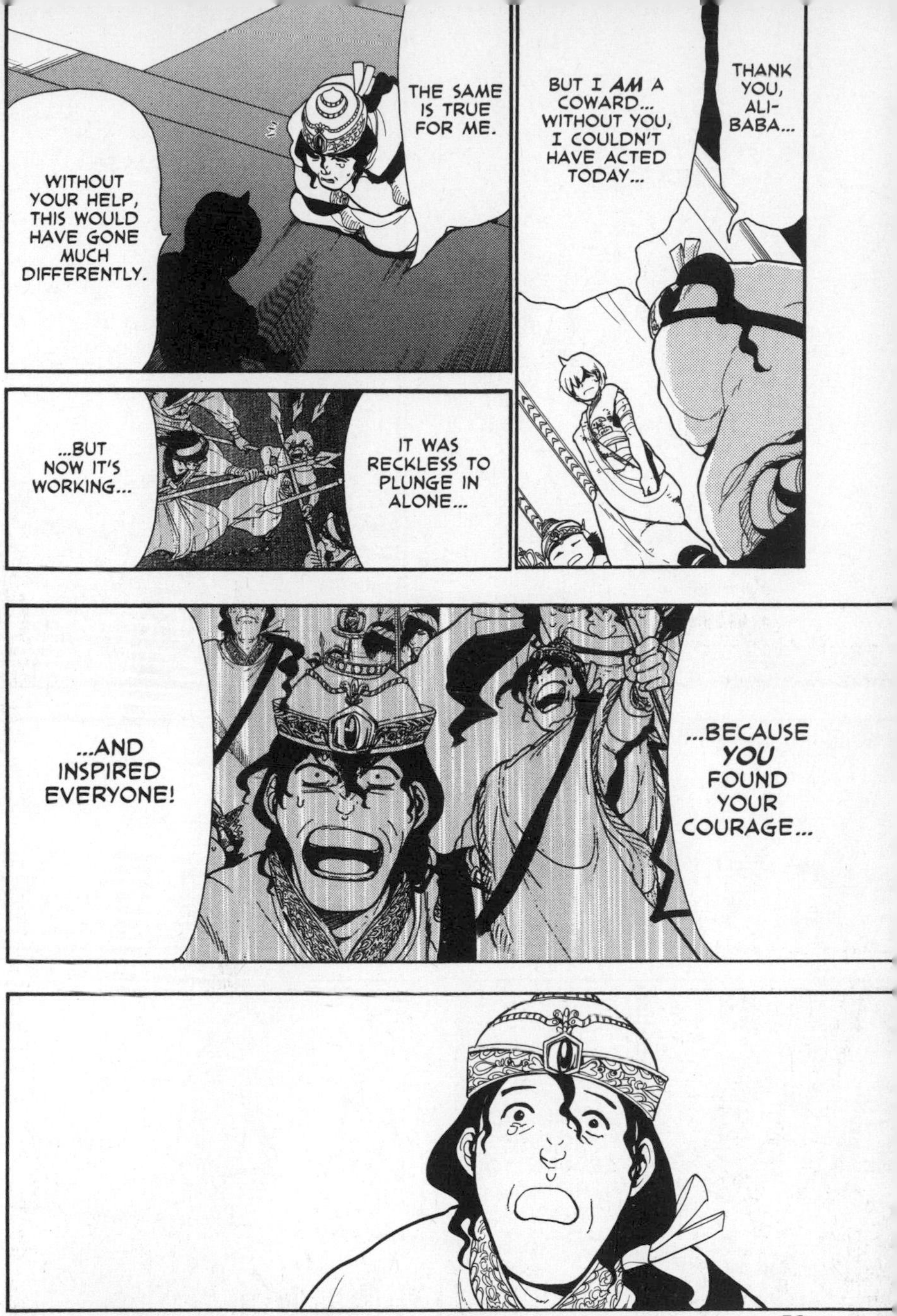
THANK YOU, ALI-BABA...
BUT I *AM* A COWARD... WITHOUT YOU, I COULDN'T HAVE ACTED TODAY...
THE SAME IS TRUE FOR ME.
WITHOUT YOUR HELP, THIS WOULD HAVE GONE MUCH DIFFERENTLY.
IT WAS RECKLESS TO PLUNGE IN ALONE...
...BUT NOW IT'S WORKING...
...BECAUSE *YOU* FOUND YOUR COURAGE...
...AND INSPIRED EVERYONE!

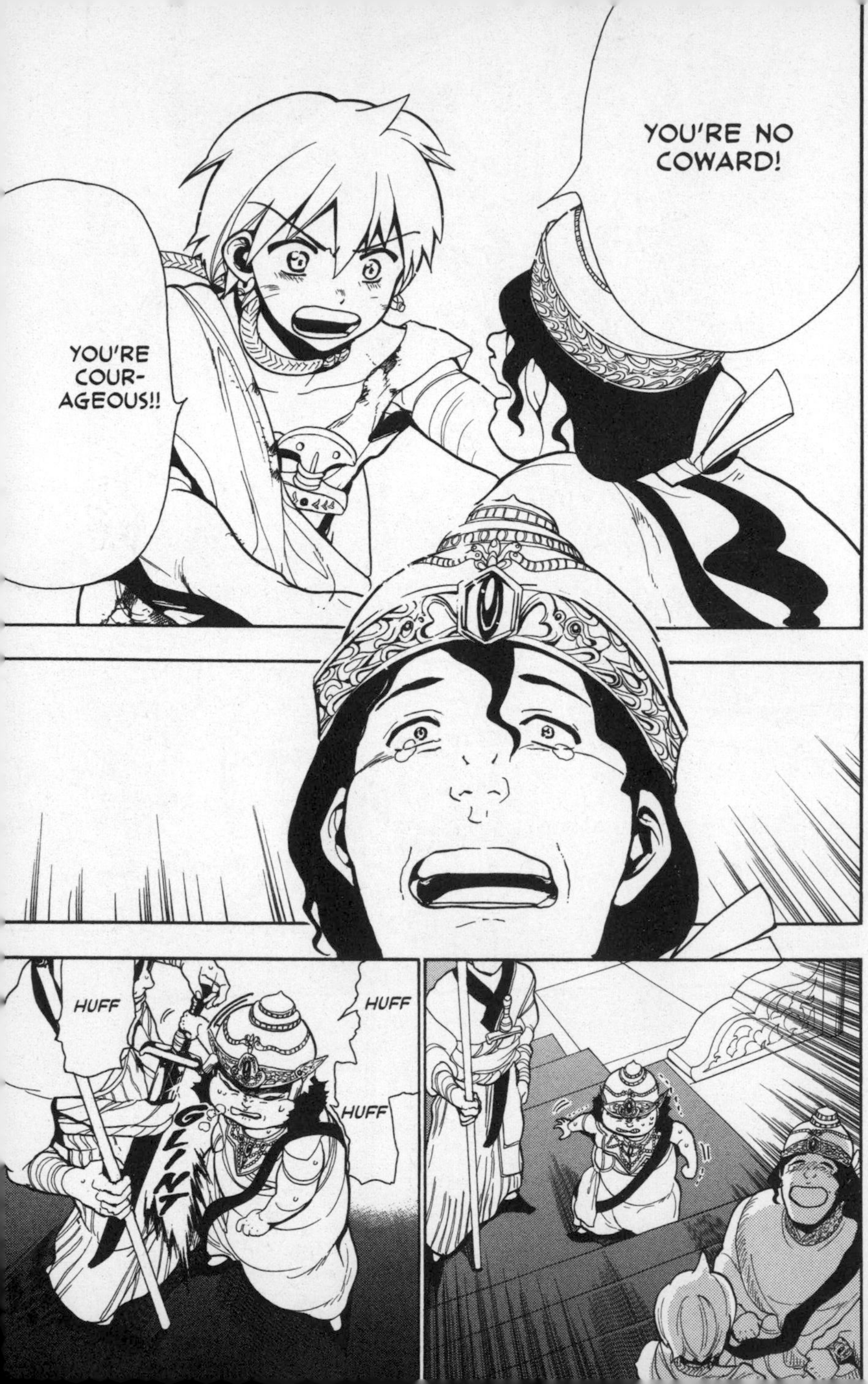
YOU'RE NO COWARD!
YOU'RE COUR-AGEOUS!!
HUFF
HUFF
HUFF
GLINT

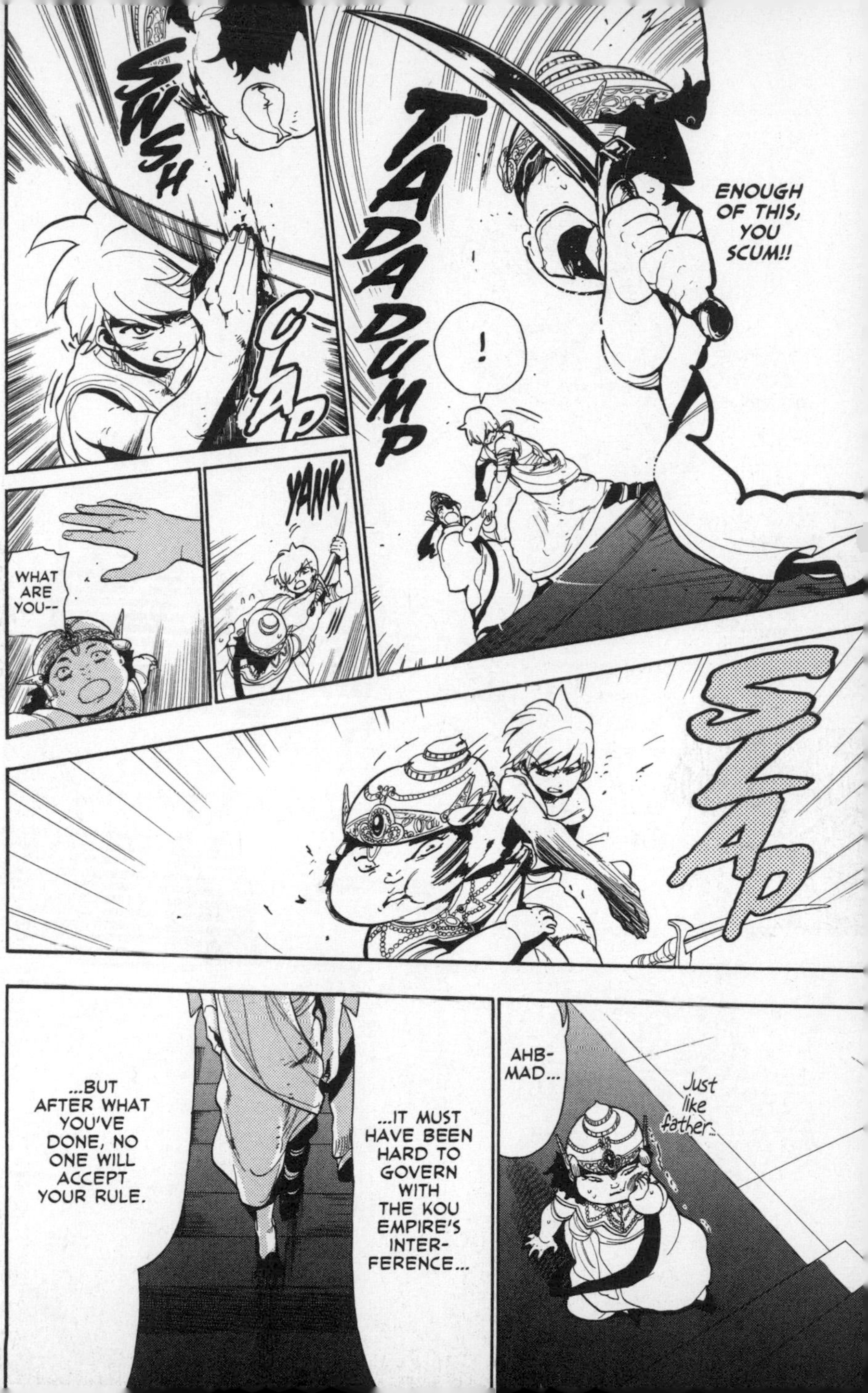
ENOUGH OF THIS, YOU SCUM!!
!
TADADUMP
SWSH
CLAP
YANK
WHAT ARE YOU--
SLAP
AHB-MAD...
Just like father...
...IT MUST HAVE BEEN HARD TO GOVERN WITH THE KOU EMPIRE'S INTER-FERENCE...
...BUT AFTER WHAT YOU'VE DONE, NO ONE WILL ACCEPT YOUR RULE.

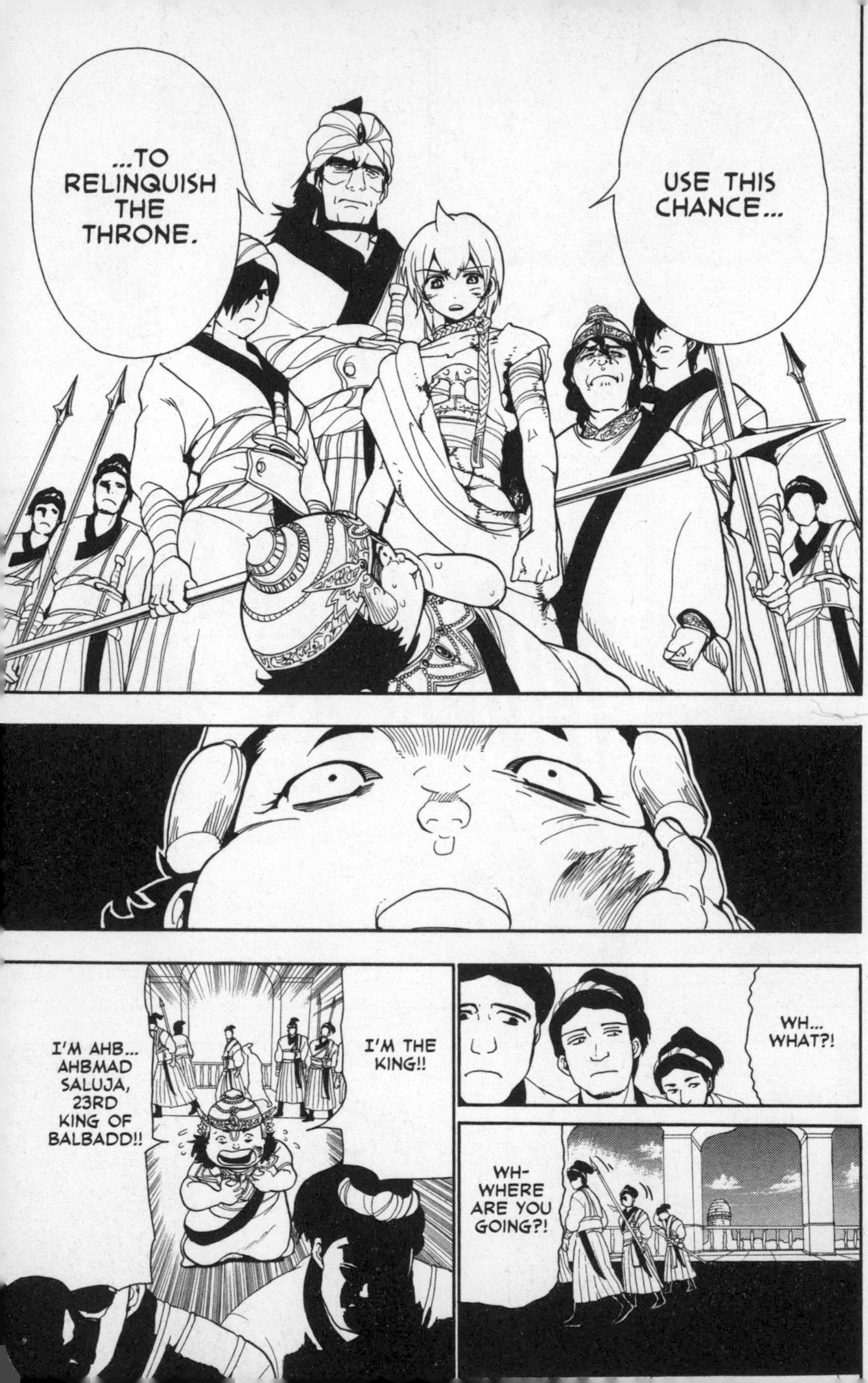
USE THIS CHANCE...
...TO RELINQUISH THE THRONE.
WH... WHAT?!
WH- WHERE ARE YOU GOING?!
I'M THE KING!!
I'M AHB... AHBMAD SALUJA, 23RD KING OF BALBADD!!

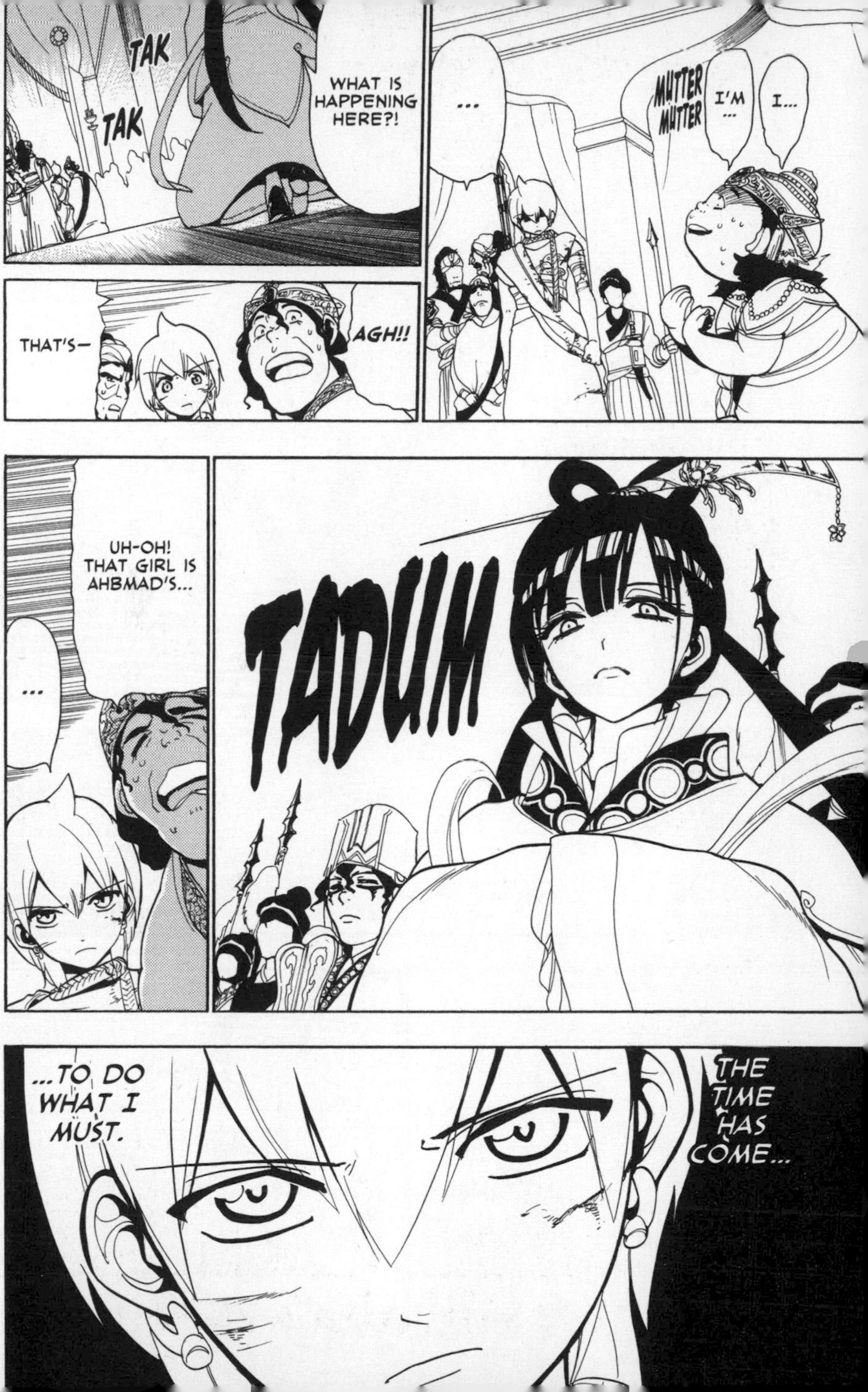
I...
I'M ...
MUTTER MUTTER
...
TAK
TAK
WHAT IS HAPPENING HERE?!
AGH!!
THAT'S—
TADUM
UH-OH! THAT GIRL IS AHBMAD'S...
...
THE TIME HAS COME...
...TO DO WHAT I MUST.

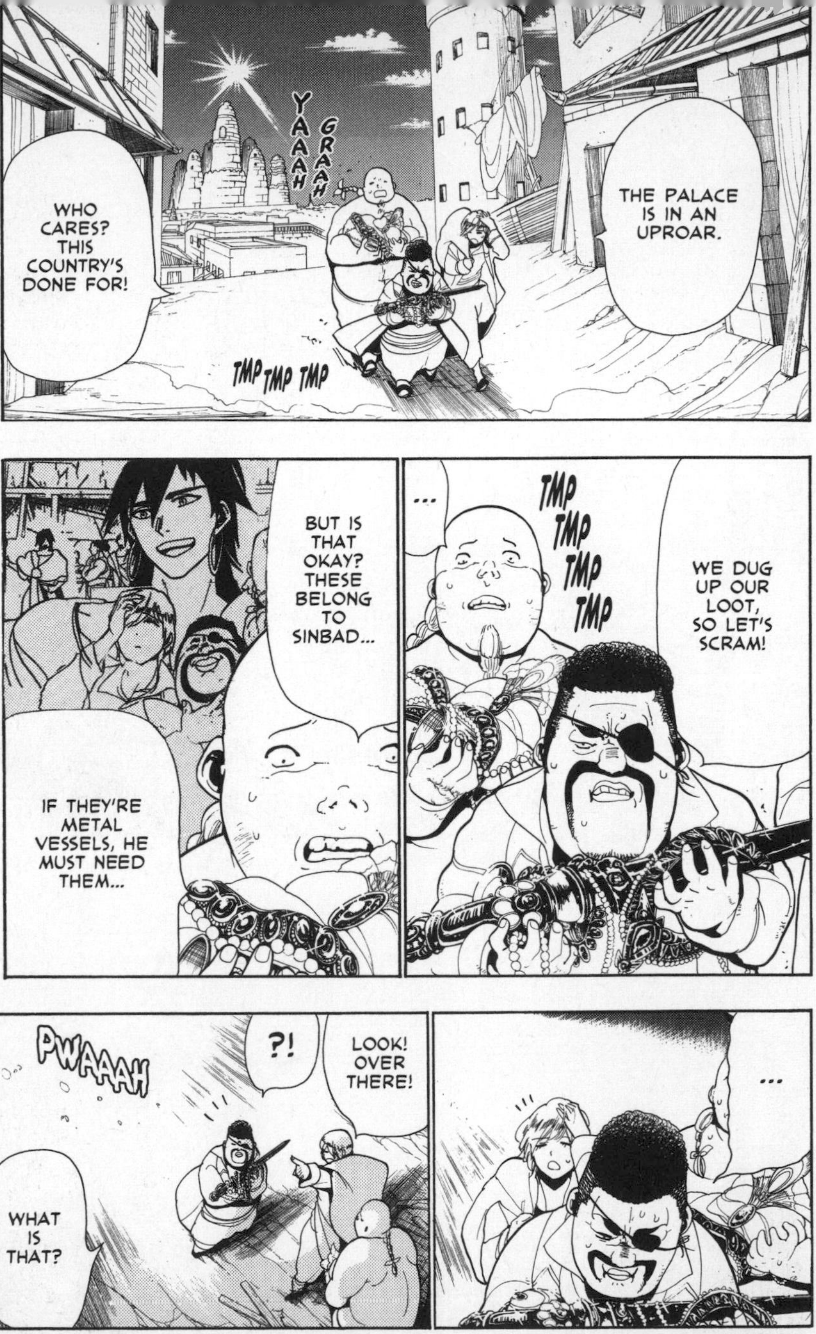
THE PALACE IS IN AN UPROAR.
YAAAAH
GRAAH
WHO CARES? THIS COUNTRY'S DONE FOR!
TMP TMP TMP
TMP TMP TMP TMP
WE DUG UP OUR LOOT, SO LET'S SCRAM!
...
BUT IS THAT OKAY? THESE BELONG TO SINBAD...
IF THEY'RE METAL VESSELS, HE MUST NEED THEM...
...
LOOK! OVER THERE!
?!
PWAAAH
WHAT IS THAT?

Night 62: Alibaba's Answer

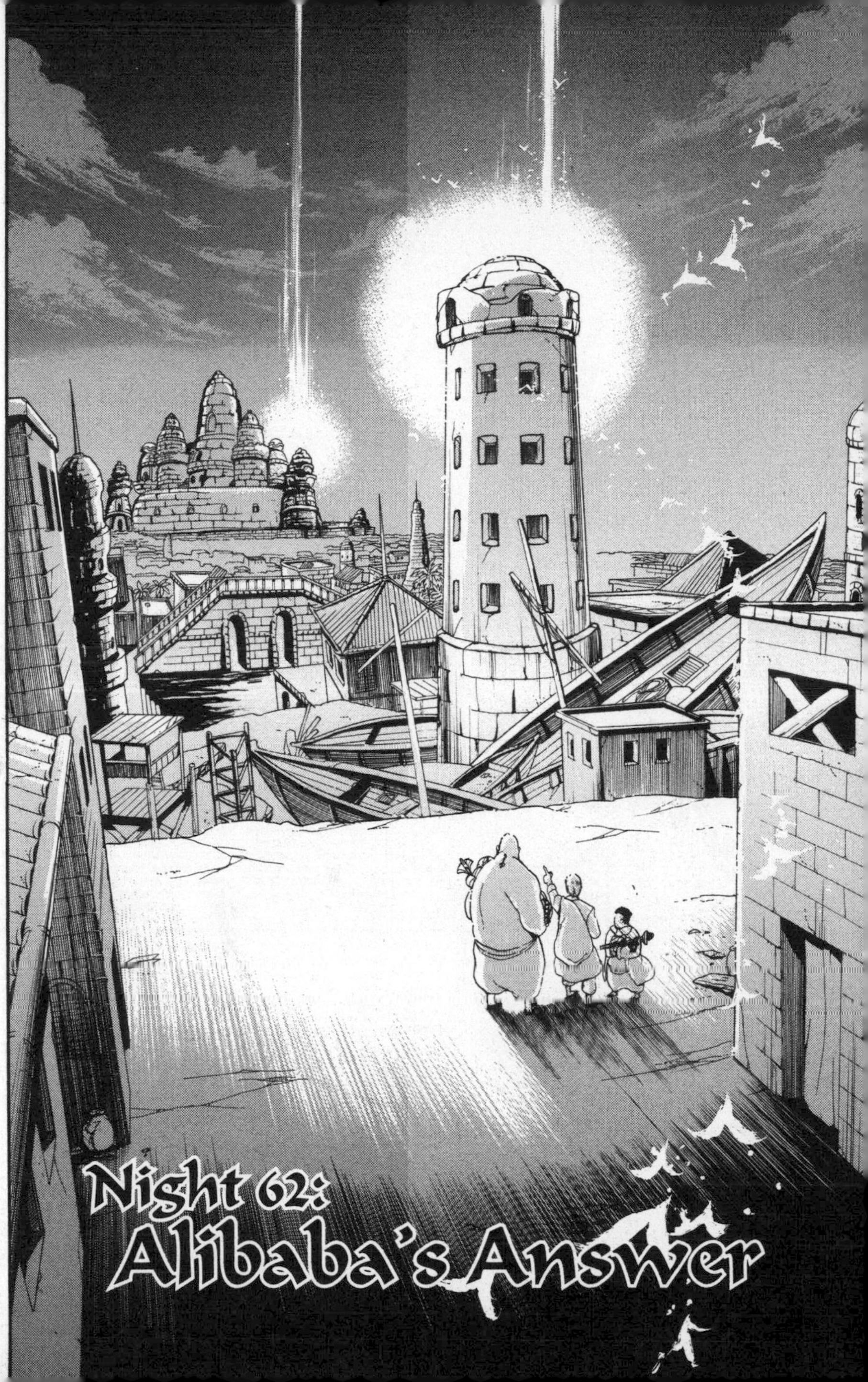
Night 62:
Alibaba's Answer

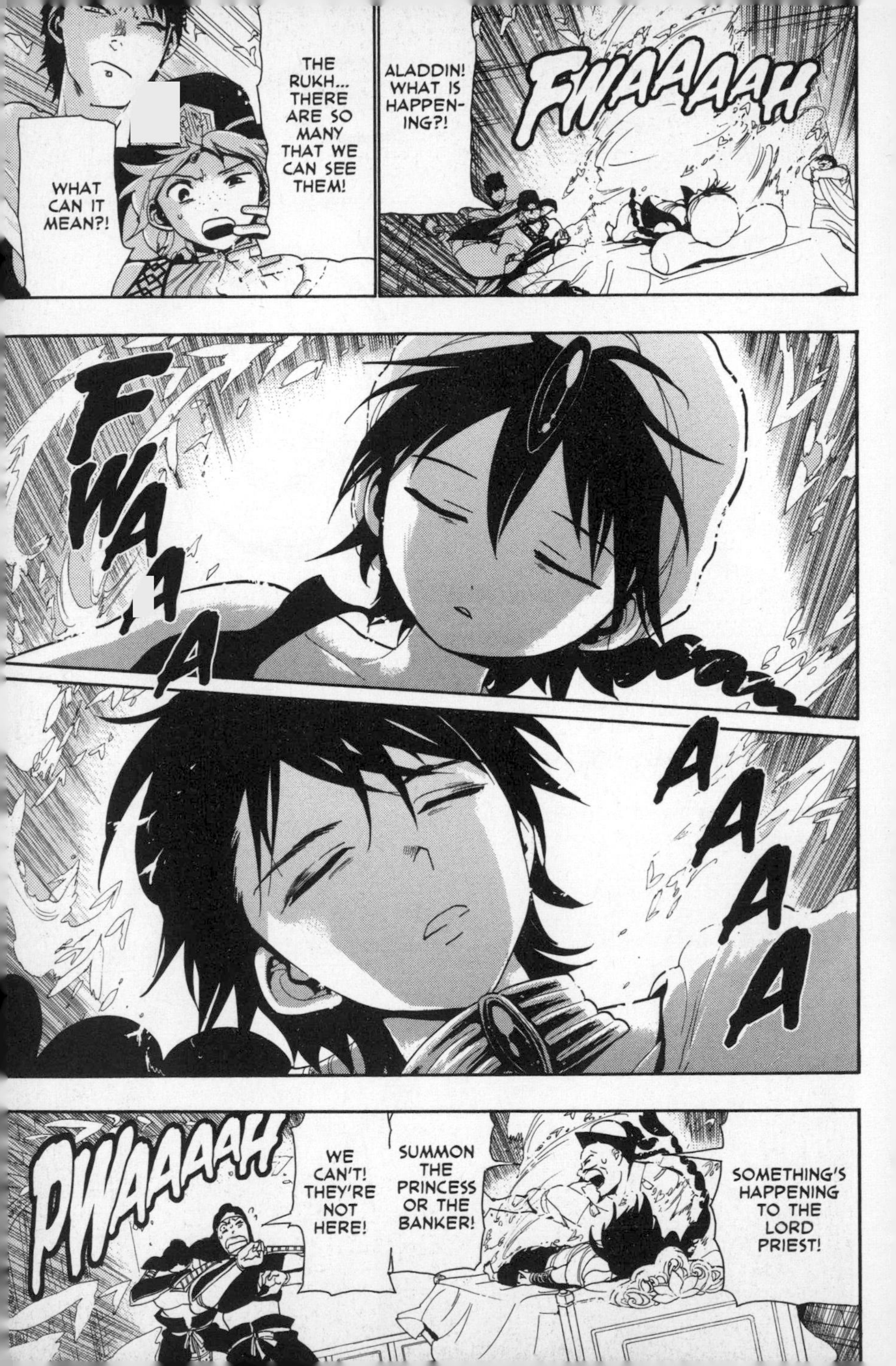
FWAAAAAH
ALADDIN! WHAT IS HAPPEN-ING?!
THE RUKH... THERE ARE SO MANY THAT WE CAN SEE THEM!
WHAT CAN IT MEAN?!
FWAAAA
AAAAA
SOMETHING'S HAPPENING TO THE LORD PRIEST!
SUMMON THE PRINCESS OR THE BANKER!
WE CAN'T! THEY'RE NOT HERE!
PWAAAAAH

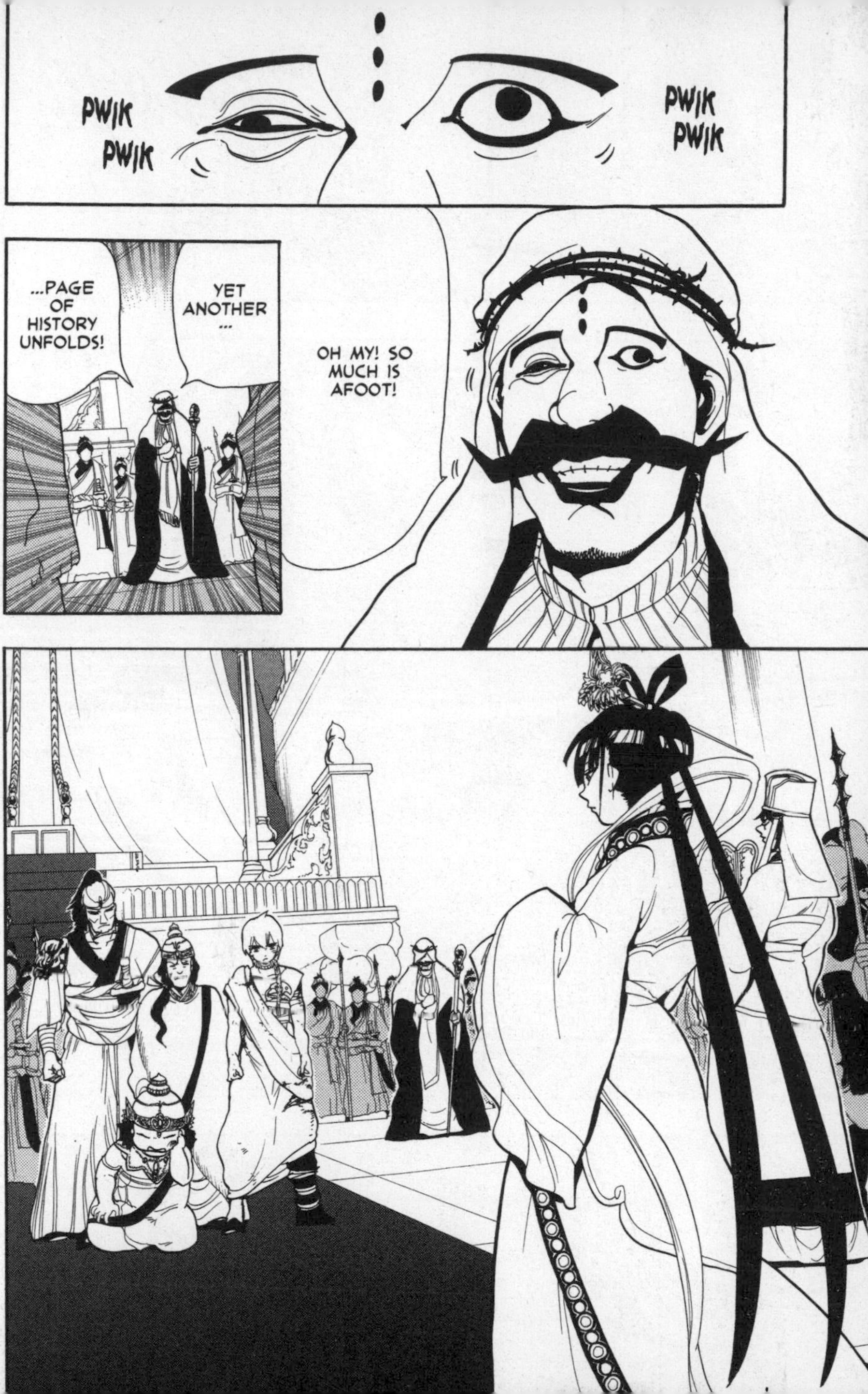
PWIK PWIK
PWIK PWIK
OH MY! SO MUCH IS AFOOT!
YET ANOTHER ...
...PAGE OF HISTORY UNFOLDS!

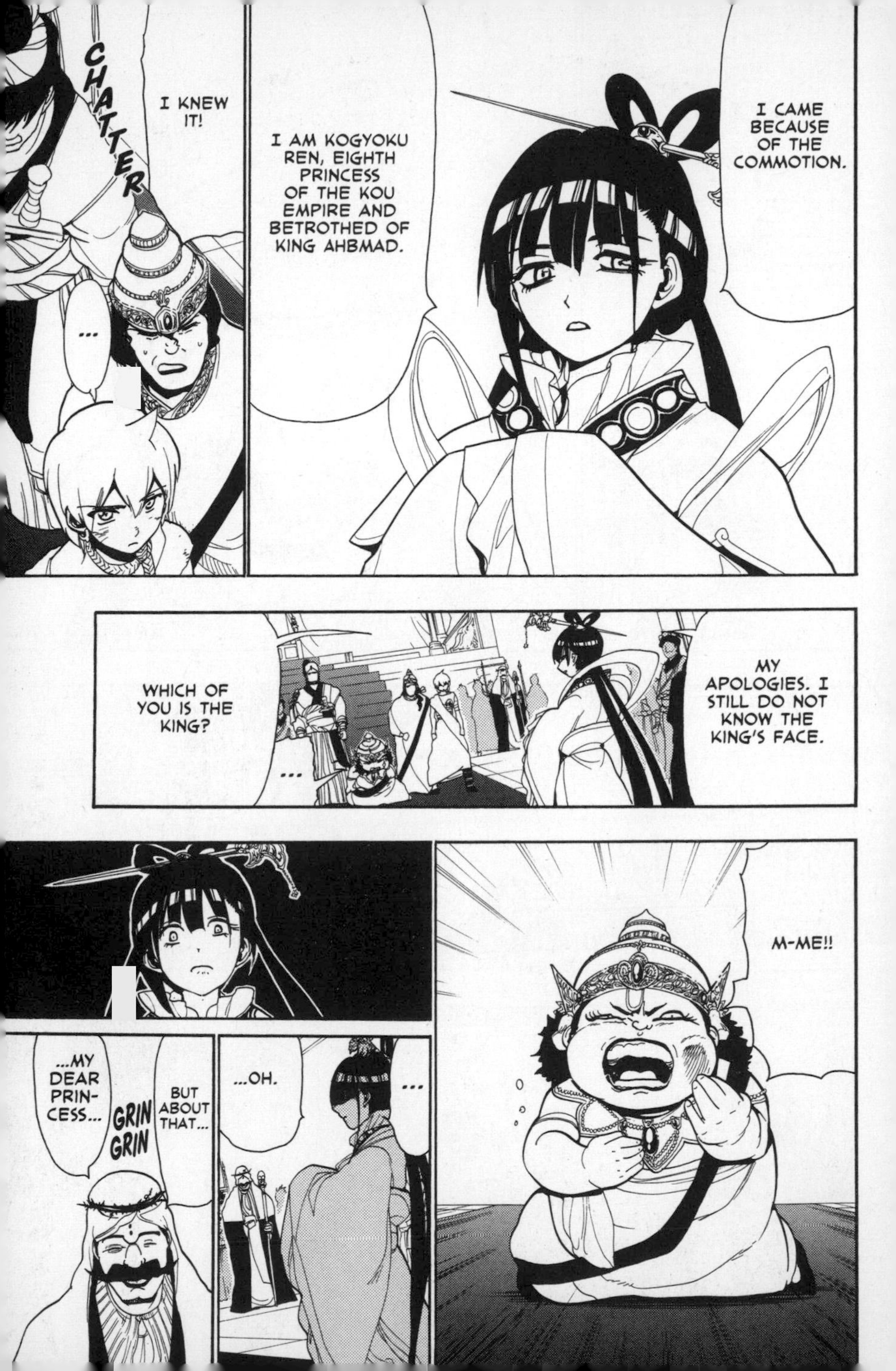
I CAME BECAUSE OF THE COMMOTION.
I AM KOGYOKU REN, EIGHTH PRINCESS OF THE KOU EMPIRE AND BETROTHED OF KING AHBMAD.
I KNEW IT!
CHATTER
...
MY APOLOGIES. I STILL DO NOT KNOW THE KING'S FACE.
WHICH OF YOU IS THE KING?
...
M-ME!!
...
...OH.
BUT ABOUT THAT...
GRIN GRIN
...MY DEAR PRIN-CESS...

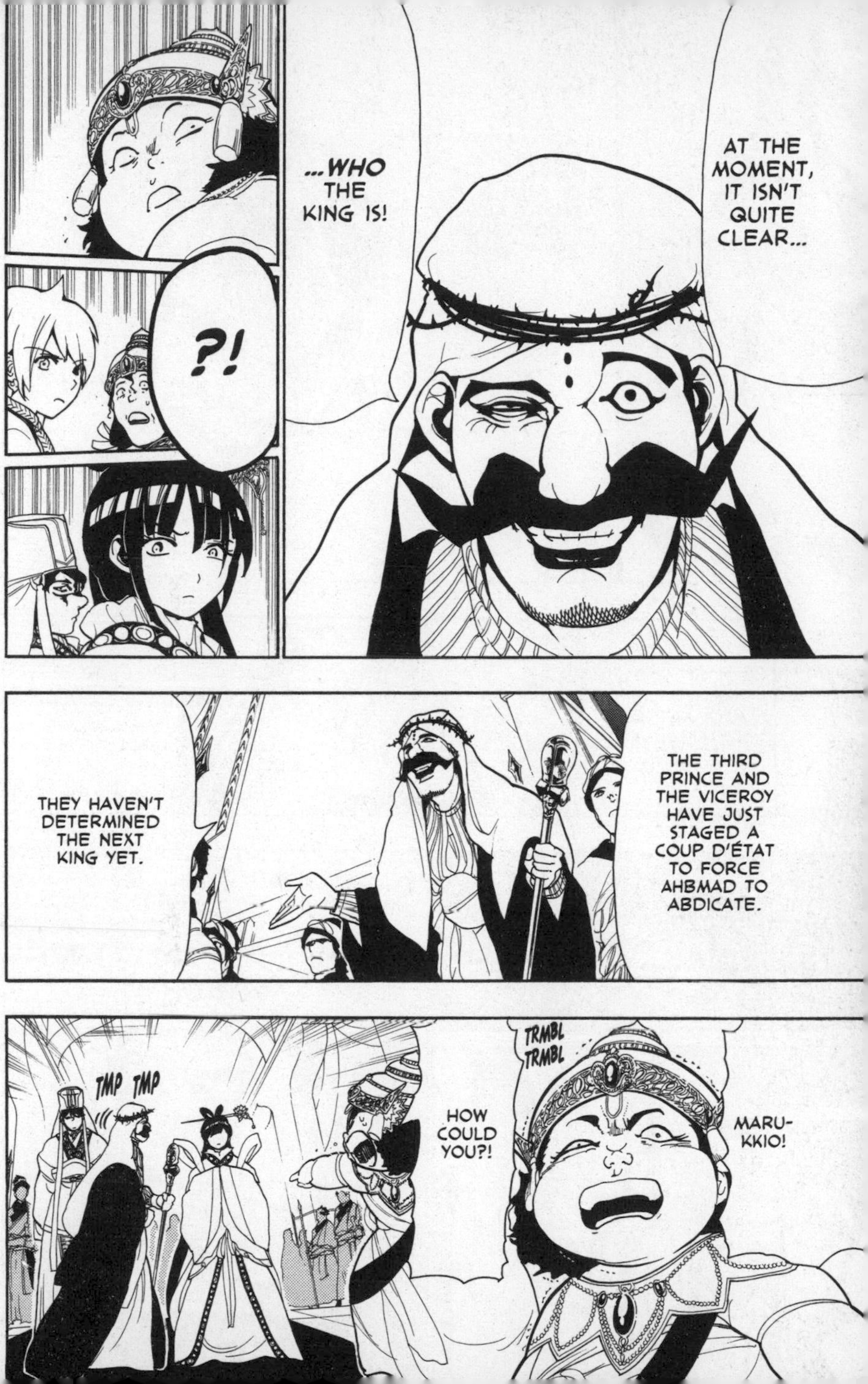
AT THE MOMENT, IT ISN'T QUITE CLEAR...
...WHO THE KING IS!
?!
THE THIRD PRINCE AND THE VICEROY HAVE JUST STAGED A COUP D'ÉTAT TO FORCE AHBMAD TO ABDICATE.
THEY HAVEN'T DETERMINED THE NEXT KING YET.
TRMBL TRMBL
MARU-KKIO!
HOW COULD YOU?!
TMP TMP

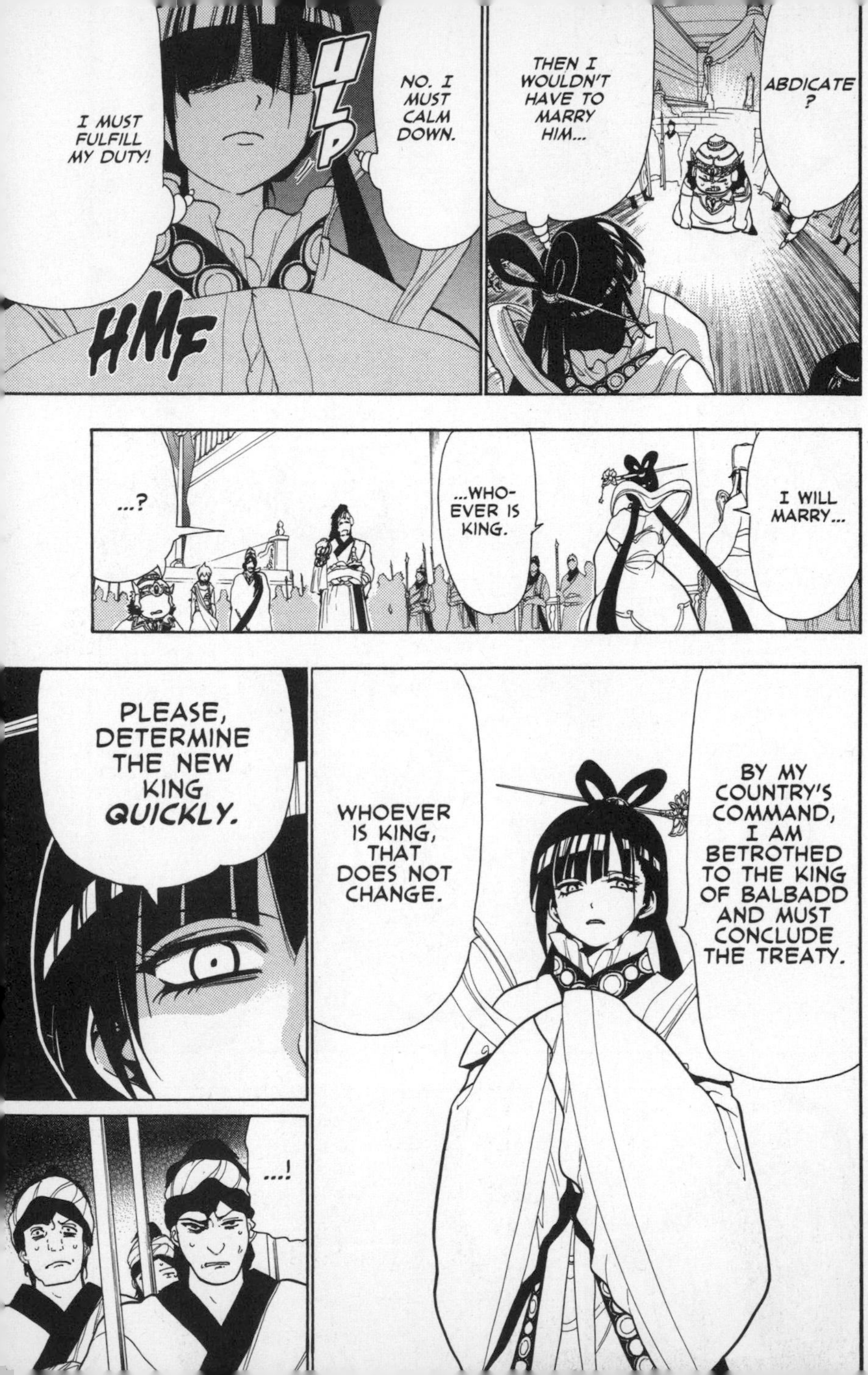
ABDICATE?
THEN I WOULDN'T HAVE TO MARRY HIM...
NO. I MUST CALM DOWN.
ULP
I MUST FULFILL MY DUTY!
HMF
I WILL MARRY...
...WHOEVER IS KING.
...?
BY MY COUNTRY'S COMMAND, I AM BETROTHED TO THE KING OF BALBADD AND MUST CONCLUDE THE TREATY.
WHOEVER IS KING, THAT DOES NOT CHANGE.
PLEASE, DETERMINE THE NEW KING QUICKLY.
...!

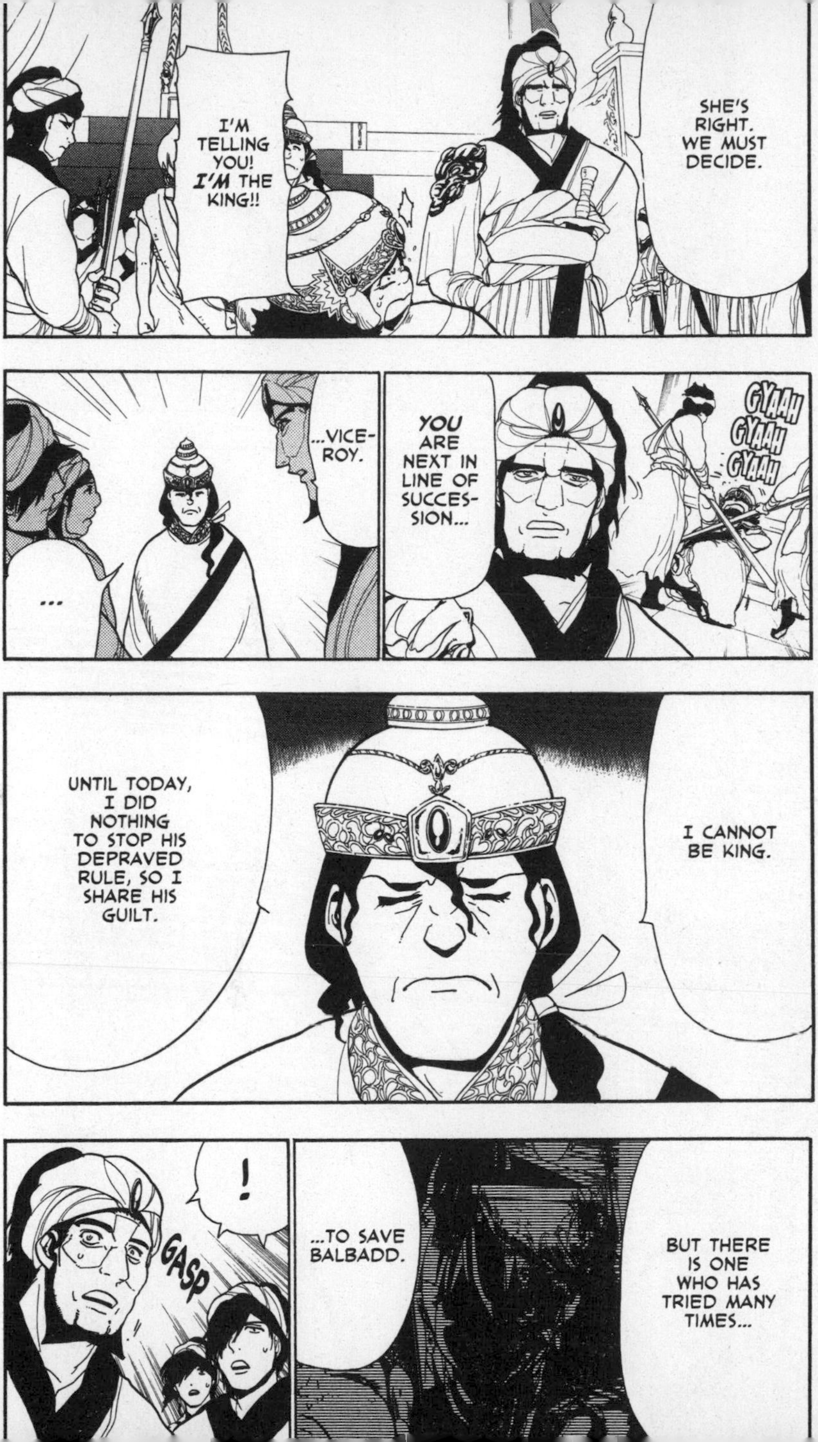
SHE'S RIGHT. WE MUST DECIDE.
I'M TELLING YOU! *I'M* THE KING!!
GYAAH GYAAH GYAAH
YOU ARE NEXT IN LINE OF SUCCES-SION...
...VICE-ROY.
...
I CANNOT BE KING.
UNTIL TODAY, I DID NOTHING TO STOP HIS DEPRAVED RULE, SO I SHARE HIS GUILT.
BUT THERE IS ONE WHO HAS TRIED MANY TIMES...
...TO SAVE BALBADD.
!
GASP

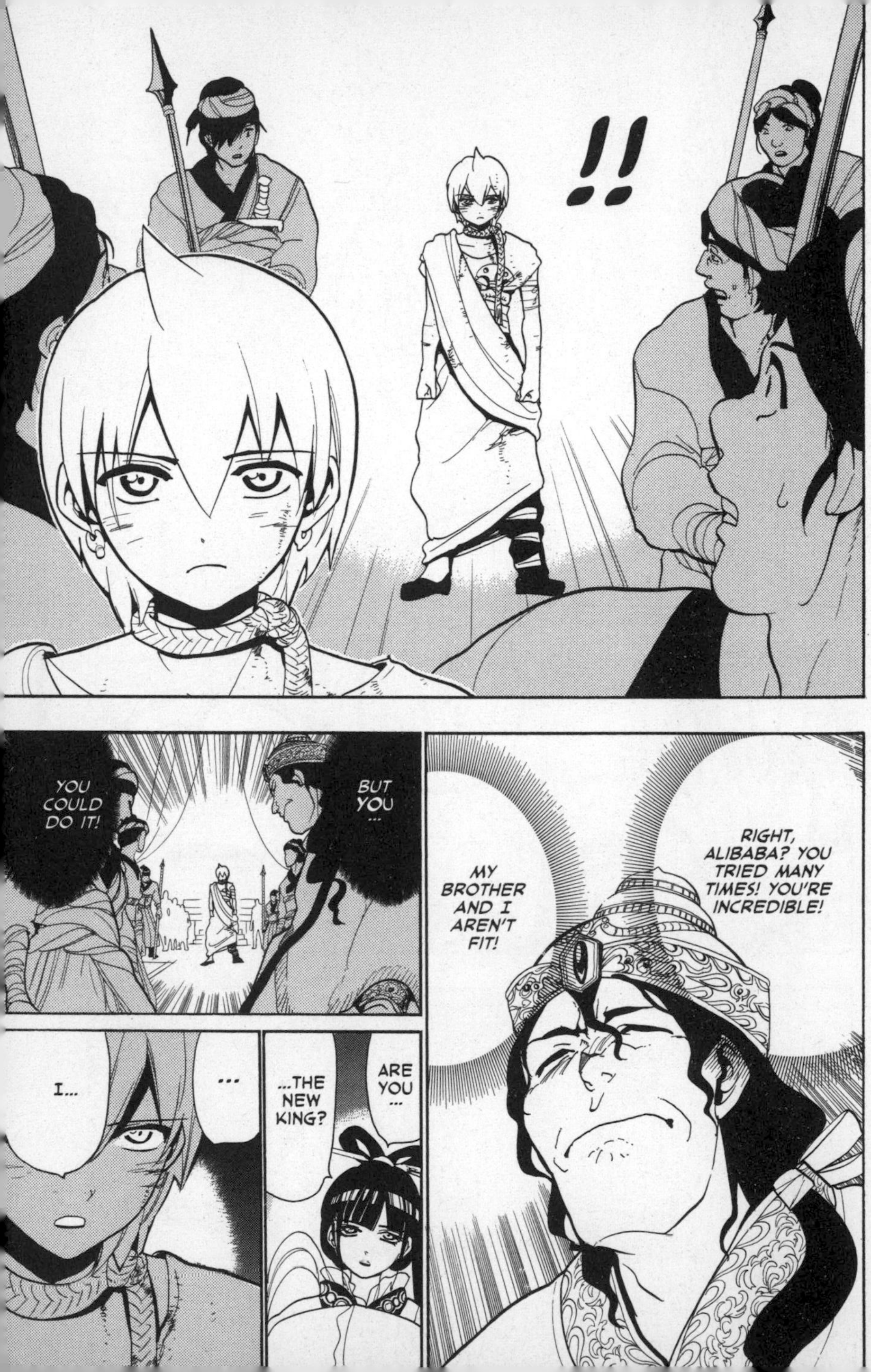
!!
RIGHT, ALIBABA? YOU TRIED MANY TIMES! YOU'RE INCREDIBLE!
MY BROTHER AND I AREN'T FIT!
BUT YOU ...
YOU COULD DO IT!
ARE YOU ...
...THE NEW KING?
...
I...

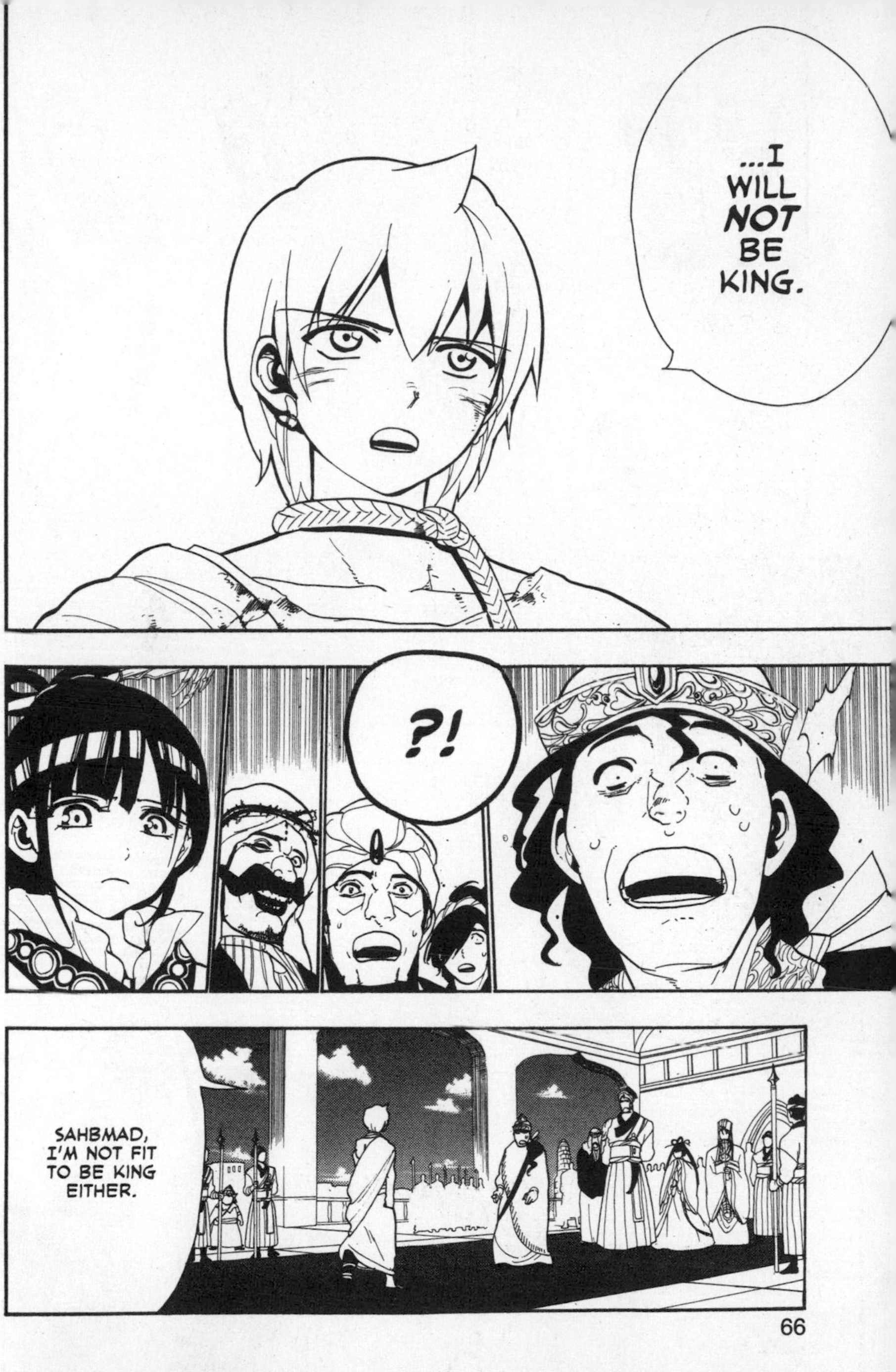
...I WILL NOT BE KING.
?!
SAHBMAD, I'M NOT FIT TO BE KING EITHER.

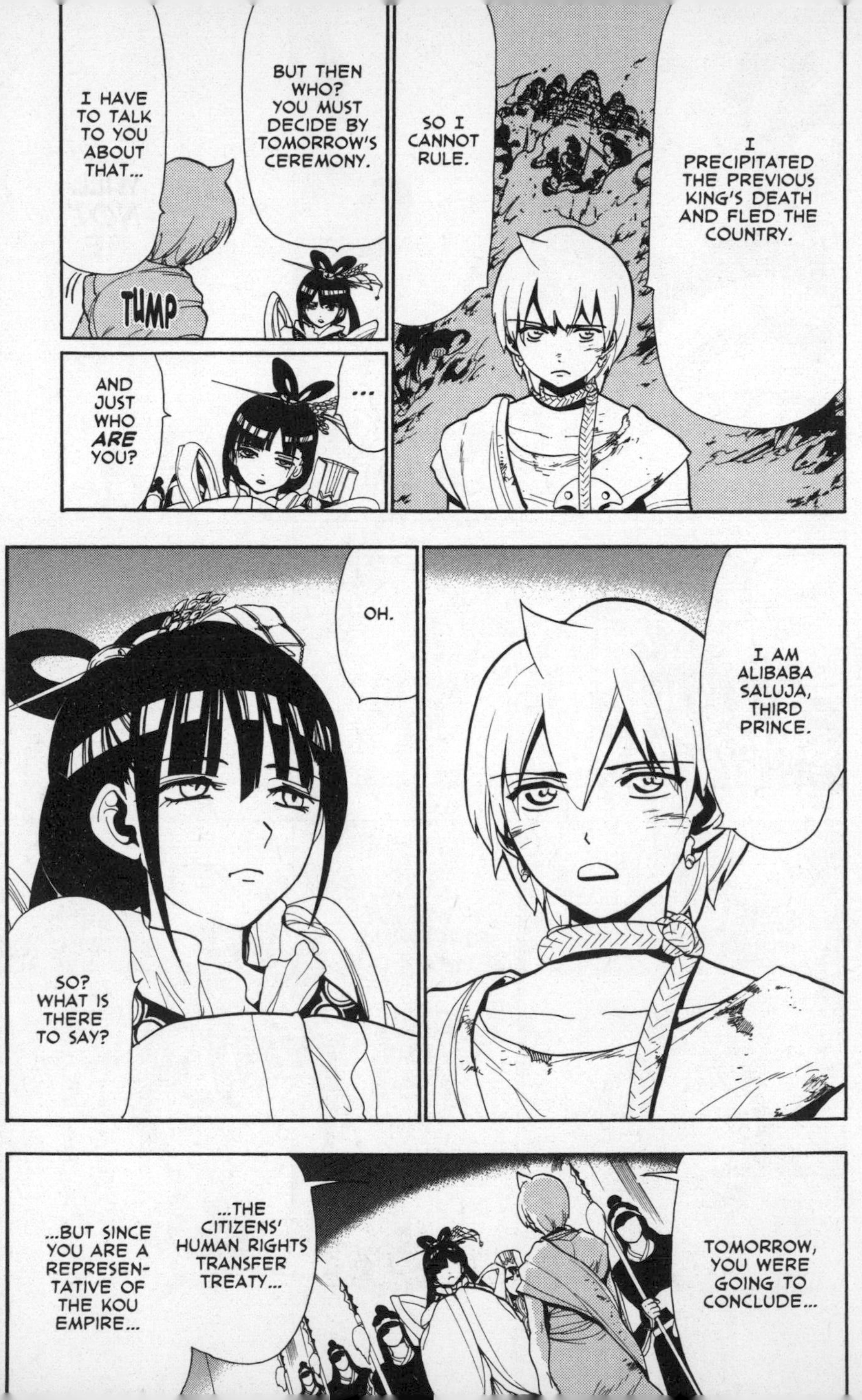
I PRECIPITATED THE PREVIOUS KING'S DEATH AND FLED THE COUNTRY.
SO I CANNOT RULE.
BUT THEN WHO? YOU MUST DECIDE BY TOMORROW'S CEREMONY.
I HAVE TO TALK TO YOU ABOUT THAT...
THUMP
...
AND JUST WHO *ARE* YOU?
I AM ALIBABA SALUJA, THIRD PRINCE.
OH.
SO? WHAT IS THERE TO SAY?
TOMORROW, YOU WERE GOING TO CONCLUDE...
...THE CITIZENS' HUMAN RIGHTS TRANSFER TREATY...
...BUT SINCE YOU ARE A REPRESEN-TATIVE OF THE KOU EMPIRE...

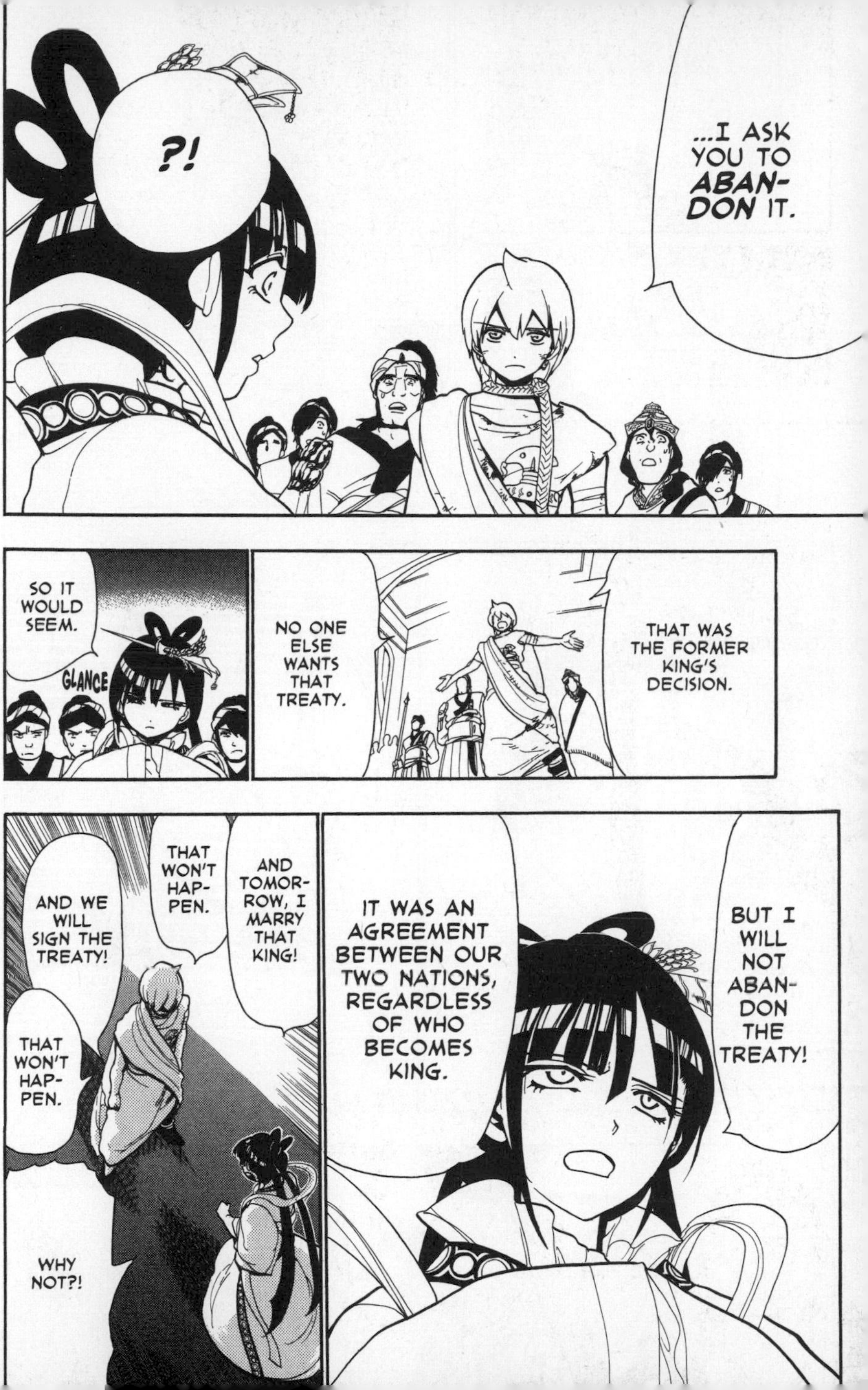
...I ASK YOU TO ABANDON IT.
?!
THAT WAS THE FORMER KING'S DECISION.
NO ONE ELSE WANTS THAT TREATY.
SO IT WOULD SEEM.
GLANCE
BUT I WILL NOT ABANDON THE TREATY!
IT WAS AN AGREEMENT BETWEEN OUR TWO NATIONS, REGARDLESS OF WHO BECOMES KING.
AND TOMORROW, I MARRY THAT KING!
THAT WON'T HAPPEN.
AND WE WILL SIGN THE TREATY!
THAT WON'T HAPPEN.
WHY NOT?!

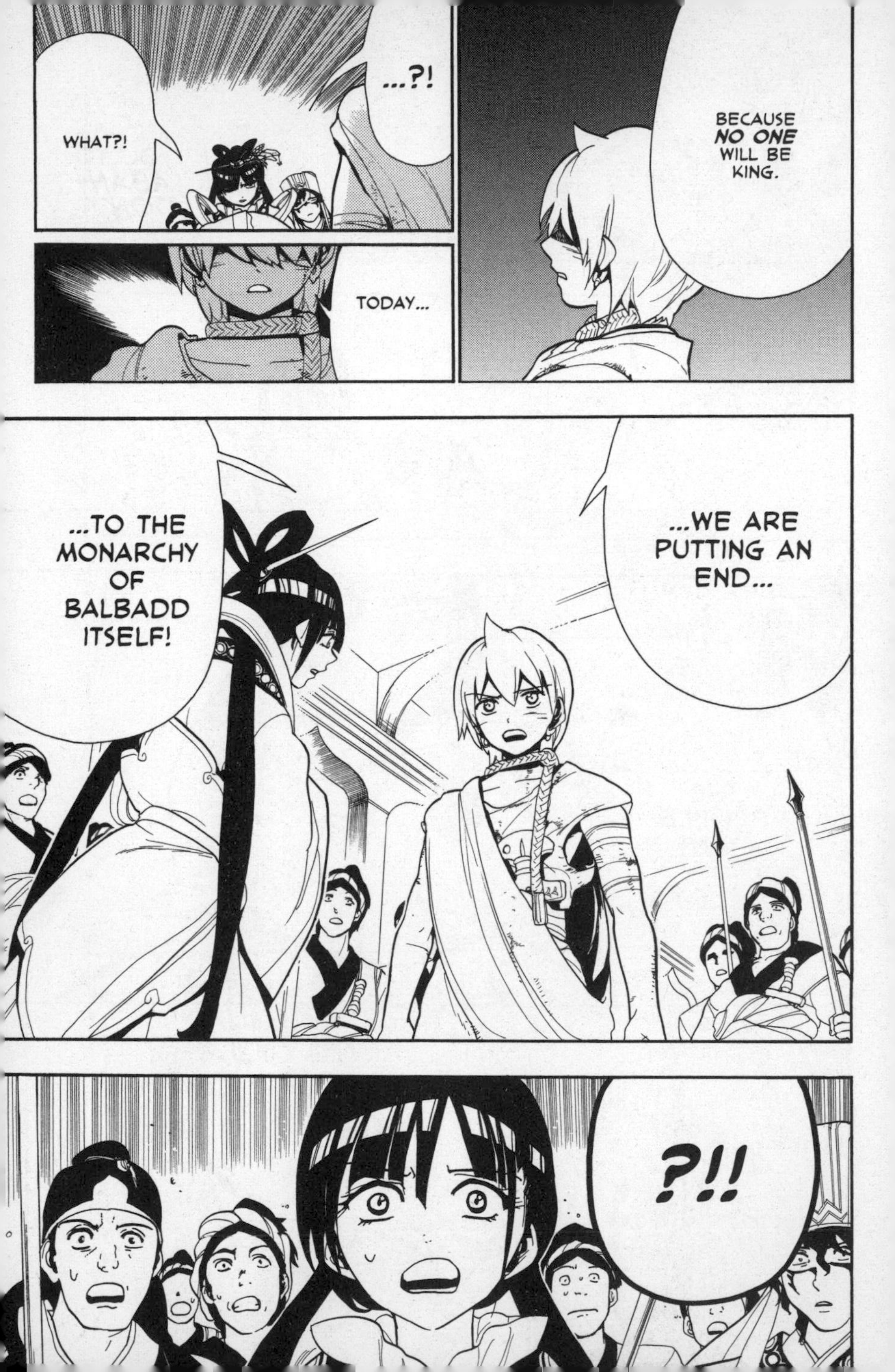
BECAUSE NO ONE WILL BE KING.
...?!
WHAT?!
TODAY...
...WE ARE PUTTING AN END...
...TO THE MONARCHY OF BALBADD ITSELF!
?!!

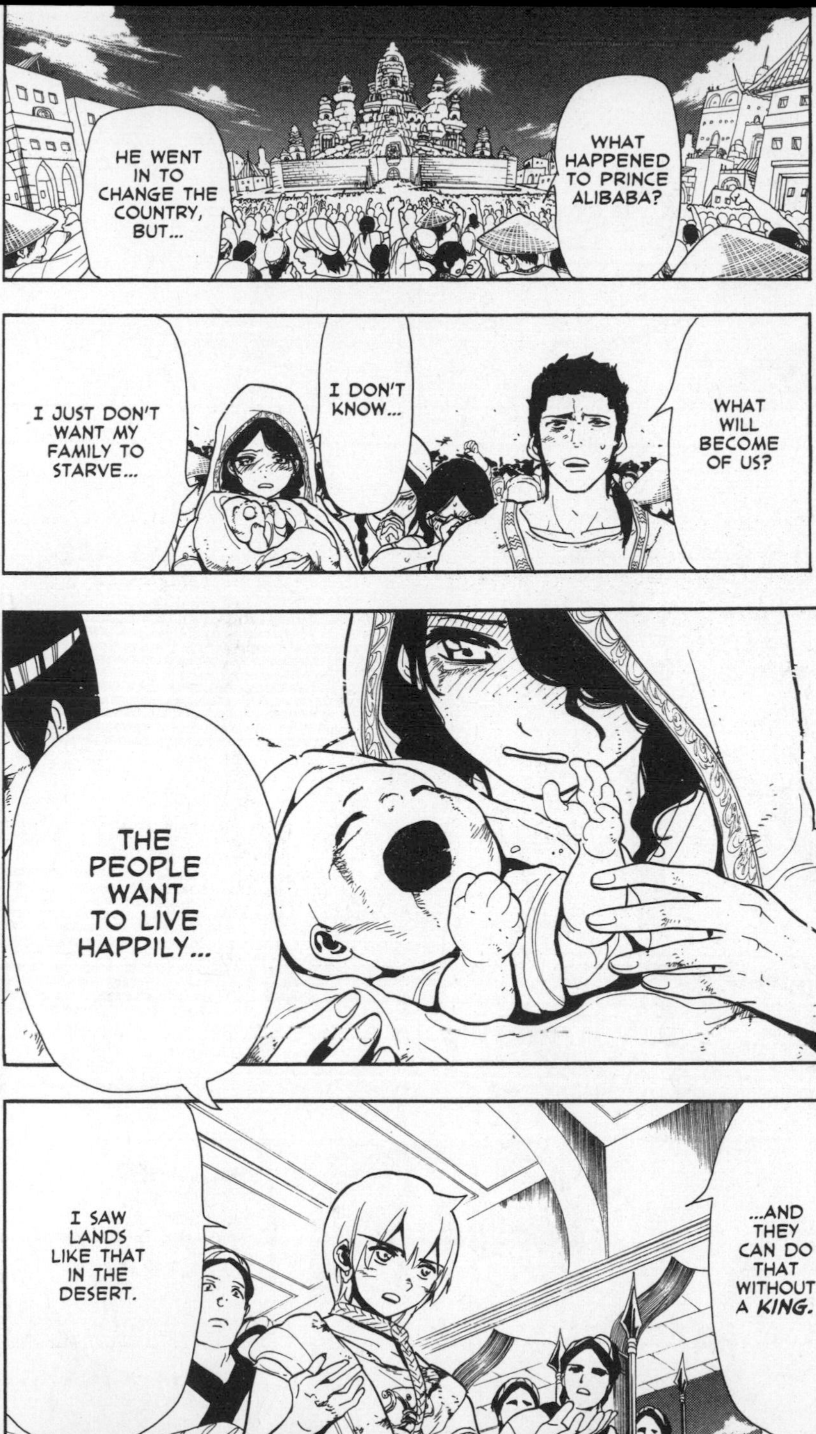
WHAT HAPPENED TO PRINCE ALIBABA?
HE WENT IN TO CHANGE THE COUNTRY, BUT...
WHAT WILL BECOME OF US?
I DON'T KNOW...
I JUST DON'T WANT MY FAMILY TO STARVE...
THE PEOPLE WANT TO LIVE HAPPILY...
I SAW LANDS LIKE THAT IN THE DESERT.
...AND THEY CAN DO THAT WITHOUT A *KING.*

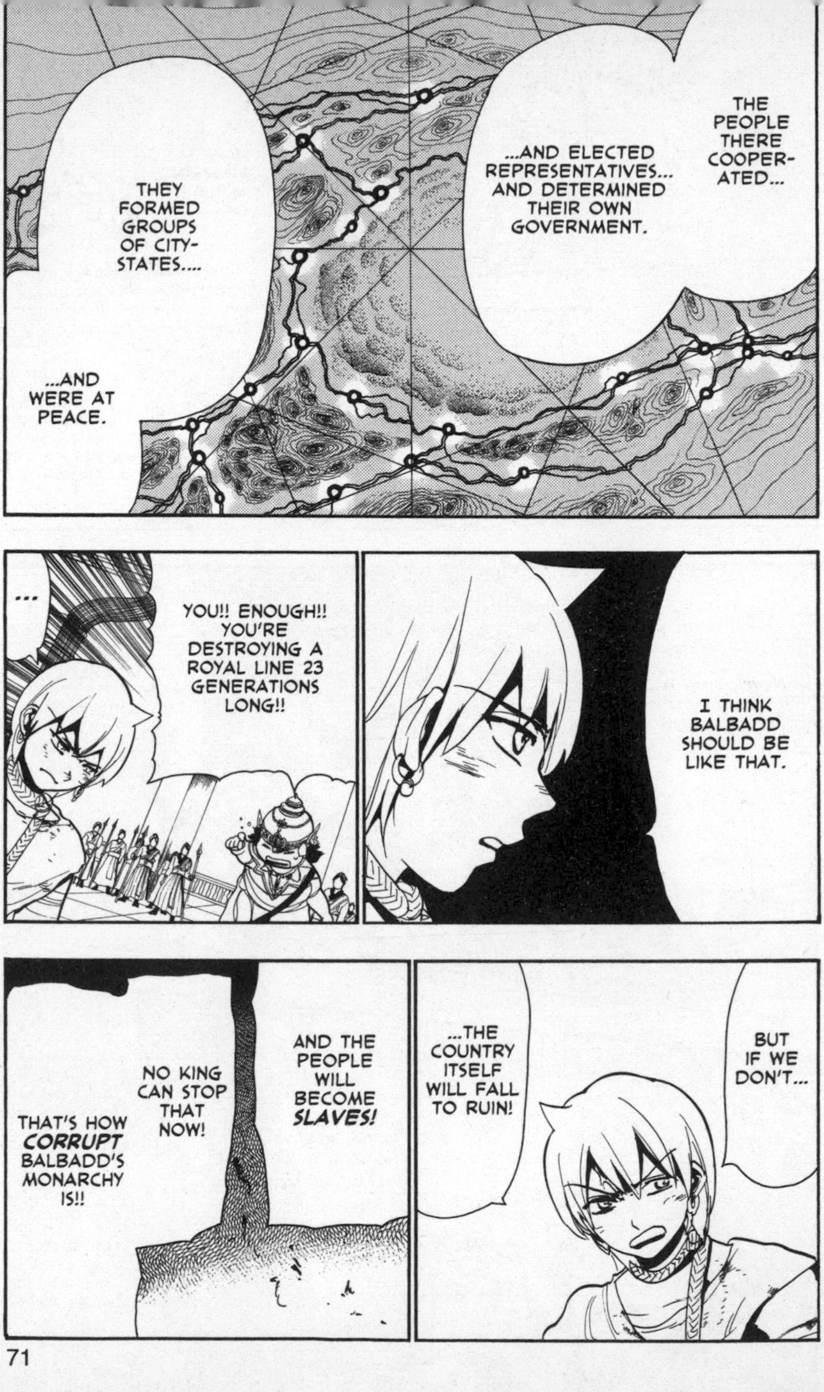
THE PEOPLE THERE COOPER-ATED...
...AND ELECTED REPRESENTATIVES... AND DETERMINED THEIR OWN GOVERNMENT.
THEY FORMED GROUPS OF CITY-STATES....
...AND WERE AT PEACE.
I THINK BALBADD SHOULD BE LIKE THAT.
YOU!! ENOUGH!! YOU'RE DESTROYING A ROYAL LINE 23 GENERATIONS LONG!!
...
BUT IF WE DON'T...
...THE COUNTRY ITSELF WILL FALL TO RUIN!
AND THE PEOPLE WILL BECOME *SLAVES!*
NO KING CAN STOP THAT NOW!
THAT'S HOW ***CORRUPT*** BALBADD'S MONARCHY IS!!

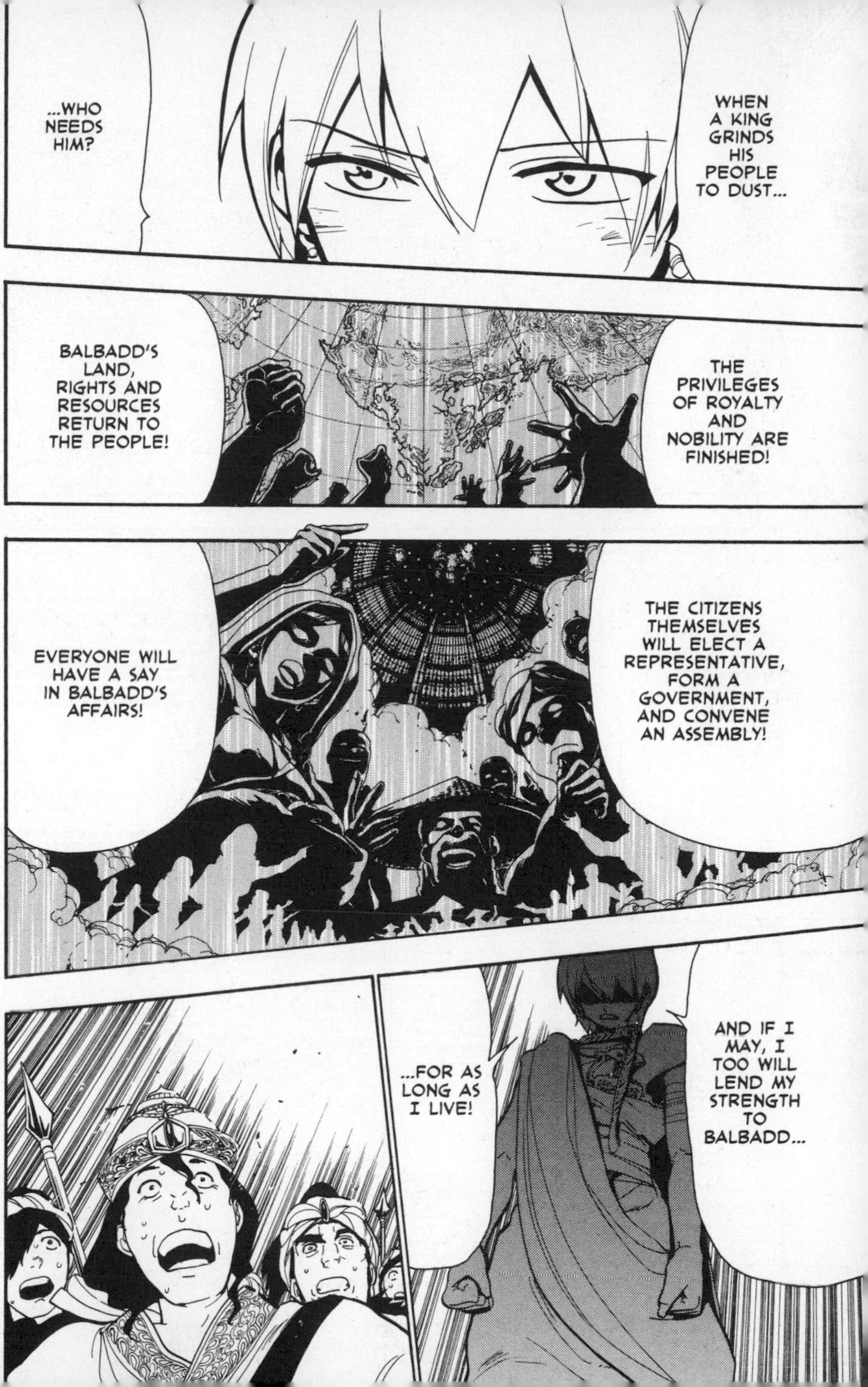
WHEN A KING GRINDS HIS PEOPLE TO DUST...
...WHO NEEDS HIM?
THE PRIVILEGES OF ROYALTY AND NOBILITY ARE FINISHED!
BALBADD'S LAND, RIGHTS AND RESOURCES RETURN TO THE PEOPLE!
THE CITIZENS THEMSELVES WILL ELECT A REPRESENTATIVE, FORM A GOVERNMENT, AND CONVENE AN ASSEMBLY!
EVERYONE WILL HAVE A SAY IN BALBADD'S AFFAIRS!
AND IF I MAY, I TOO WILL LEND MY STRENGTH TO BALBADD...
...FOR AS LONG AS I LIVE!

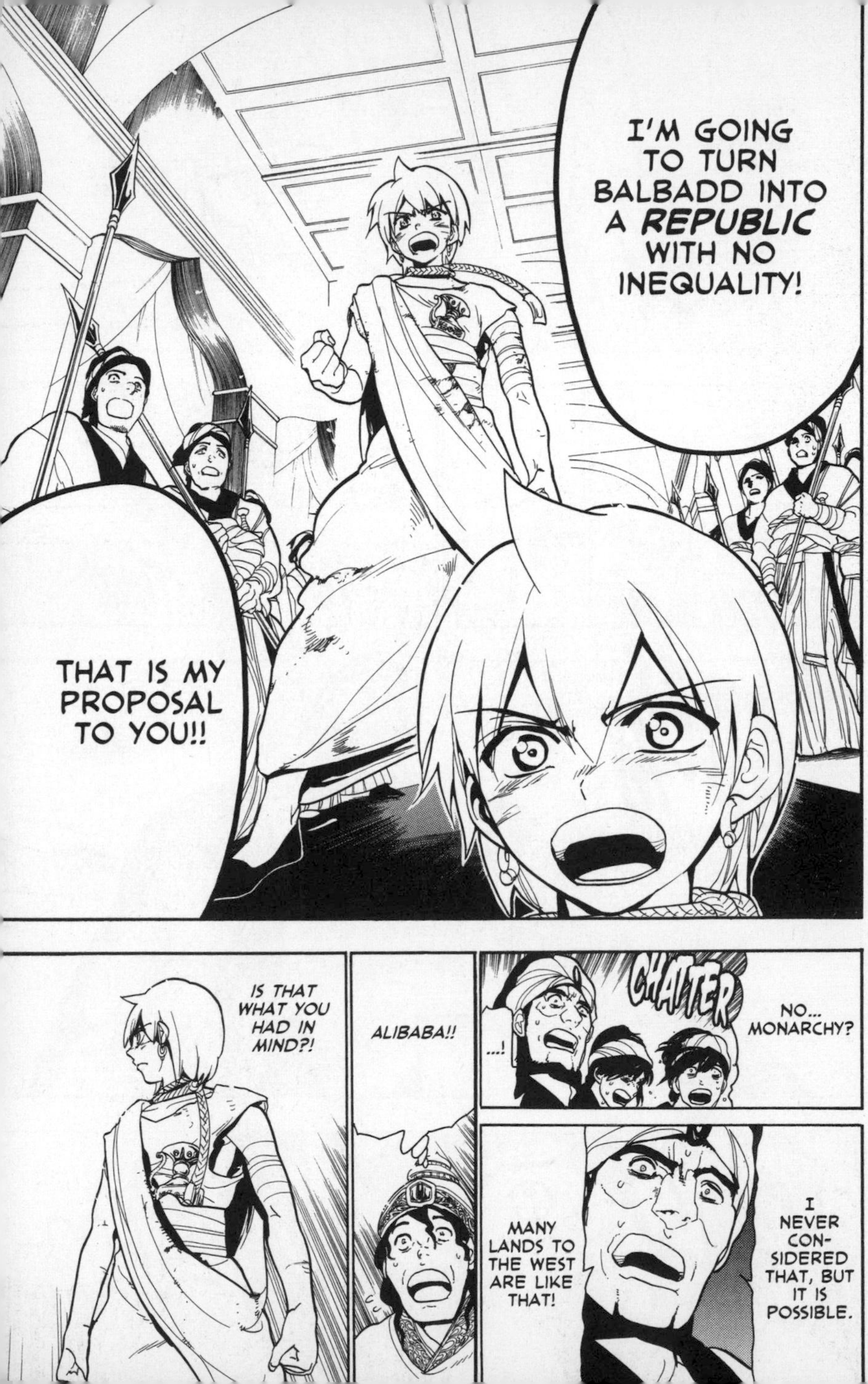
I'M GOING TO TURN BALBADD INTO A *REPUBLIC* WITH NO INEQUALITY!
THAT IS MY PROPOSAL TO YOU!!
NO... MONARCHY?
CHATTER
...!
I NEVER CON-SIDERED THAT, BUT IT IS POSSIBLE.
MANY LANDS TO THE WEST ARE LIKE THAT!
ALIBABA!!
IS THAT WHAT YOU HAD IN MIND?!

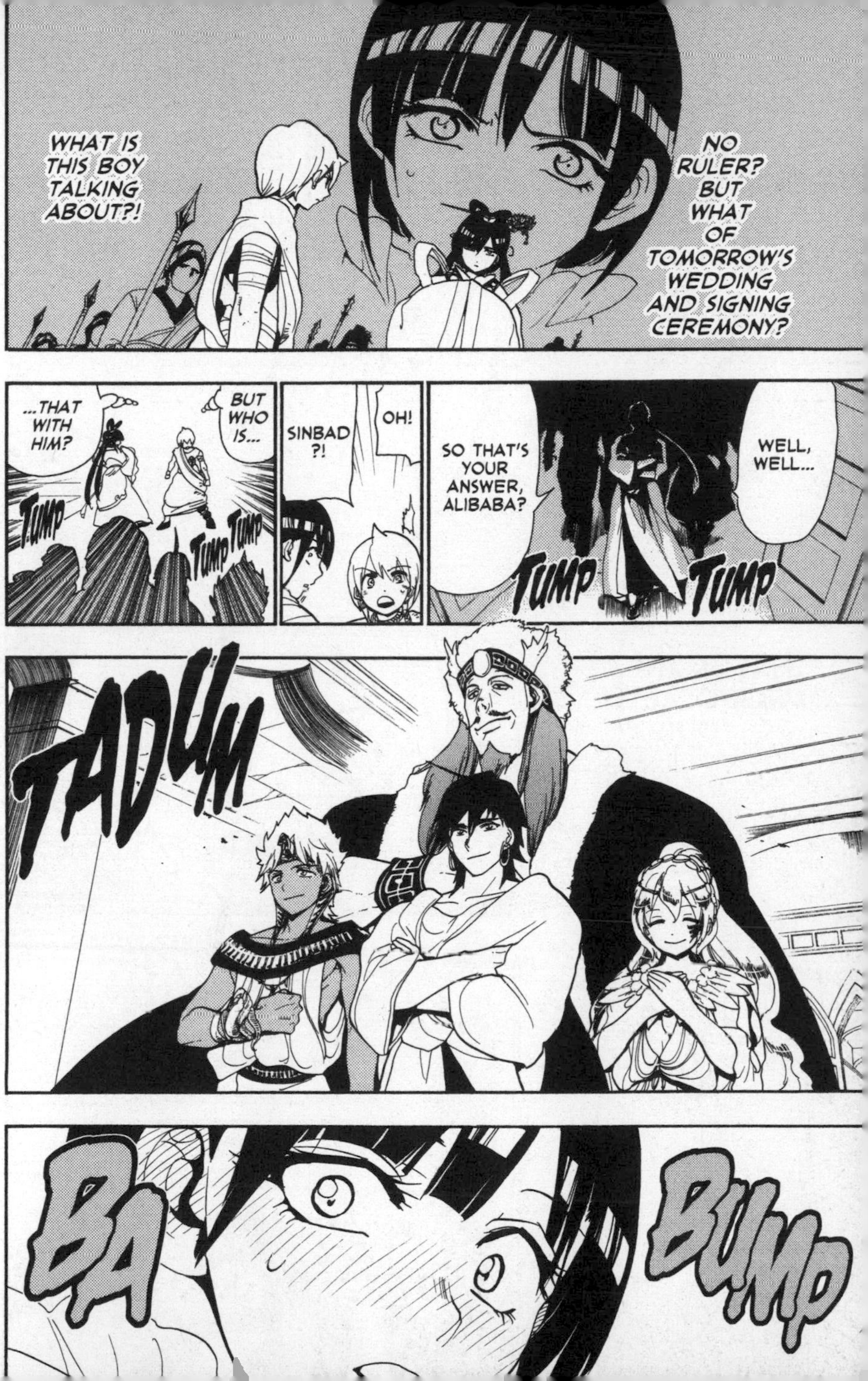
NO RULER? BUT WHAT OF TOMORROW'S WEDDING AND SIGNING CEREMONY?
WHAT IS THIS BOY TALKING ABOUT?!
WELL, WELL...
SO THAT'S YOUR ANSWER, ALIBABA?
TUMP
TUMP
OH!
SINBAD?!
BUT WHO IS...
...THAT WITH HIM?
TUMP
TUMP
TUMP
TUMP
TADUM
BA
BUMP

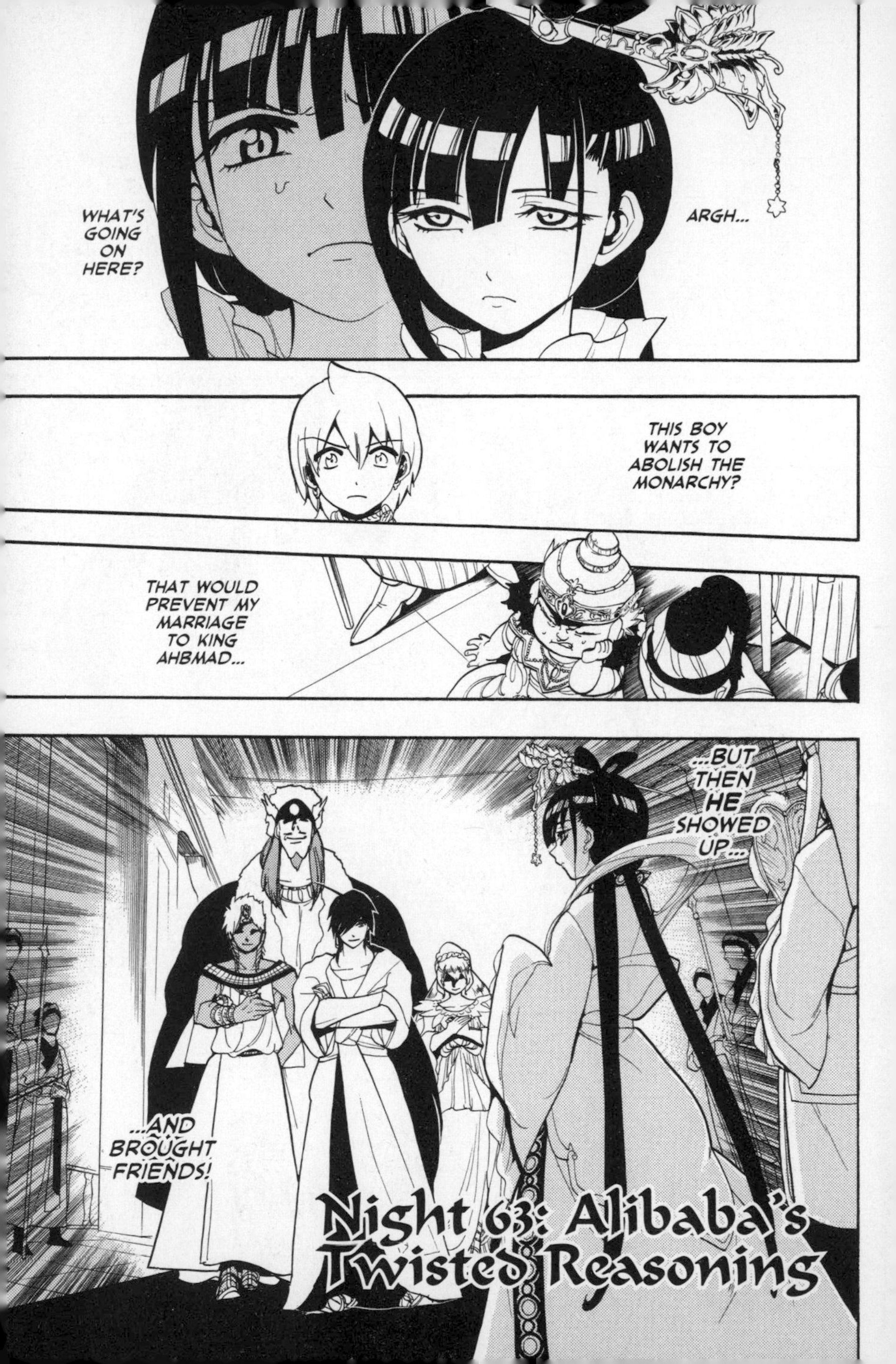
ARGH...
WHAT'S GOING ON HERE?
THIS BOY WANTS TO ABOLISH THE MONARCHY?
THAT WOULD PREVENT MY MARRIAGE TO KING AHBMAD...
...BUT THEN HE SHOWED UP...
...AND BROUGHT FRIENDS!
Night 63: Alibaba's Twisted Reasoning

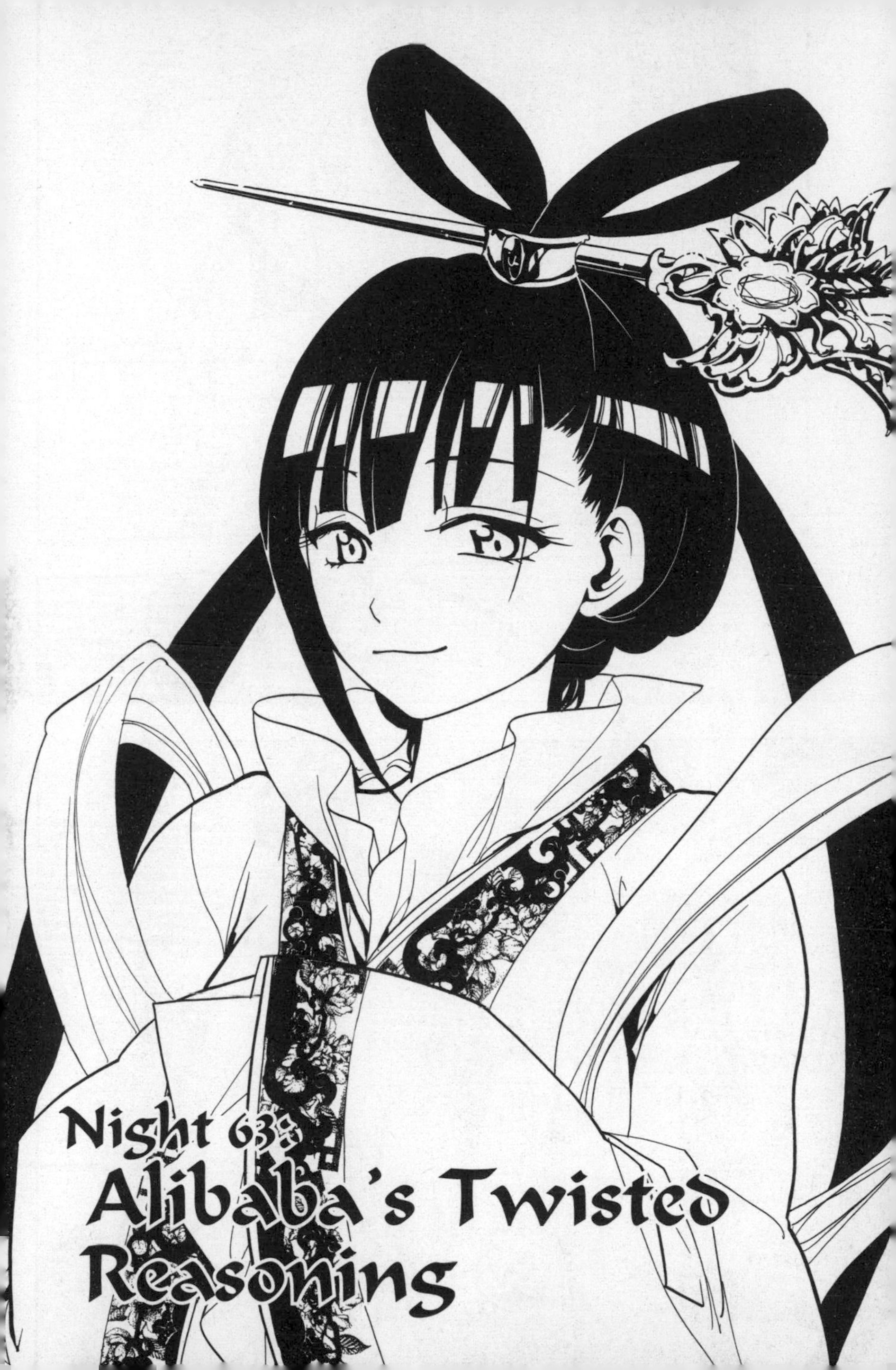
Night 63:
Alibaba's Twisted Reasoning

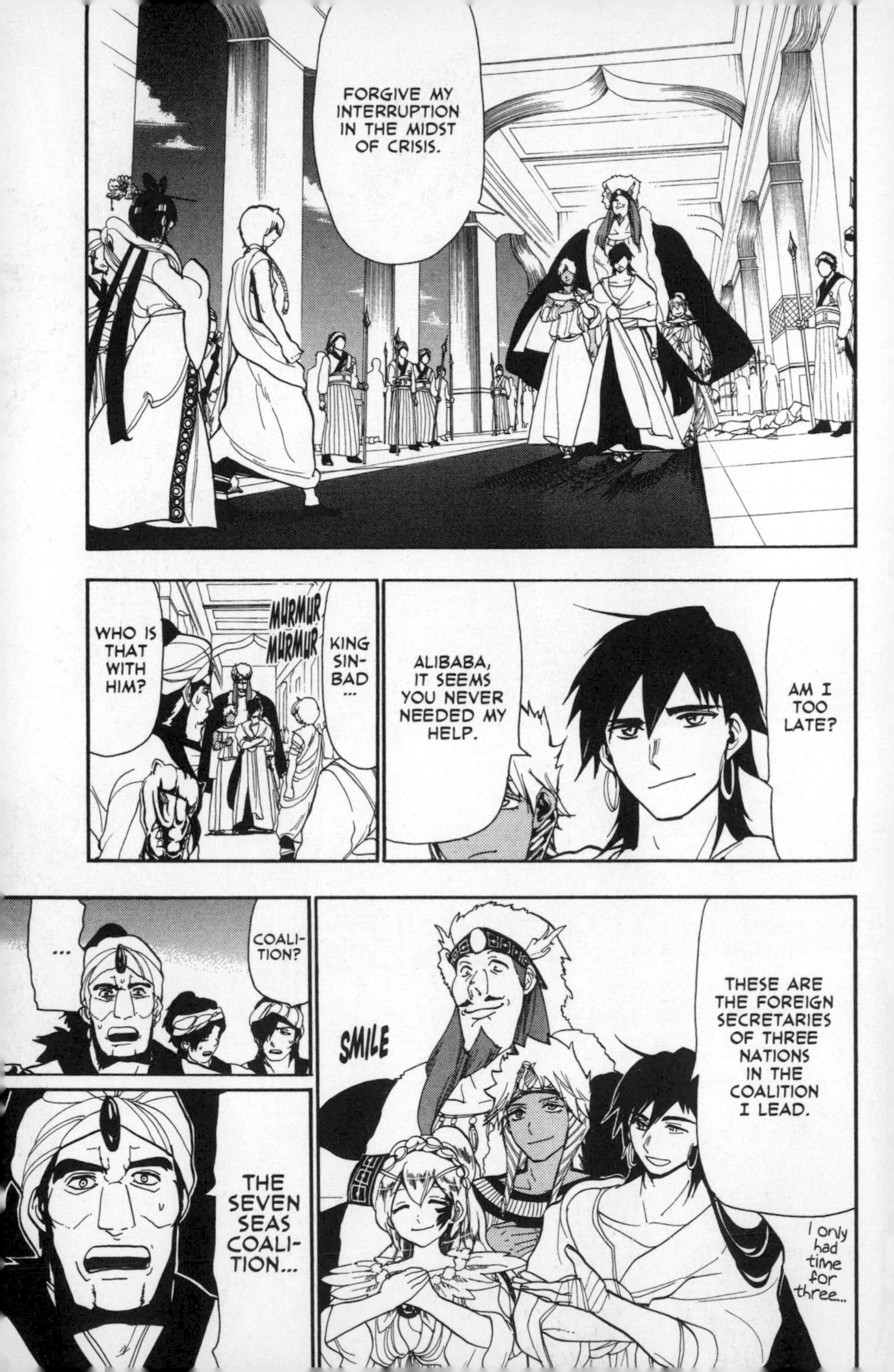
FORGIVE MY INTERRUPTION IN THE MIDST OF CRISIS.
AM I TOO LATE?
ALIBABA, IT SEEMS YOU NEVER NEEDED MY HELP.
KING SINBAD...
MURMUR MURMUR
WHO IS THAT WITH HIM?
THESE ARE THE FOREIGN SECRETARIES OF THREE NATIONS IN THE COALITION I LEAD.
SMILE
I only had time for three...
COALITION?
...
THE SEVEN SEAS COALITION...

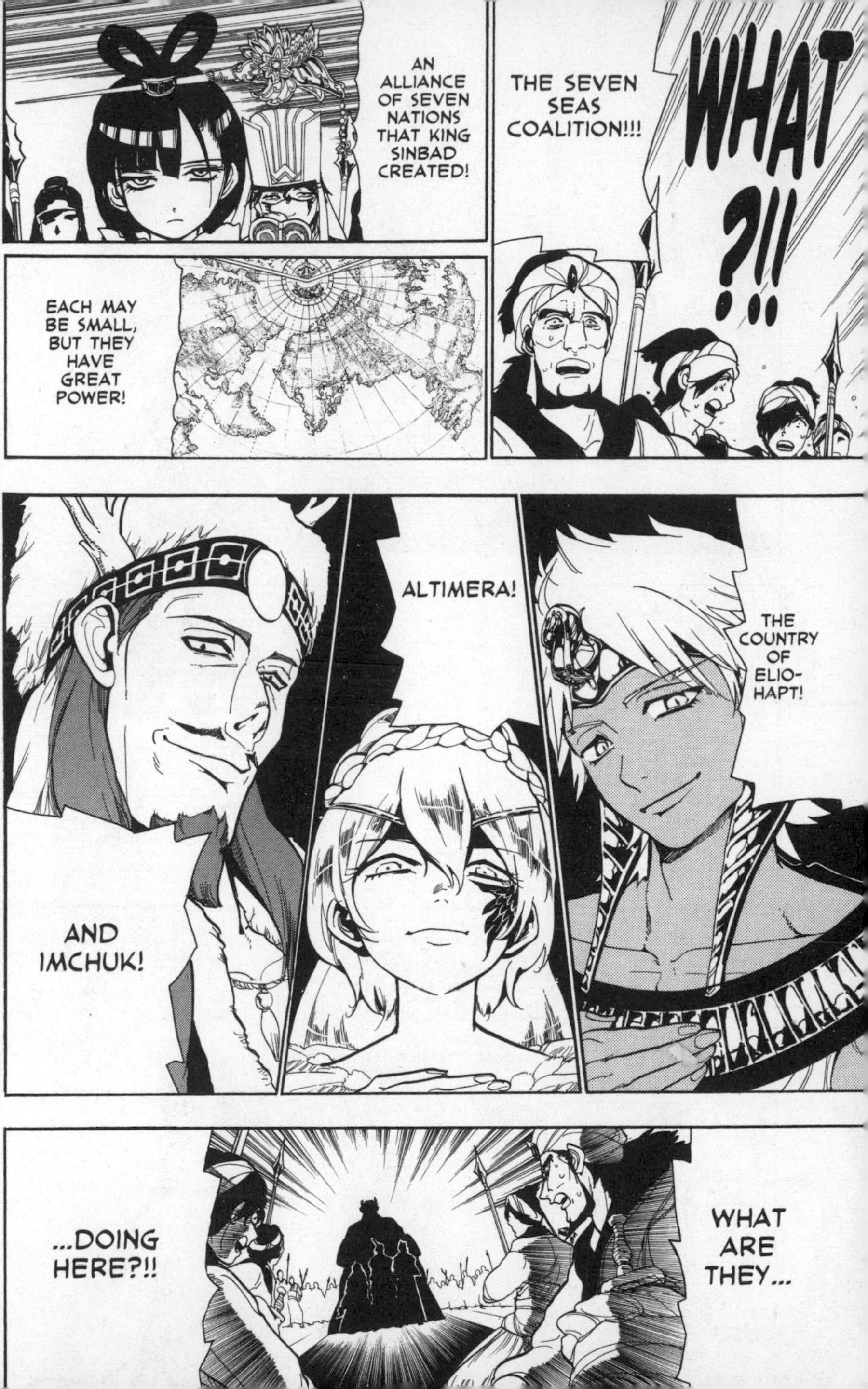
WHAT ?!!
THE SEVEN SEAS COALITION!!!
AN ALLIANCE OF SEVEN NATIONS THAT KING SINBAD CREATED!
EACH MAY BE SMALL, BUT THEY HAVE GREAT POWER!
THE COUNTRY OF ELIO-HAPT!
ALTIMERA!
AND IMCHUK!
WHAT ARE THEY...
...DOING HERE?!!

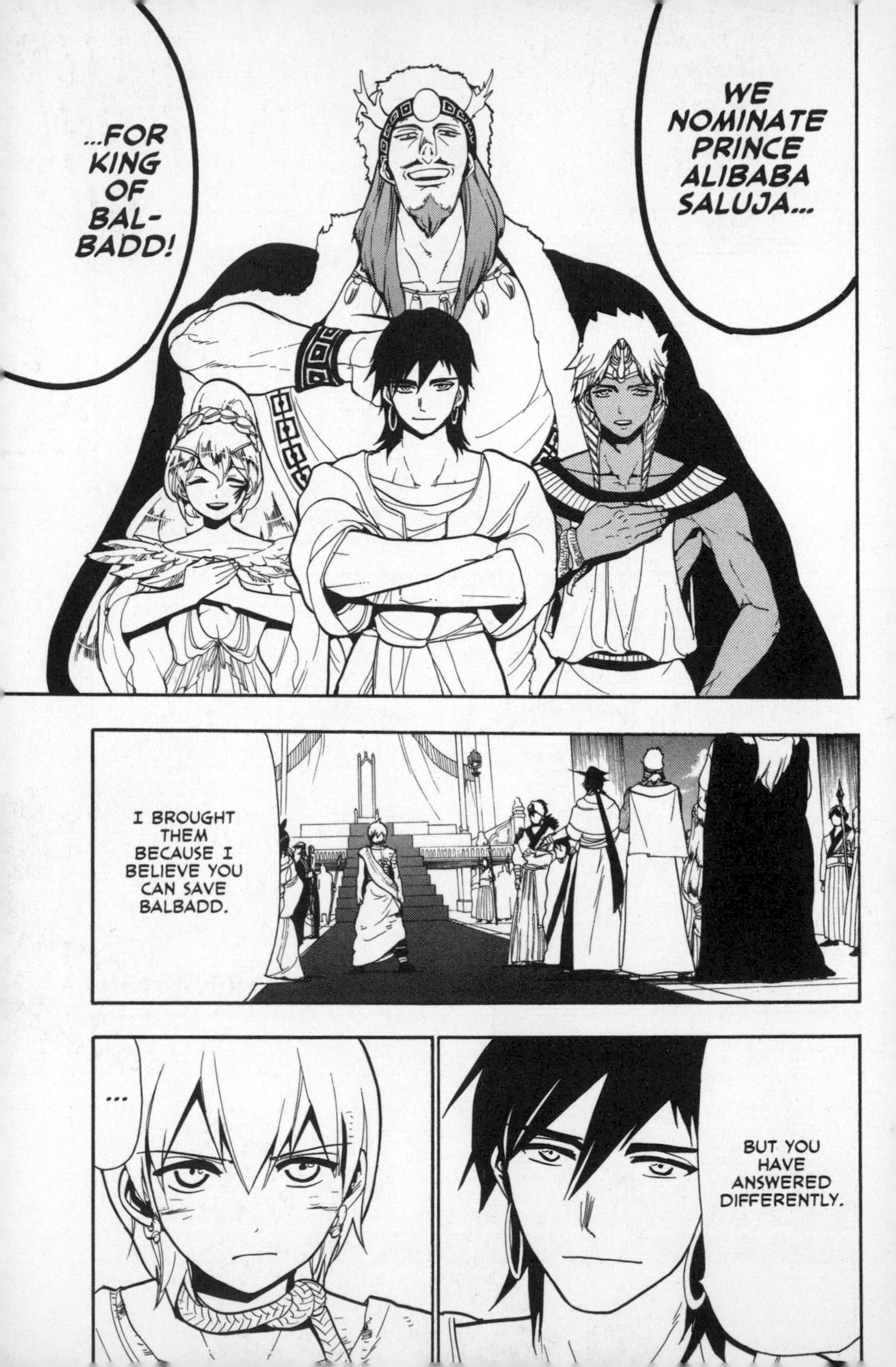
WE NOMINATE PRINCE ALIBABA SALUJA...
...FOR KING OF BAL-BADD!
I BROUGHT THEM BECAUSE I BELIEVE YOU CAN SAVE BALBADD.
BUT YOU HAVE ANSWERED DIFFERENTLY.
...

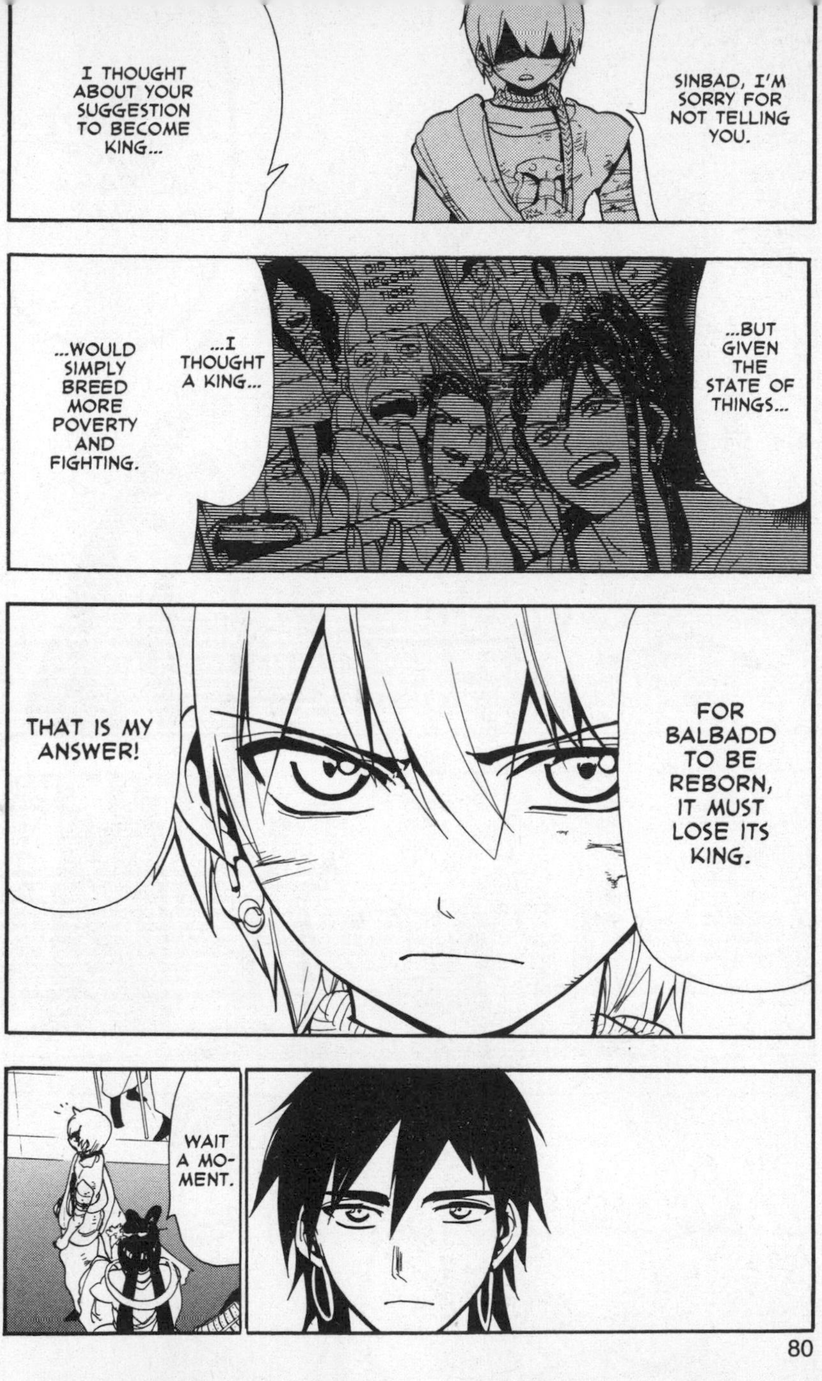
SINBAD, I'M SORRY FOR NOT TELLING YOU.
I THOUGHT ABOUT YOUR SUGGESTION TO BECOME KING...
...BUT GIVEN THE STATE OF THINGS...
...I THOUGHT A KING...
...WOULD SIMPLY BREED MORE POVERTY AND FIGHTING.
FOR BALBADD TO BE REBORN, IT MUST LOSE ITS KING.
THAT IS MY ANSWER!
WAIT A MO-MENT.

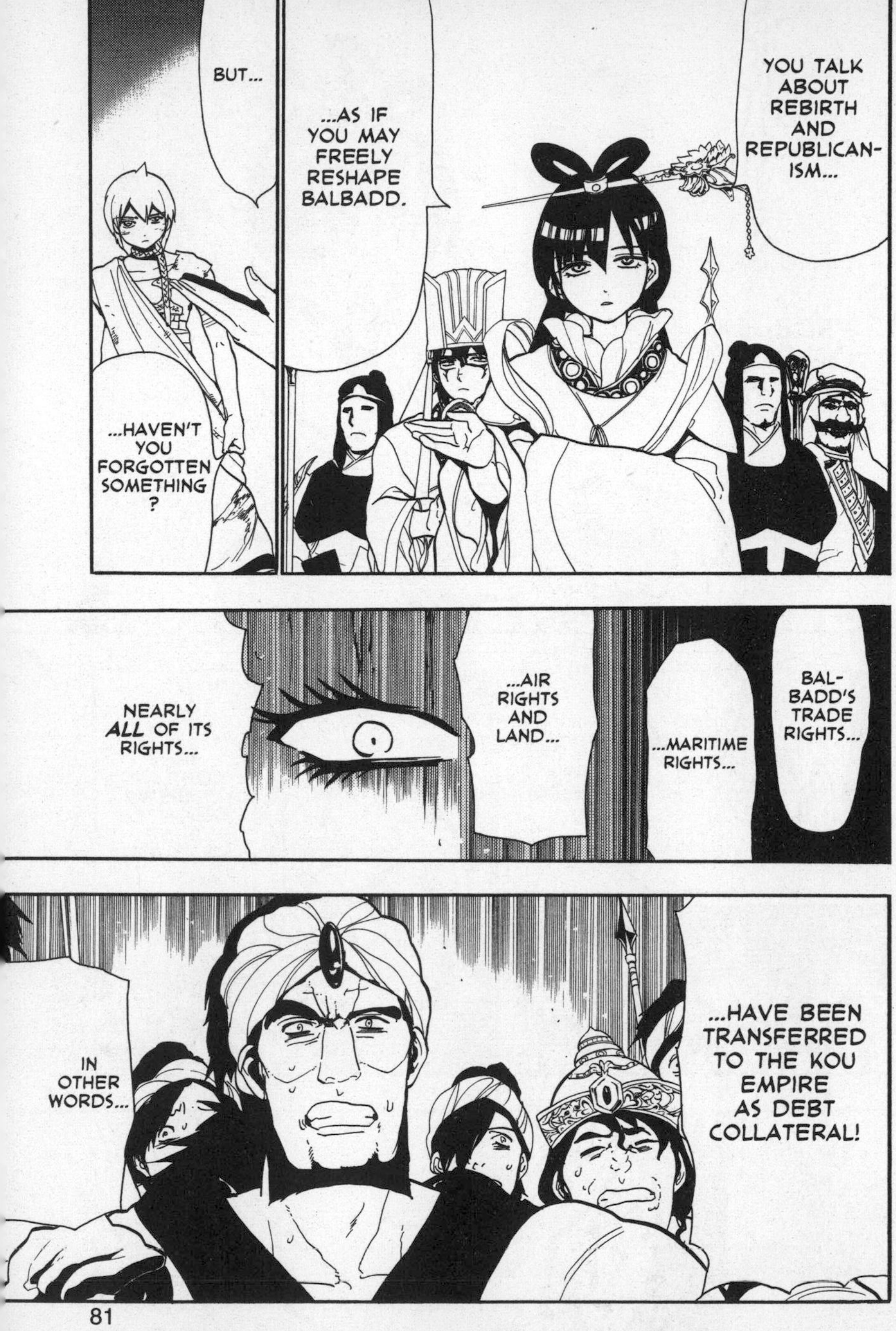
YOU TALK ABOUT REBIRTH AND REPUBLICAN-ISM...
...AS IF YOU MAY FREELY RESHAPE BALBADD.
BUT...
...HAVEN'T YOU FORGOTTEN SOMETHING?
BAL-BADD'S TRADE RIGHTS...
...MARITIME RIGHTS...
...AIR RIGHTS AND LAND...
NEARLY ALL OF ITS RIGHTS...
...HAVE BEEN TRANSFERRED TO THE KOU EMPIRE AS DEBT COLLATERAL!
IN OTHER WORDS...

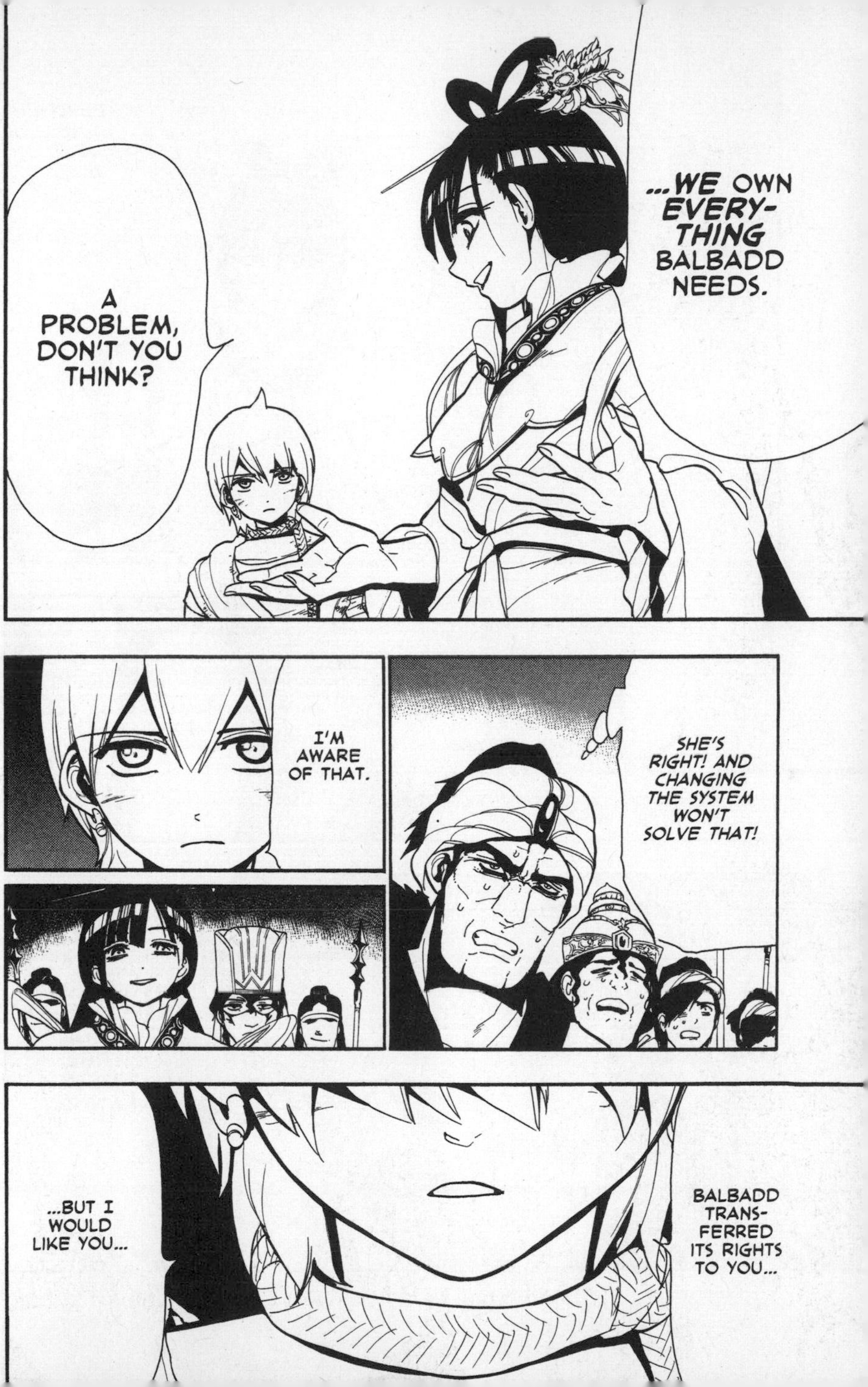
...WE OWN EVERYTHING BALBADD NEEDS.
A PROBLEM, DON'T YOU THINK?
SHE'S RIGHT! AND CHANGING THE SYSTEM WON'T SOLVE THAT!
I'M AWARE OF THAT.
BALBADD TRANSFERRED ITS RIGHTS TO YOU...
...BUT I WOULD LIKE YOU...

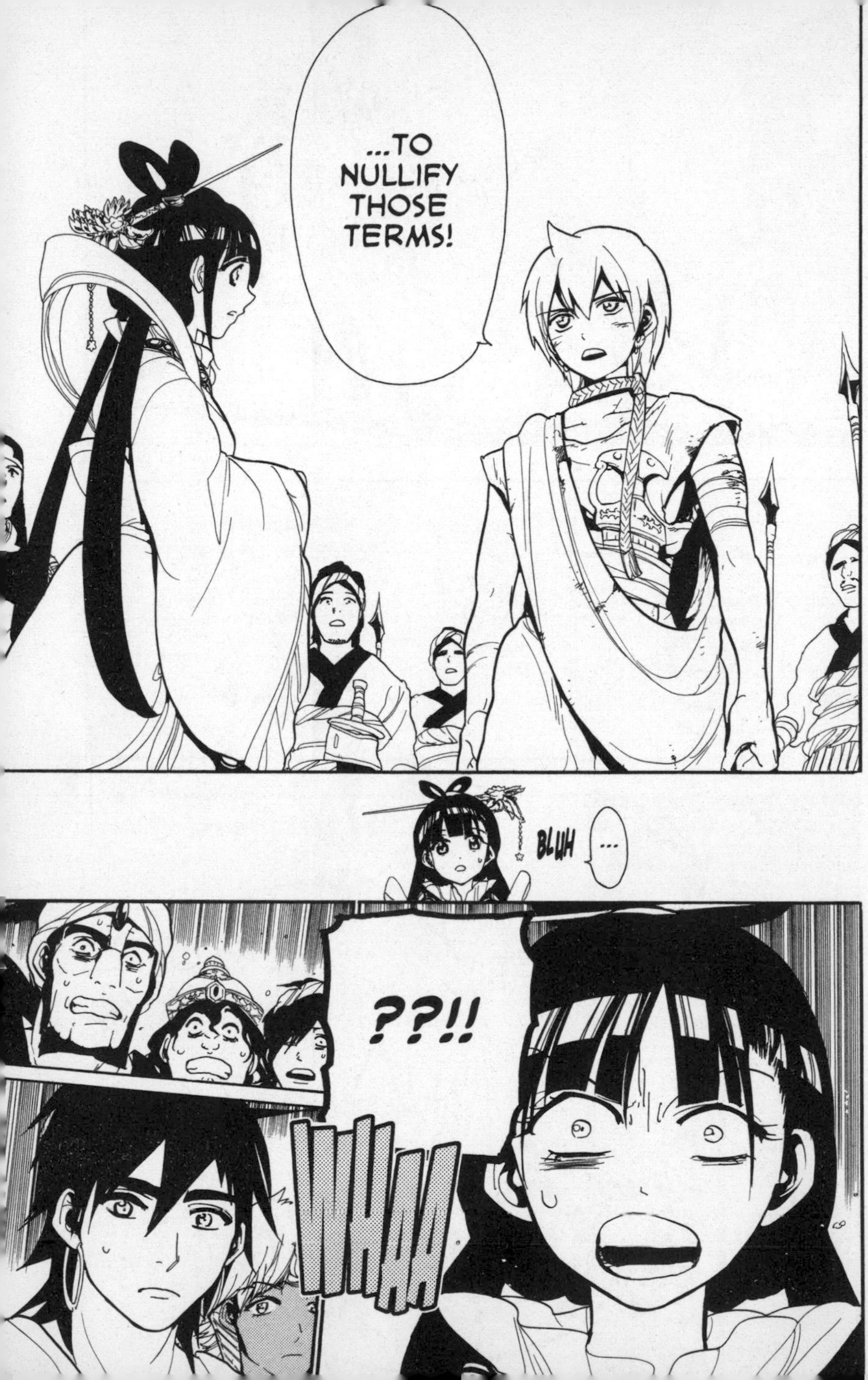
...TO NULLIFY THOSE TERMS!
...
BLUH
??!!
WHAA

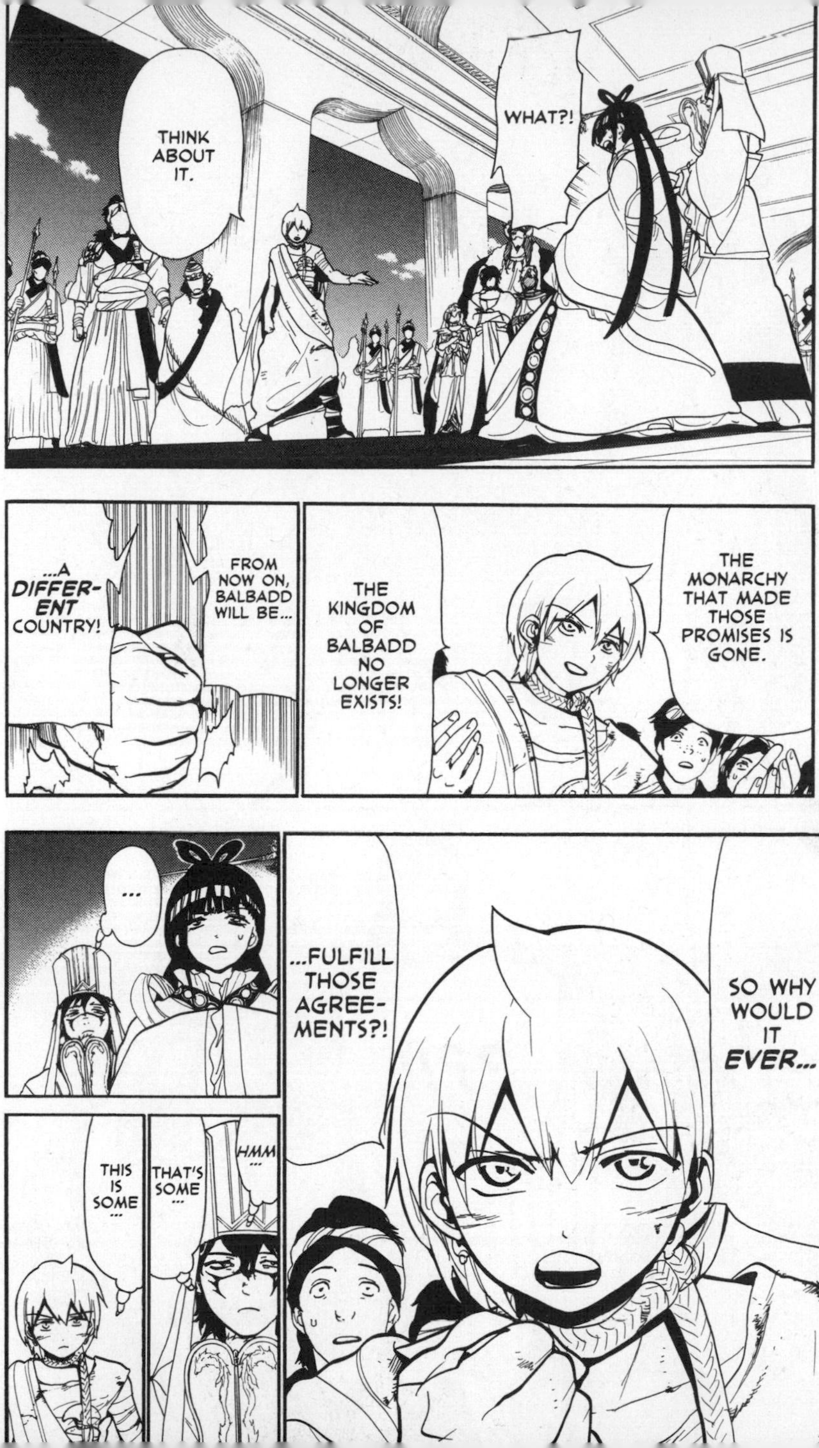
WHAT?!
THINK ABOUT IT.
THE MONARCHY THAT MADE THOSE PROMISES IS GONE.
THE KINGDOM OF BALBADD NO LONGER EXISTS!
FROM NOW ON, BALBADD WILL BE...
...A *DIFFERENT* COUNTRY!
SO WHY WOULD IT *EVER...*
...FULFILL THOSE AGREEMENTS?!
...
HMM...
THAT'S SOME...
THIS IS SOME...

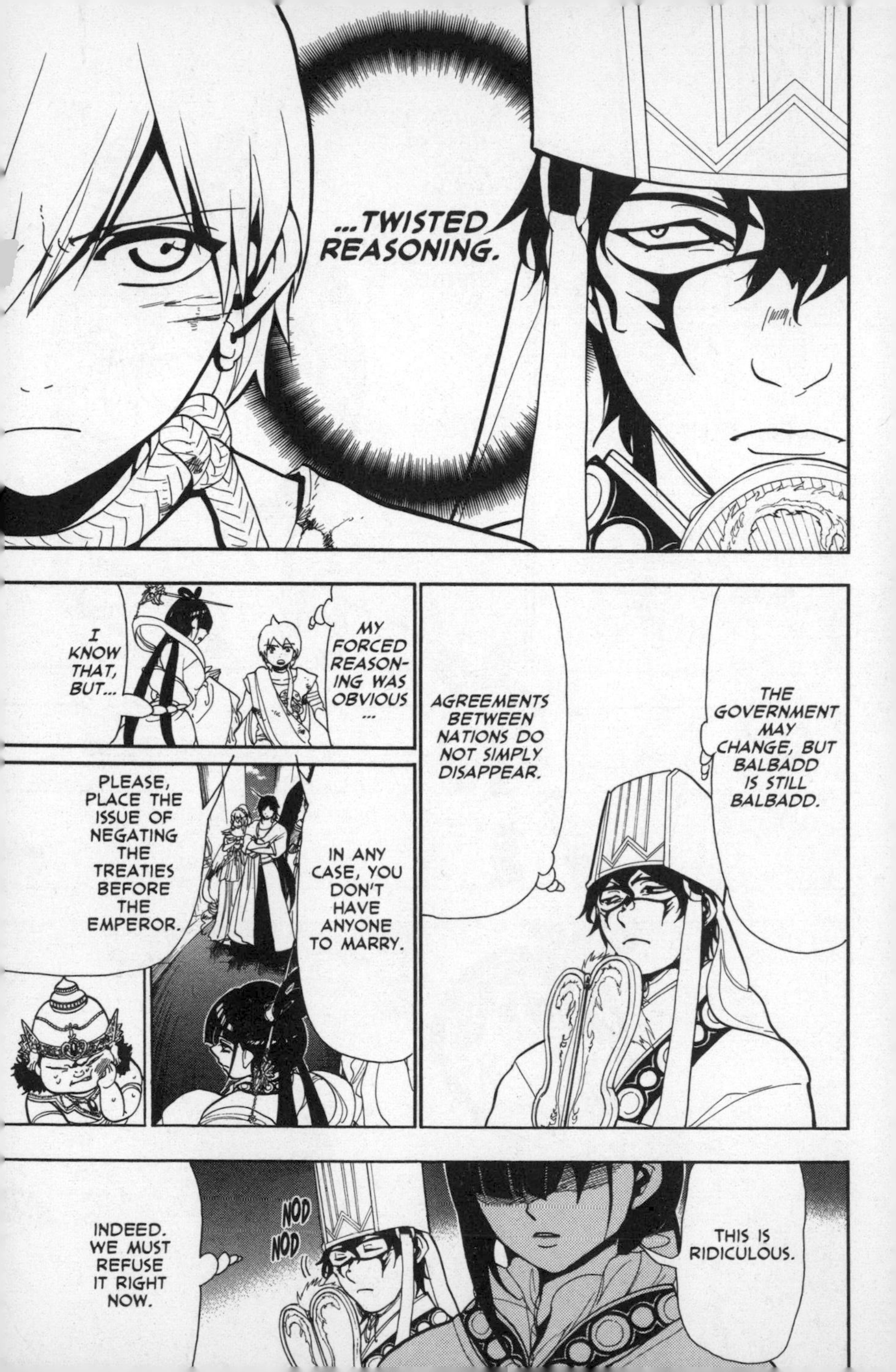
...TWISTED REASONING.
THE GOVERNMENT MAY CHANGE, BUT BALBADD IS STILL BALBADD.
AGREEMENTS BETWEEN NATIONS DO NOT SIMPLY DISAPPEAR.
MY FORCED REASONING WAS OBVIOUS...
I KNOW THAT, BUT...
IN ANY CASE, YOU DON'T HAVE ANYONE TO MARRY.
PLEASE, PLACE THE ISSUE OF NEGATING THE TREATIES BEFORE THE EMPEROR.
THIS IS RIDICULOUS.
NOD NOD
INDEED. WE MUST REFUSE IT RIGHT NOW.

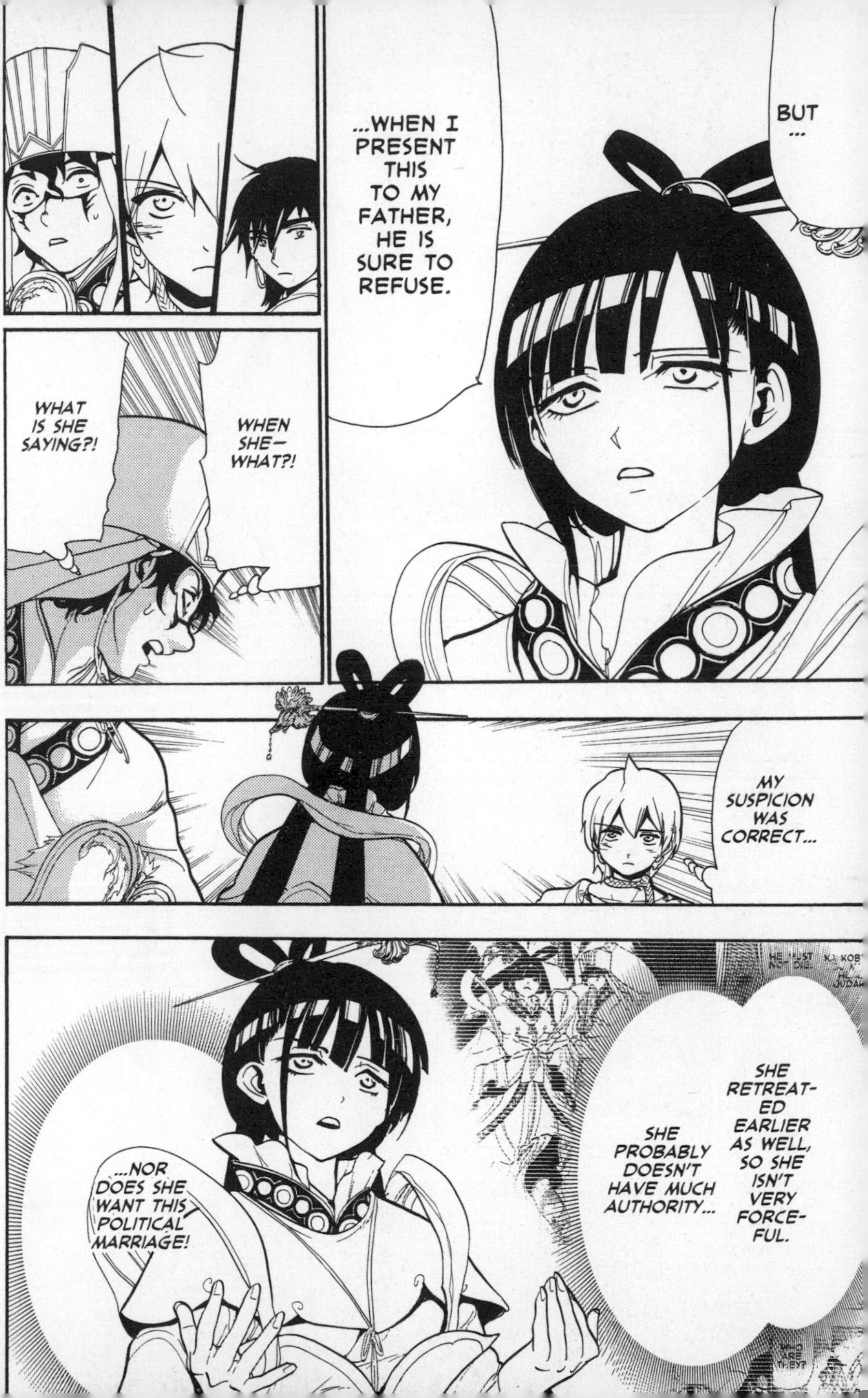
BUT ...
...WHEN I PRESENT THIS TO MY FATHER, HE IS SURE TO REFUSE.
WHEN SHE— WHAT?!
WHAT IS SHE SAYING?!
MY SUSPICION WAS CORRECT...
HE MUST NOT DIE!
SHE RETREAT-ED EARLIER AS WELL, SO SHE ISN'T VERY FORCE-FUL.
SHE PROBABLY DOESN'T HAVE MUCH AUTHORITY...
...NOR DOES SHE WANT THIS POLITICAL MARRIAGE!
WHO ARE THEY?

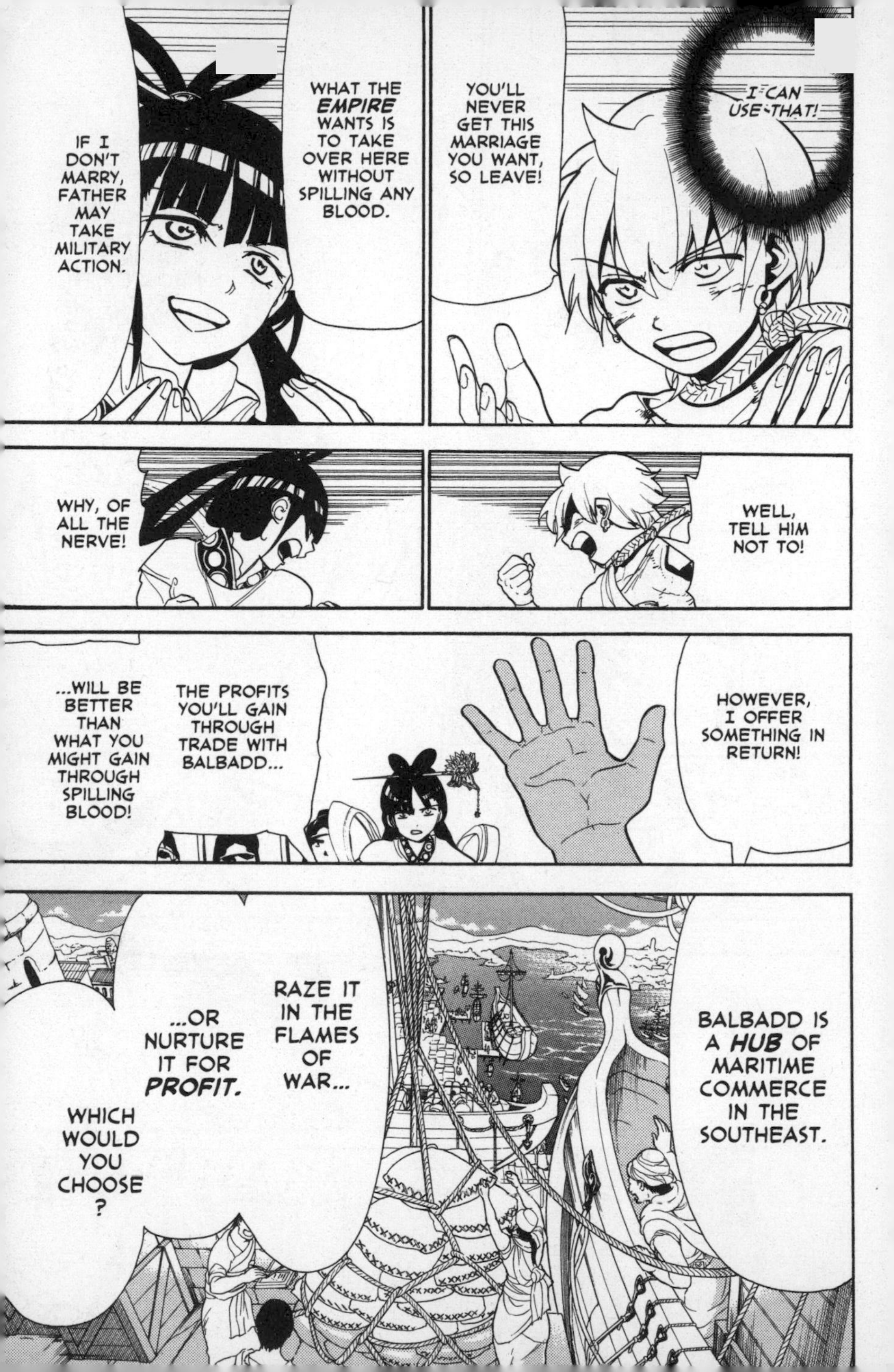
I CAN USE THAT!
YOU'LL NEVER GET THIS MARRIAGE YOU WANT, SO LEAVE!
WHAT THE EMPIRE WANTS IS TO TAKE OVER HERE WITHOUT SPILLING ANY BLOOD.
IF I DON'T MARRY, FATHER MAY TAKE MILITARY ACTION.
WELL, TELL HIM NOT TO!
WHY, OF ALL THE NERVE!
HOWEVER, I OFFER SOMETHING IN RETURN!
THE PROFITS YOU'LL GAIN THROUGH TRADE WITH BALBADD...
...WILL BE BETTER THAN WHAT YOU MIGHT GAIN THROUGH SPILLING BLOOD!
BALBADD IS A HUB OF MARITIME COMMERCE IN THE SOUTHEAST.
RAZE IT IN THE FLAMES OF WAR...
...OR NURTURE IT FOR PROFIT.
WHICH WOULD YOU CHOOSE ?

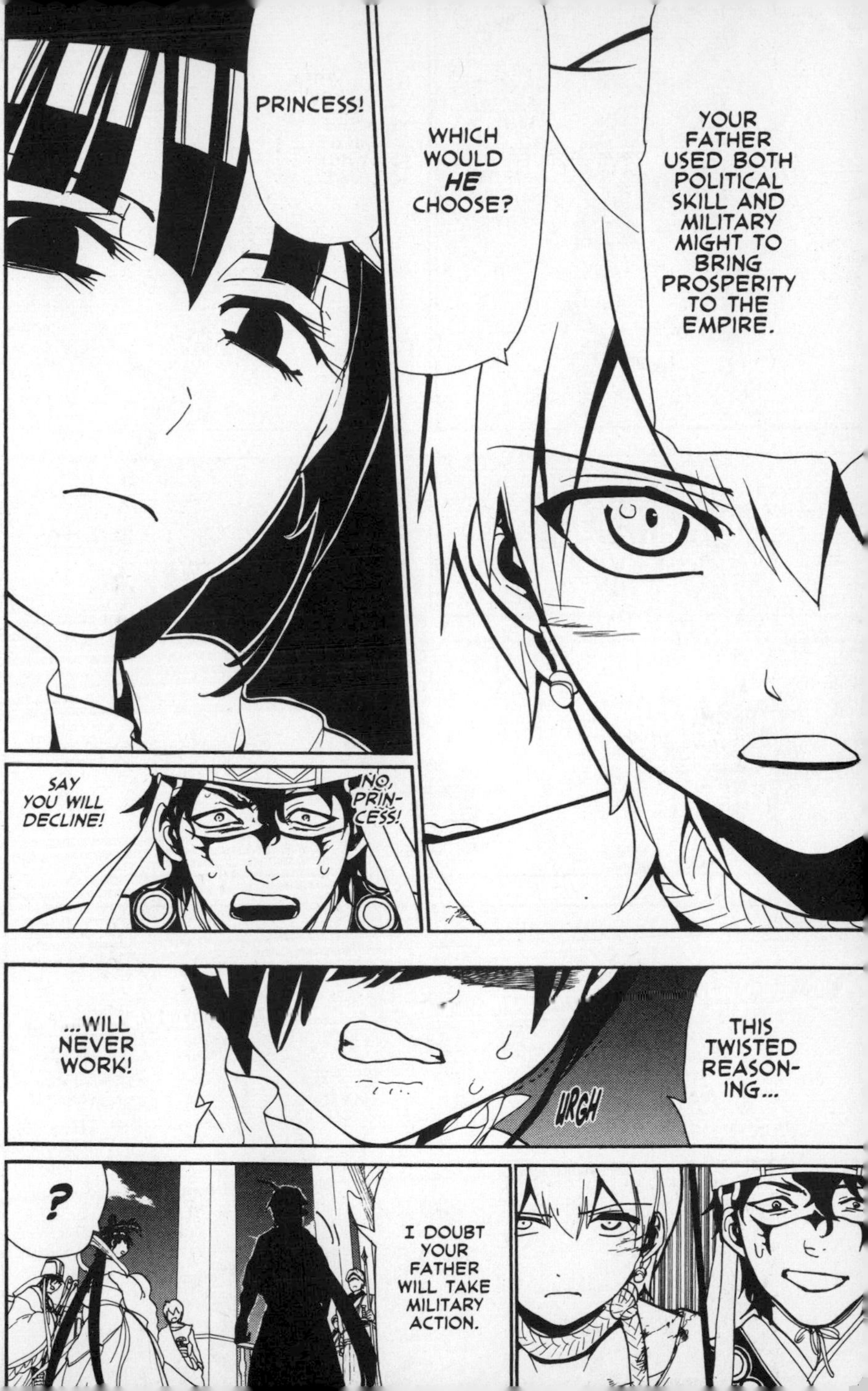
YOUR FATHER USED BOTH POLITICAL SKILL AND MILITARY MIGHT TO BRING PROSPERITY TO THE EMPIRE.
WHICH WOULD *HE* CHOOSE?
PRINCESS!
NO, PRIN-CESS!
SAY YOU WILL DECLINE!
THIS TWISTED REASON-ING...
URGH
...WILL NEVER WORK!
I DOUBT YOUR FATHER WILL TAKE MILITARY ACTION.
?

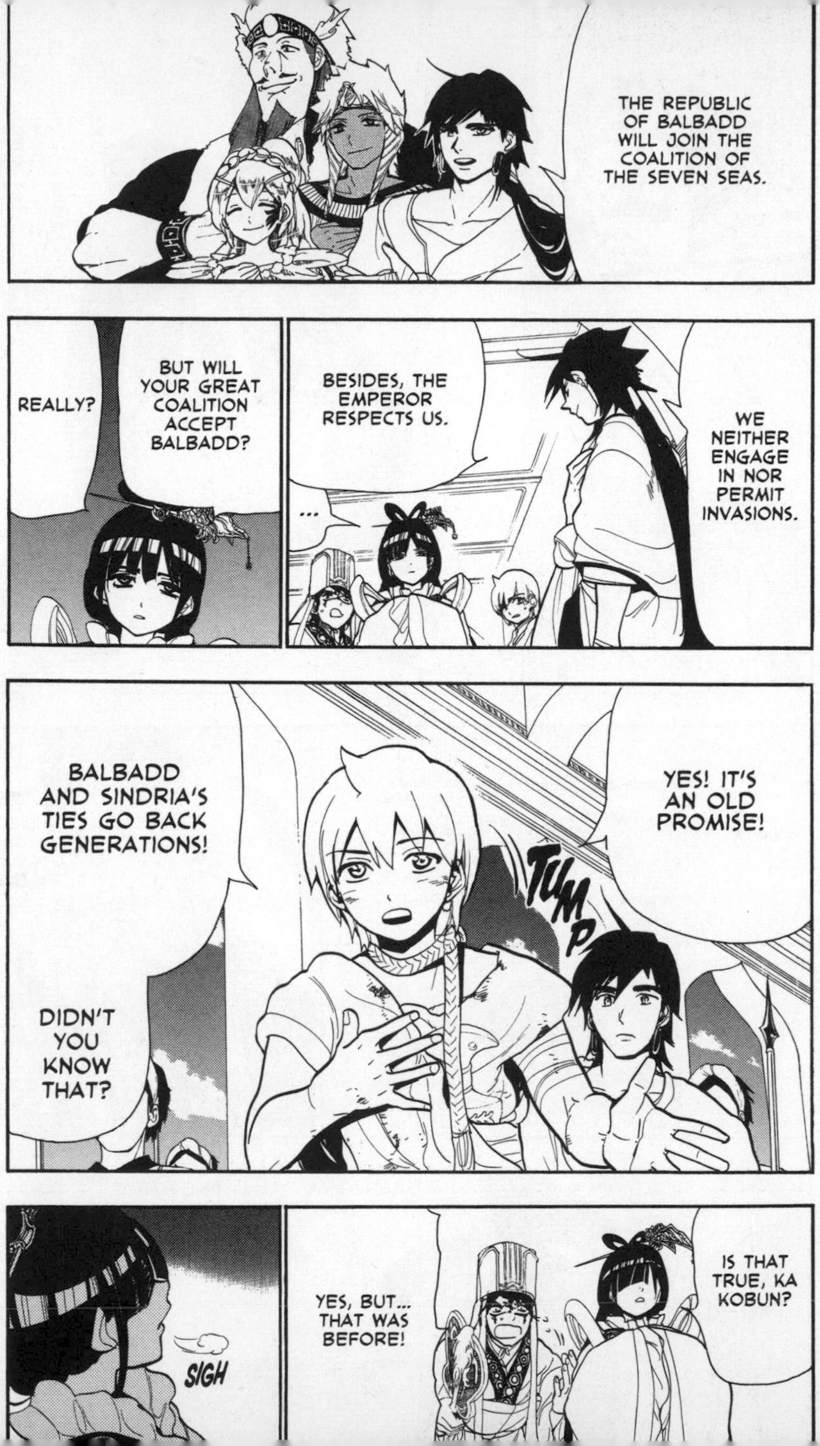
THE REPUBLIC OF BALBADD WILL JOIN THE COALITION OF THE SEVEN SEAS.
WE NEITHER ENGAGE IN NOR PERMIT INVASIONS.
BESIDES, THE EMPEROR RESPECTS US.
...
BUT WILL YOUR GREAT COALITION ACCEPT BALBADD?
REALLY?
YES! IT'S AN OLD PROMISE!
TUMP
BALBADD AND SINDRIA'S TIES GO BACK GENERATIONS!
DIDN'T YOU KNOW THAT?
IS THAT TRUE, KA KOBUN?
YES, BUT... THAT WAS BEFORE!
SIGH

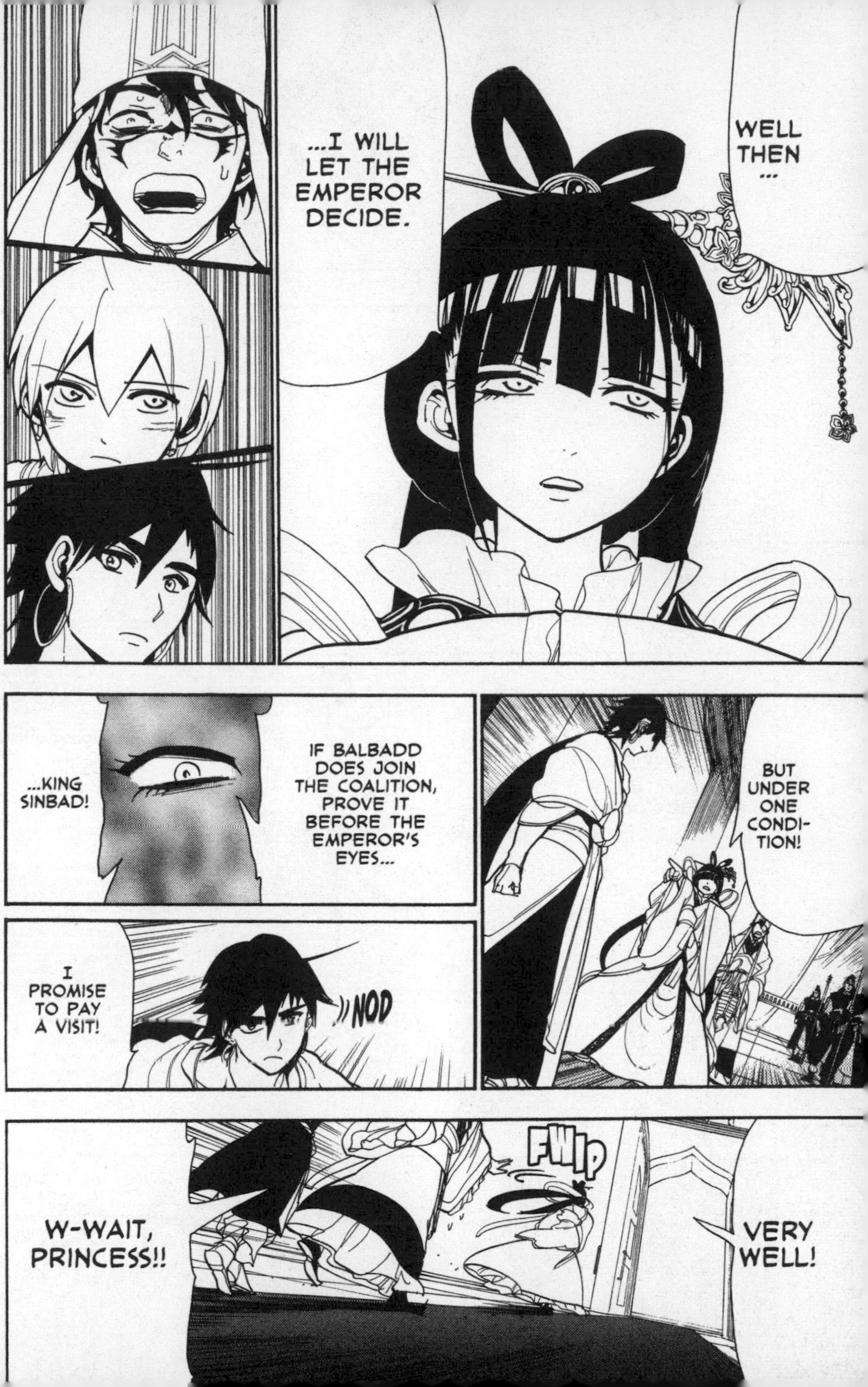
WELL THEN ...
...I WILL LET THE EMPEROR DECIDE.
BUT UNDER ONE CONDITION!
IF BALBADD DOES JOIN THE COALITION, PROVE IT BEFORE THE EMPEROR'S EYES...
...KING SINBAD!
NOD
I PROMISE TO PAY A VISIT!
VERY WELL!
FWIP
W-WAIT, PRINCESS!!

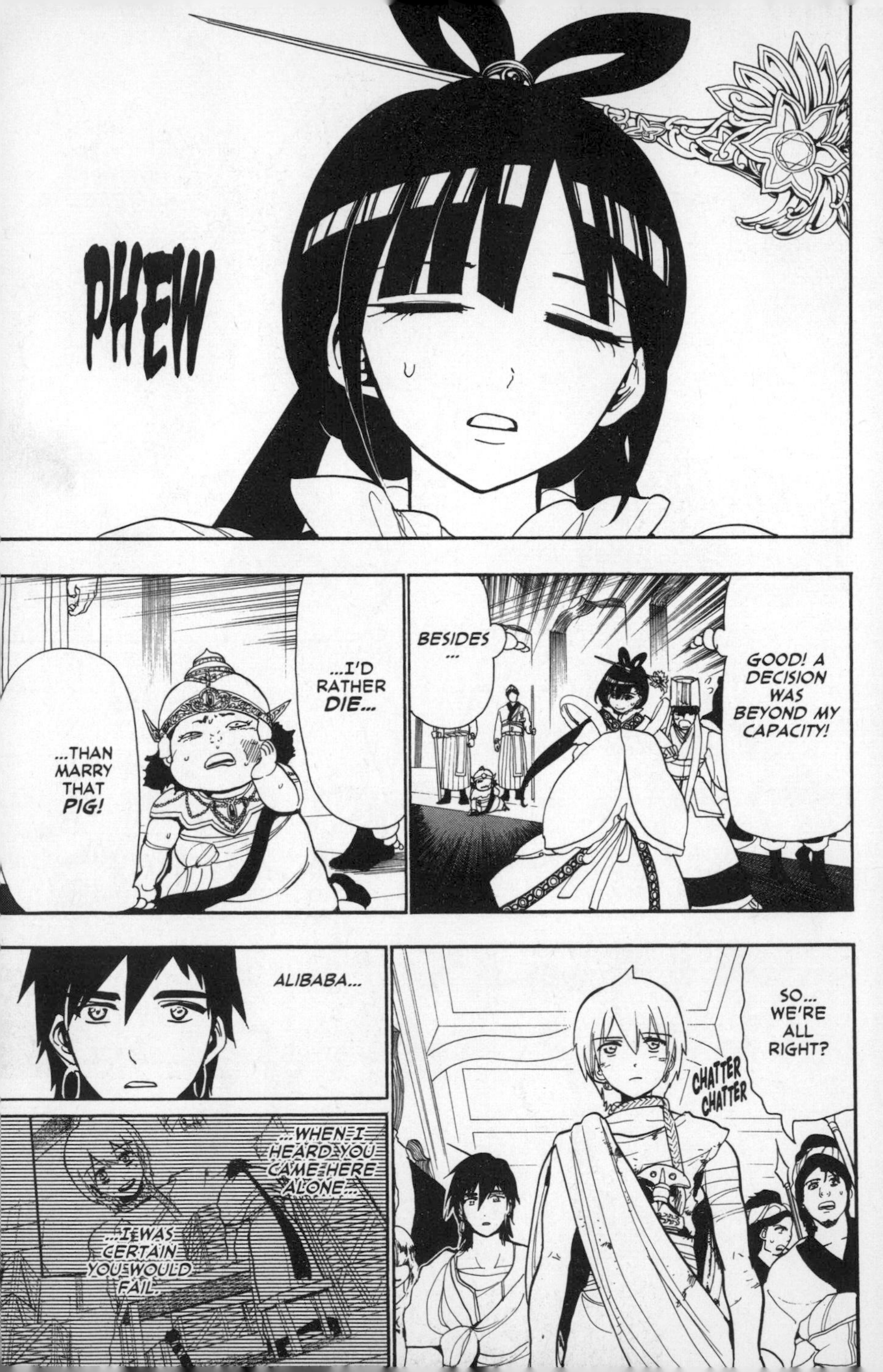
PHEW
GOOD! A DECISION WAS BEYOND MY CAPACITY!
BESIDES ...
...I'D RATHER DIE...
...THAN MARRY THAT PIG!
SO... WE'RE ALL RIGHT?
CHATTER CHATTER
ALIBABA...
...WHEN I HEARD YOU CAME HERE ALONE...
...I WAS CERTAIN YOU WOULD FAIL.

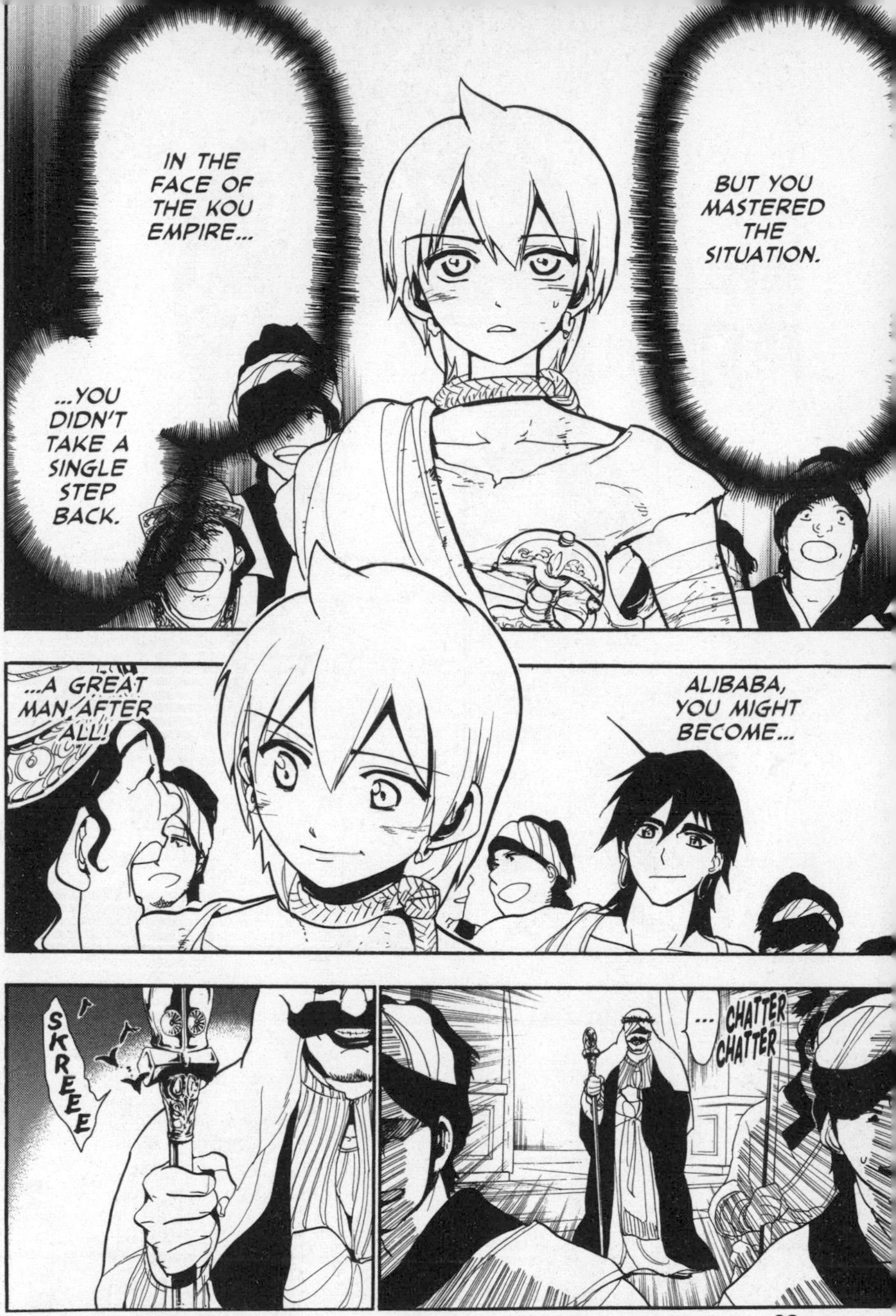
BUT YOU MASTERED THE SITUATION.
IN THE FACE OF THE KOU EMPIRE...
...YOU DIDN'T TAKE A SINGLE STEP BACK.
ALIBABA, YOU MIGHT BECOME...
...A GREAT MAN AFTER ALL!
...
CHATTER CHATTER
SKREEE

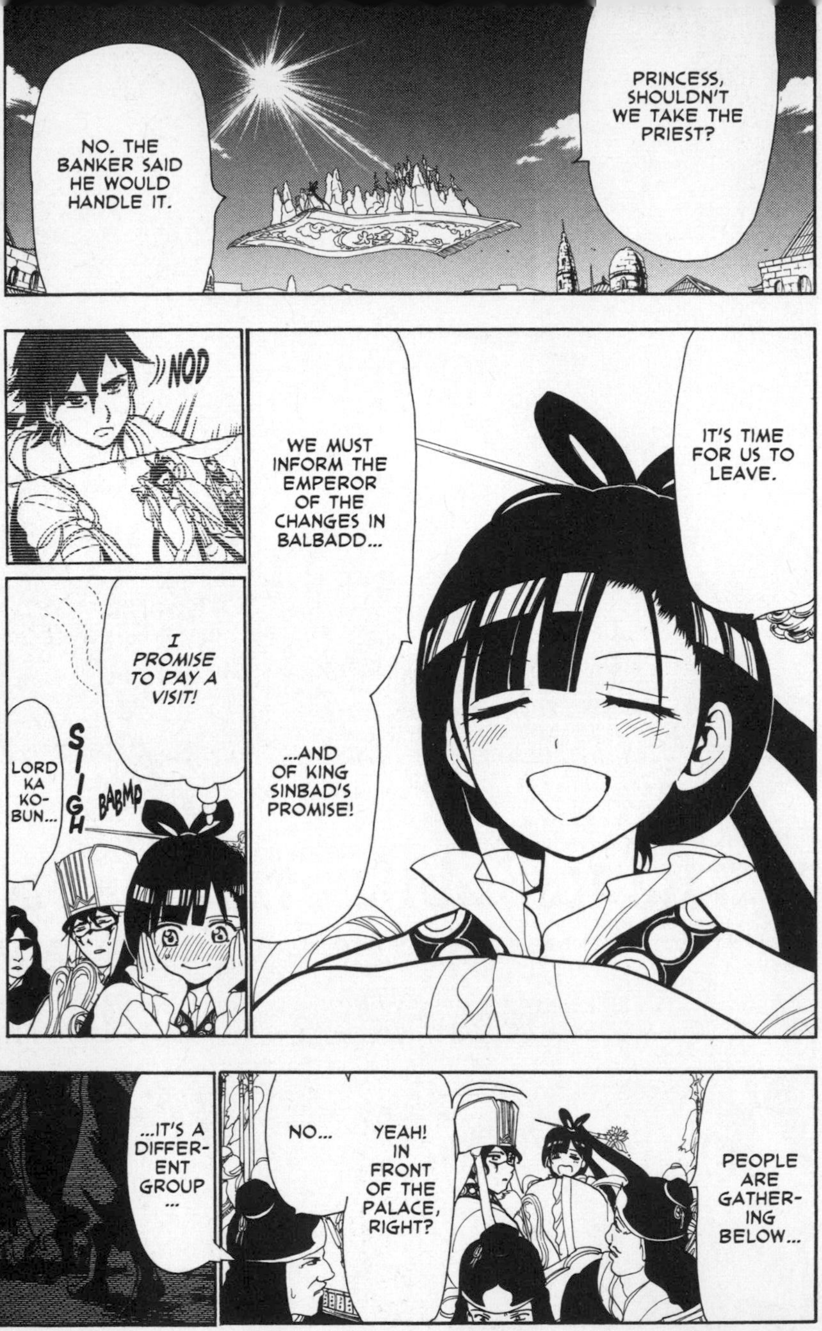
PRINCESS, SHOULDN'T WE TAKE THE PRIEST?
NO. THE BANKER SAID HE WOULD HANDLE IT.
IT'S TIME FOR US TO LEAVE.
WE MUST INFORM THE EMPEROR OF THE CHANGES IN BALBADD...
...AND OF KING SINBAD'S PROMISE!
NOD
I PROMISE TO PAY A VISIT!
SIGH
BABMP
LORD KA KO-BUN...
PEOPLE ARE GATHER-ING BELOW...
YEAH! IN FRONT OF THE PALACE, RIGHT?
NO...
...IT'S A DIFFER-ENT GROUP ...

Night 64: The Republic of Balbadd

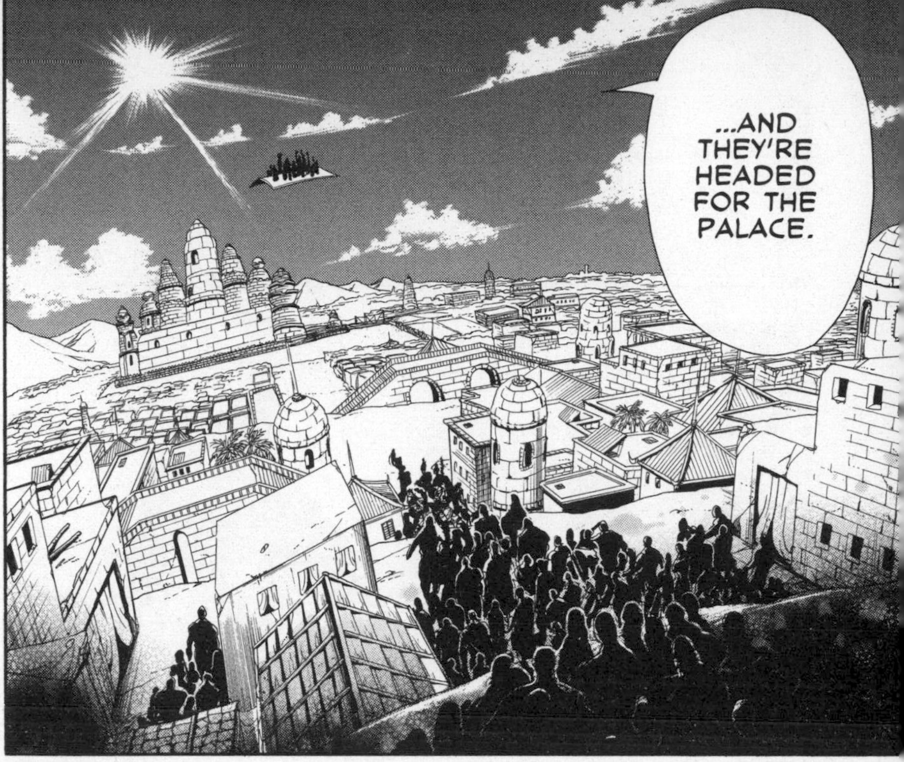
...AND THEY'RE HEADED FOR THE PALACE.

Night 64: The Republic of Balbadd

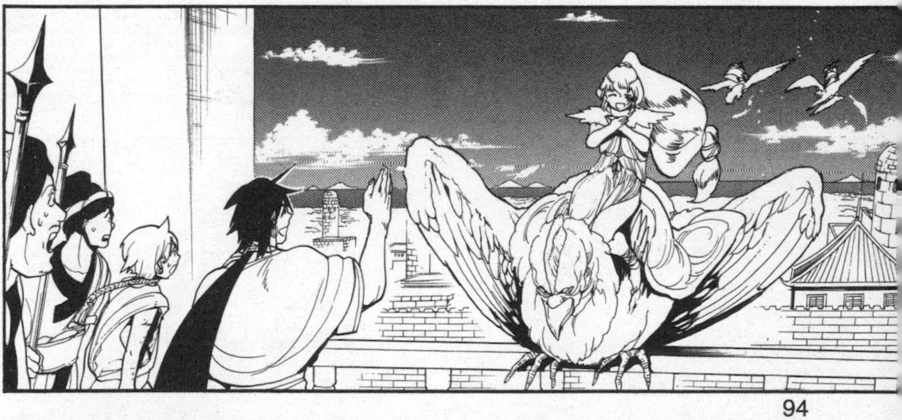

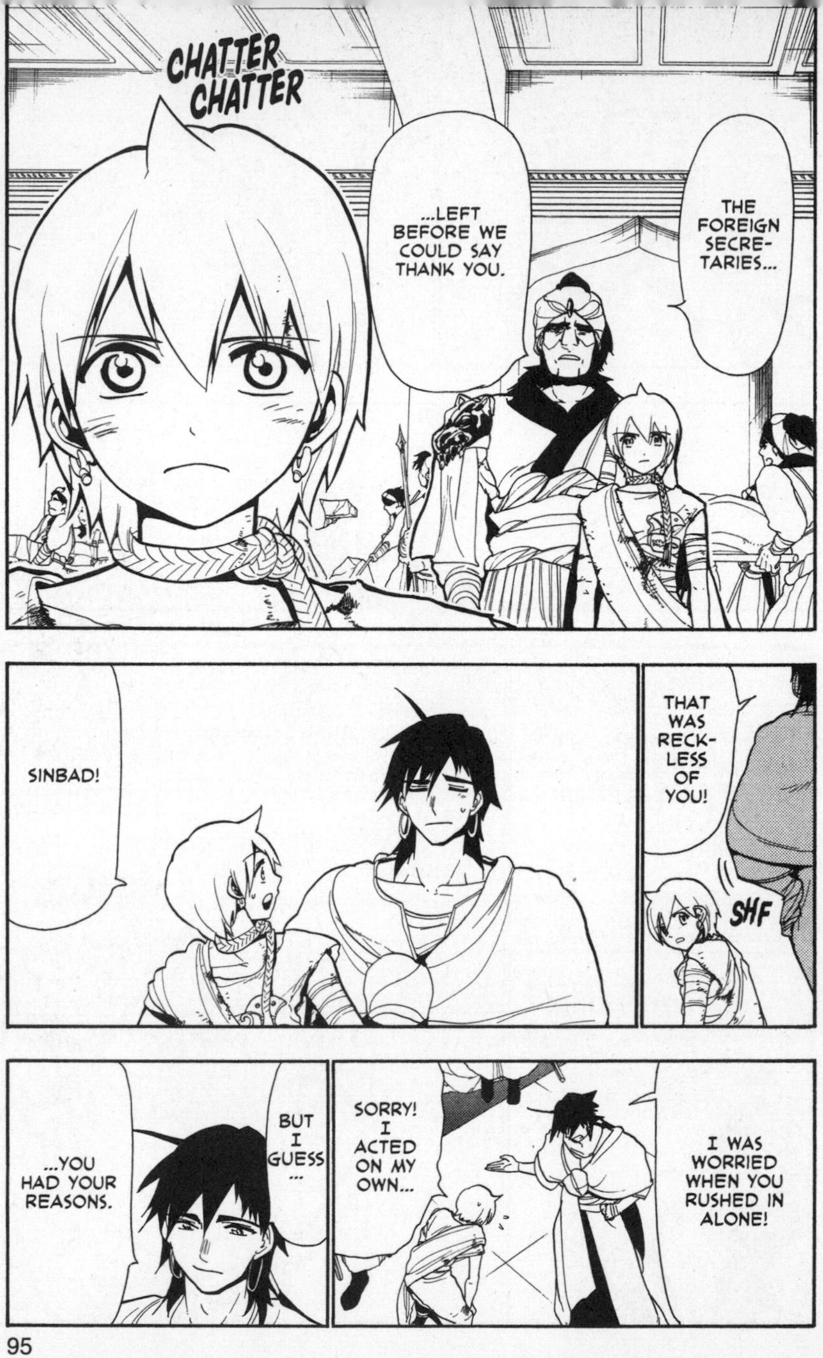
THE FOREIGN SECRE-TARIES...
...LEFT BEFORE WE COULD SAY THANK YOU.
CHATTER CHATTER
THAT WAS RECK-LESS OF YOU!
SHF
SINBAD!
I WAS WORRIED WHEN YOU RUSHED IN ALONE!
SORRY! I ACTED ON MY OWN...
BUT I GUESS ...
...YOU HAD YOUR REASONS.

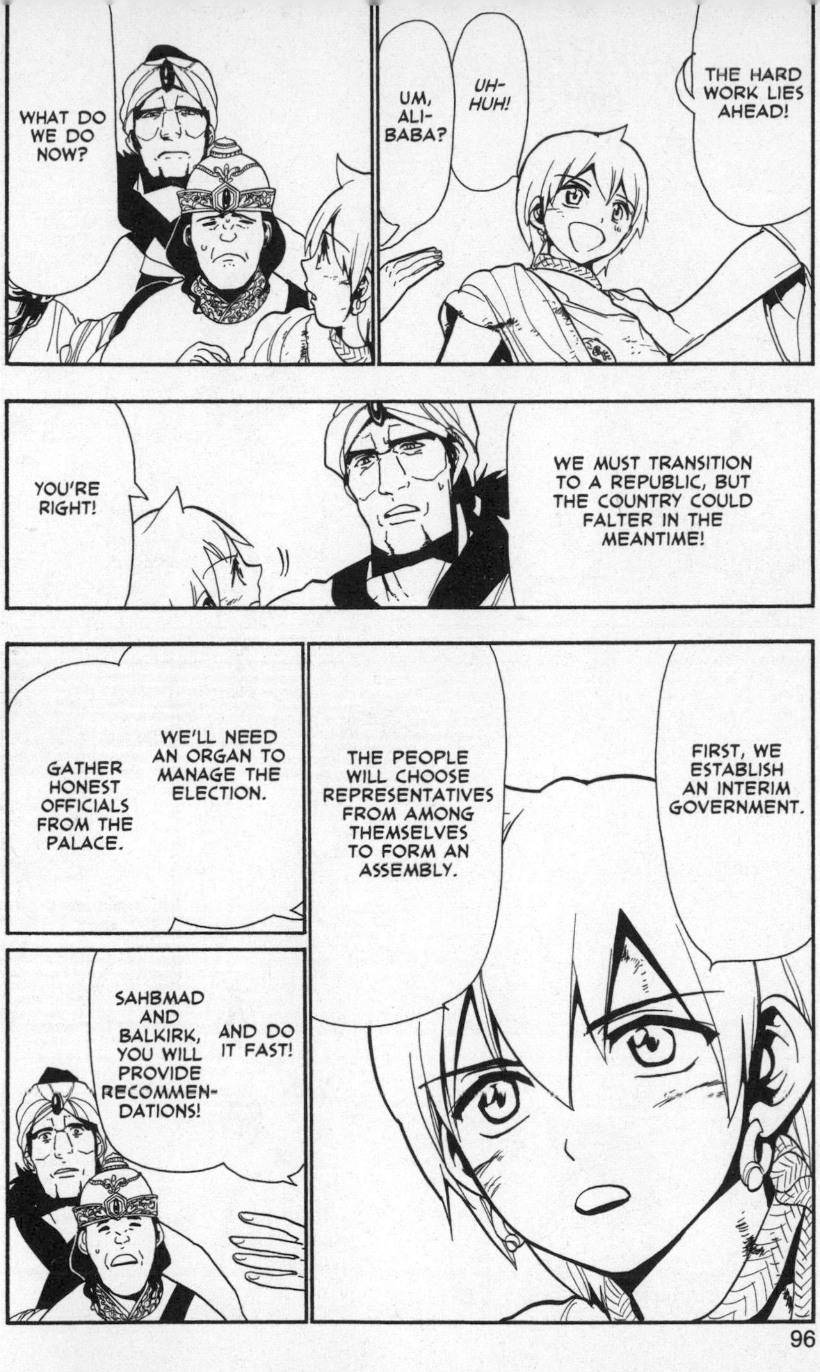
THE HARD WORK LIES AHEAD!
UH-HUH!
UM, ALI-BABA?
WHAT DO WE DO NOW?
WE MUST TRANSITION TO A REPUBLIC, BUT THE COUNTRY COULD FALTER IN THE MEANTIME!
YOU'RE RIGHT!
FIRST, WE ESTABLISH AN INTERIM GOVERNMENT.
THE PEOPLE WILL CHOOSE REPRESENTATIVES FROM AMONG THEMSELVES TO FORM AN ASSEMBLY.
WE'LL NEED AN ORGAN TO MANAGE THE ELECTION.
GATHER HONEST OFFICIALS FROM THE PALACE.
SAHBMAD AND BALKIRK, YOU WILL PROVIDE RECOMMEN-DATIONS!
AND DO IT FAST!

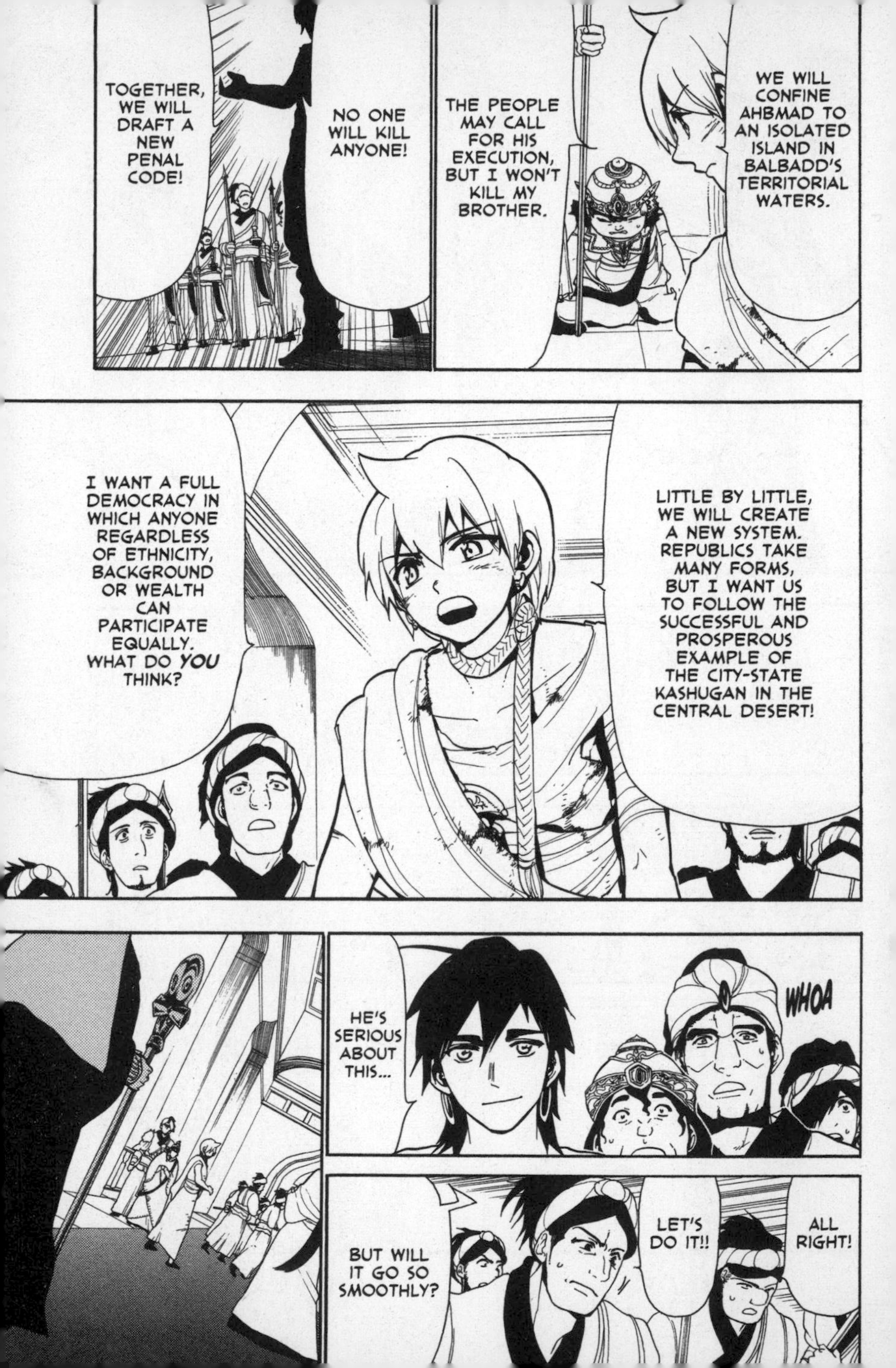
WE WILL CONFINE AHBMAD TO AN ISOLATED ISLAND IN BALBADD'S TERRITORIAL WATERS.
THE PEOPLE MAY CALL FOR HIS EXECUTION, BUT I WON'T KILL MY BROTHER.
NO ONE WILL KILL ANYONE!
TOGETHER, WE WILL DRAFT A NEW PENAL CODE!
LITTLE BY LITTLE, WE WILL CREATE A NEW SYSTEM. REPUBLICS TAKE MANY FORMS, BUT I WANT US TO FOLLOW THE SUCCESSFUL AND PROSPEROUS EXAMPLE OF THE CITY-STATE KASHUGAN IN THE CENTRAL DESERT!
I WANT A FULL DEMOCRACY IN WHICH ANYONE REGARDLESS OF ETHNICITY, BACKGROUND OR WEALTH CAN PARTICIPATE EQUALLY. WHAT DO *YOU* THINK?
WHOA
HE'S SERIOUS ABOUT THIS...
ALL RIGHT!
LET'S DO IT!!
BUT WILL IT GO SO SMOOTHLY?

DO YOU REALLY THINK...
...A REPUBLIC WILL BE SO EASY TO ESTABLISH?
I HAVE TRAVELED TO MANY LANDS...
...AND REPUBLICS TOUTING EQUALITY ALWAYS END UP UNDER ONE PERSON'S CONTROL AND FALL APART.
HOPE FOR EQUALITY ALL YOU LIKE...
...BUT SOMEONE WILL SEEK TO BECOME RULER...
...OR THE PEOPLE THEMSELVES WILL DEMAND ONE!

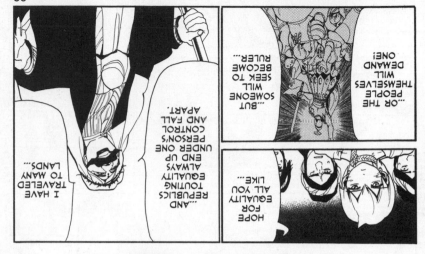

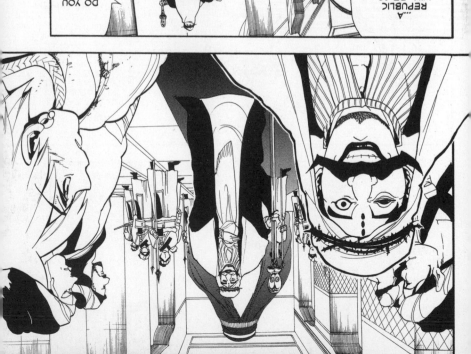

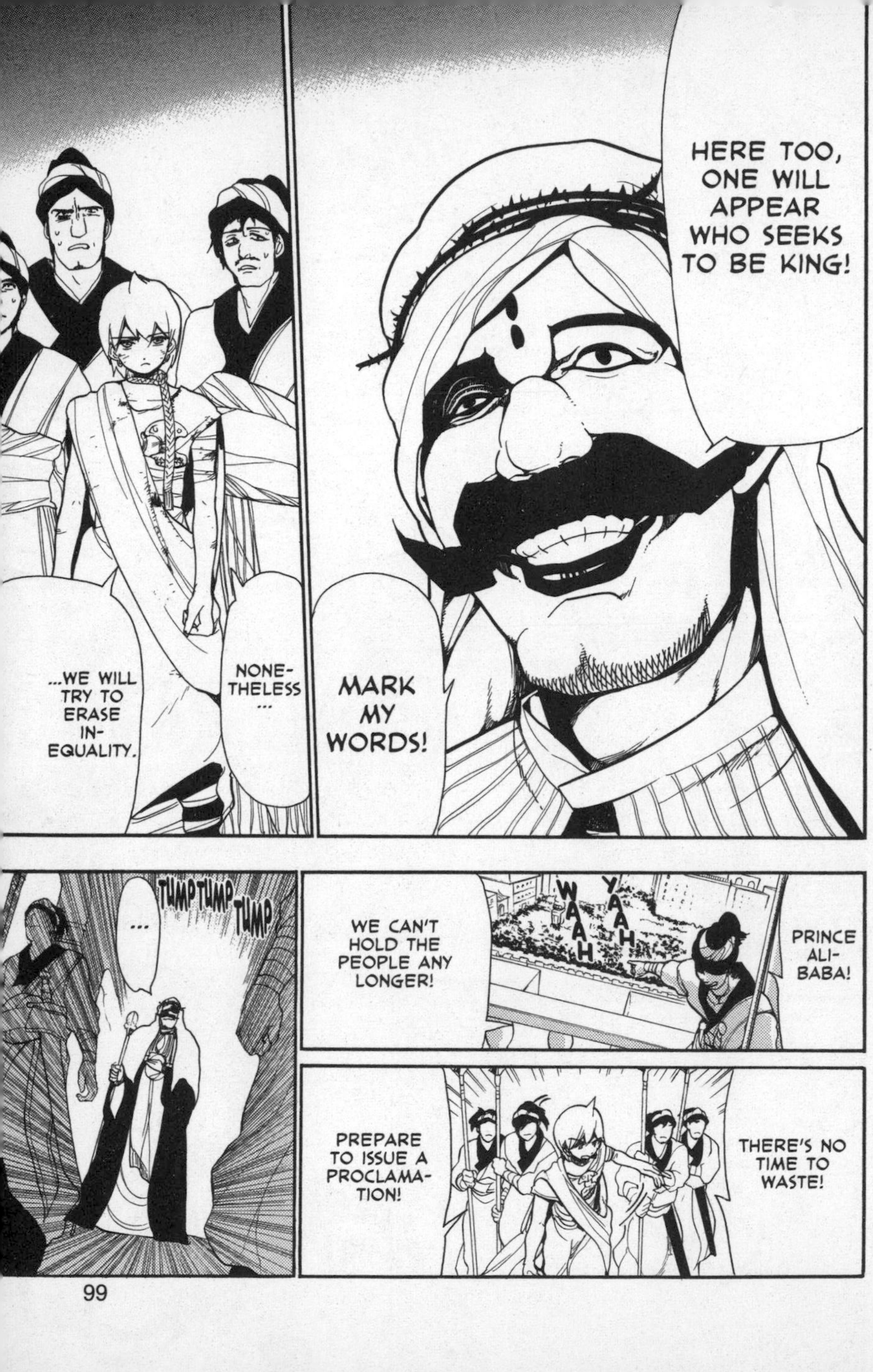
HERE TOO, ONE WILL APPEAR WHO SEEKS TO BE KING!
MARK MY WORDS!
NONE-THELESS ...
...WE WILL TRY TO ERASE IN-EQUALITY.
PRINCE ALI-BABA!
YAAH
WAAH
WE CAN'T HOLD THE PEOPLE ANY LONGER!
THERE'S NO TIME TO WASTE!
PREPARE TO ISSUE A PROCLAMA-TION!
TUMP TUMP TUMP
...

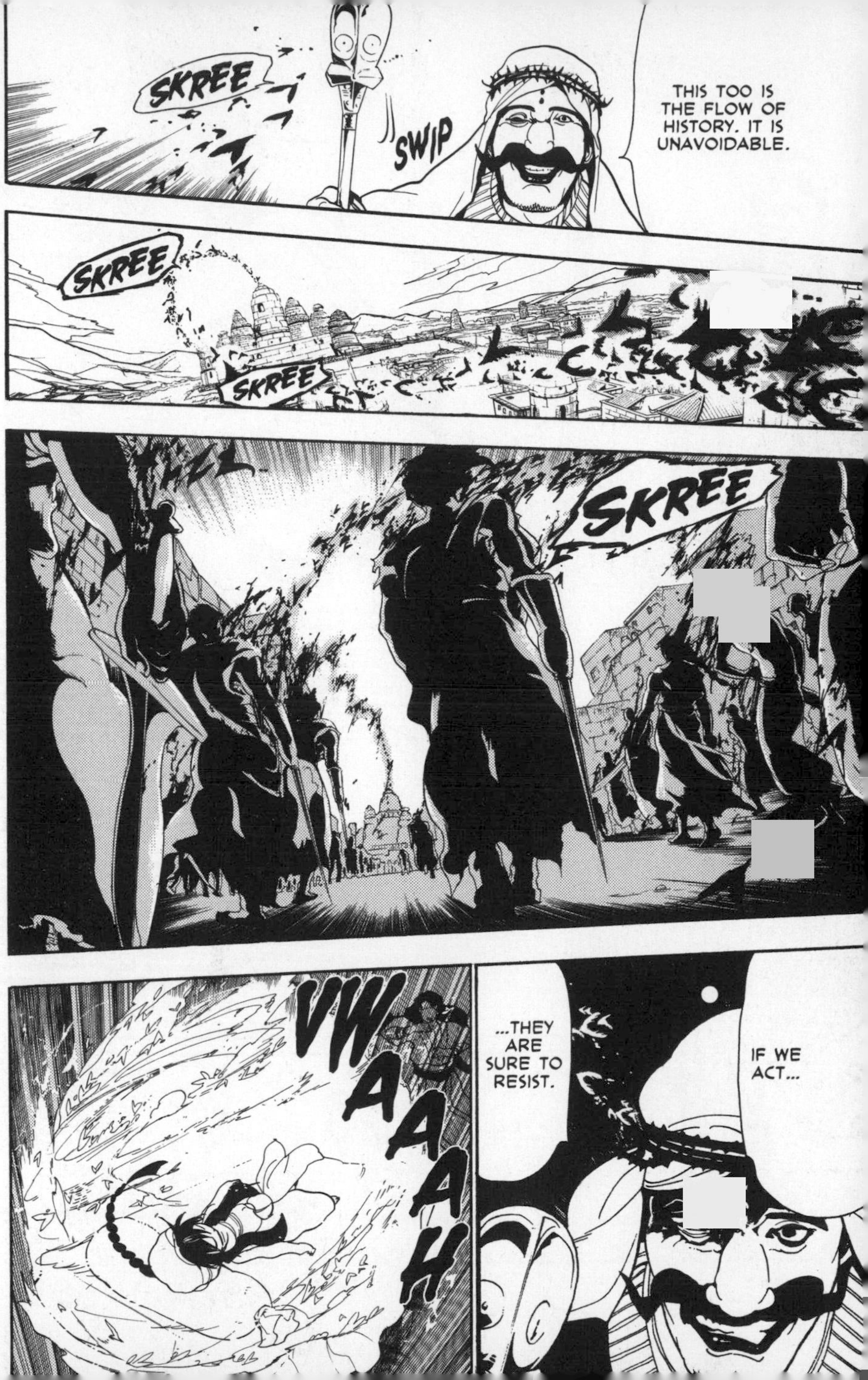
THIS TOO IS THE FLOW OF HISTORY. IT IS UNAVOIDABLE.
SWIP
SKREE
SKREE
SKREE
SKREE
IF WE ACT...
...THEY ARE SURE TO RESIST.
VWAAAH

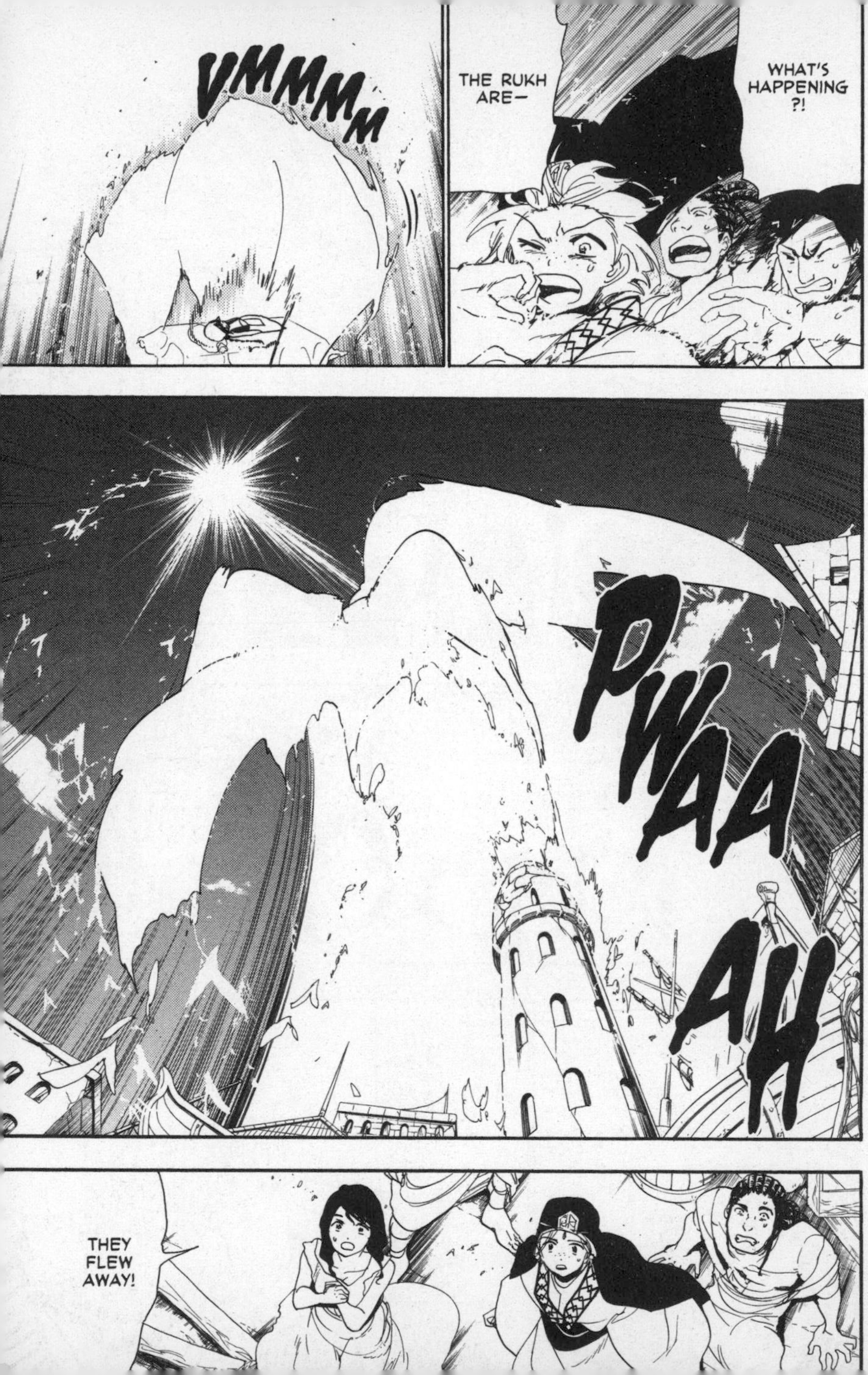
WHAT'S HAPPENING ?!
THE RUKH ARE—
VMMMM
PWAAAH
THEY FLEW AWAY!

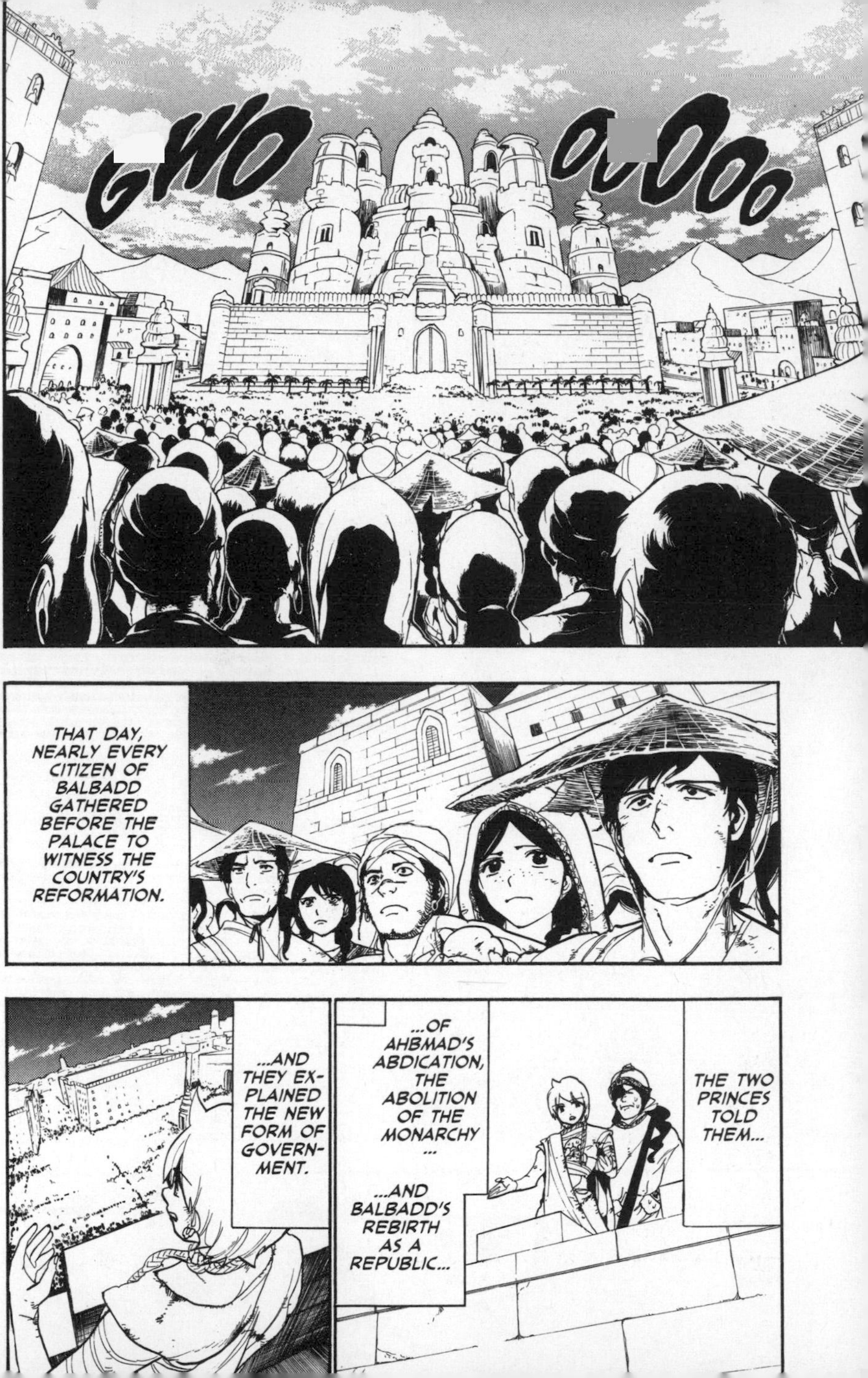
GWO
OOOoo
THAT DAY, NEARLY EVERY CITIZEN OF BALBADD GATHERED BEFORE THE PALACE TO WITNESS THE COUNTRY'S REFORMATION.
THE TWO PRINCES TOLD THEM...
...OF AHBMAD'S ABDICATION, THE ABOLITION OF THE MONARCHY...
...AND BALBADD'S REBIRTH AS A REPUBLIC...
...AND THEY EX-PLAINED THE NEW FORM OF GOVERN-MENT.

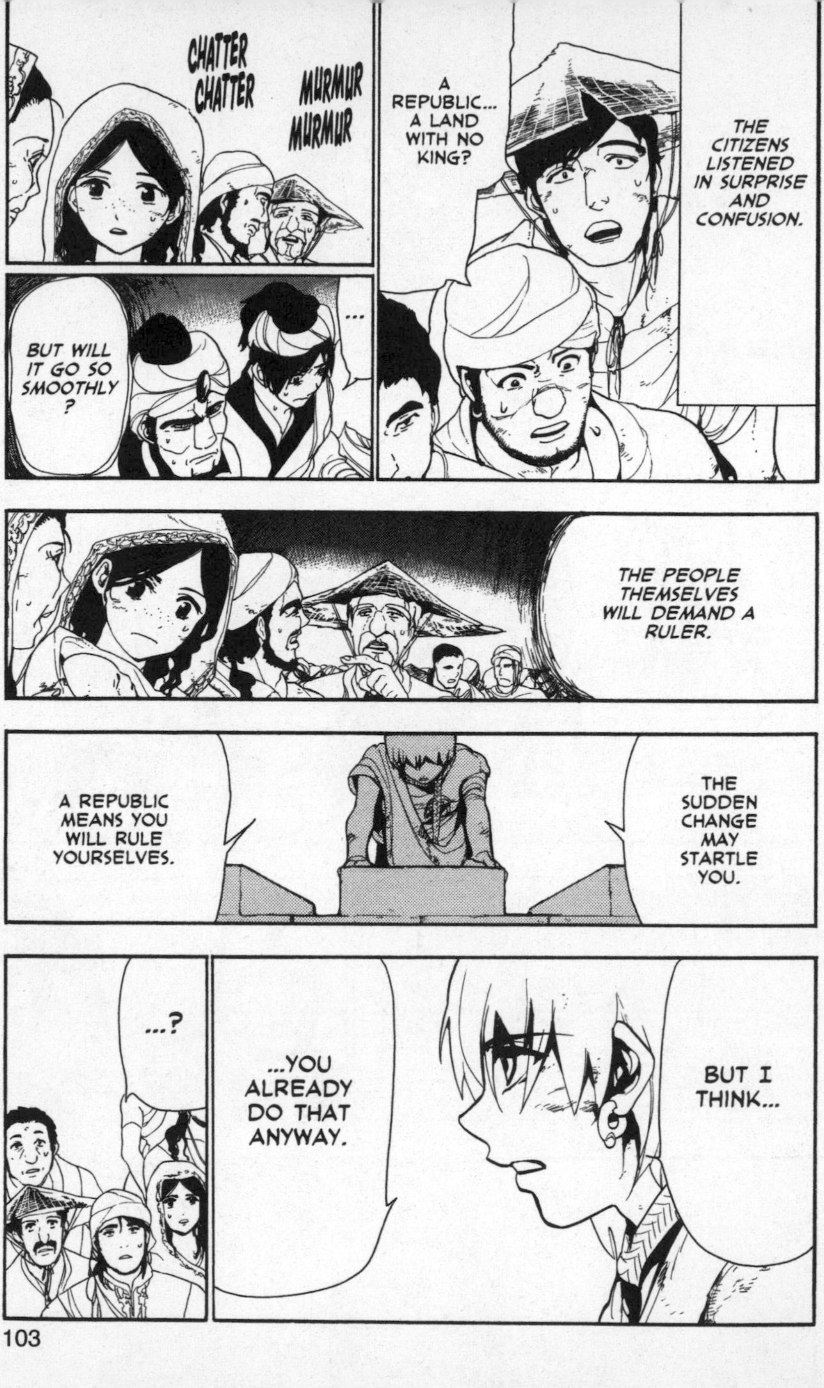
THE CITIZENS LISTENED IN SURPRISE AND CONFUSION.
A REPUBLIC... A LAND WITH NO KING?
CHATTER CHATTER
MURMUR MURMUR
...
BUT WILL IT GO SO SMOOTHLY?
THE PEOPLE THEMSELVES WILL DEMAND A RULER.
THE SUDDEN CHANGE MAY STARTLE YOU.
A REPUBLIC MEANS YOU WILL RULE YOURSELVES.
BUT I THINK...
...YOU ALREADY DO THAT ANYWAY.
...?

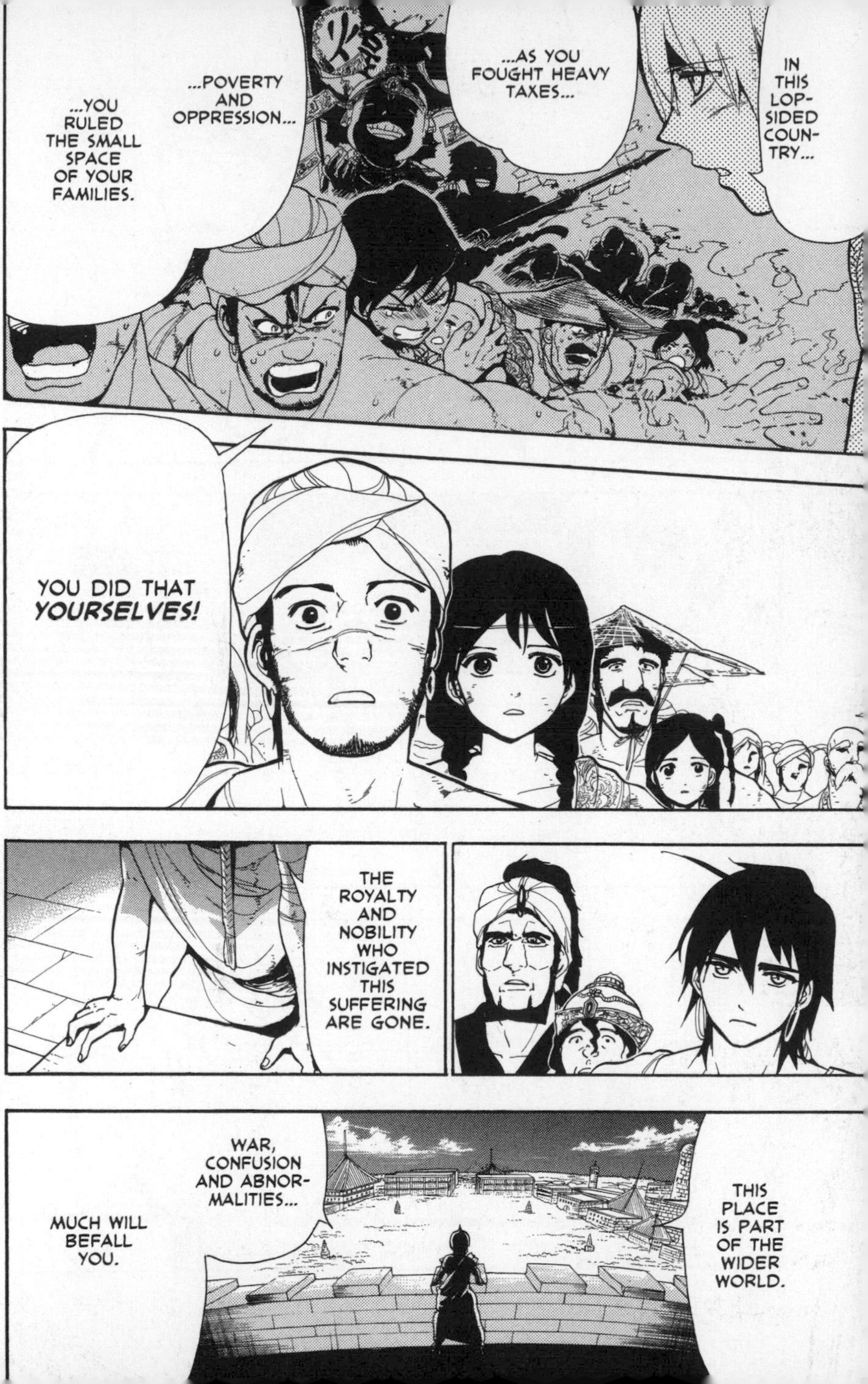
IN THIS LOP-SIDED COUNTRY...
...AS YOU FOUGHT HEAVY TAXES...
...POVERTY AND OPPRESSION...
...YOU RULED THE SMALL SPACE OF YOUR FAMILIES.
YOU DID THAT *YOURSELVES!*
THE ROYALTY AND NOBILITY WHO INSTIGATED THIS SUFFERING ARE GONE.
THIS PLACE IS PART OF THE WIDER WORLD.
WAR, CONFUSION AND ABNORMALITIES...
MUCH WILL BEFALL YOU.

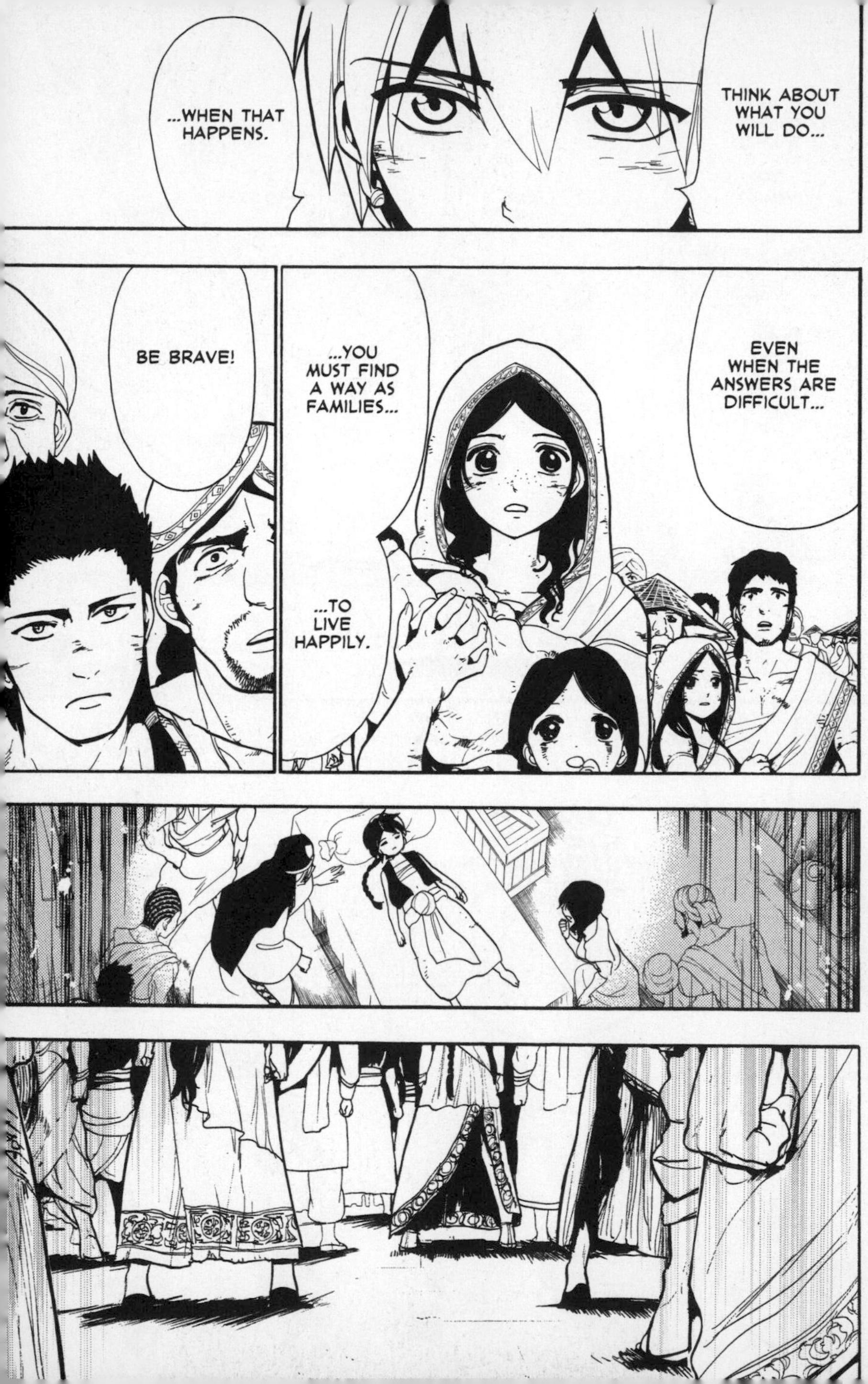
THINK ABOUT WHAT YOU WILL DO...
...WHEN THAT HAPPENS.
EVEN WHEN THE ANSWERS ARE DIFFICULT...
...YOU MUST FIND A WAY AS FAMILIES...
...TO LIVE HAPPILY.
BE BRAVE!

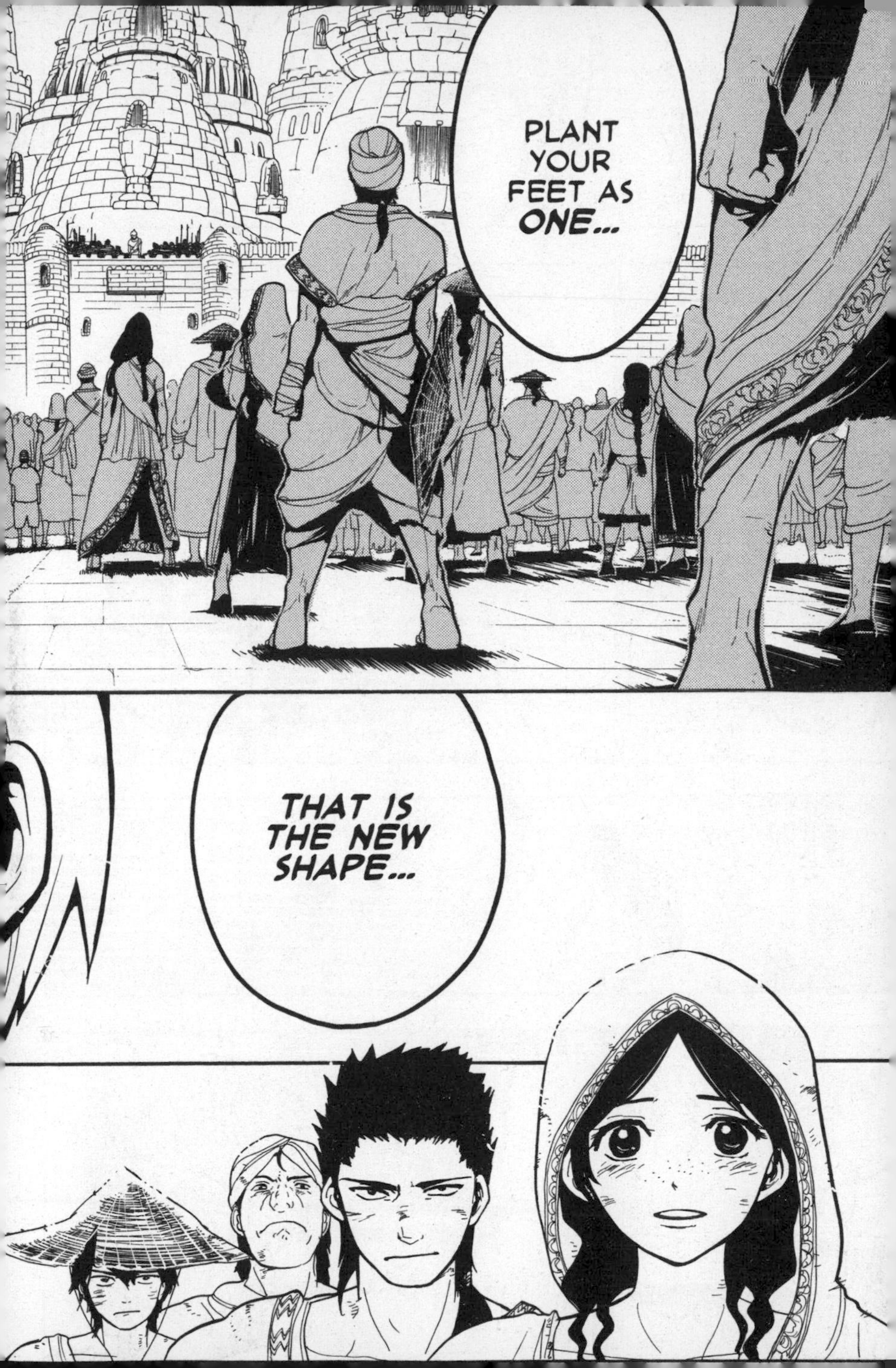
PLANT YOUR FEET AS ONE...
THAT IS THE NEW SHAPE...

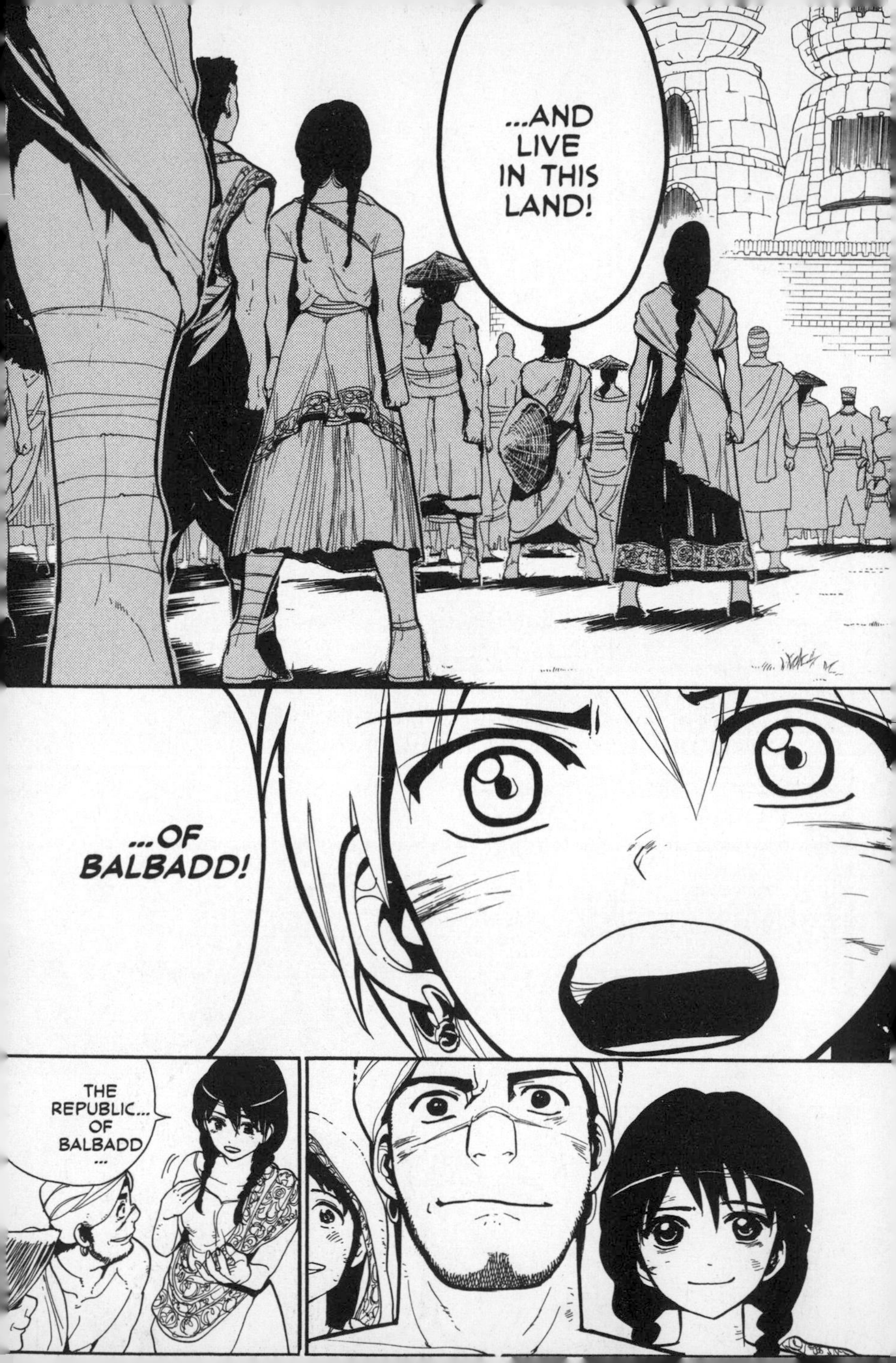
...AND LIVE IN THIS LAND!
...OF BALBADD!
THE REPUBLIC... OF BALBADD ...

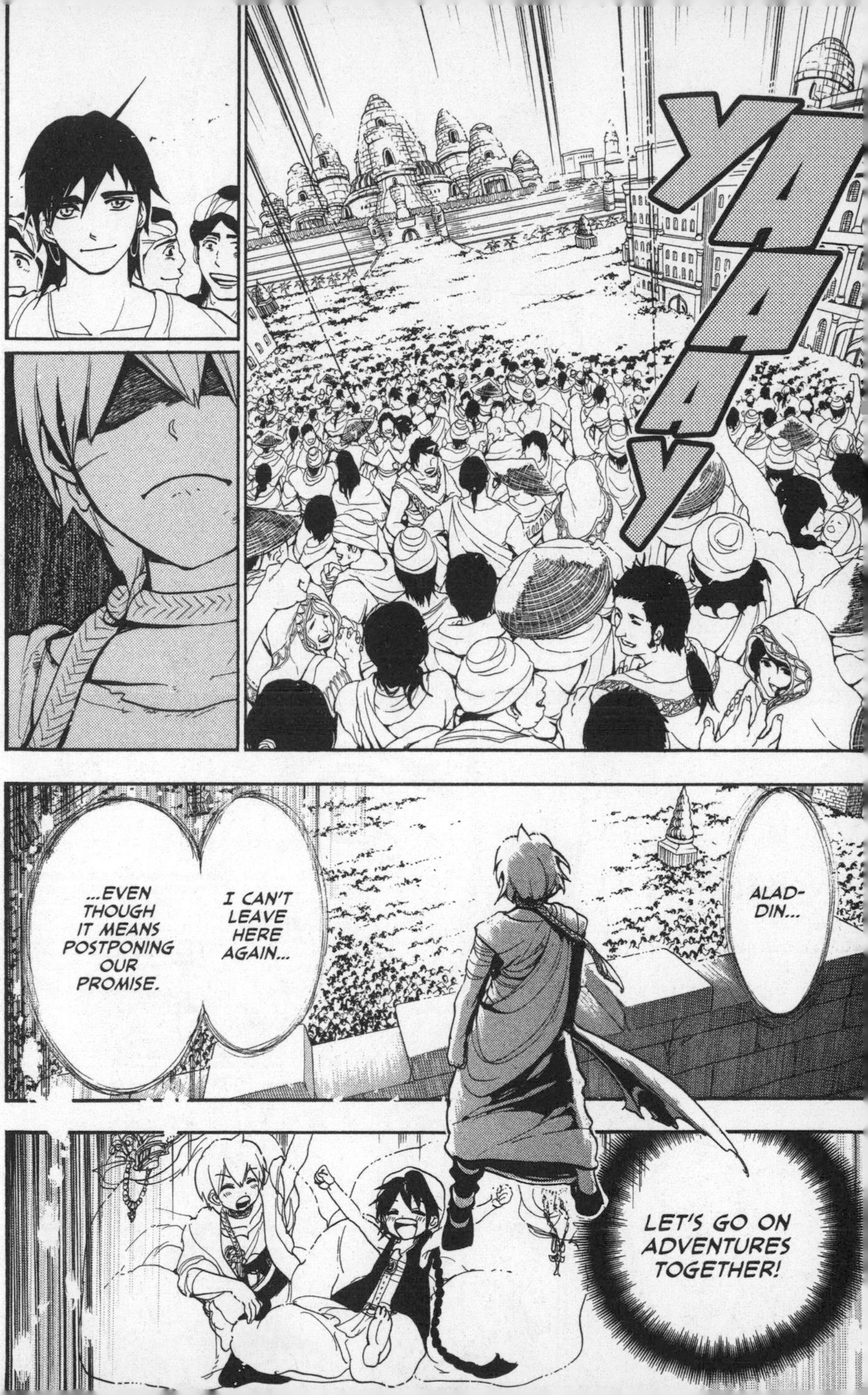
YAAAY
ALAD-DIN...
I CAN'T LEAVE HERE AGAIN...
...EVEN THOUGH IT MEANS POSTPONING OUR PROMISE.
LET'S GO ON ADVENTURES TOGETHER!

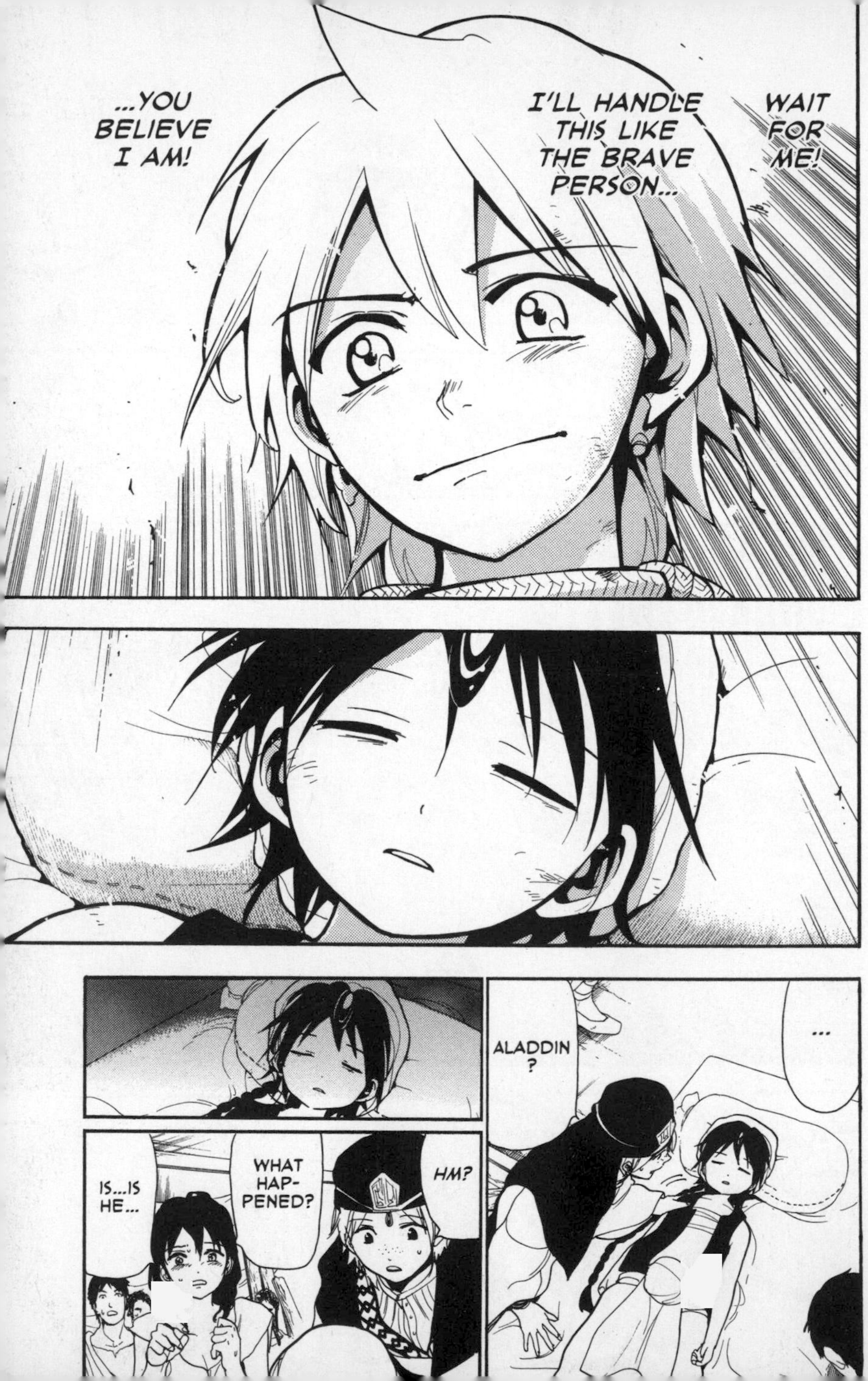
WAIT FOR ME!
I'LL HANDLE THIS LIKE THE BRAVE PERSON...
...YOU BELIEVE I AM!
...
ALADDIN?
HM?
WHAT HAP-PENED?
IS...IS HE...

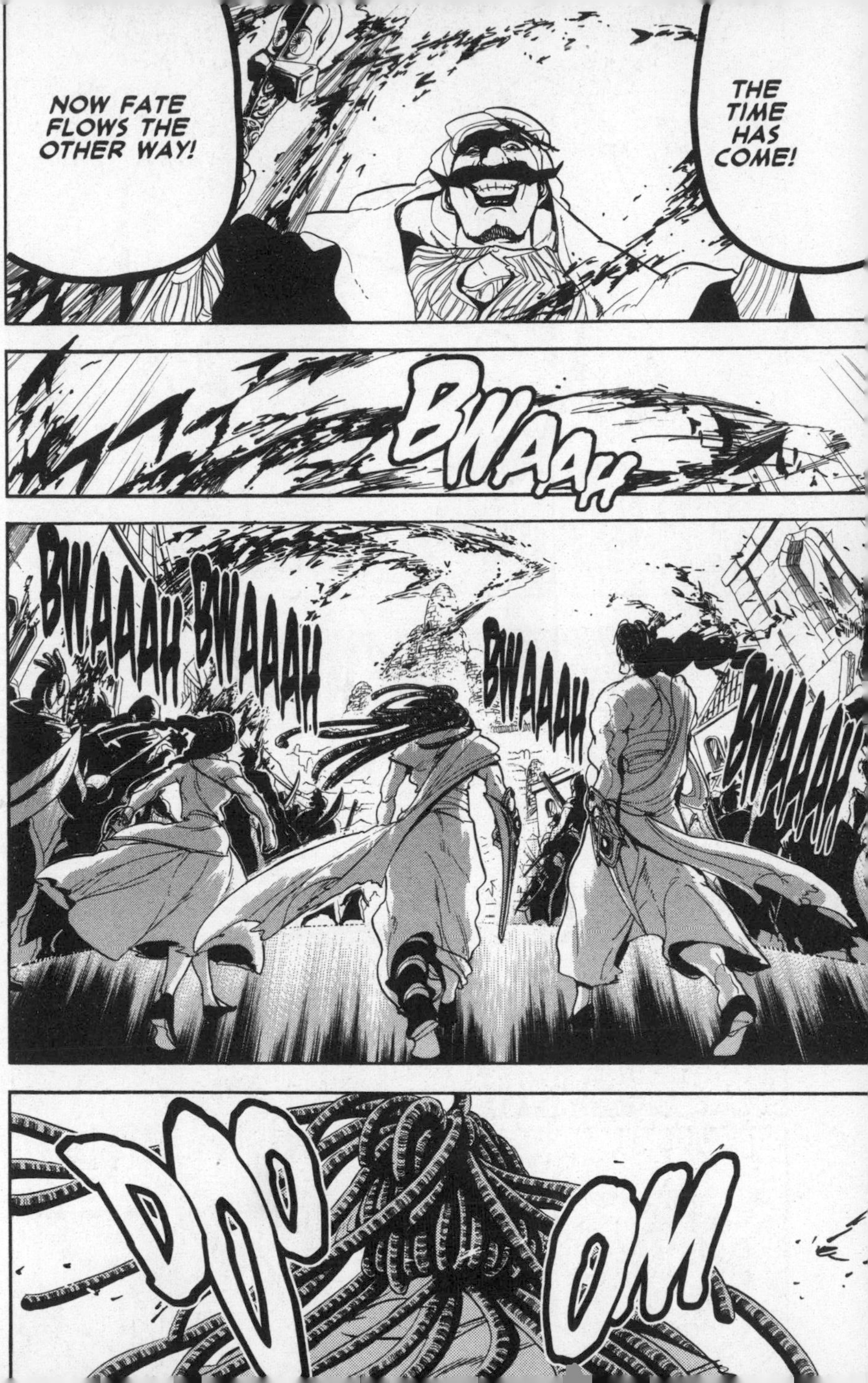
THE TIME HAS COME!
NOW FATE FLOWS THE OTHER WAY!
BWAAH
BWAAAH
BWAAAH
BWAAAH
BWAAAH
DOOOM

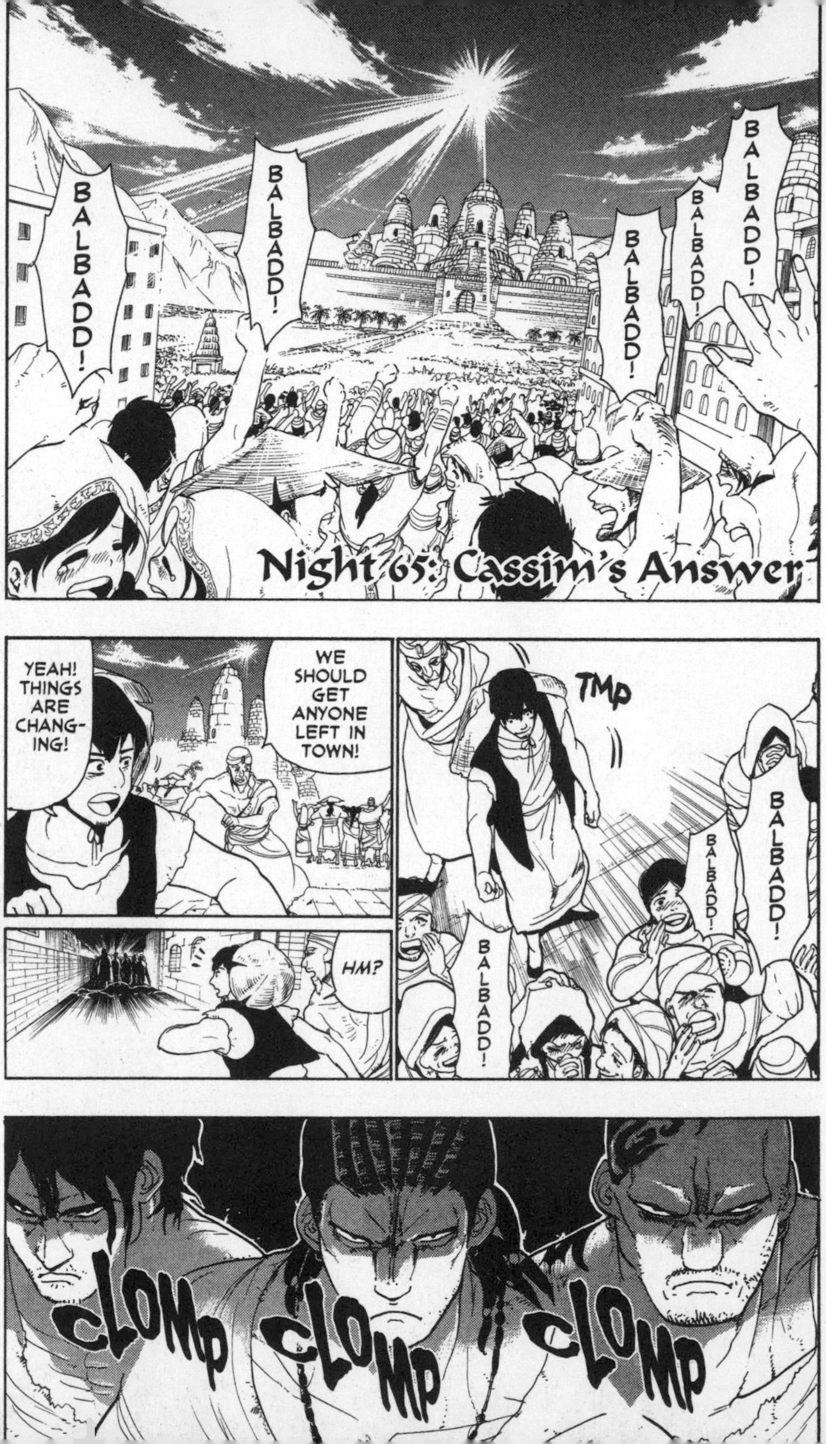
BALBADD!
BALBADD!
BALBADD!
BALBADD!
BALBADD!
Night 65: Cassim's Answer
TMP
BALBADD!
BALBADD!
BALBADD!
WE SHOULD GET ANYONE LEFT IN TOWN!
YEAH! THINGS ARE CHANGING!
HM?
CLOMP CLOMP CLOMP

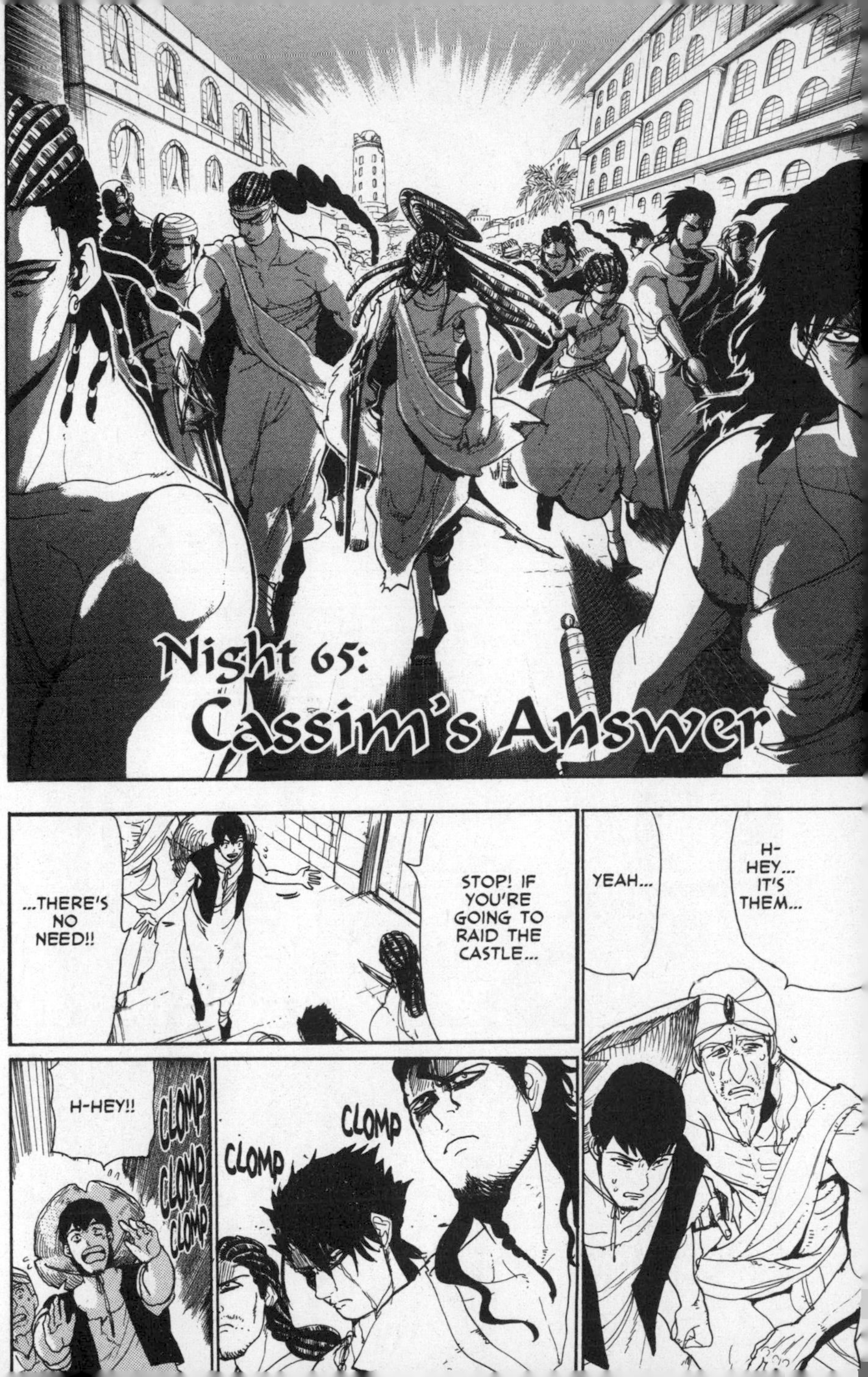
Night 65:
Cassim's Answer
H-HEY... IT'S THEM...
YEAH...
STOP! IF YOU'RE GOING TO RAID THE CASTLE...
...THERE'S NO NEED!!
CLOMP
CLOMP
H-HEY!!
CLOMP
CLOMP
CLOMP
CLOMP

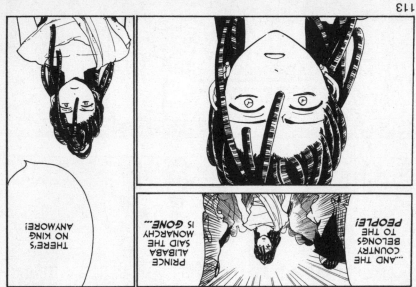

CLOMP
LISTEN! BALBADD HAS BEEN...
...RE-BORN!
THERE'S NO KING ANYMORE!
PRINCE ALIBABA SAID THE MONARCHY IS GONE...
...AND THE COUNTRY BELONGS TO THE PEOPLE!

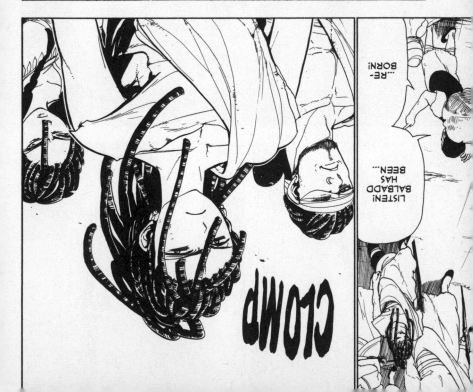

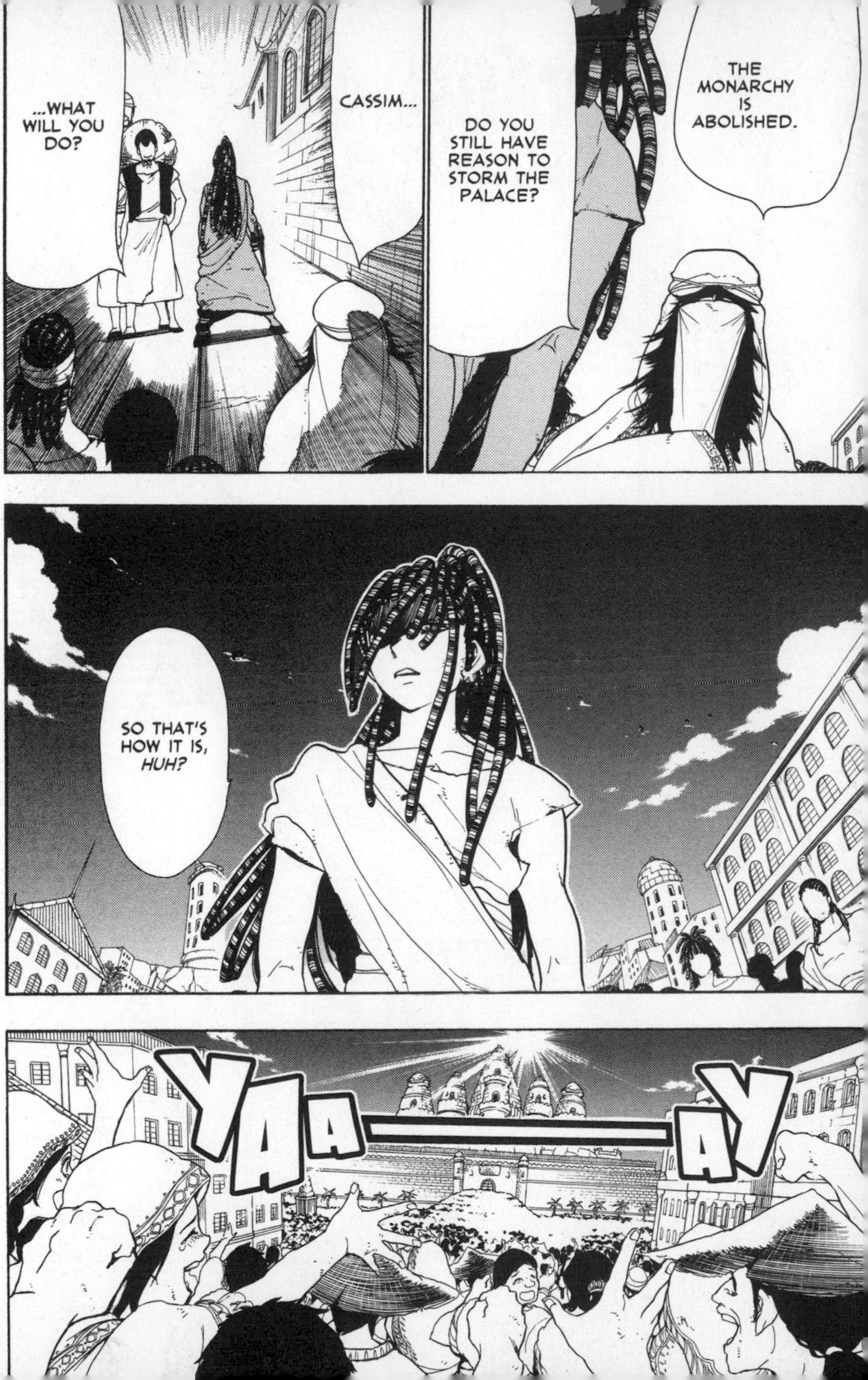
THE MONARCHY IS ABOLISHED.
DO YOU STILL HAVE REASON TO STORM THE PALACE?
CASSIM...
...WHAT WILL YOU DO?
SO THAT'S HOW IT IS, *HUH?*
YAA—AY

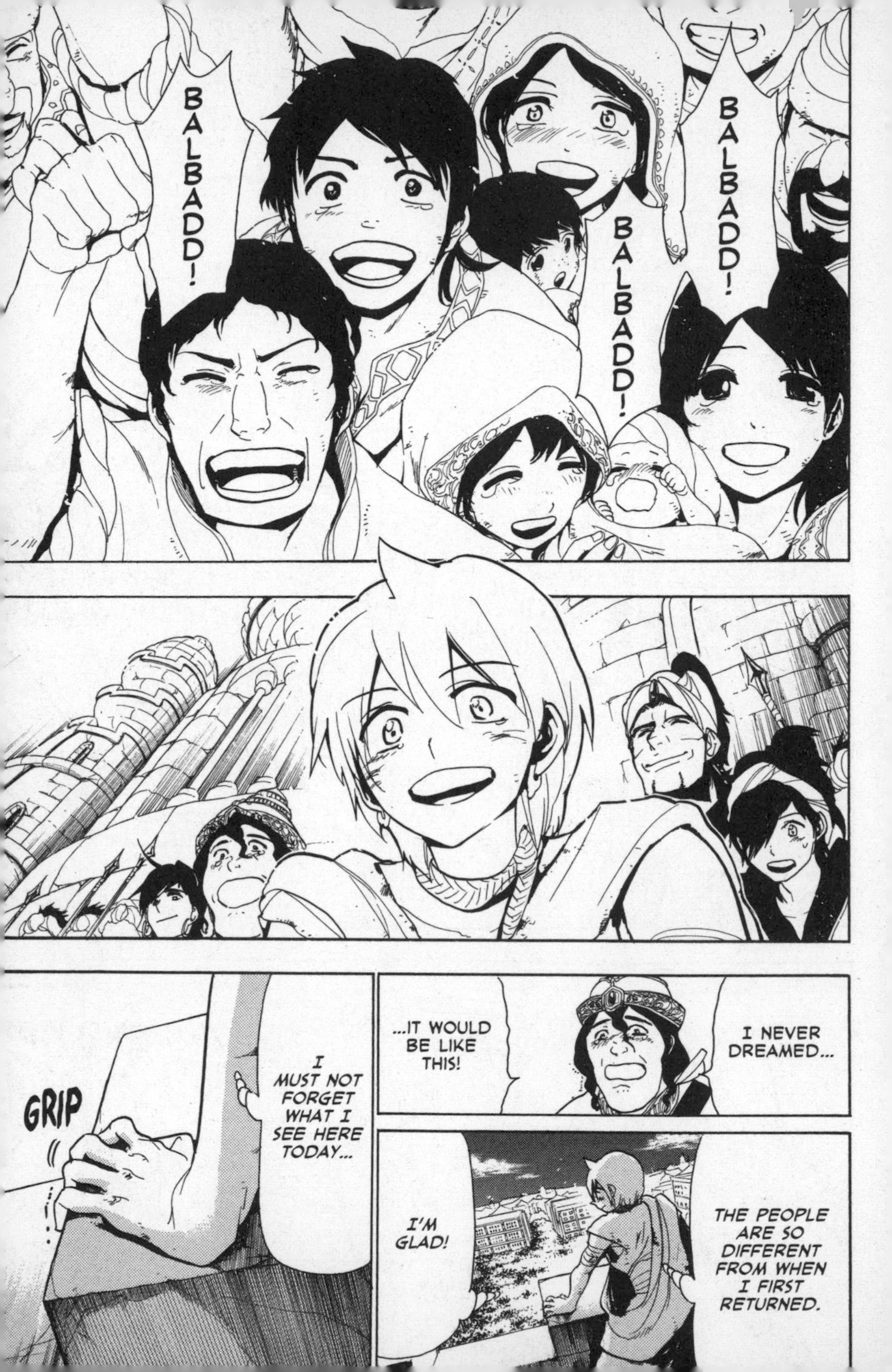
BALBADD!
BALBADD!
BALBADD!
I NEVER DREAMED...
...IT WOULD BE LIKE THIS!
THE PEOPLE ARE SO DIFFERENT FROM WHEN I FIRST RETURNED.
I'M GLAD!
I MUST NOT FORGET WHAT I SEE HERE TODAY...
GRIP
...!

I MUST KEEP THIS VISION IN MIND...
...SO IT LASTS FOREVER!
ALI-BABA!
ALI-BABA!
ALI-BABA!
ALIBABA!
ALIBABA!
CLOMP
HUH?
!!
HE'S HERE.

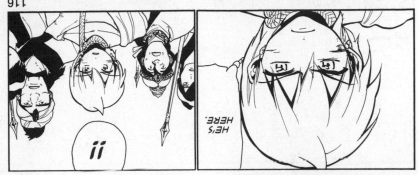

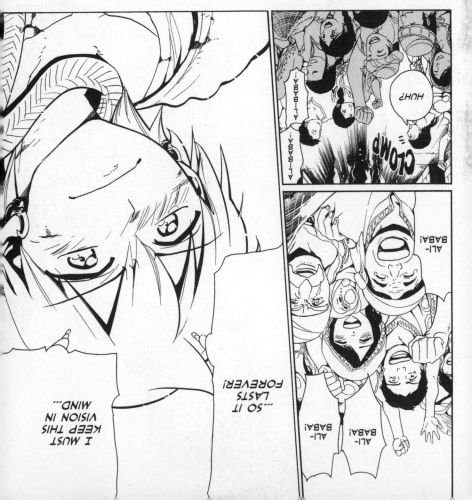

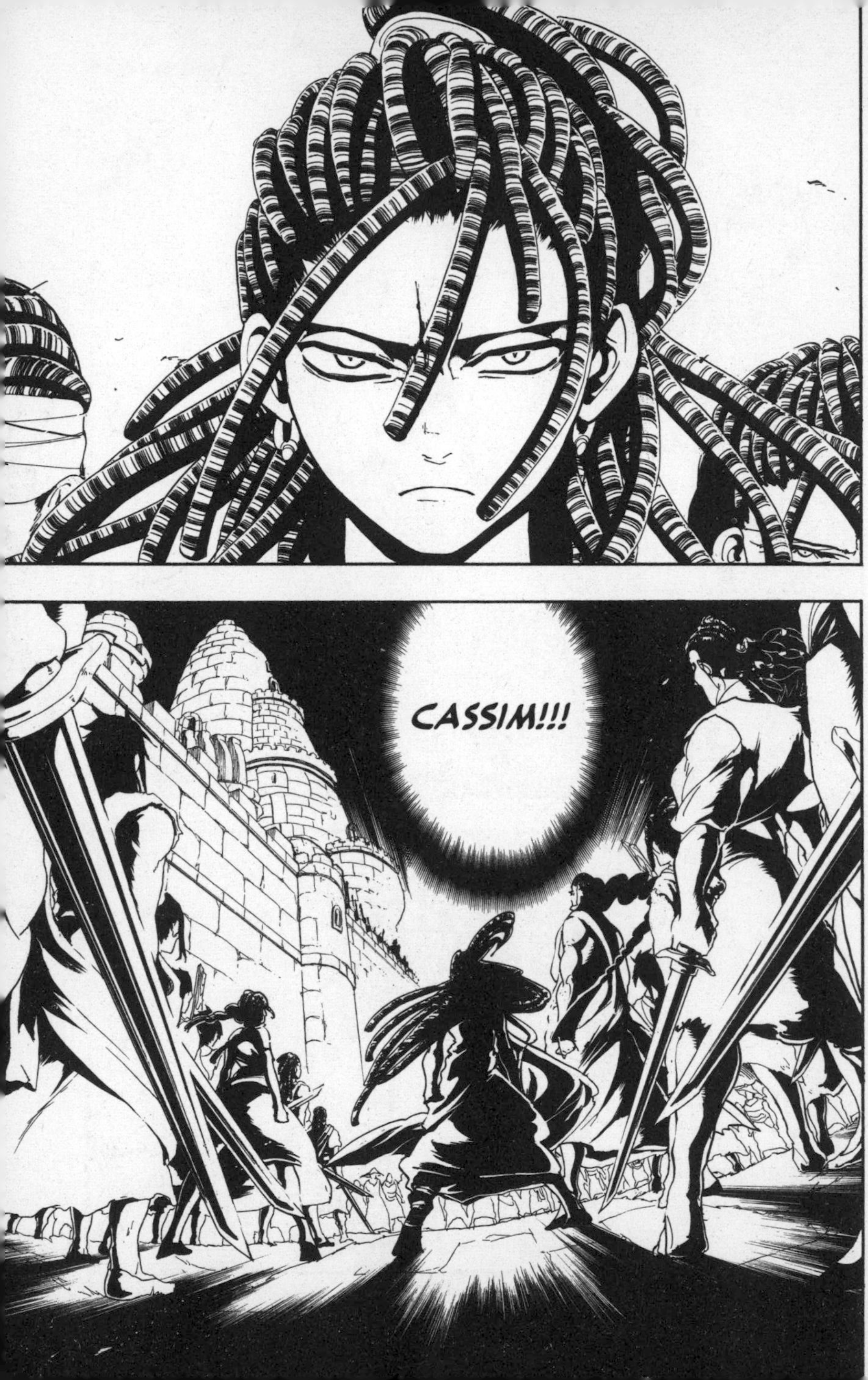
CASSIM!!!

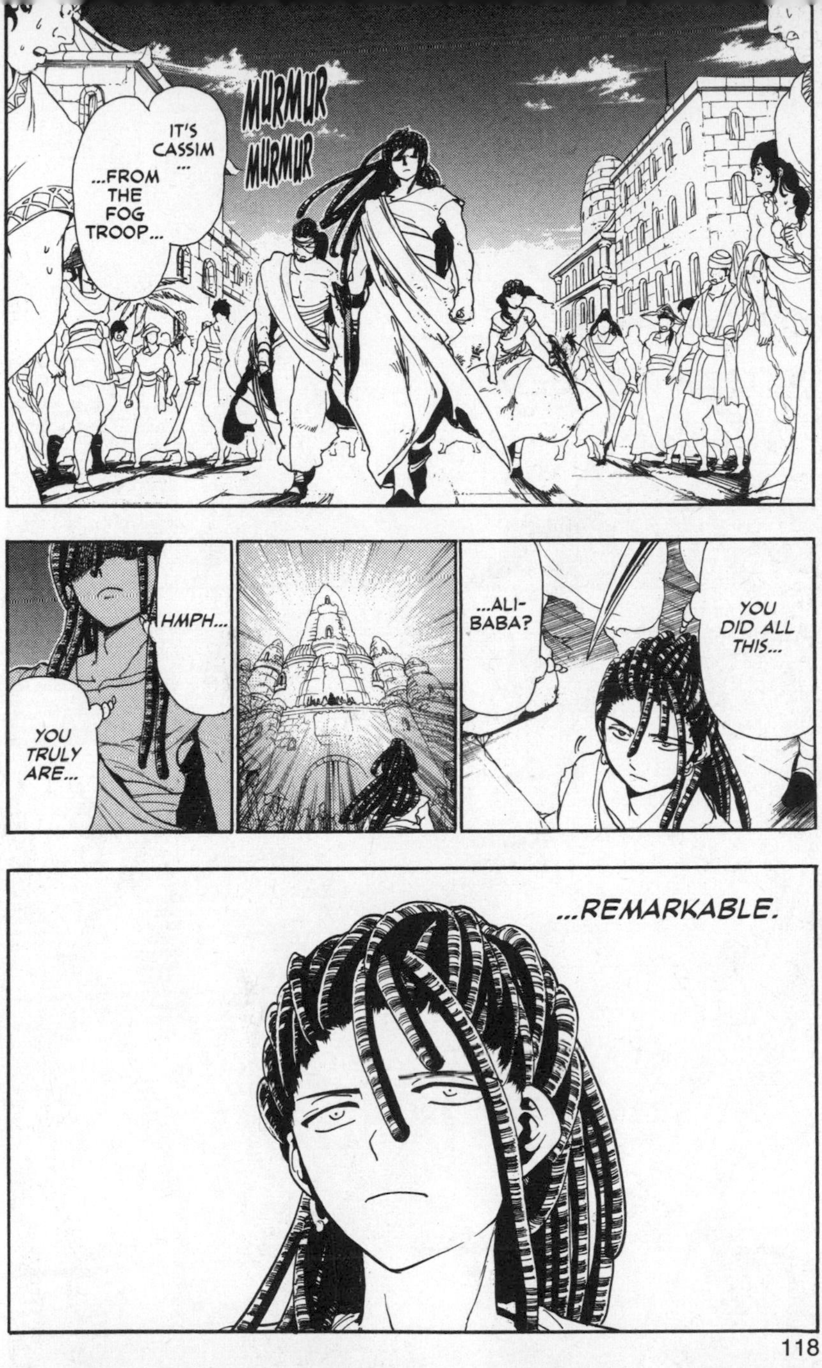
IT'S CASSIM ... ...FROM THE FOG TROOP...
MURMUR MURMUR
YOU DID ALL THIS...
...ALI-BABA?
HMPH...
YOU TRULY ARE...
...REMARKABLE.

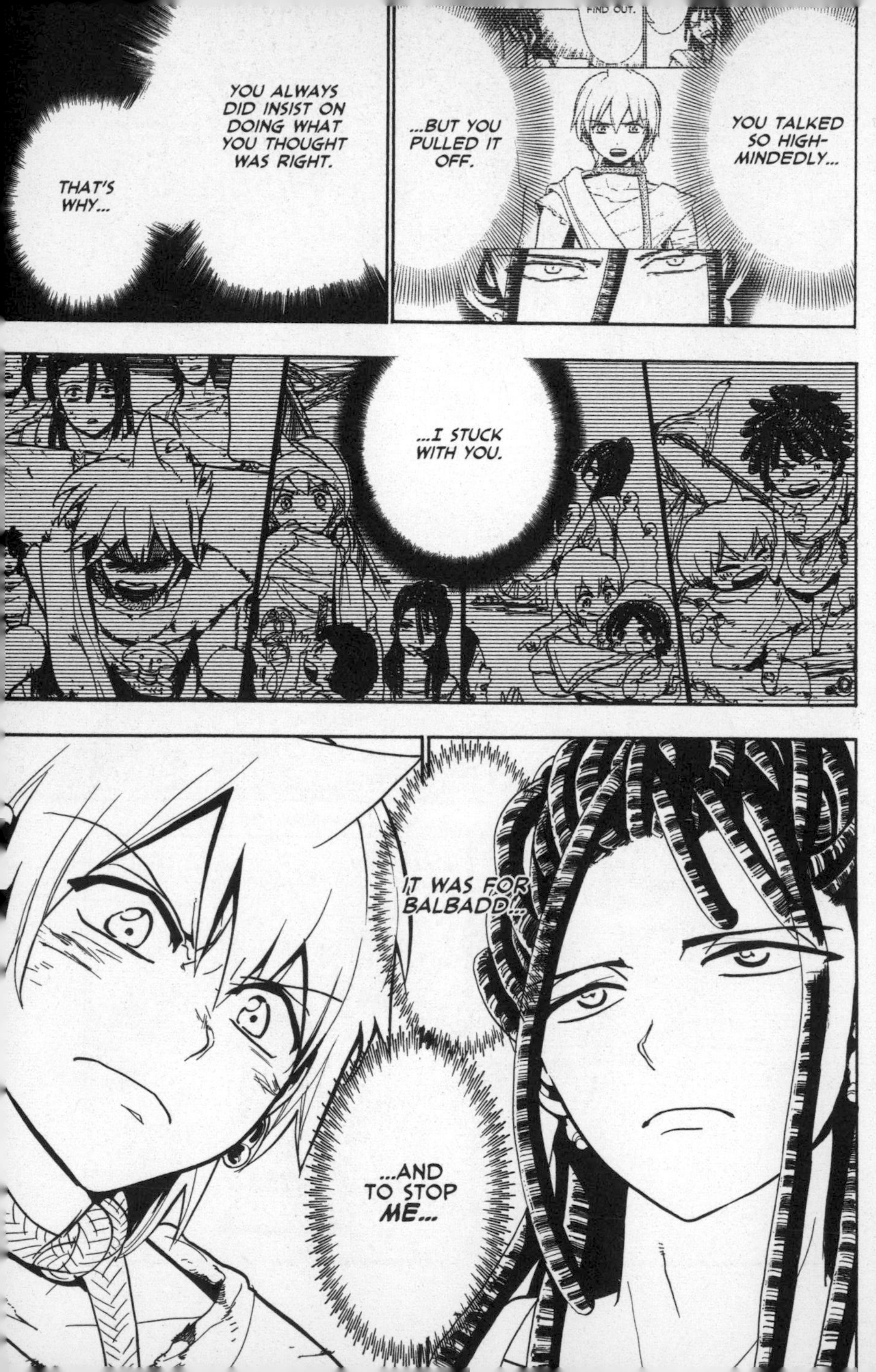
FIND OUT.
YOU TALKED SO HIGH-MINDEDLY...
...BUT YOU PULLED IT OFF.
YOU ALWAYS DID INSIST ON DOING WHAT YOU THOUGHT WAS RIGHT.
THAT'S WHY...
...I STUCK WITH YOU.
IT WAS FOR BALBADD...
...AND TO STOP ME...

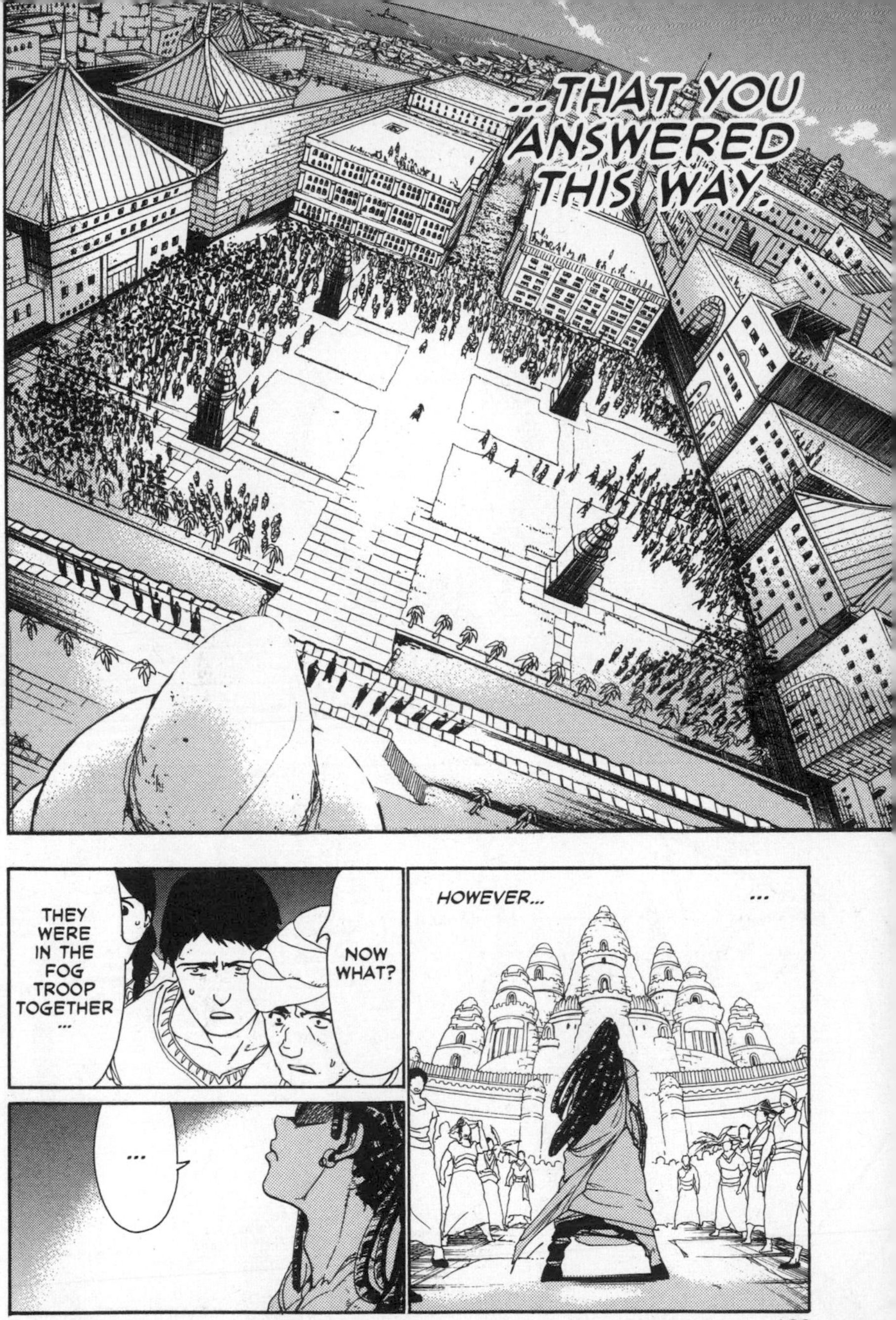
...THAT YOU ANSWERED THIS WAY.
HOWEVER...
...
NOW WHAT?
THEY WERE IN THE FOG TROOP TOGETHER ...
...

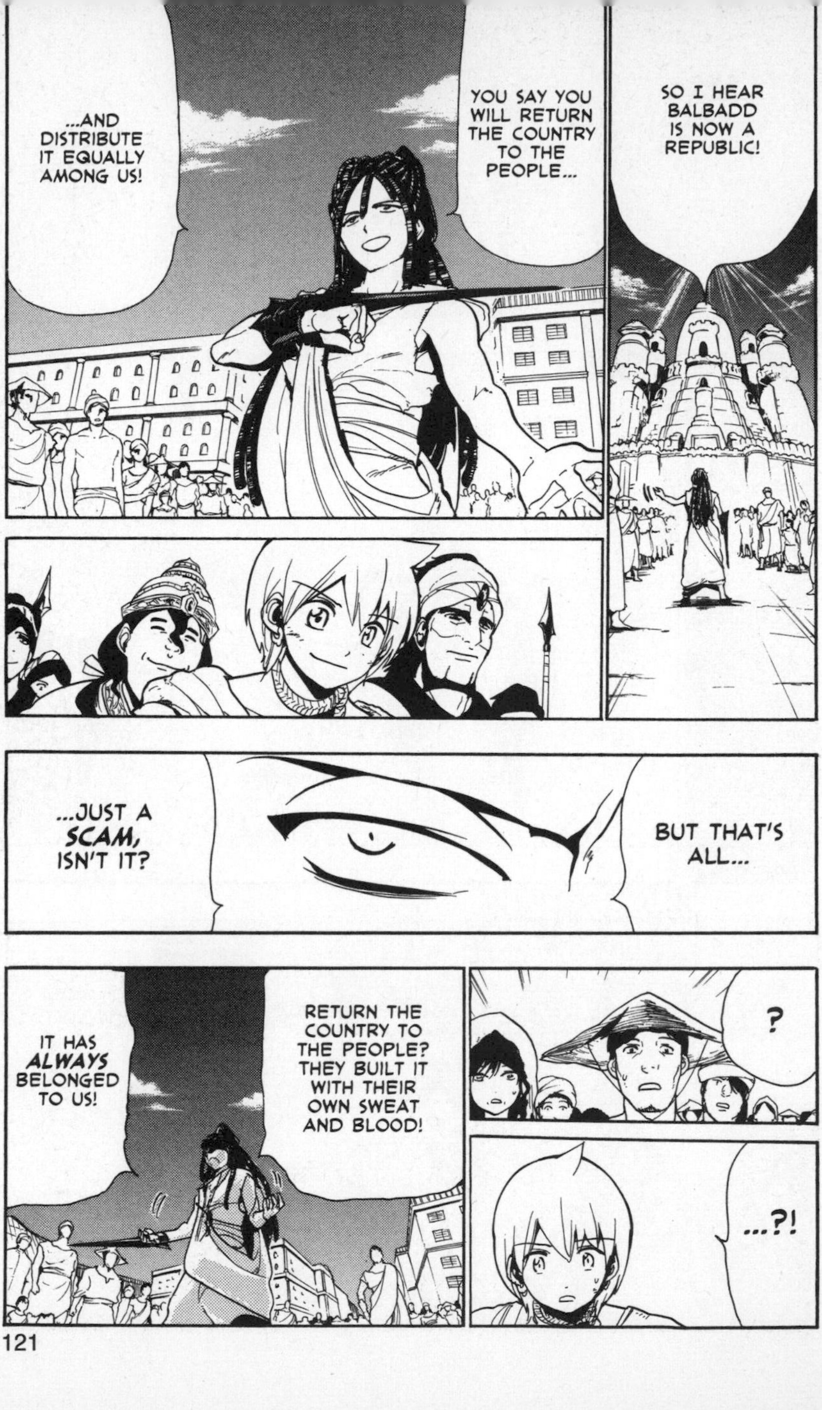
SO I HEAR BALBADD IS NOW A REPUBLIC!
YOU SAY YOU WILL RETURN THE COUNTRY TO THE PEOPLE...
...AND DISTRIBUTE IT EQUALLY AMONG US!
BUT THAT'S ALL...
...JUST A *SCAM,* ISN'T IT?
?
...?!
RETURN THE COUNTRY TO THE PEOPLE? THEY BUILT IT WITH THEIR OWN SWEAT AND BLOOD!
IT HAS *ALWAYS* BELONGED TO US!

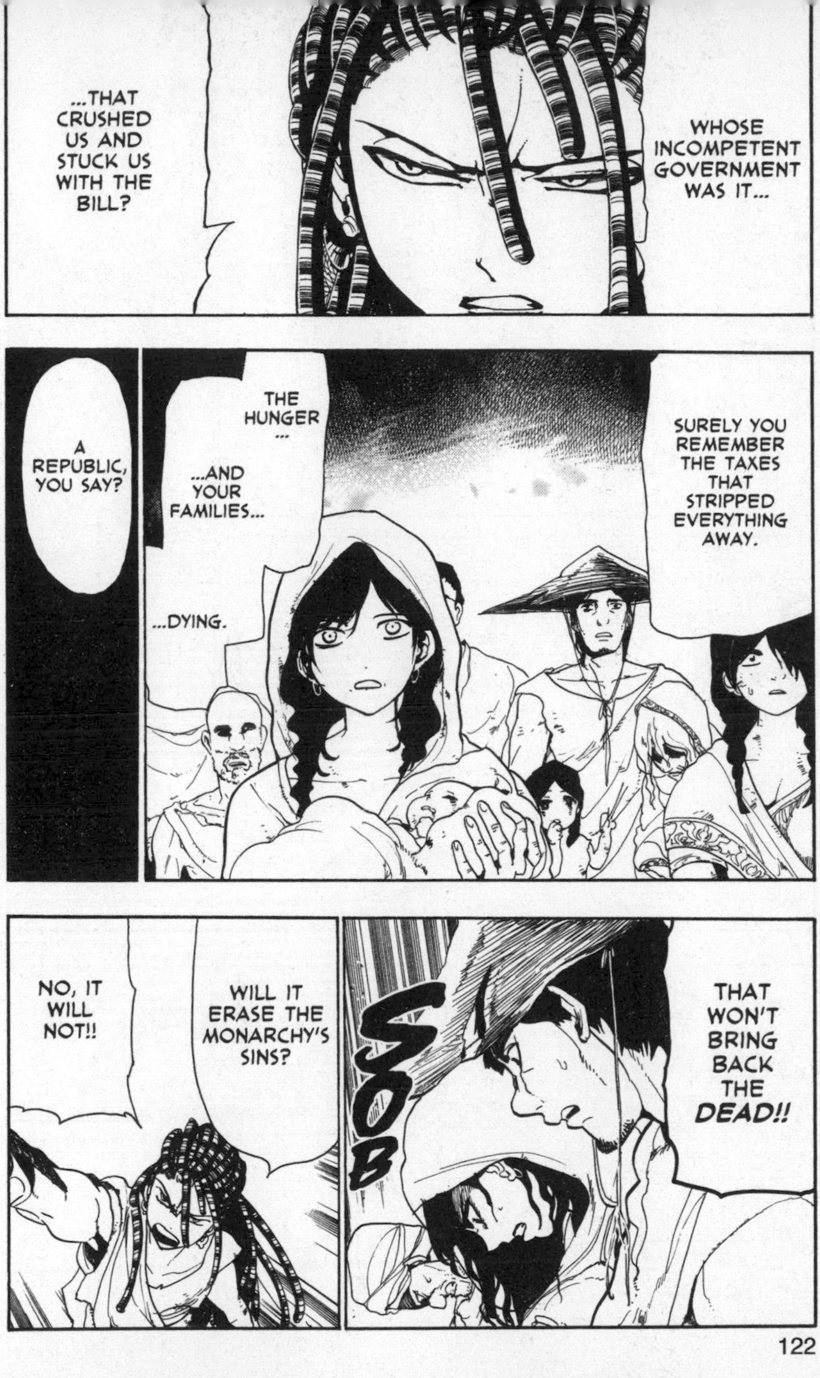
WHOSE INCOMPETENT GOVERNMENT WAS IT...
...THAT CRUSHED US AND STUCK US WITH THE BILL?
SURELY YOU REMEMBER THE TAXES THAT STRIPPED EVERYTHING AWAY.
THE HUNGER...
...AND YOUR FAMILIES...
...DYING.
A REPUBLIC, YOU SAY?
THAT WON'T BRING BACK THE DEAD!!
SOB
WILL IT ERASE THE MONARCHY'S SINS?
NO, IT WILL NOT!!

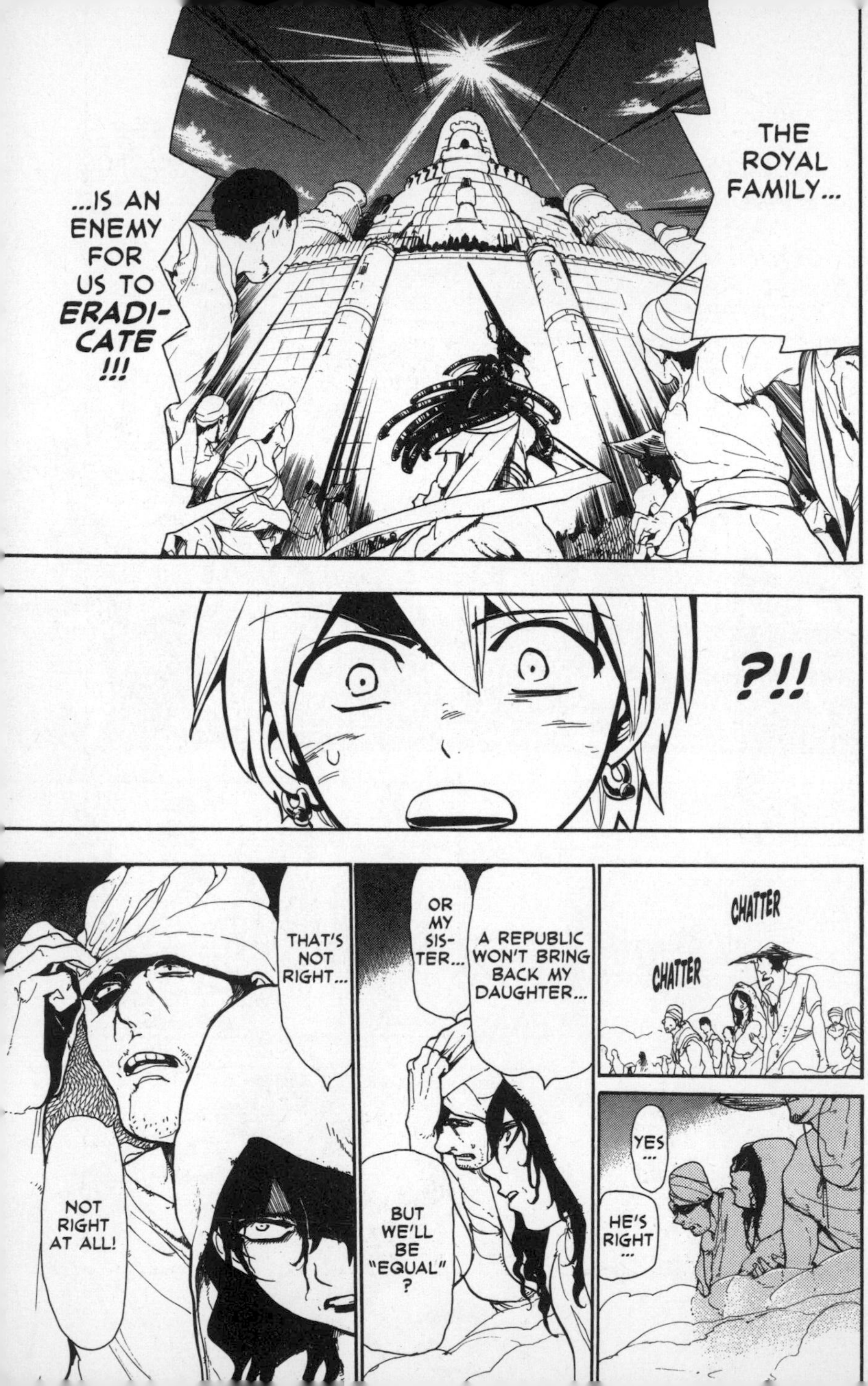
THE ROYAL FAMILY...
...IS AN ENEMY FOR US TO *ERADICATE* !!!
?!!
CHATTER
CHATTER
YES...
HE'S RIGHT...
A REPUBLIC WON'T BRING BACK MY DAUGHTER...
OR MY SISTER...
BUT WE'LL BE "EQUAL"?
THAT'S NOT RIGHT...
NOT RIGHT AT ALL!

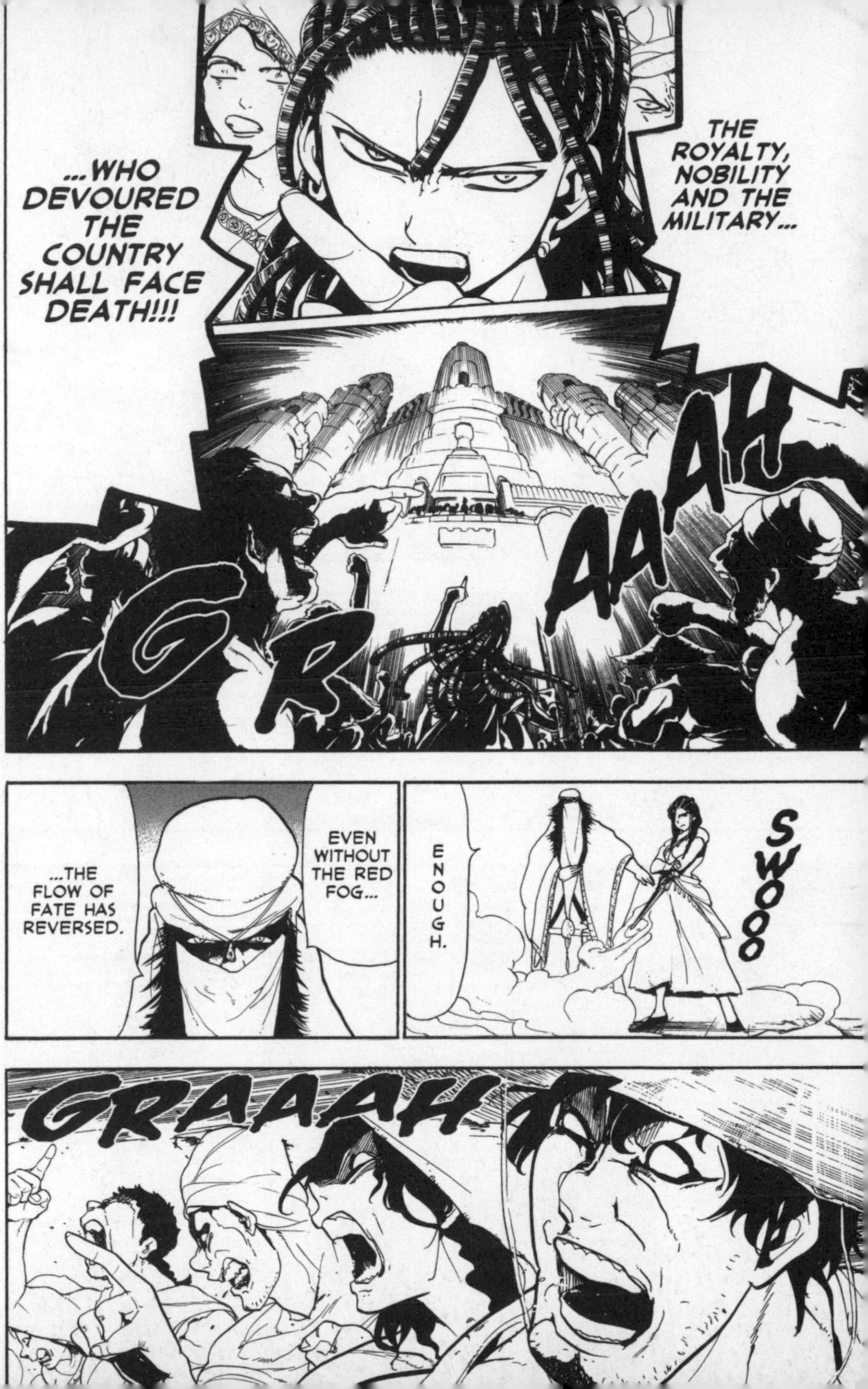
THE ROYALTY, NOBILITY AND THE MILITARY...
...WHO DEVOURED THE COUNTRY SHALL FACE DEATH!!!
GRAAAH
SWOOO
ENOUGH.
EVEN WITHOUT THE RED FOG...
...THE FLOW OF FATE HAS REVERSED.
GRAAAH

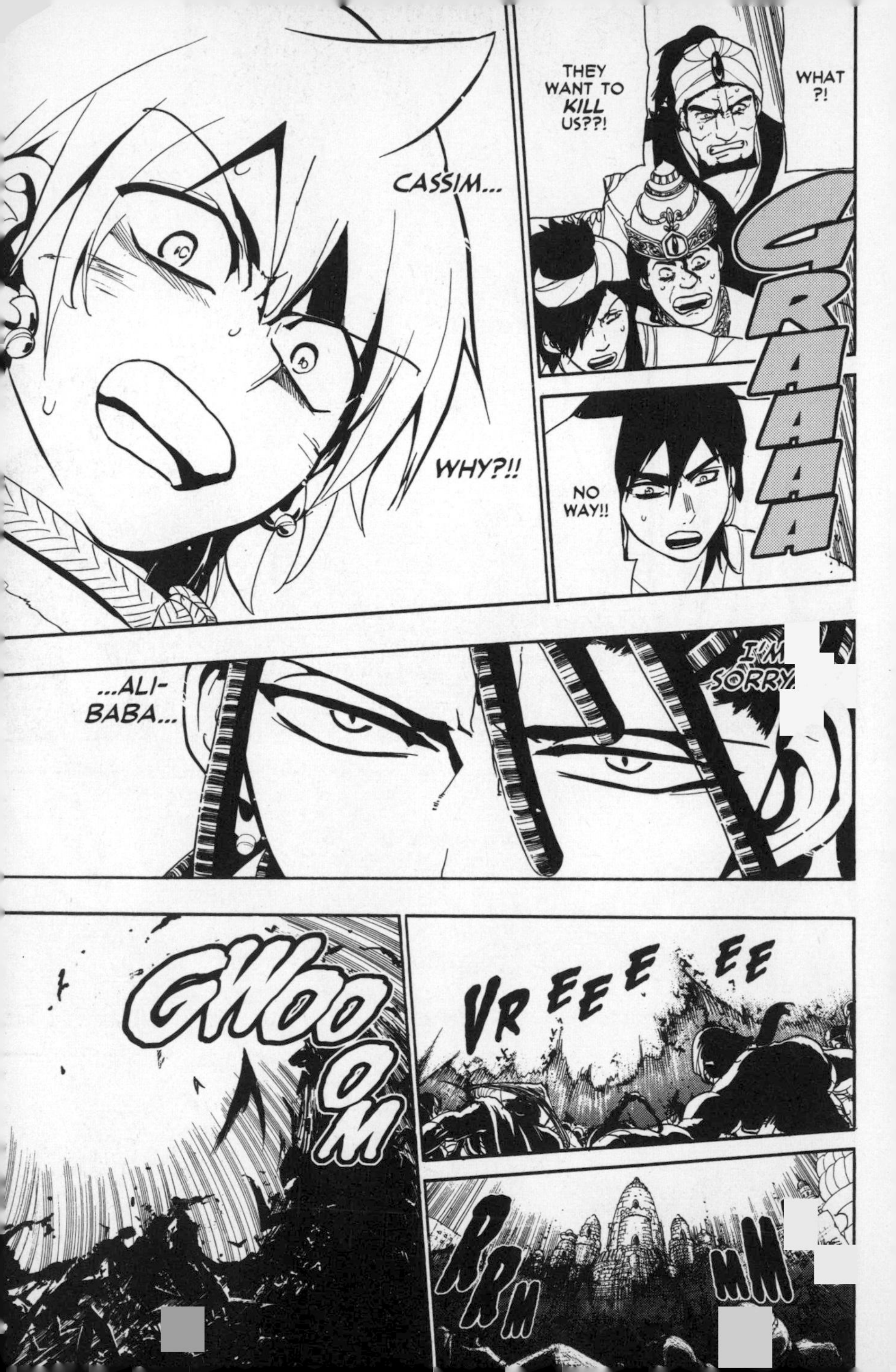
WHAT ?!
THEY WANT TO KILL US??!
GRAAAAA
NO WAY!!
CASSIM...
WHY?!!
I'M SORRY
...ALI-BABA...
VREEEEEE
RRM
MM
GWOOOM

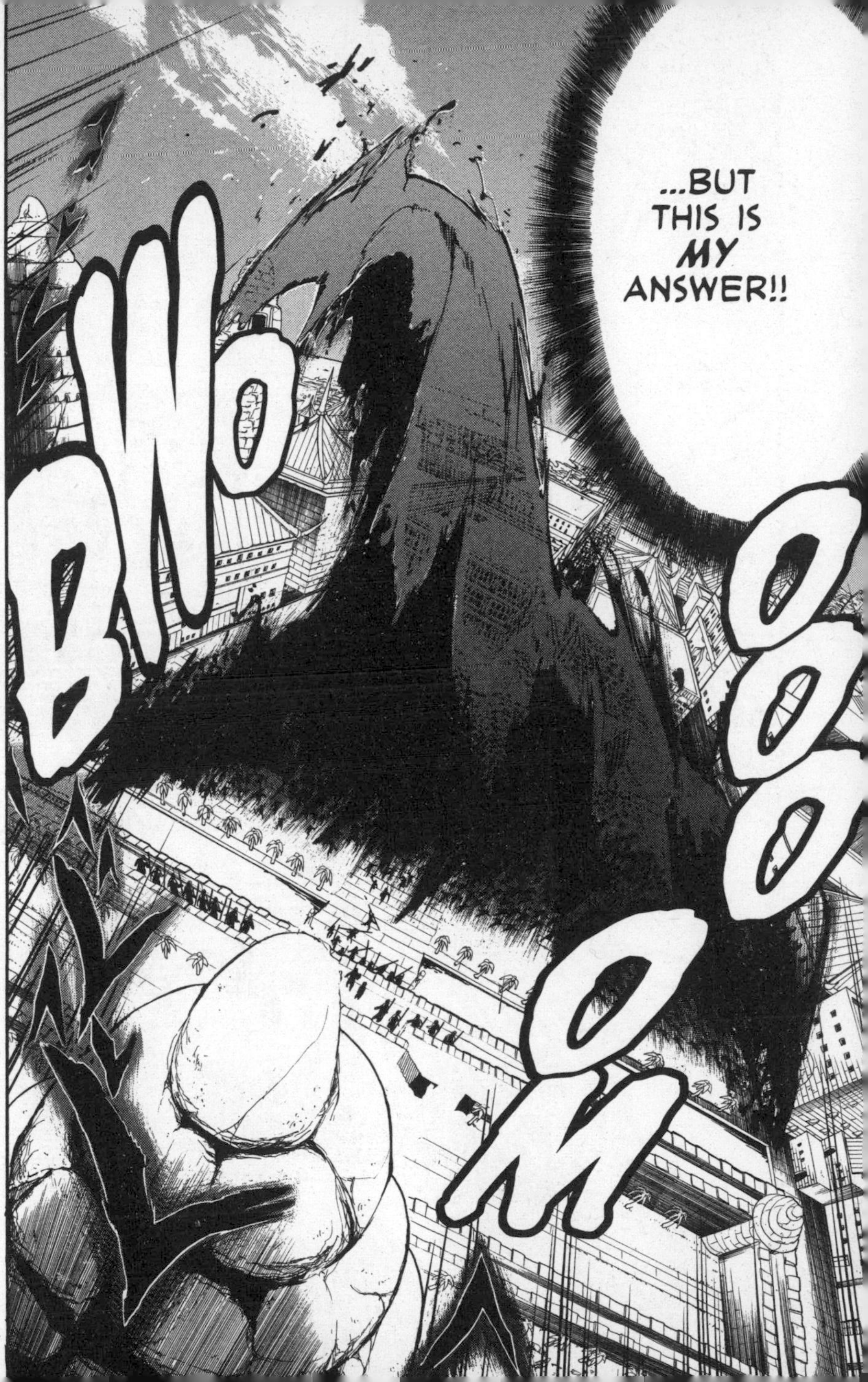
...BUT THIS IS MY ANSWER!!
BWOOOOM

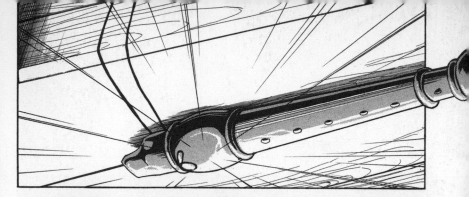

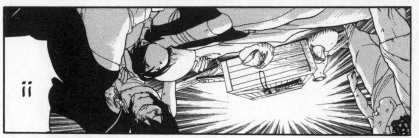

11

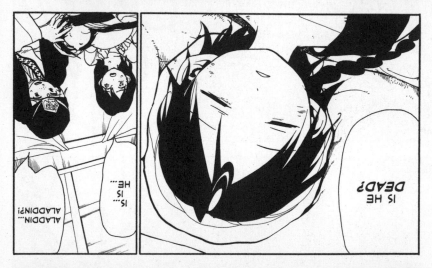

ALADDIN...
ALADDIN?!

...IS
HE...

IS HE
DEAD?

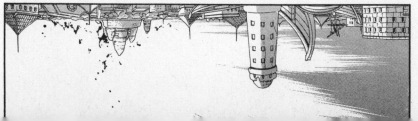

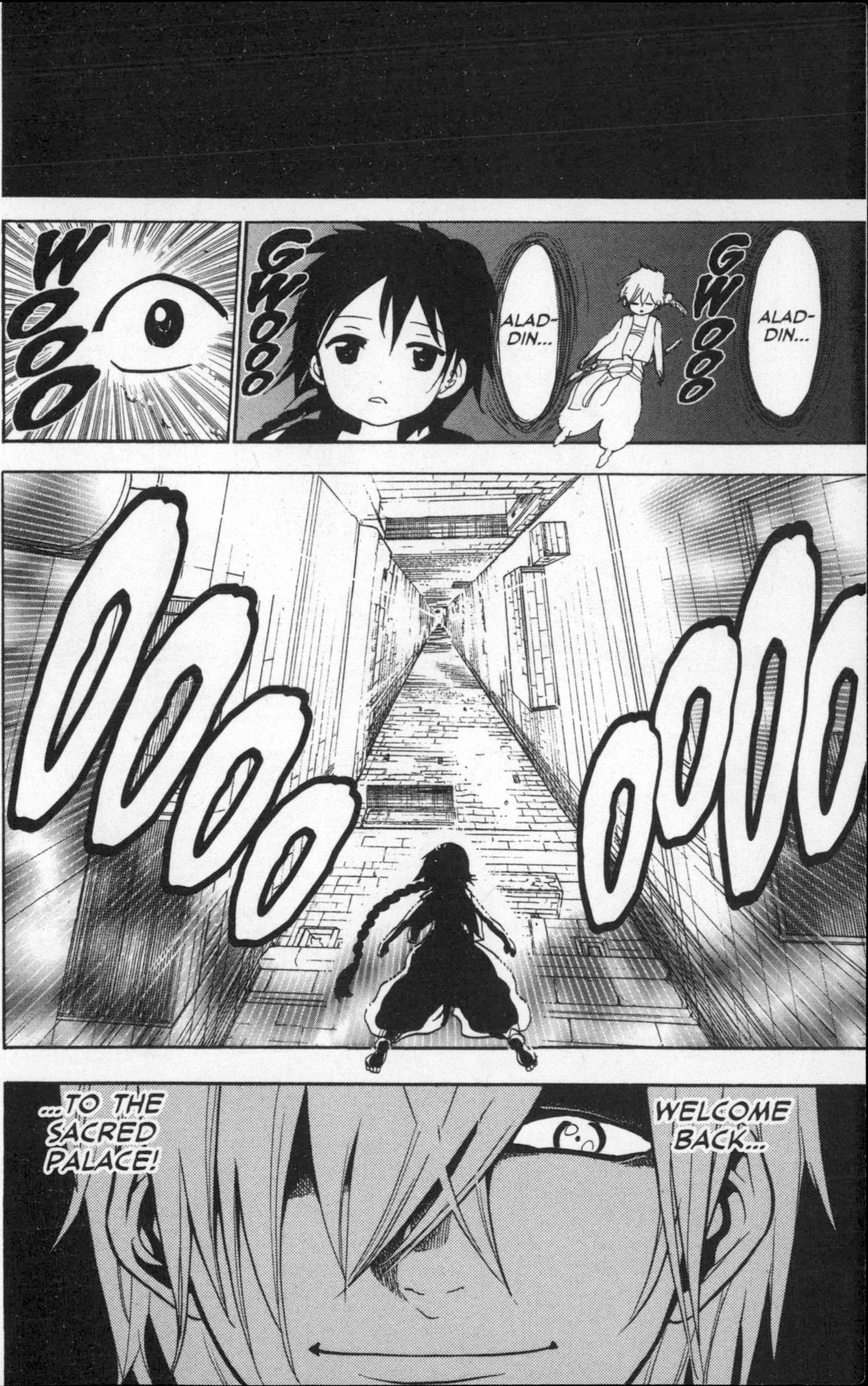
ALAD-DIN...
GWOOOO
ALAD-DIN...
GWOOOO
WOOOO
OOOOOO
OOOOOO
WELCOME BACK...
...TO THE SACRED PALACE!

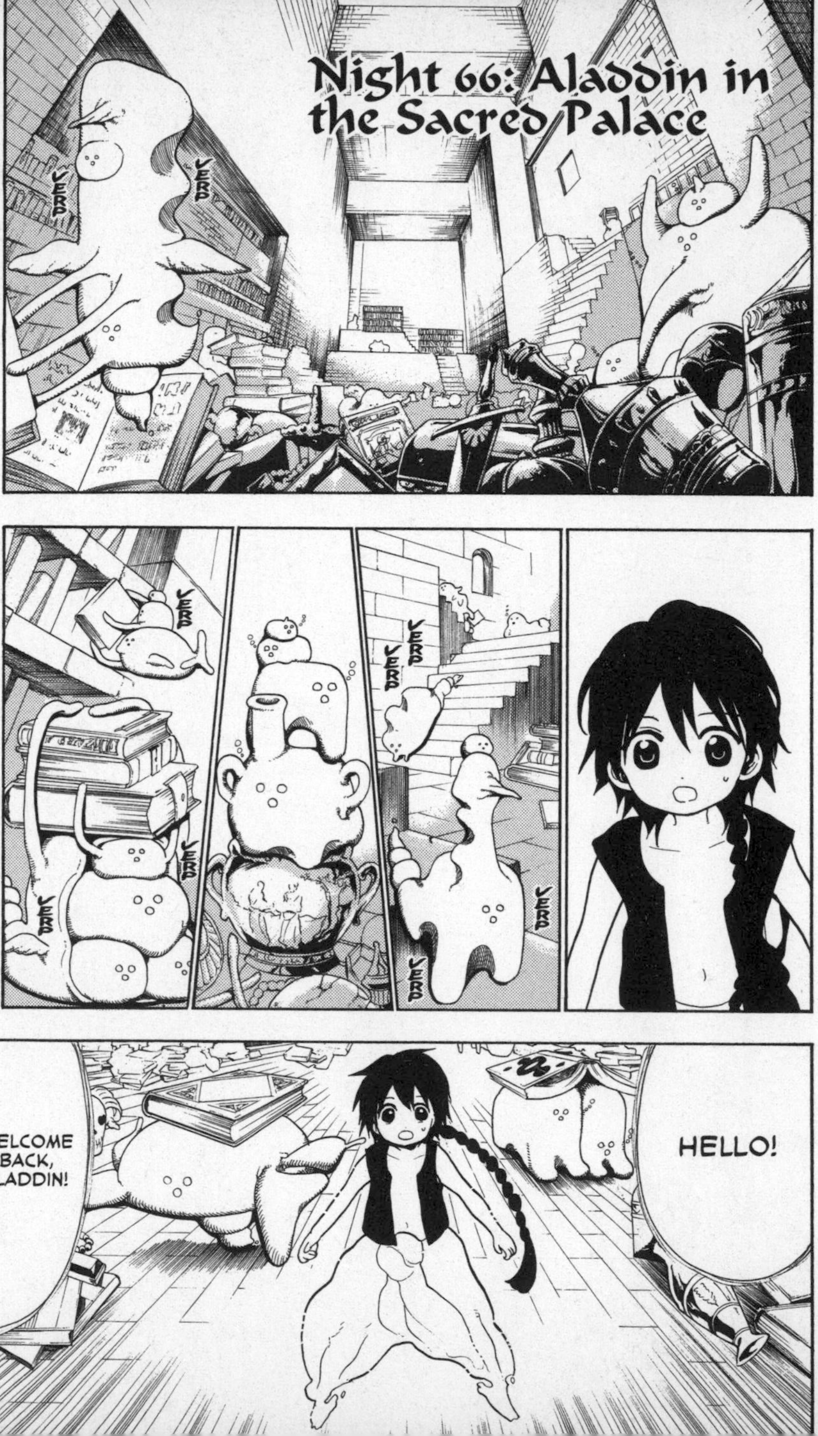
Night 66: Aladdin in the Sacred Palace
VERP
VERP
VERP
VERP
VERP
VERP
VERP
VERP
VERP
HELLO!
WELCOME BACK, ALADDIN!

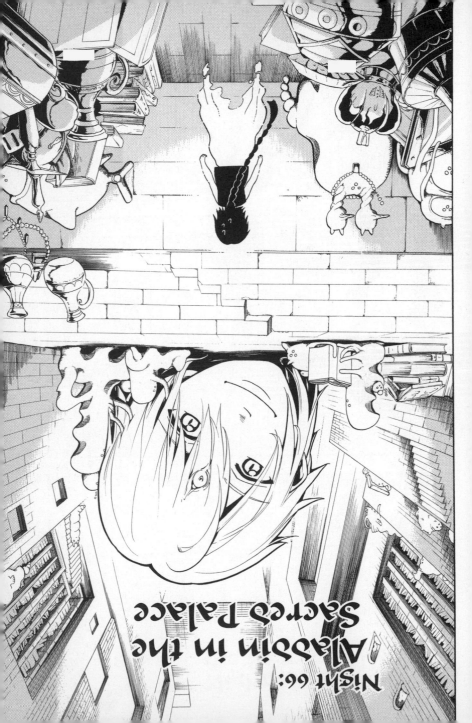

Night 66:
Aladdin in the
Sacred Palace

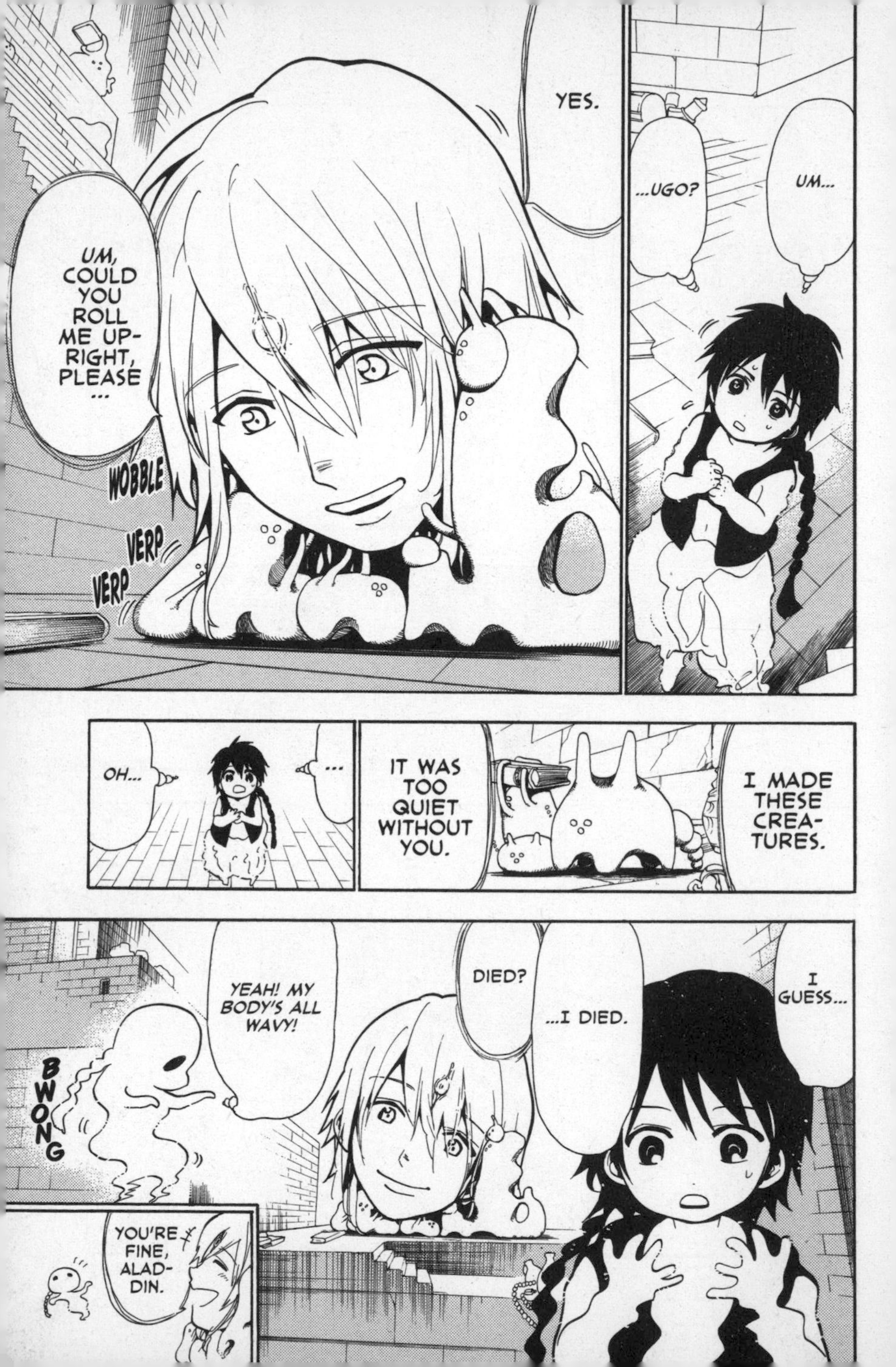
UM...
...UGO?
YES.
UM, COULD YOU ROLL ME UP-RIGHT, PLEASE...
WOBBLE
VERP
VERP
I MADE THESE CREA-TURES.
IT WAS TOO QUIET WITHOUT YOU.
...
OH...
I GUESS...
...I DIED.
DIED?
YEAH! MY BODY'S ALL WAVY!
BWONG
YOU'RE FINE, ALAD-DIN.

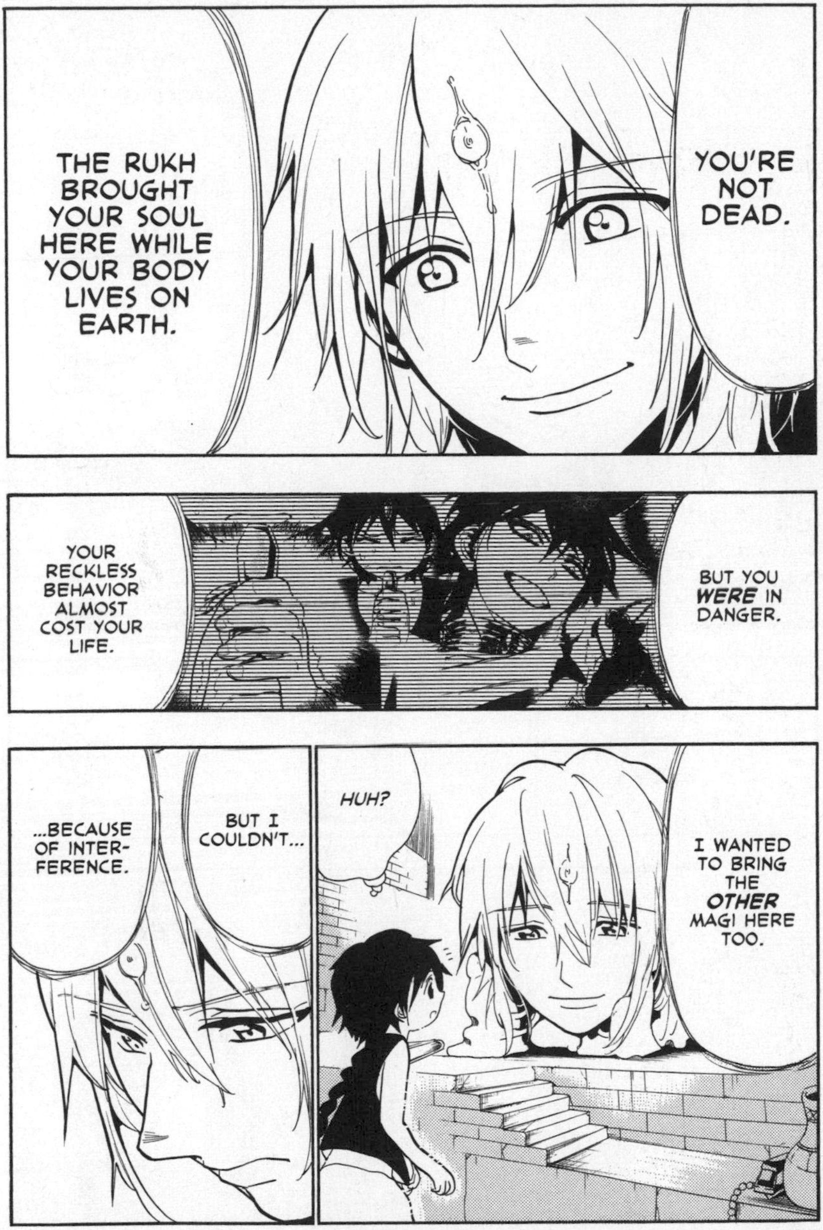
YOU'RE NOT DEAD.
THE RUKH BROUGHT YOUR SOUL HERE WHILE YOUR BODY LIVES ON EARTH.
BUT YOU *WERE* IN DANGER.
YOUR RECKLESS BEHAVIOR ALMOST COST YOUR LIFE.
I WANTED TO BRING THE *OTHER* MAGI HERE TOO.
HUH?
BUT I COULDN'T...
...BECAUSE OF INTER-FERENCE.

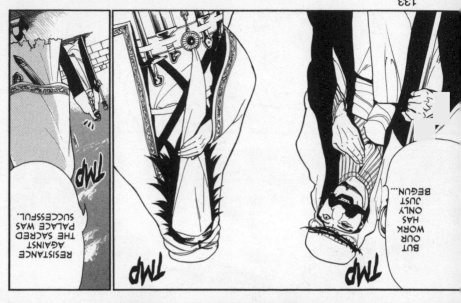

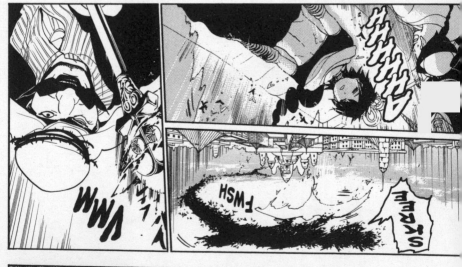

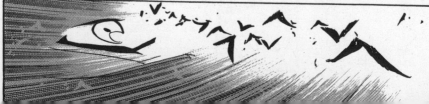

VMM
SKREE
FWSH
AHHHHH
RESISTANCE AGAINST THE SACRED PALACE WAS SUCCESSFUL.
TMP
TMP
TMP
BUT OUR WORK HAS ONLY JUST BEGUN...

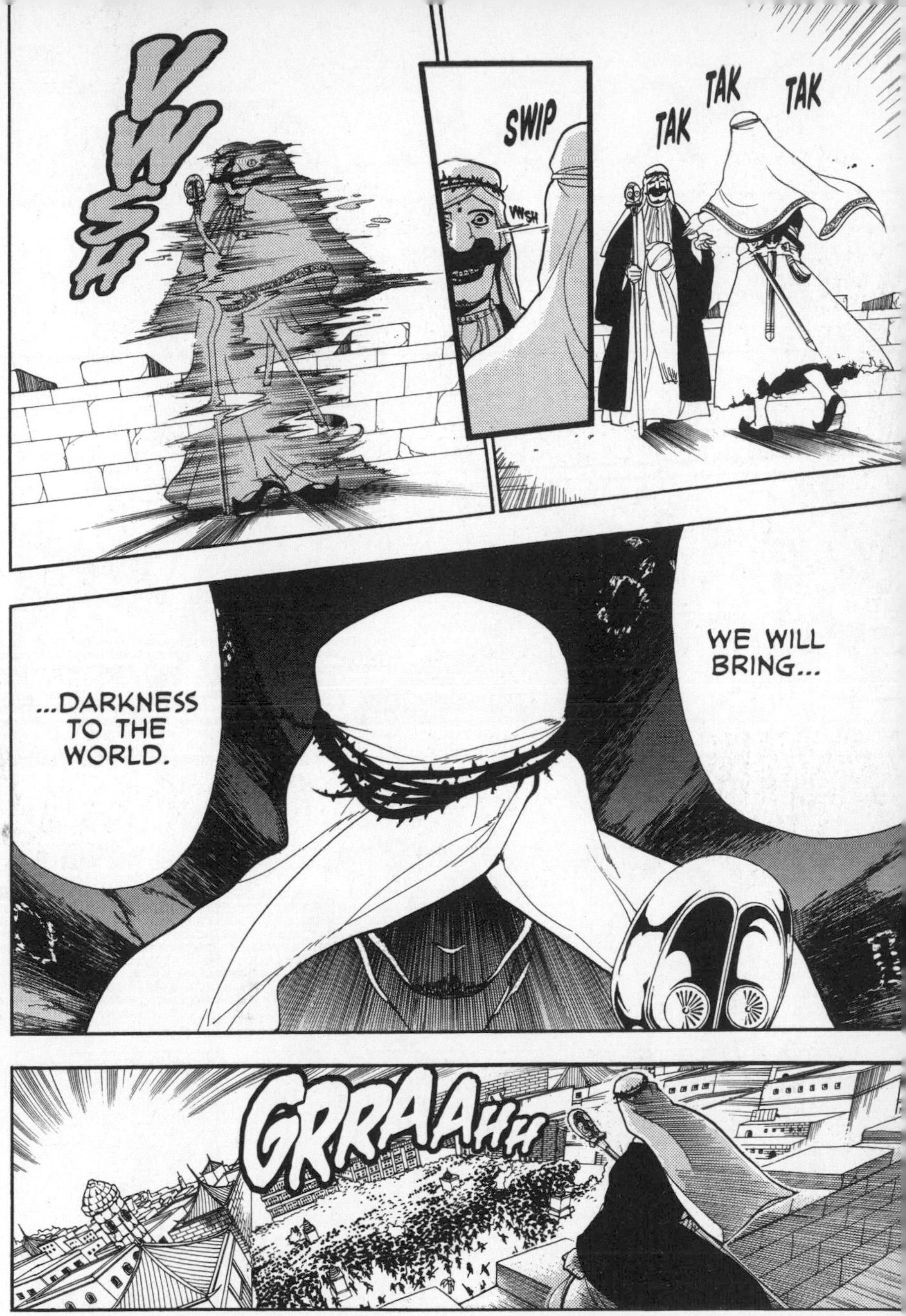
TAK
TAK
TAK
SWIP
VWSH
VWSH
WE WILL BRING...
...DARKNESS TO THE WORLD.
GRRAAHHH

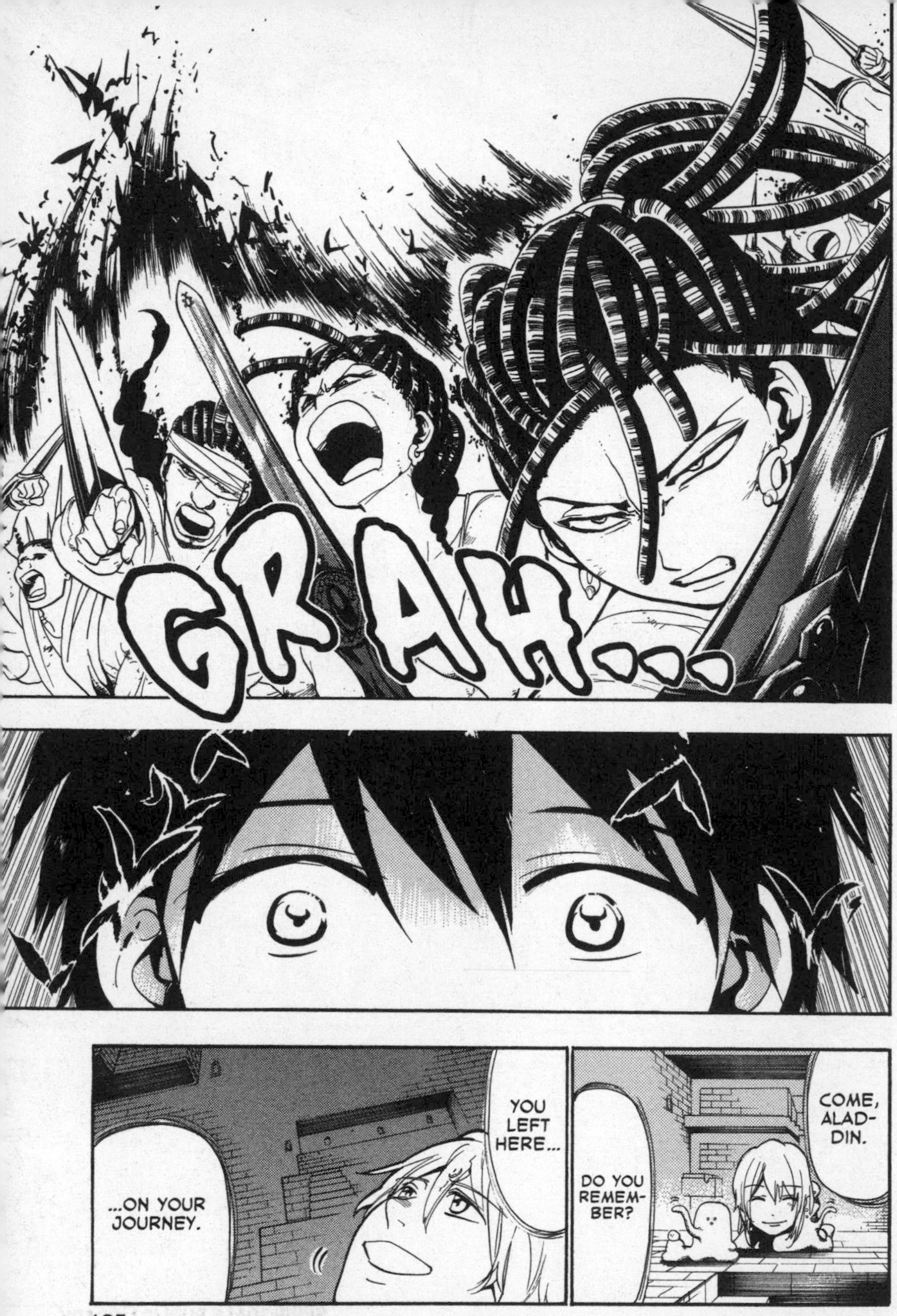
GRAH...
YOU LEFT HERE...
...ON YOUR JOURNEY.
COME, ALAD-DIN.
DO YOU REMEM-BER?

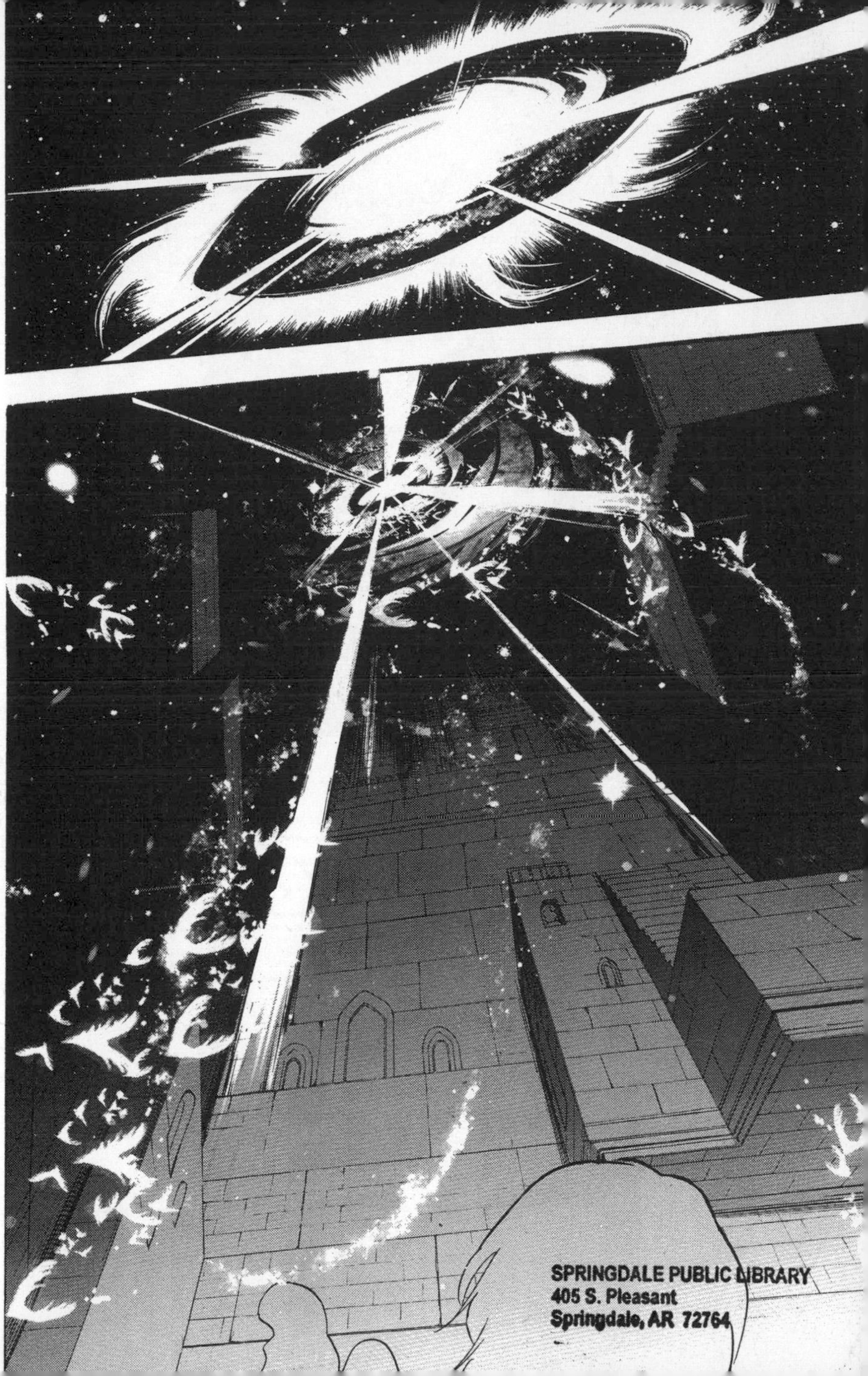

AS I WISHED...
...YOU WENT IN SEARCH OF METAL VESSELS...
...AND MET THE DJINN...
...AND THEIR MASTERS...
...JUST AS YOU WERE LED.
I DID NOT TEACH YOU BEFORE-HAND...
...BECAUSE YOUR JOURNEY NEEDED TO BE NATURAL...
...OR IT WOULD DISRUPT THE FLOW.
WHEN A LIFE BEGINS...
...IT ENTERS THE FLOW...
...AND BY ACCEPTING THAT, IT PROGRESSES EVER FORWARD.
THAT IS HOW...
...THE RUKH LEAD.

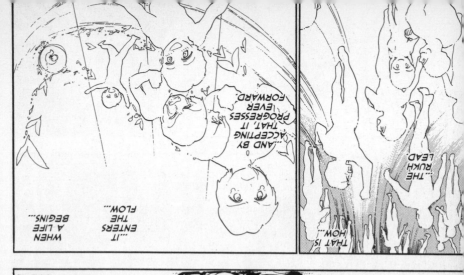

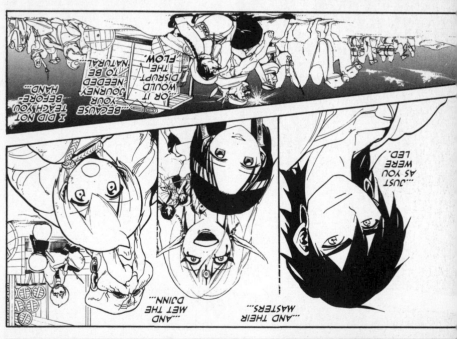

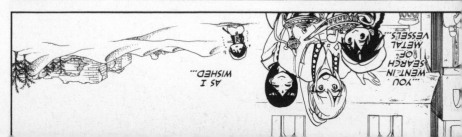

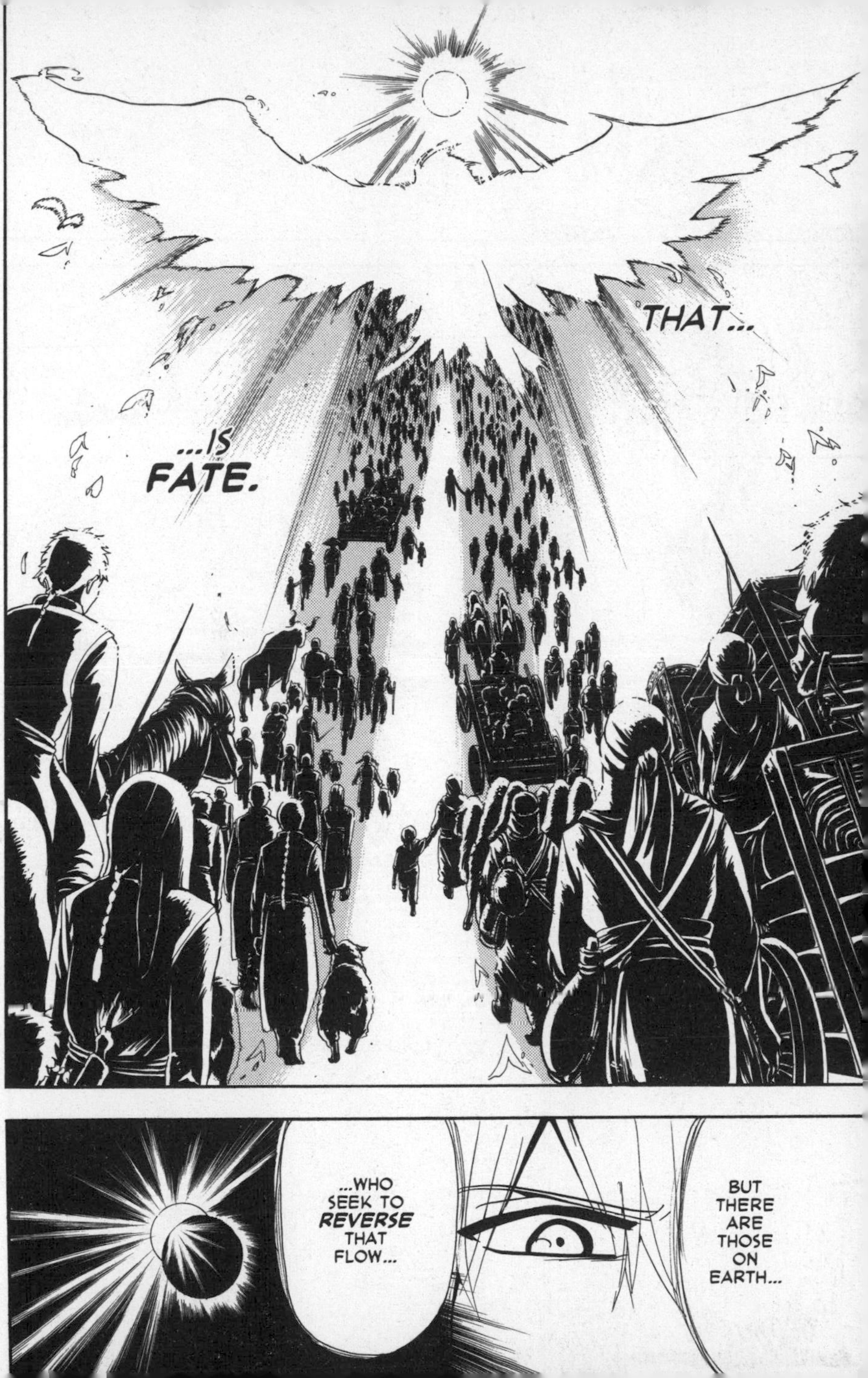
THAT...
...IS FATE.
BUT THERE ARE THOSE ON EARTH...
...WHO SEEK TO *REVERSE* THAT FLOW...

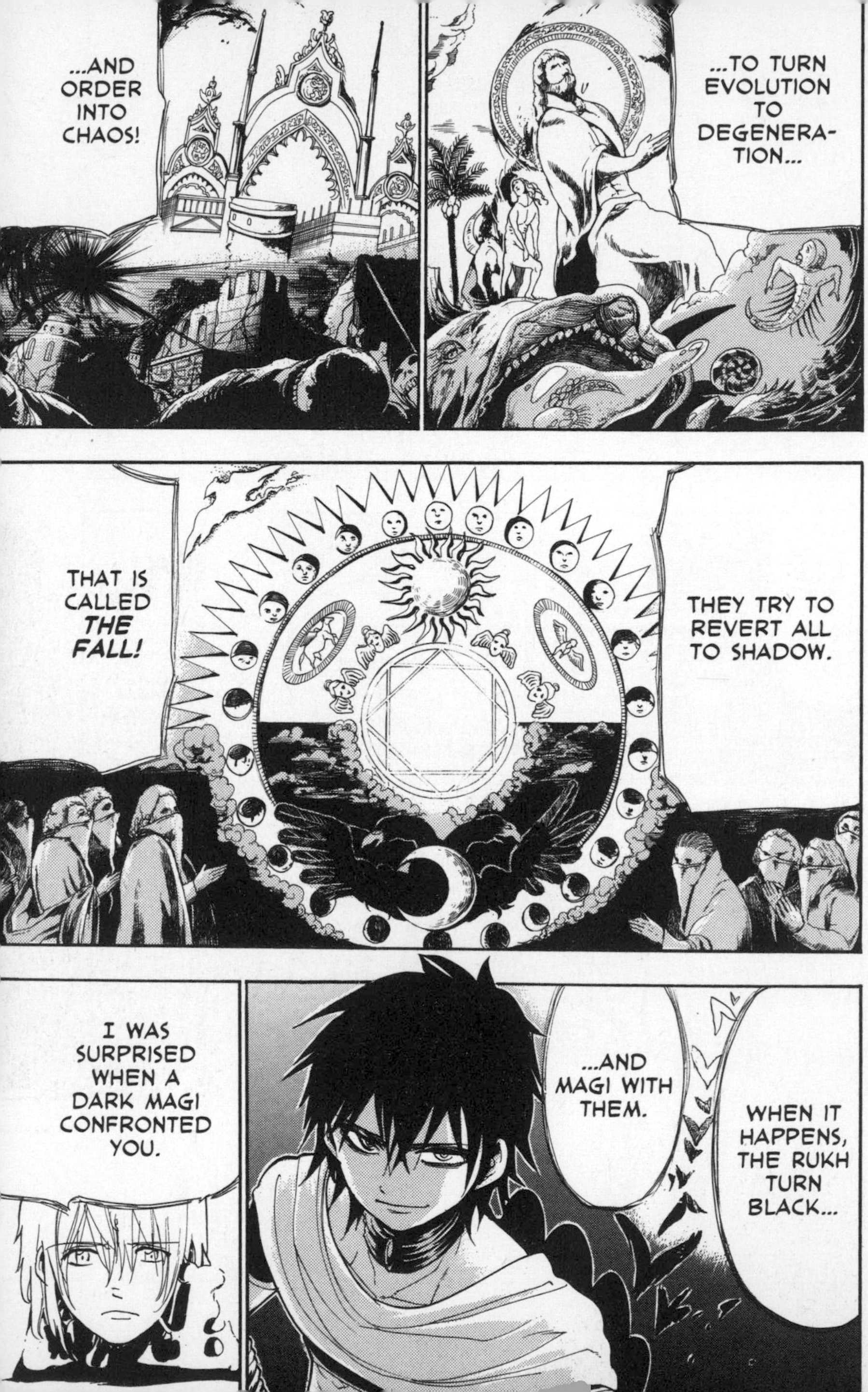
...TO TURN EVOLUTION TO DEGENERA-TION...
...AND ORDER INTO CHAOS!
THEY TRY TO REVERT ALL TO SHADOW.
THAT IS CALLED *THE FALL!*
WHEN IT HAPPENS, THE RUKH TURN BLACK...
...AND MAGI WITH THEM.
I WAS SURPRISED WHEN A DARK MAGI CONFRONTED YOU.

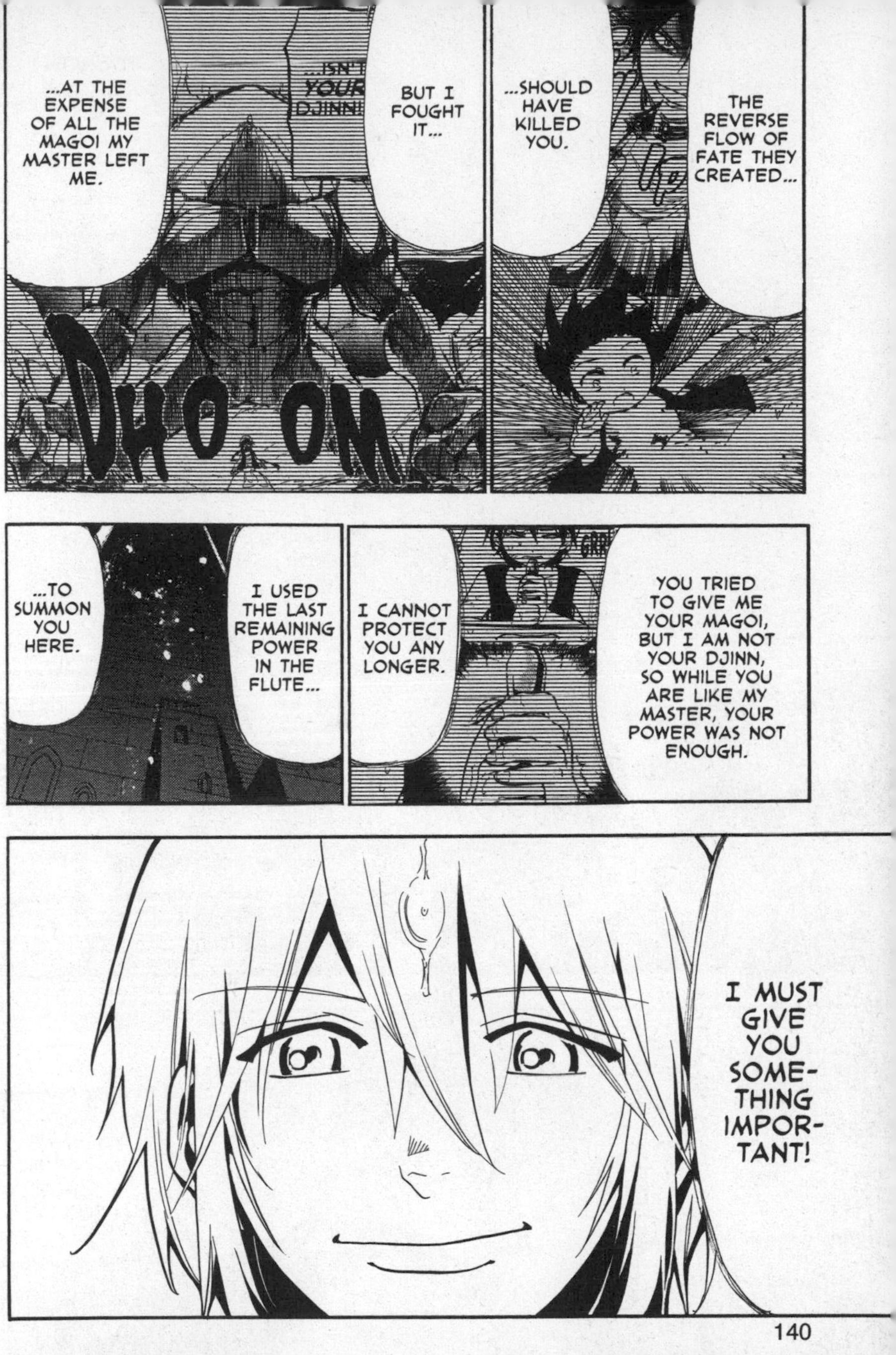
THE REVERSE FLOW OF FATE THEY CREATED...
...SHOULD HAVE KILLED YOU.
BUT I FOUGHT IT...
...ISN'T YOUR DJINN!
...AT THE EXPENSE OF ALL THE MAGOI MY MASTER LEFT ME.
DHO OM
YOU TRIED TO GIVE ME YOUR MAGOI, BUT I AM NOT YOUR DJINN, SO WHILE YOU ARE LIKE MY MASTER, YOUR POWER WAS NOT ENOUGH.
GRR
I CANNOT PROTECT YOU ANY LONGER.
I USED THE LAST REMAINING POWER IN THE FLUTE...
...TO SUMMON YOU HERE.
I MUST GIVE YOU SOME-THING IMPOR-TANT!

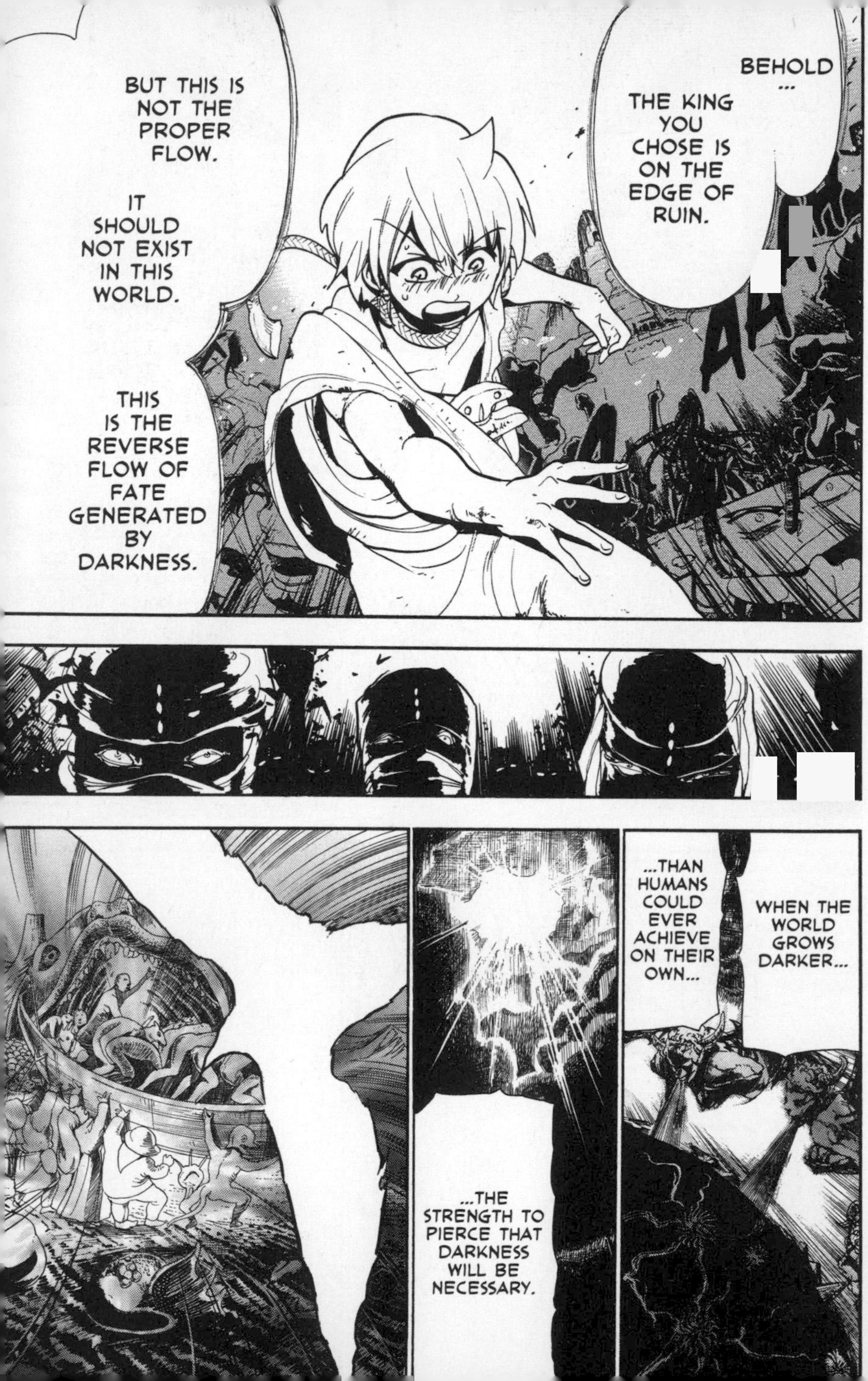
BEHOLD ...
THE KING YOU CHOSE IS ON THE EDGE OF RUIN.
BUT THIS IS NOT THE PROPER FLOW.
IT SHOULD NOT EXIST IN THIS WORLD.
THIS IS THE REVERSE FLOW OF FATE GENERATED BY DARKNESS.
WHEN THE WORLD GROWS DARKER...
...THAN HUMANS COULD EVER ACHIEVE ON THEIR OWN...
...THE STRENGTH TO PIERCE THAT DARKNESS WILL BE NECESSARY.

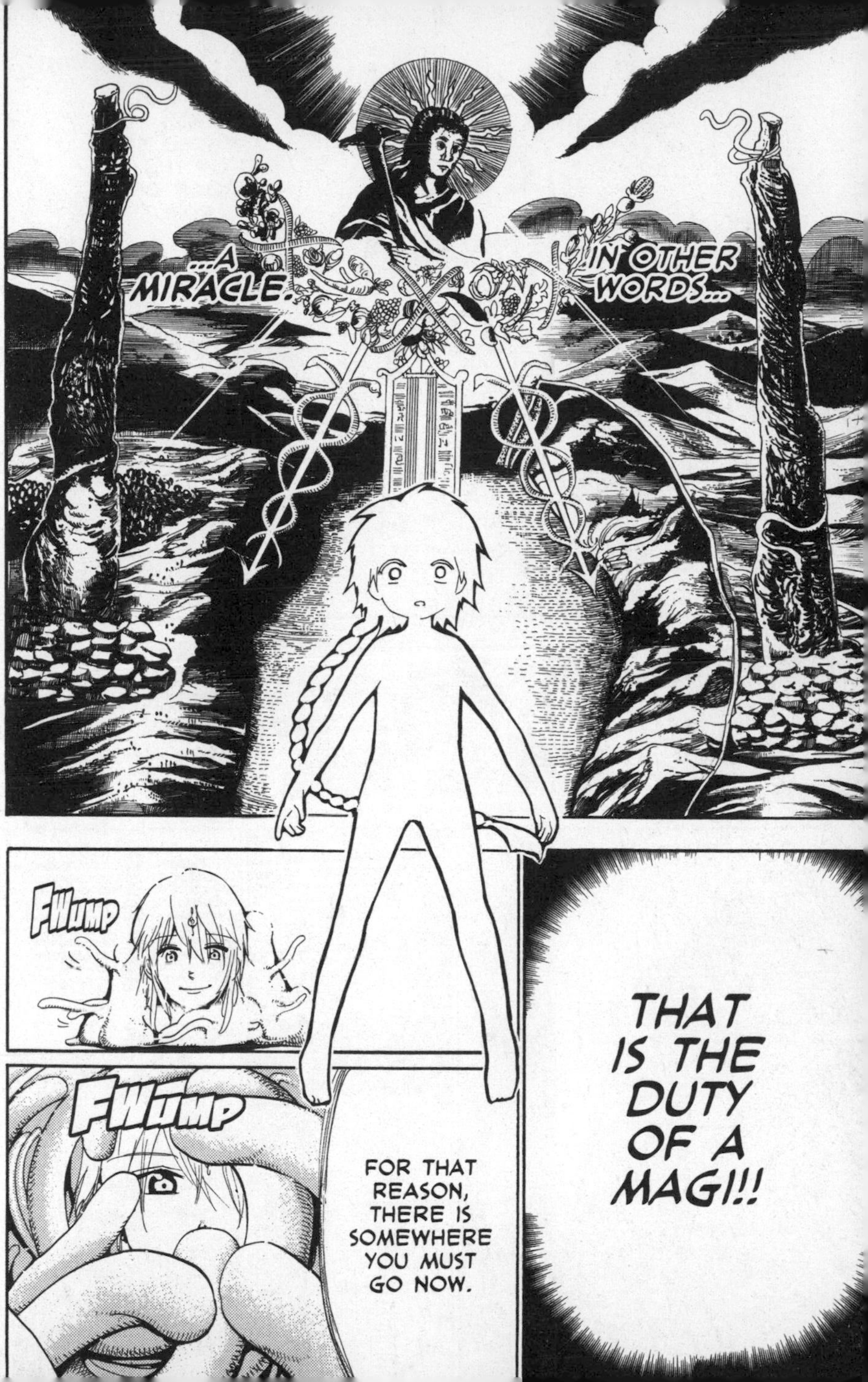
IN OTHER WORDS...
...A MIRACLE.
THAT IS THE DUTY OF A MAGI!!
FWUMP
FWUMP
FOR THAT REASON, THERE IS SOMEWHERE YOU MUST GO NOW.

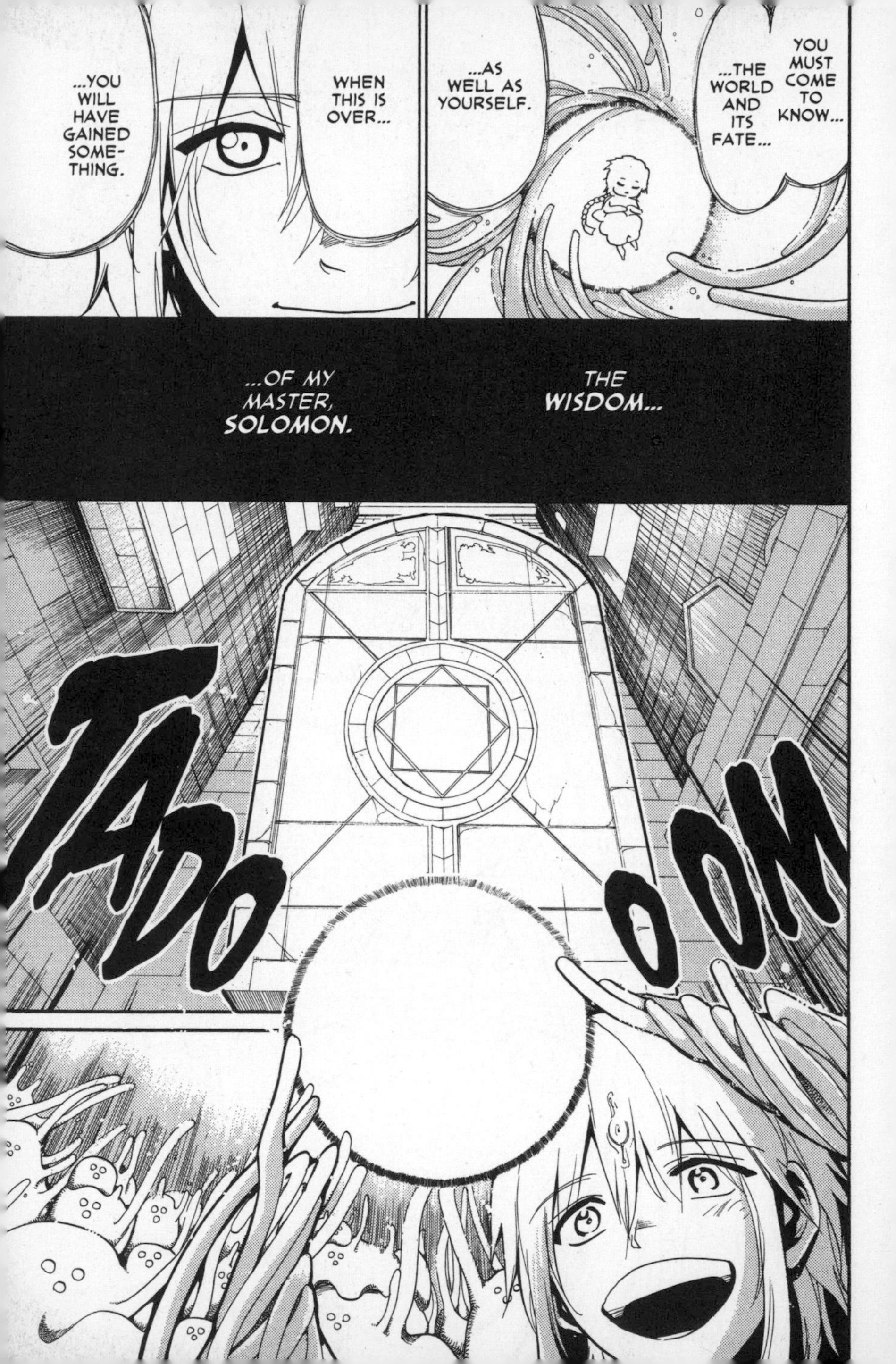
YOU MUST COME TO KNOW...
...THE WORLD AND ITS FATE...
...AS WELL AS YOURSELF.
WHEN THIS IS OVER...
...YOU WILL HAVE GAINED SOME-THING.
THE WISDOM...
...OF MY MASTER, SOLOMON.
TADOOOM

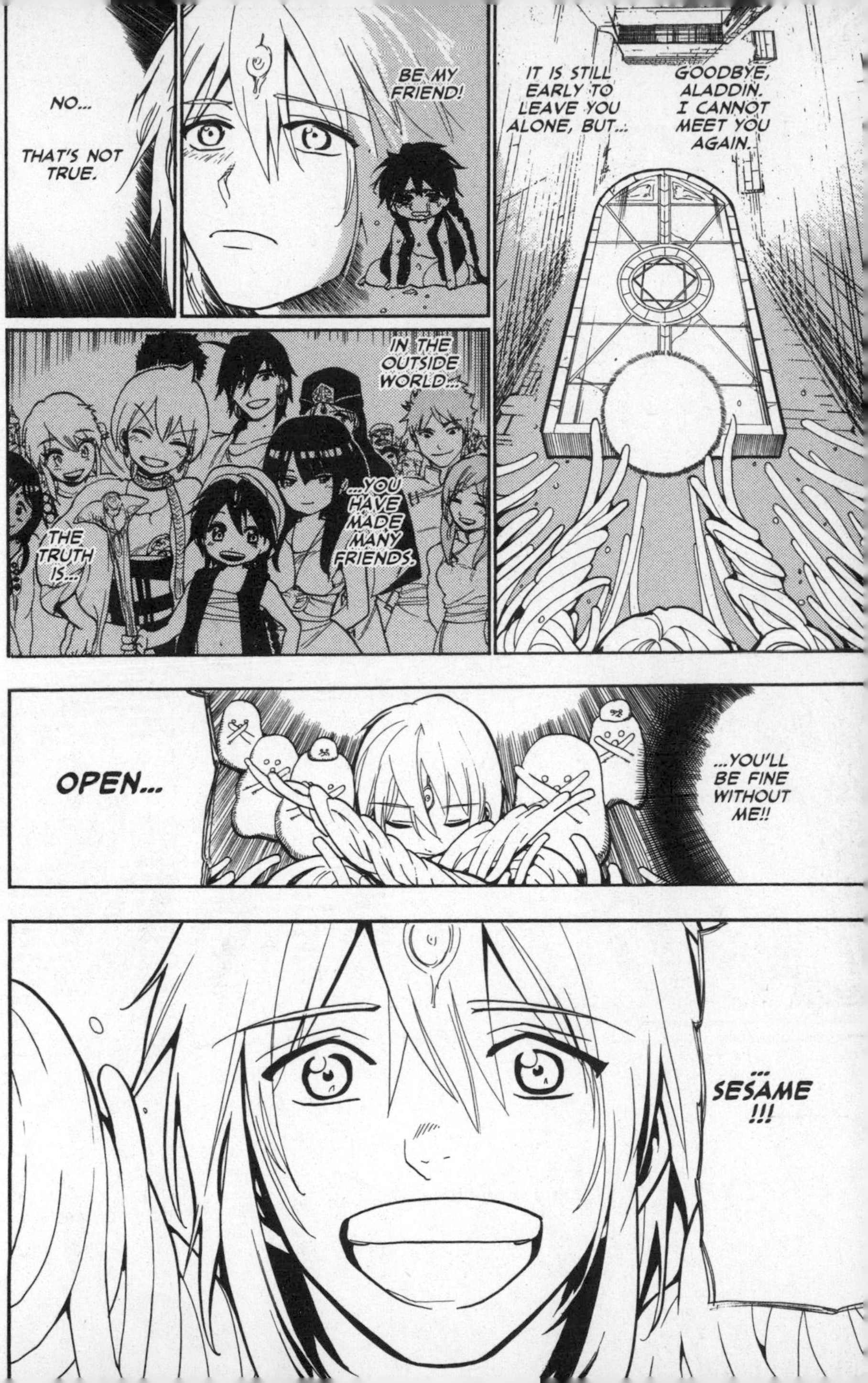
GOODBYE, ALADDIN. I CANNOT MEET YOU AGAIN.
IT IS STILL EARLY TO LEAVE YOU ALONE, BUT...
BE MY FRIEND!
NO...
THAT'S NOT TRUE.
IN THE OUTSIDE WORLD...
...YOU HAVE MADE MANY FRIENDS.
THE TRUTH IS...
...YOU'LL BE FINE WITHOUT ME!!
OPEN...
...SESAME !!!

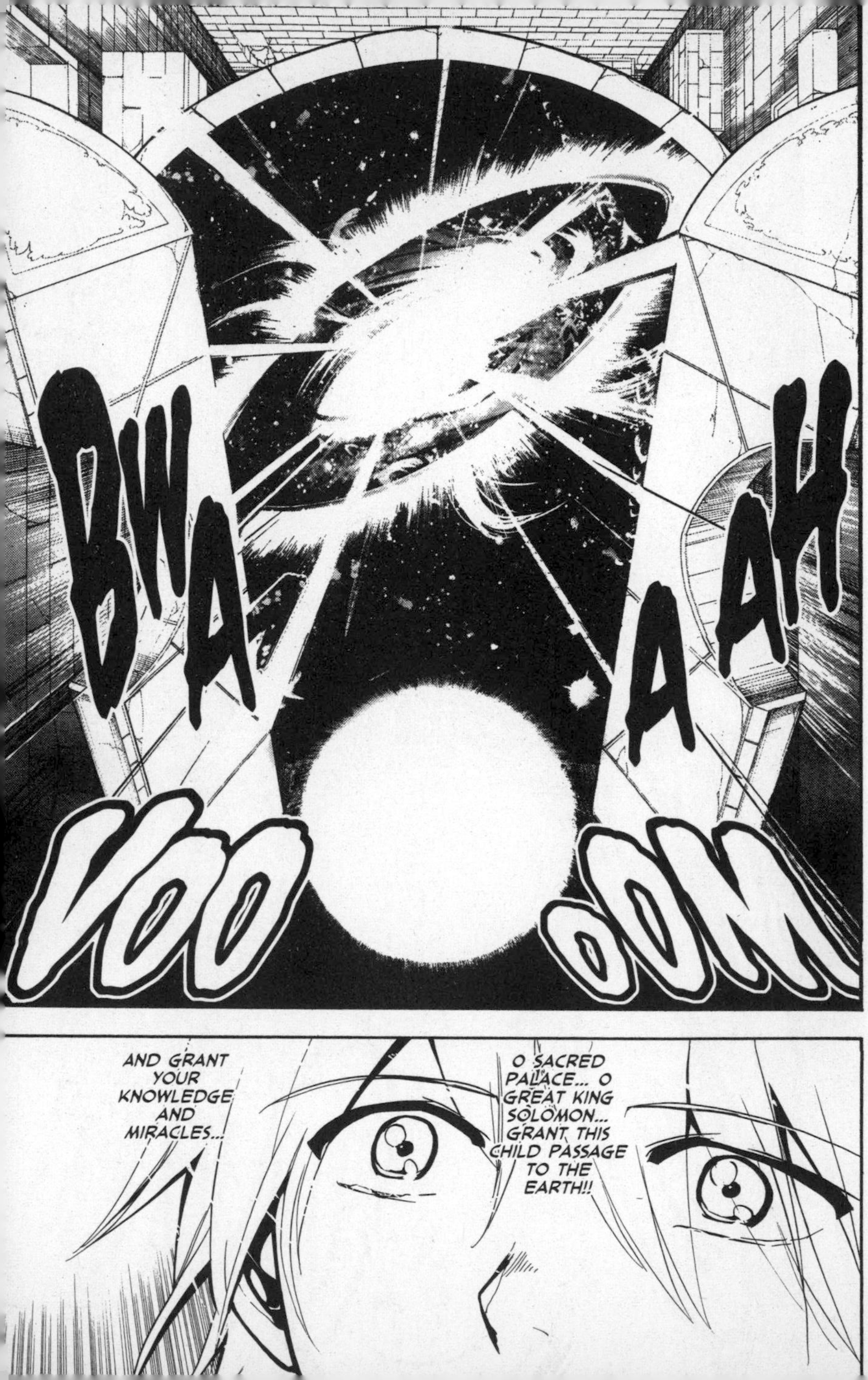
BWAAAAH
VOOOOM
O SACRED PALACE... O GREAT KING SOLOMON... GRANT THIS CHILD PASSAGE TO THE EARTH!!
AND GRANT YOUR KNOWLEDGE AND MIRACLES...

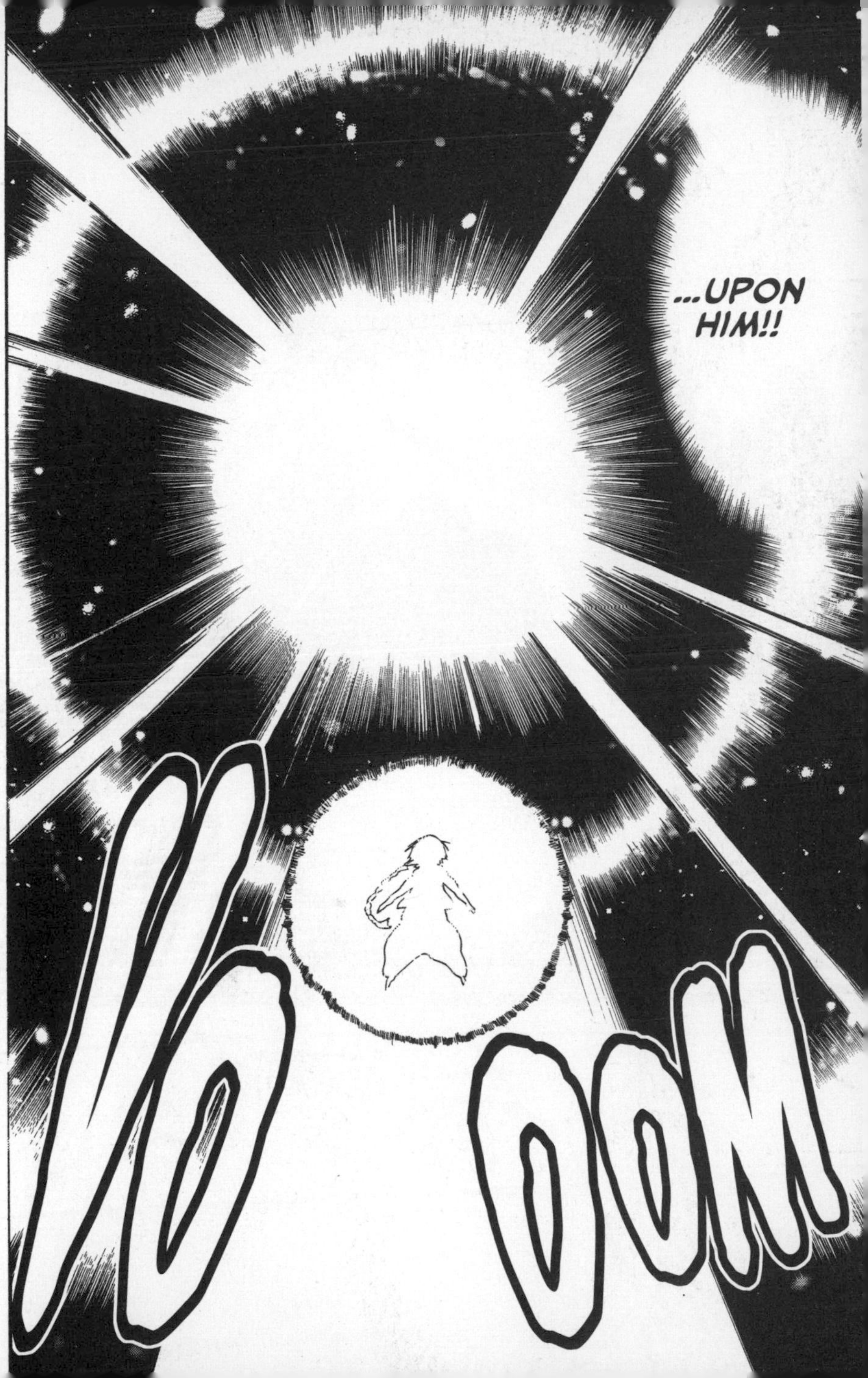
...UPON HIM!!
VOOOM

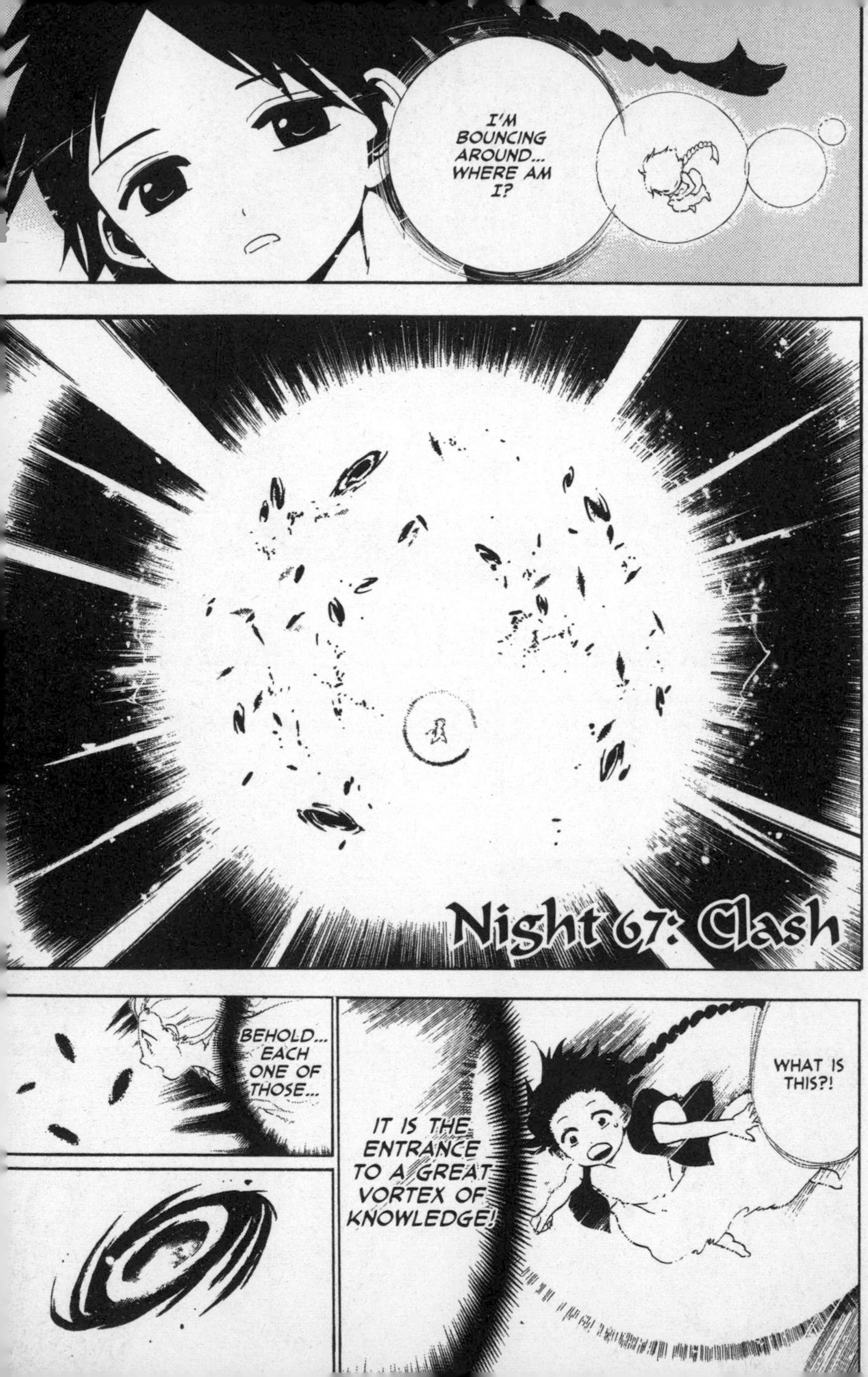
I'M BOUNCING AROUND... WHERE AM I?
Night 67: Clash
WHAT IS THIS?!
IT IS THE ENTRANCE TO A GREAT VORTEX OF KNOWLEDGE!
BEHOLD... EACH ONE OF THOSE...

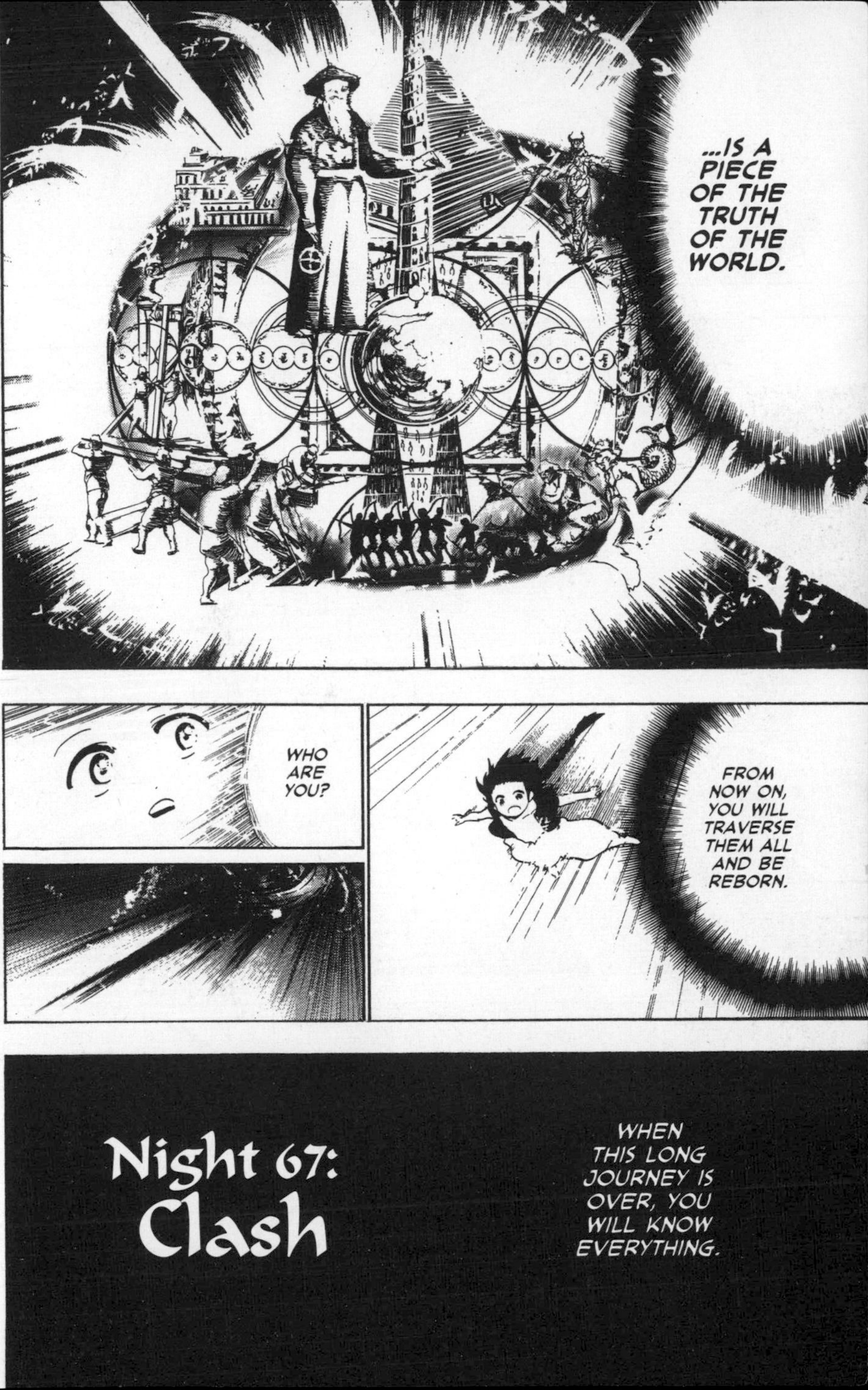
...IS A PIECE OF THE TRUTH OF THE WORLD.
FROM NOW ON, YOU WILL TRAVERSE THEM ALL AND BE REBORN.
WHO ARE YOU?
Night 67: Clash
WHEN THIS LONG JOURNEY IS OVER, YOU WILL KNOW EVERYTHING.

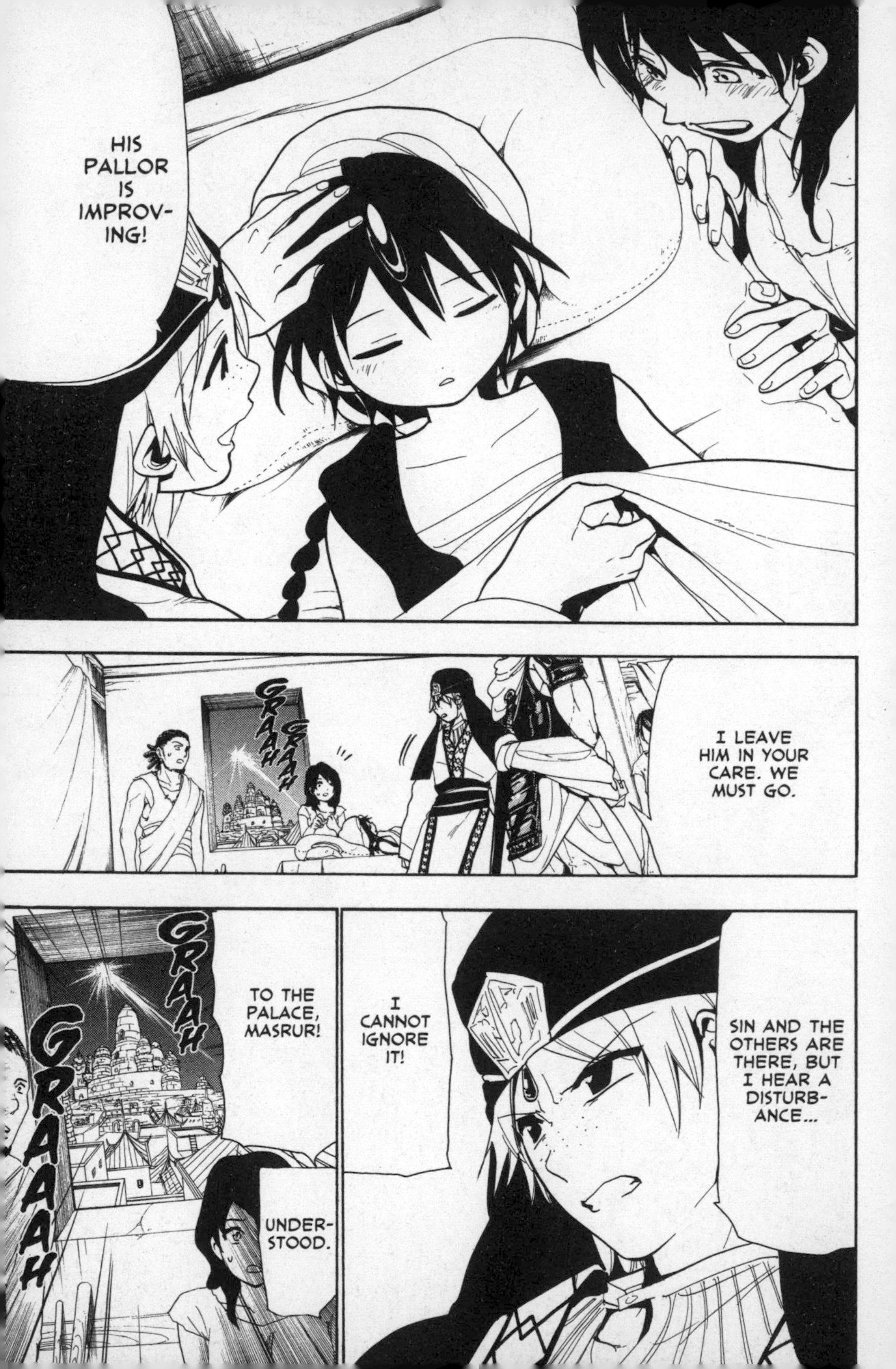
HIS PALLOR IS IMPROVING!
GRAAH GRAAH
I LEAVE HIM IN YOUR CARE. WE MUST GO.
SIN AND THE OTHERS ARE THERE, BUT I HEAR A DISTURBANCE...
I CANNOT IGNORE IT!
TO THE PALACE, MASRUR!
GRAAH
GRAAAH
UNDERSTOOD.

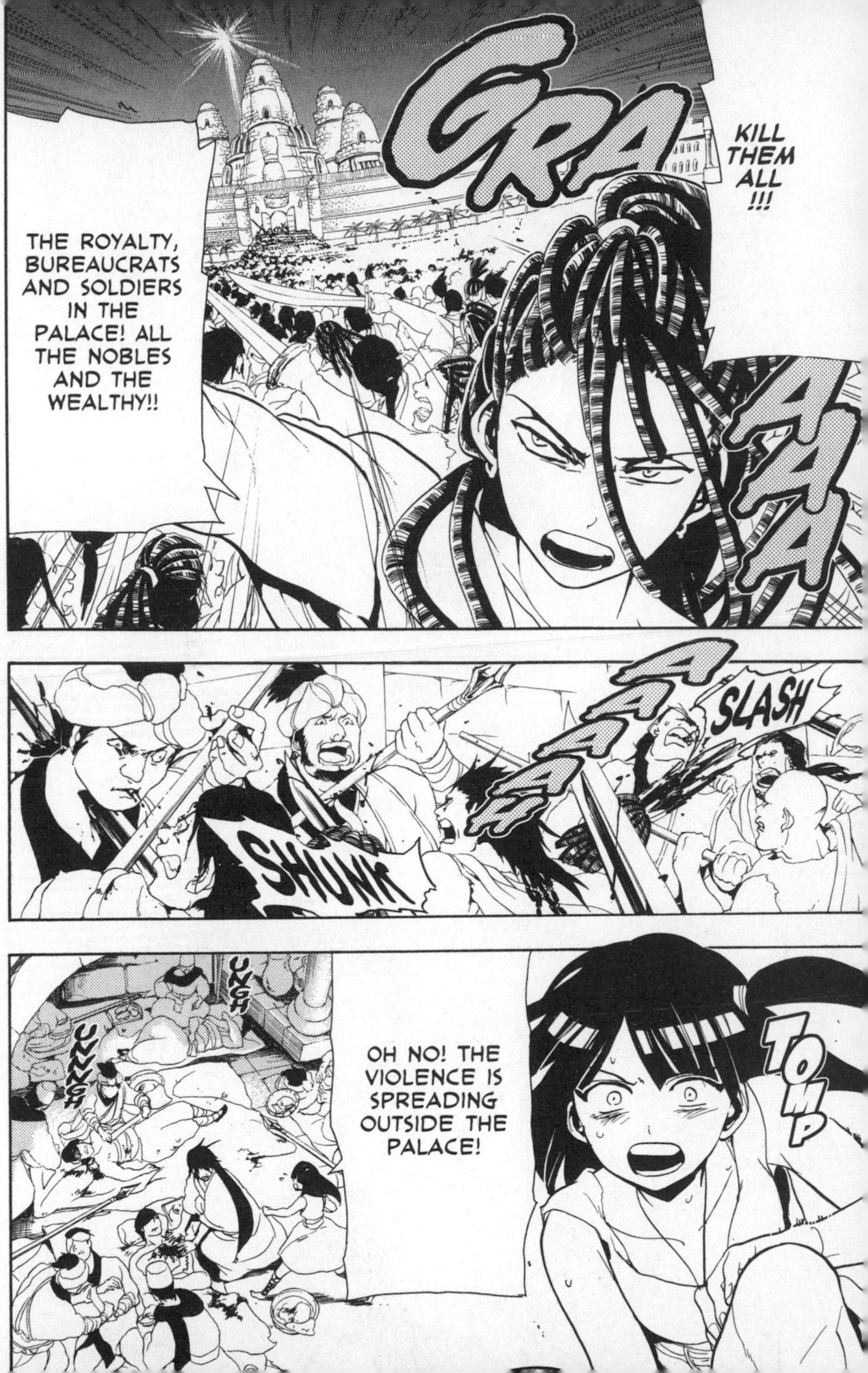
KILL THEM ALL !!!
GRAAAA
THE ROYALTY, BUREAUCRATS AND SOLDIERS IN THE PALACE! ALL THE NOBLES AND THE WEALTHY!!
SLASH
AAAAA
SHUNK
TOMP
OH NO! THE VIOLENCE IS SPREADING OUTSIDE THE PALACE!
UNGH
UNNNGH

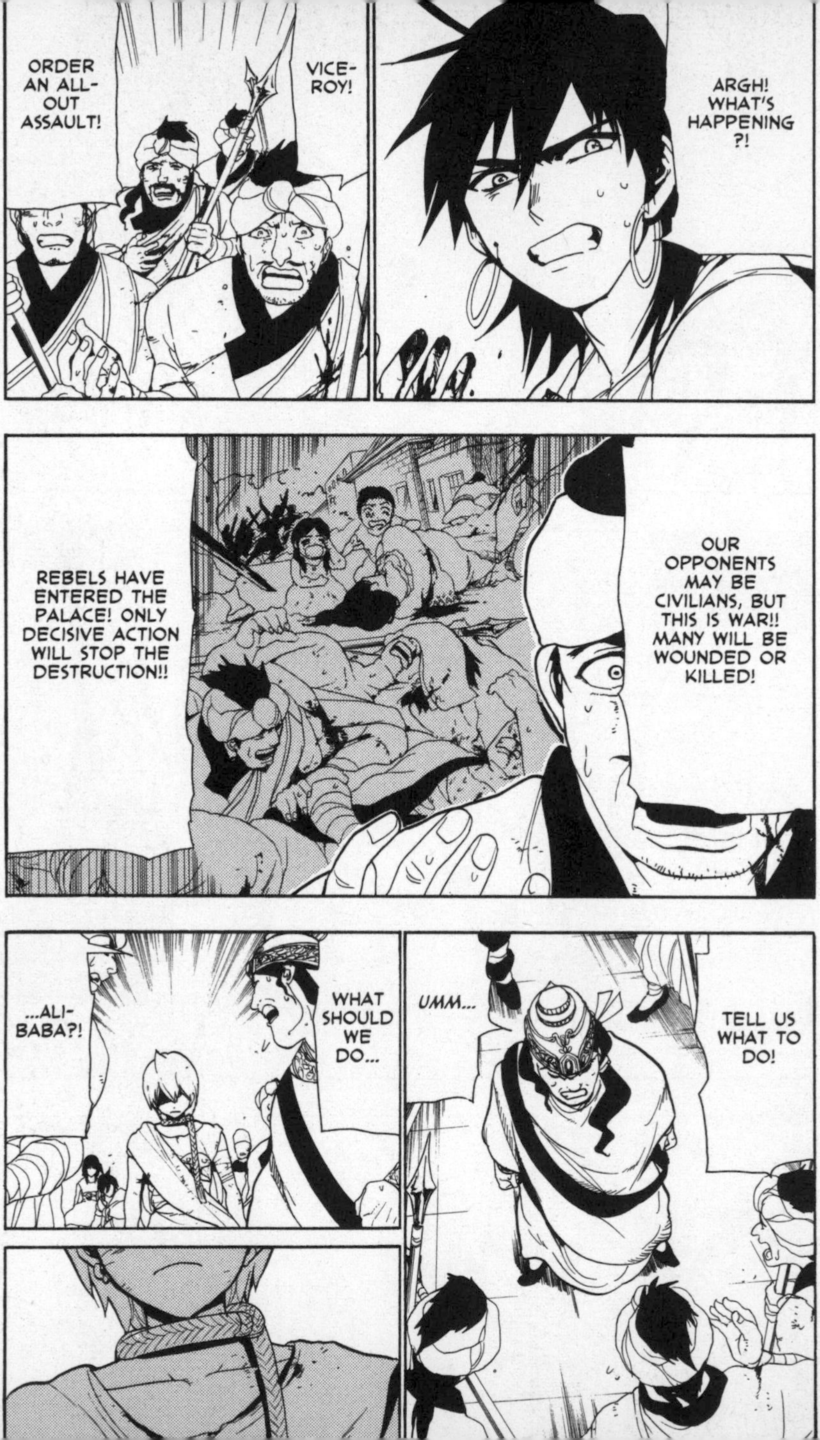
ARGH! WHAT'S HAPPENING?!
VICE-ROY!
ORDER AN ALL-OUT ASSAULT!
OUR OPPONENTS MAY BE CIVILIANS, BUT THIS IS WAR!! MANY WILL BE WOUNDED OR KILLED!
REBELS HAVE ENTERED THE PALACE! ONLY DECISIVE ACTION WILL STOP THE DESTRUCTION!!
TELL US WHAT TO DO!
UMM...
WHAT SHOULD WE DO...
...ALI-BABA?!

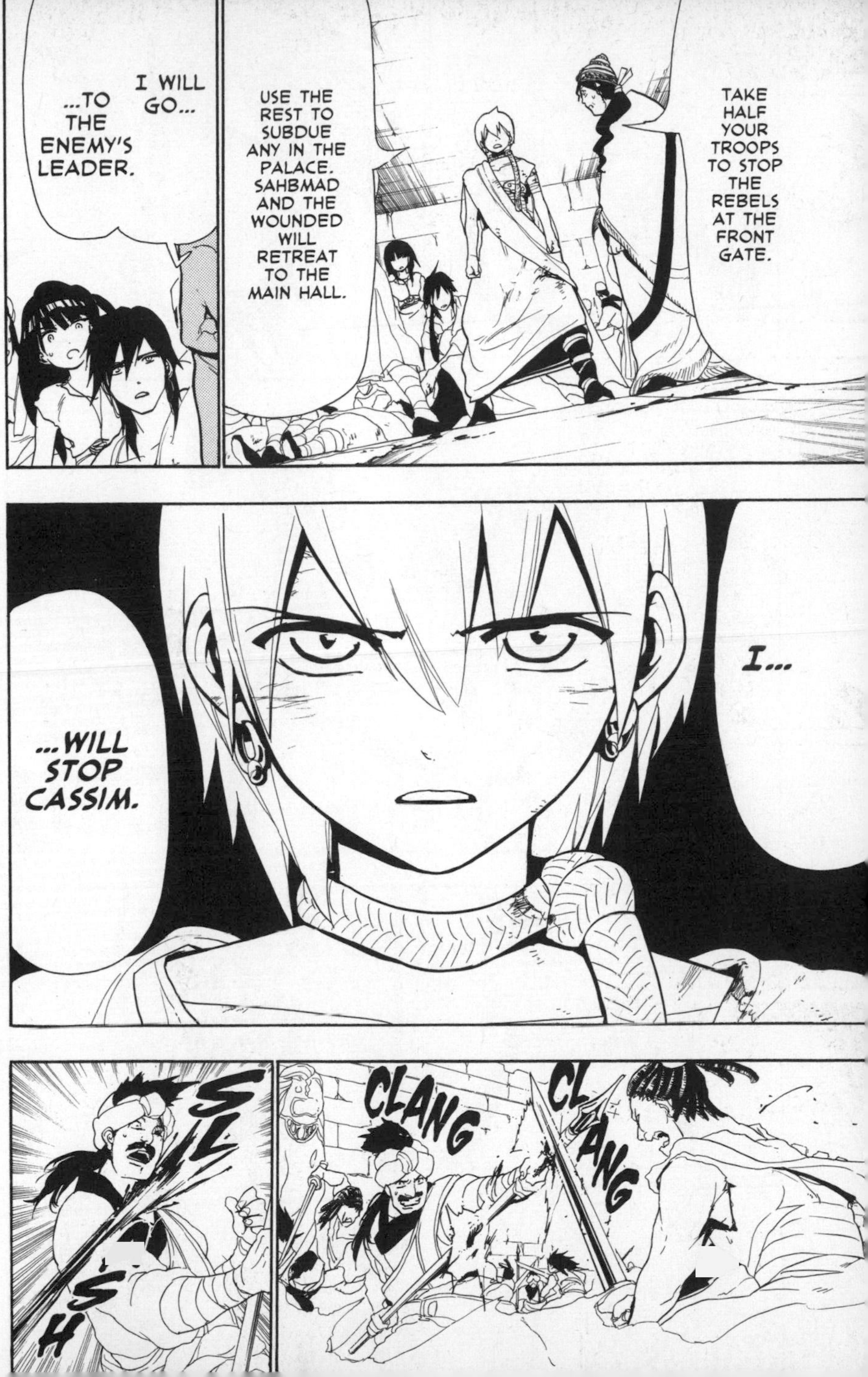
TAKE HALF YOUR TROOPS TO STOP THE REBELS AT THE FRONT GATE.
USE THE REST TO SUBDUE ANY IN THE PALACE. SAHBMAD AND THE WOUNDED WILL RETREAT TO THE MAIN HALL.
I WILL GO...
...TO THE ENEMY'S LEADER.
I...
...WILL STOP CASSIM.
CLANG
CLANG
SLISH

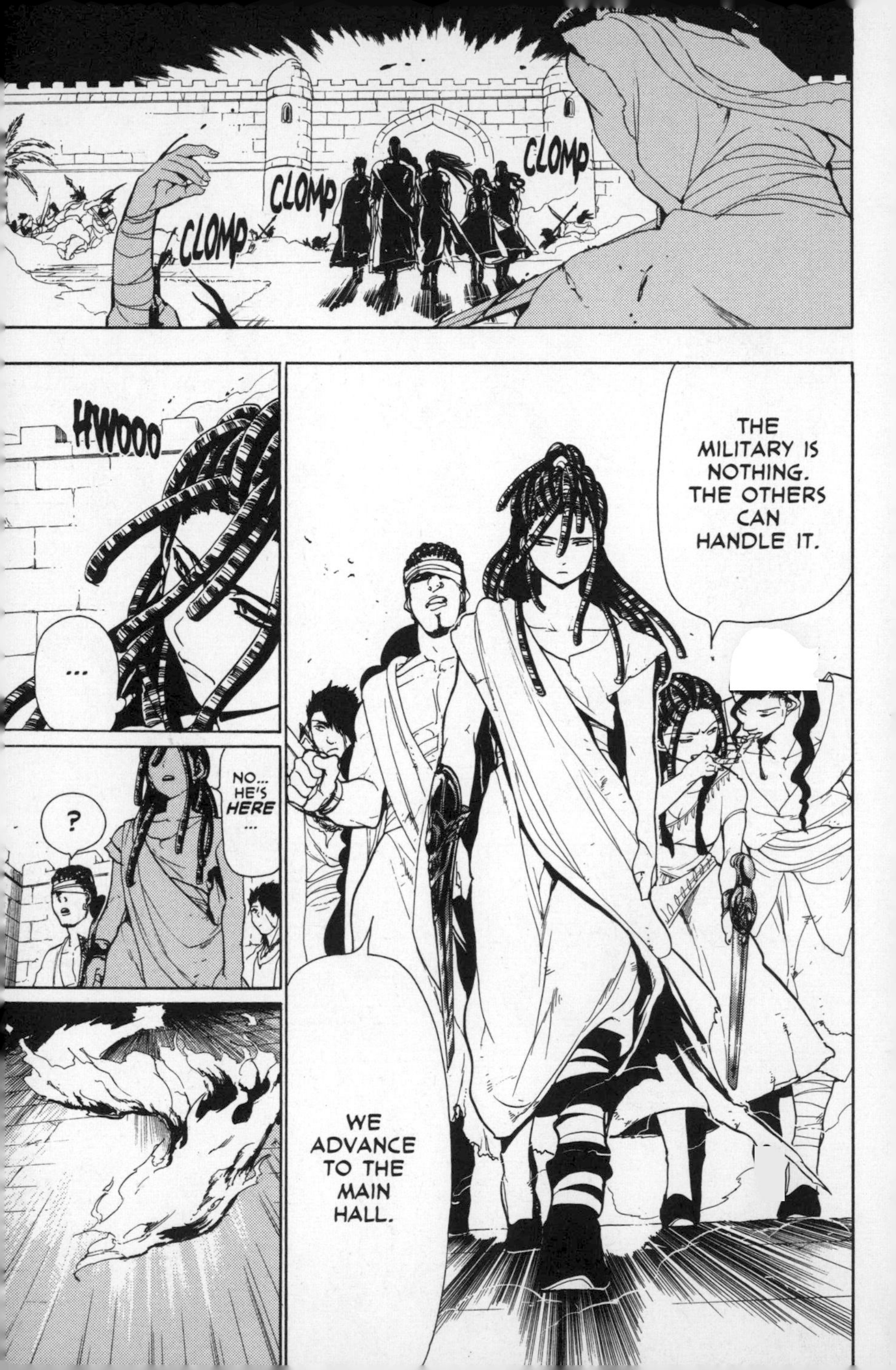
CLOMP
CLOMP
CLOMP
THE MILITARY IS NOTHING. THE OTHERS CAN HANDLE IT.
WE ADVANCE TO THE MAIN HALL.
HWOOO
...
NO... HE'S HERE...
?

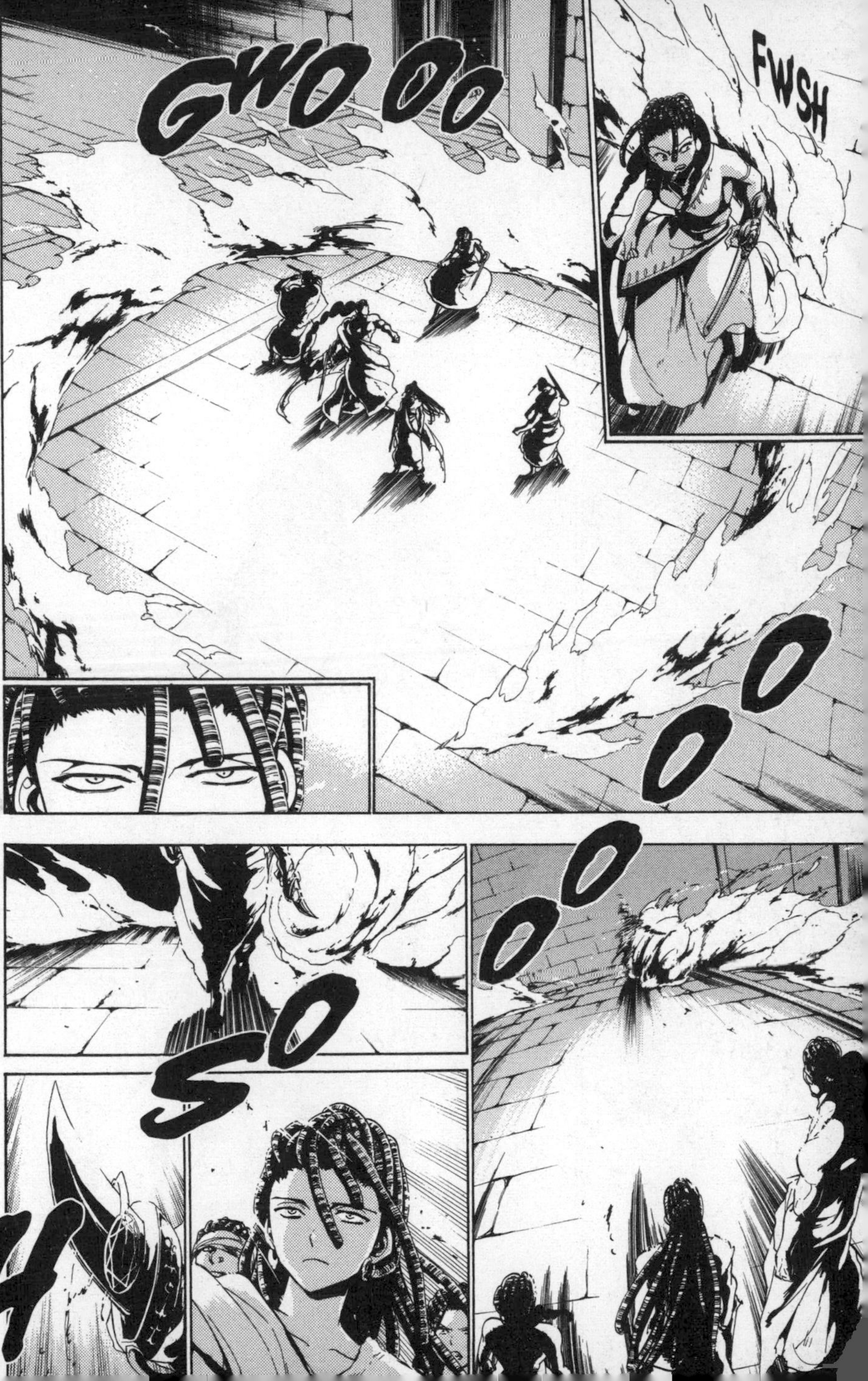
FWSH
GWO OO
OOOOOOSH

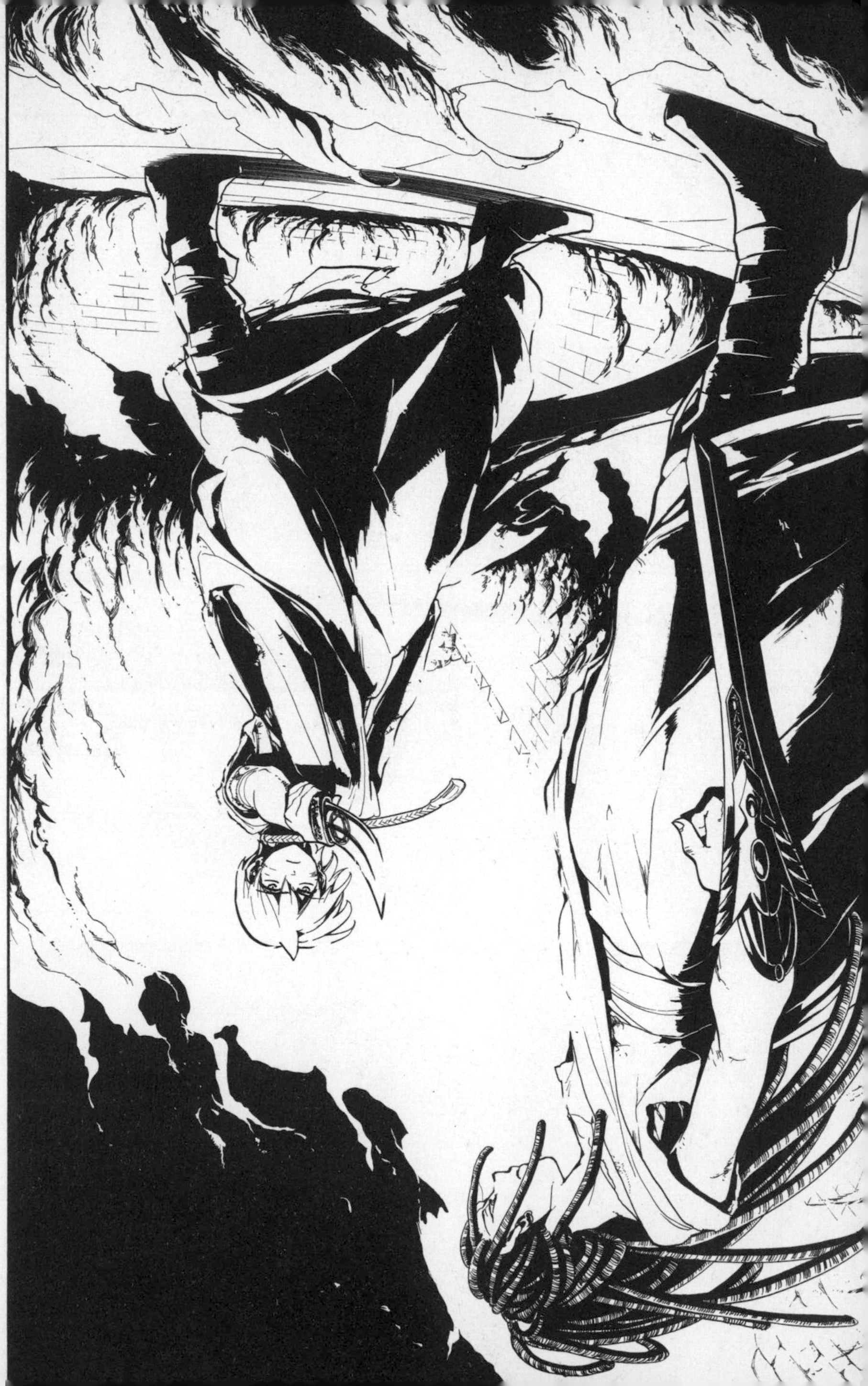

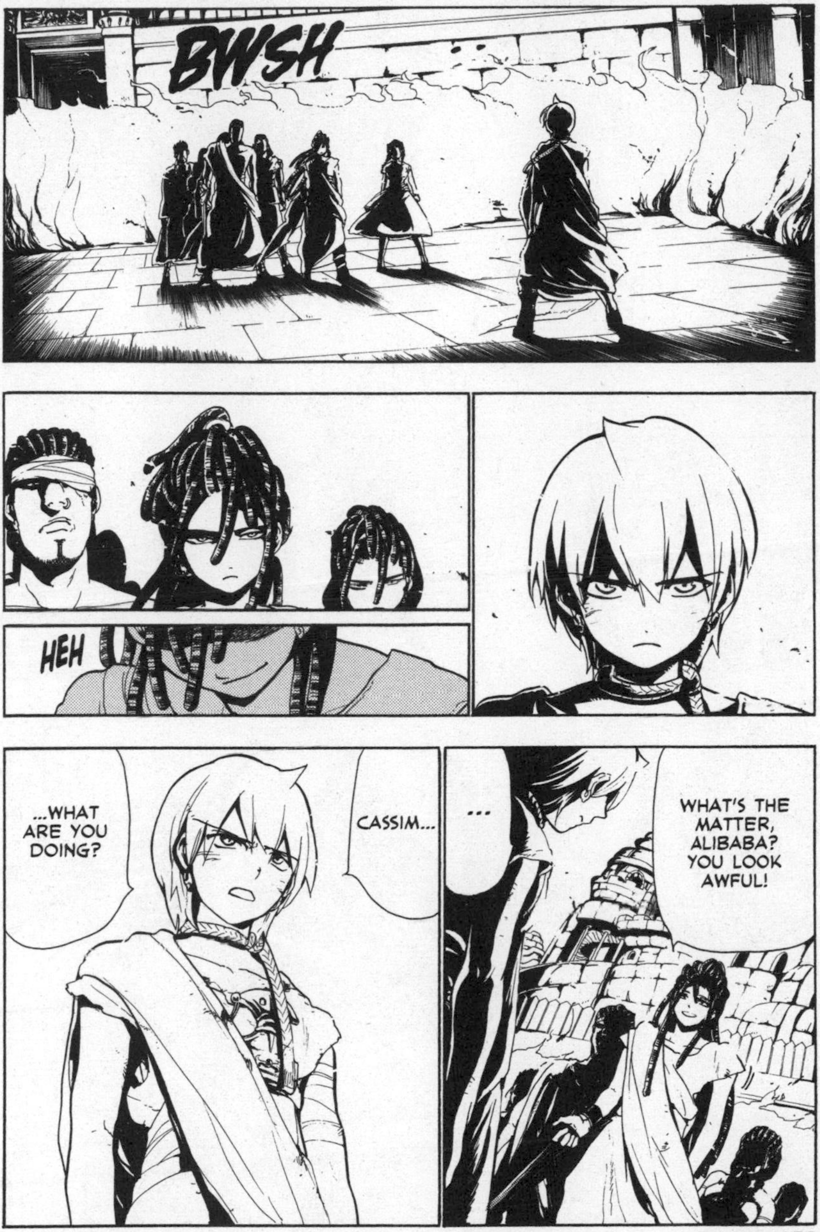
BWSH
HEH
WHAT'S THE MATTER, ALIBABA? YOU LOOK AWFUL!
...
CASSIM...
...WHAT ARE YOU DOING?

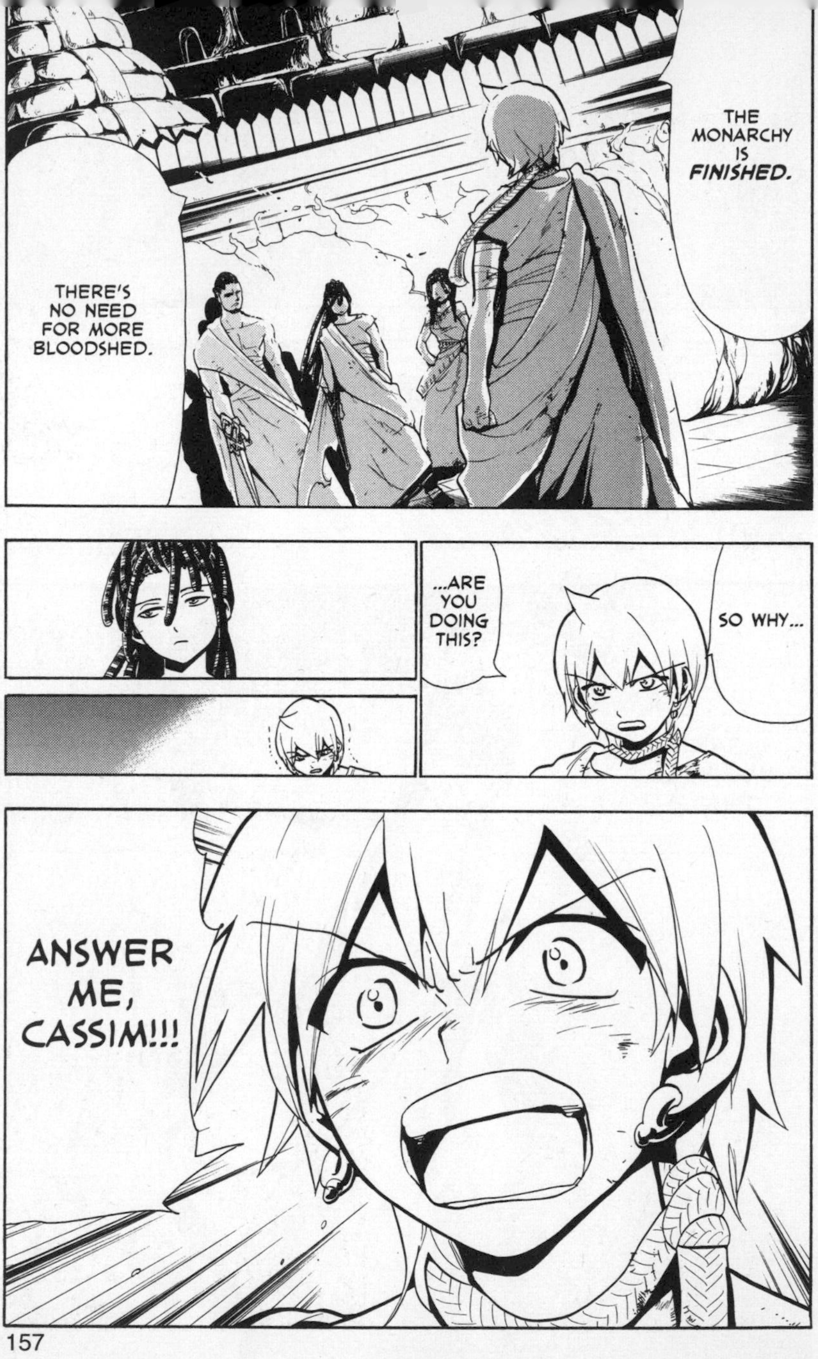
THE MONARCHY IS FINISHED.
THERE'S NO NEED FOR MORE BLOODSHED.
SO WHY...
...ARE YOU DOING THIS?
ANSWER ME, CASSIM!!!

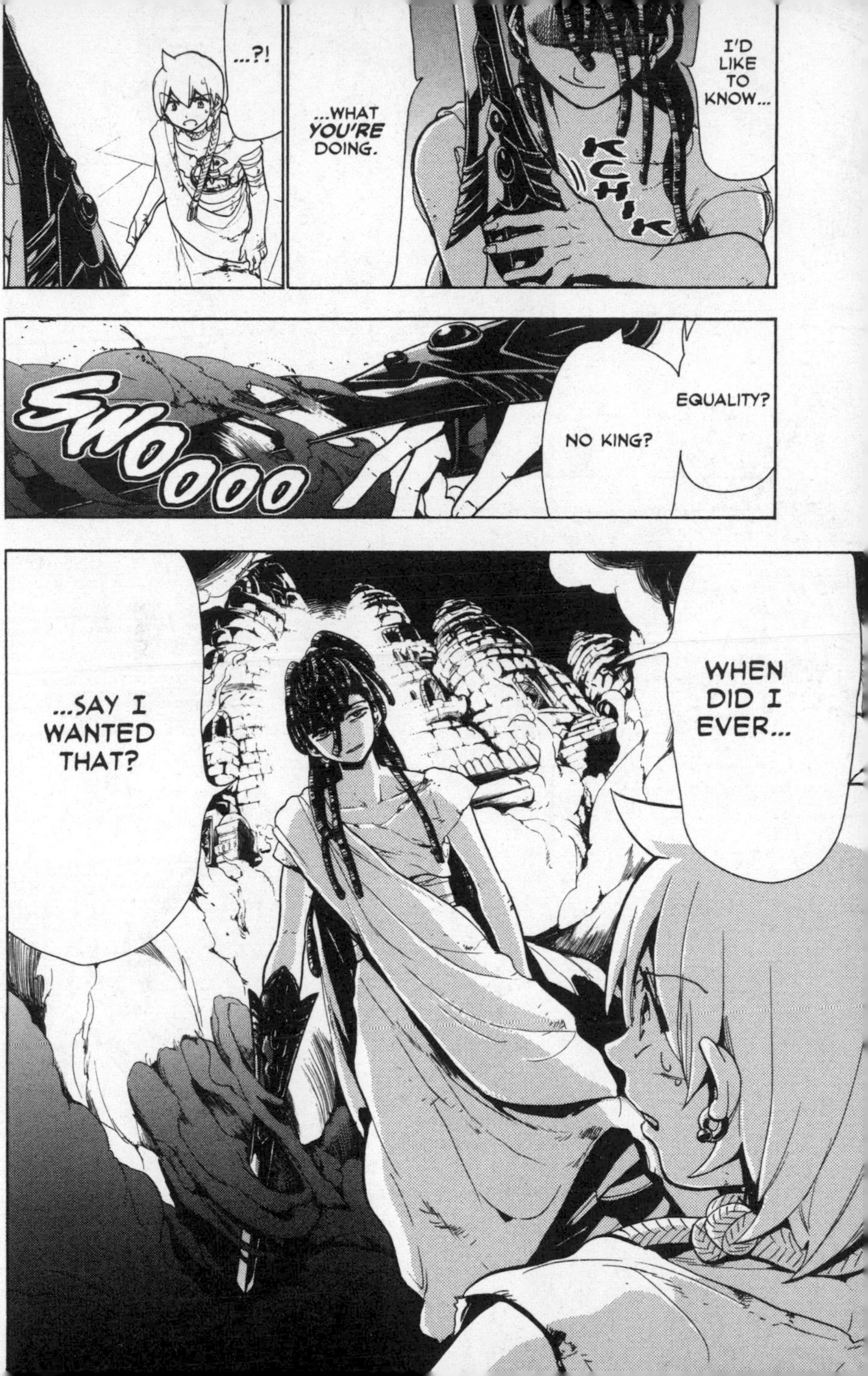
I'D LIKE TO KNOW...
KCHIK
...WHAT YOU'RE DOING.
...?!
EQUALITY?
NO KING?
SWOOOO
WHEN DID I EVER...
...SAY I WANTED THAT?

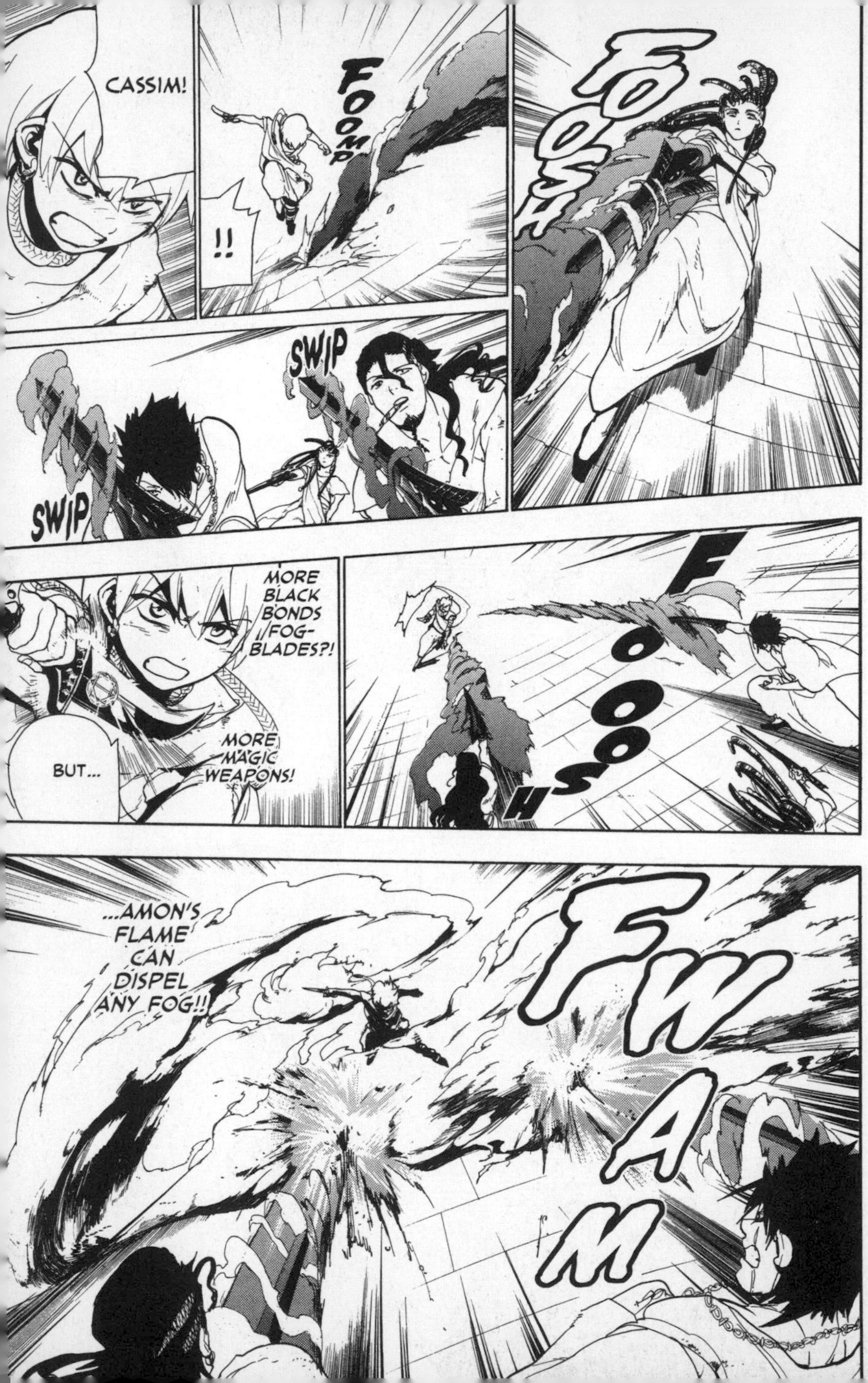
FOOOSH
!!
FOOOMP
CASSIM!
SWIP
SWIP
FOOOOSH
MORE BLACK BONDS //FOG-BLADES?!
MORE MAGIC WEAPONS!
BUT...
FWAM
...AMON'S FLAME CAN DISPEL ANY FOG!!

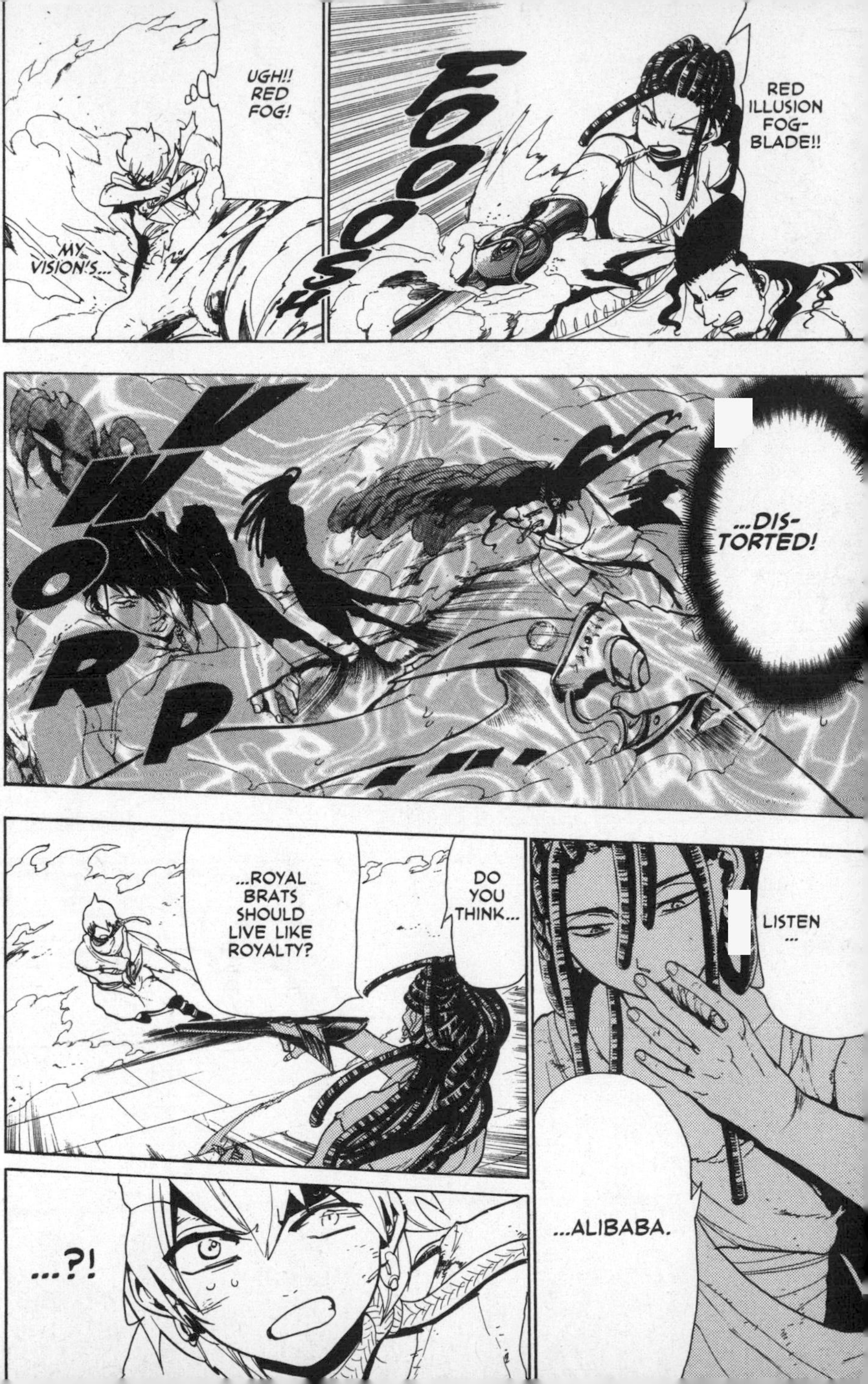
RED ILLUSION FOG-BLADE!!
FOOOOSH
UGH!! RED FOG!
MY VISION'S...
...DIS-TORTED!
WORP...
LISTEN...
...ALIBABA.
DO YOU THINK...
...ROYAL BRATS SHOULD LIVE LIKE ROYALTY?
...?!

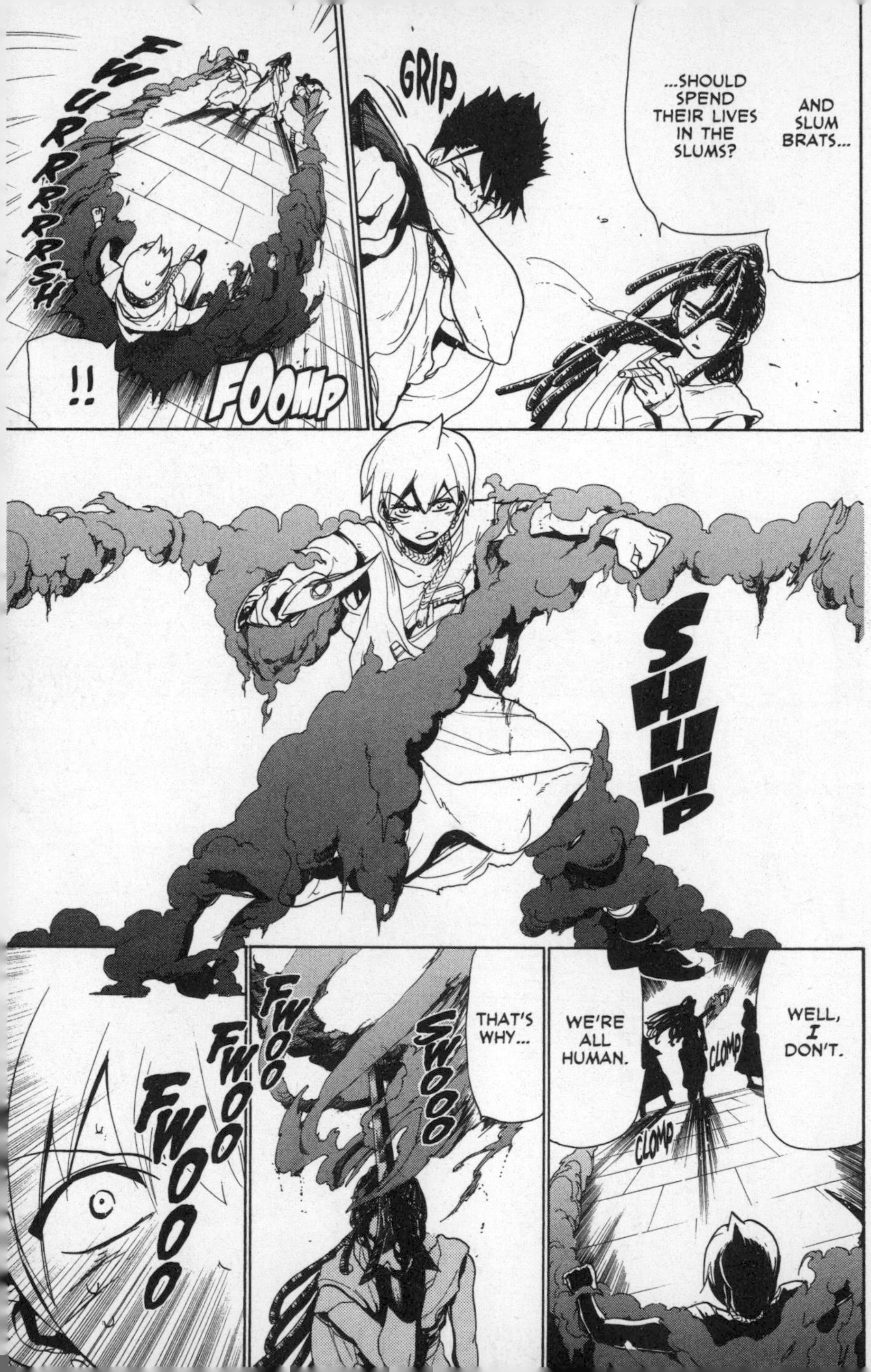
AND SLUM BRATS...
...SHOULD SPEND THEIR LIVES IN THE SLUMS?
GRIP
FWURRRRRSH
!!
FOOMP
SHUMP
WELL, I DON'T.
CLOMP
CLOMP
WE'RE ALL HUMAN.
THAT'S WHY...
SWOOO
FWOOO
FWOOO
FWOOOOO

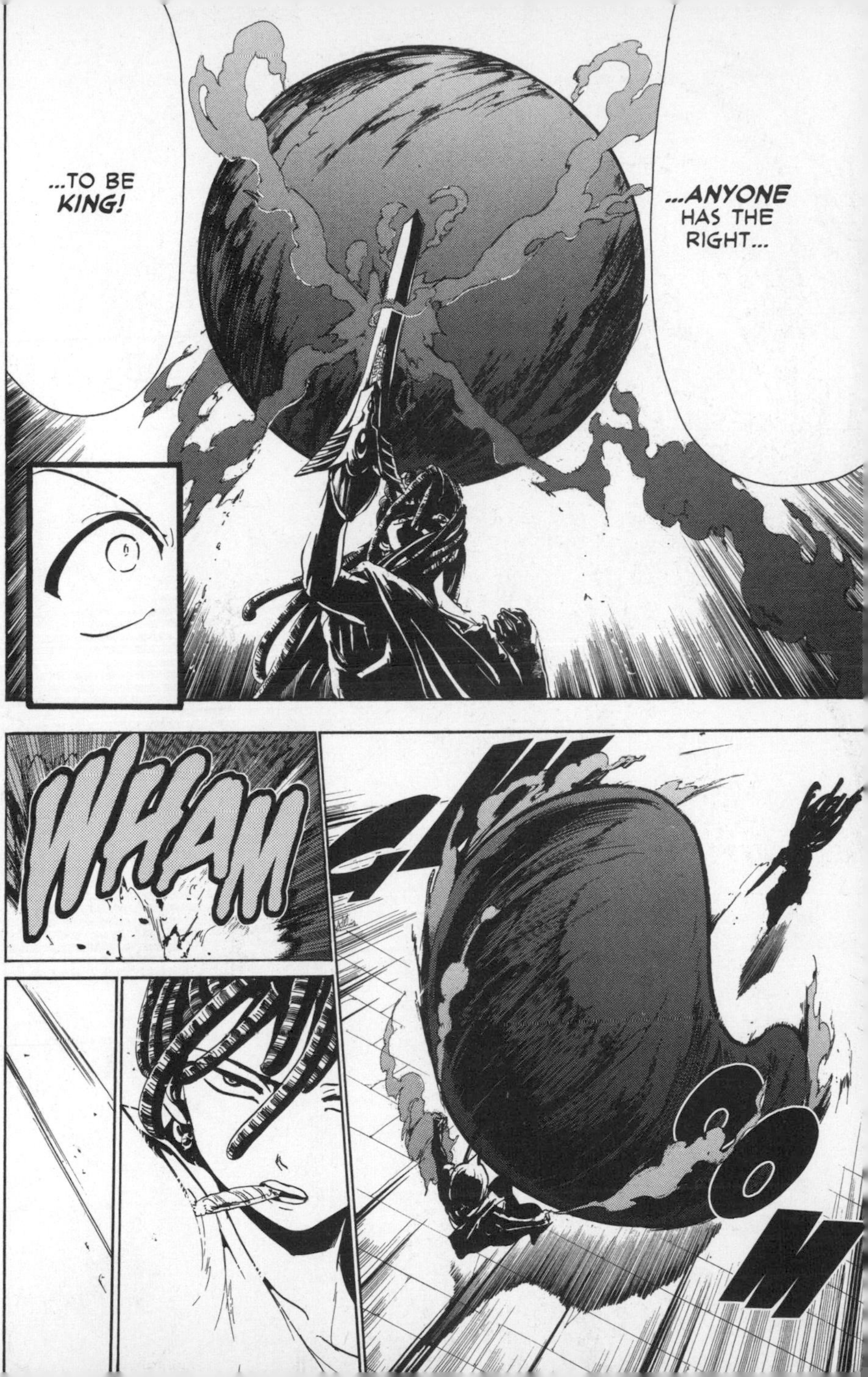
...ANYONE HAS THE RIGHT...
...TO BE KING!
WHAM

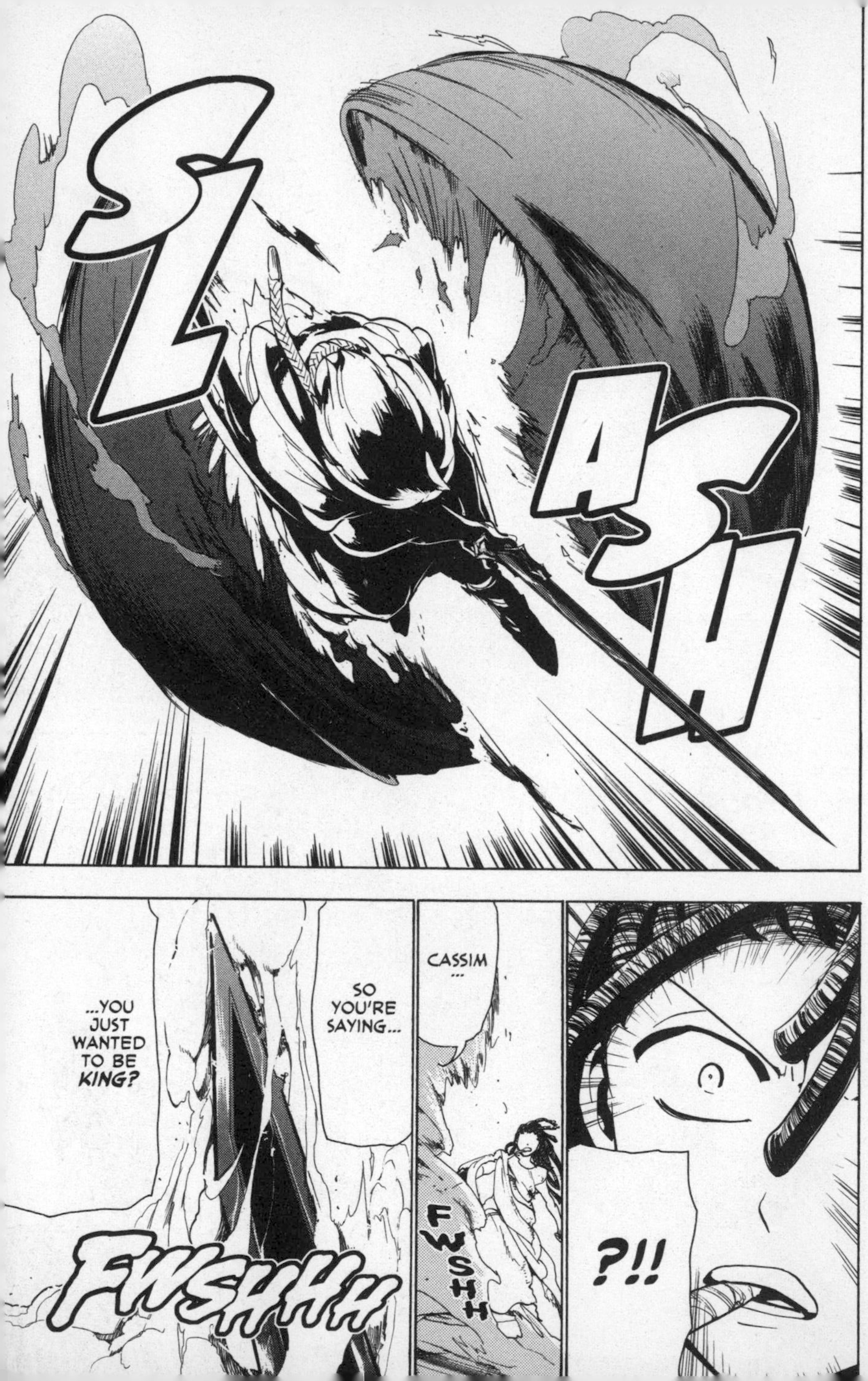
SLASH
?!!
CASSIM...
FWSHH
SO YOU'RE SAYING...
...YOU JUST WANTED TO BE KING?
FWSHHH

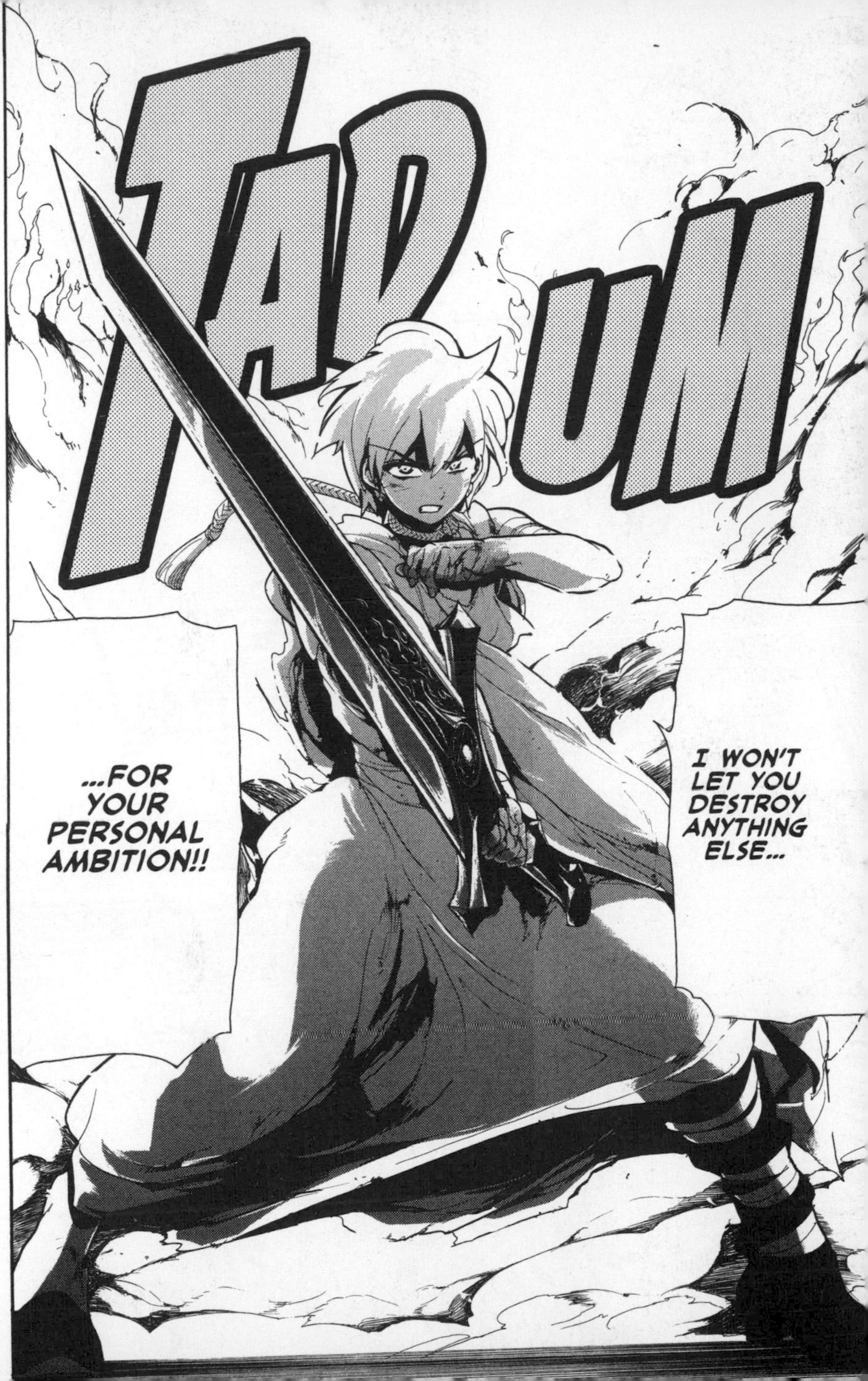
TADUM
I WON'T LET YOU DESTROY ANYTHING ELSE...
...FOR YOUR PERSONAL AMBITION!!

Night 68: Djinn of Black Rukh

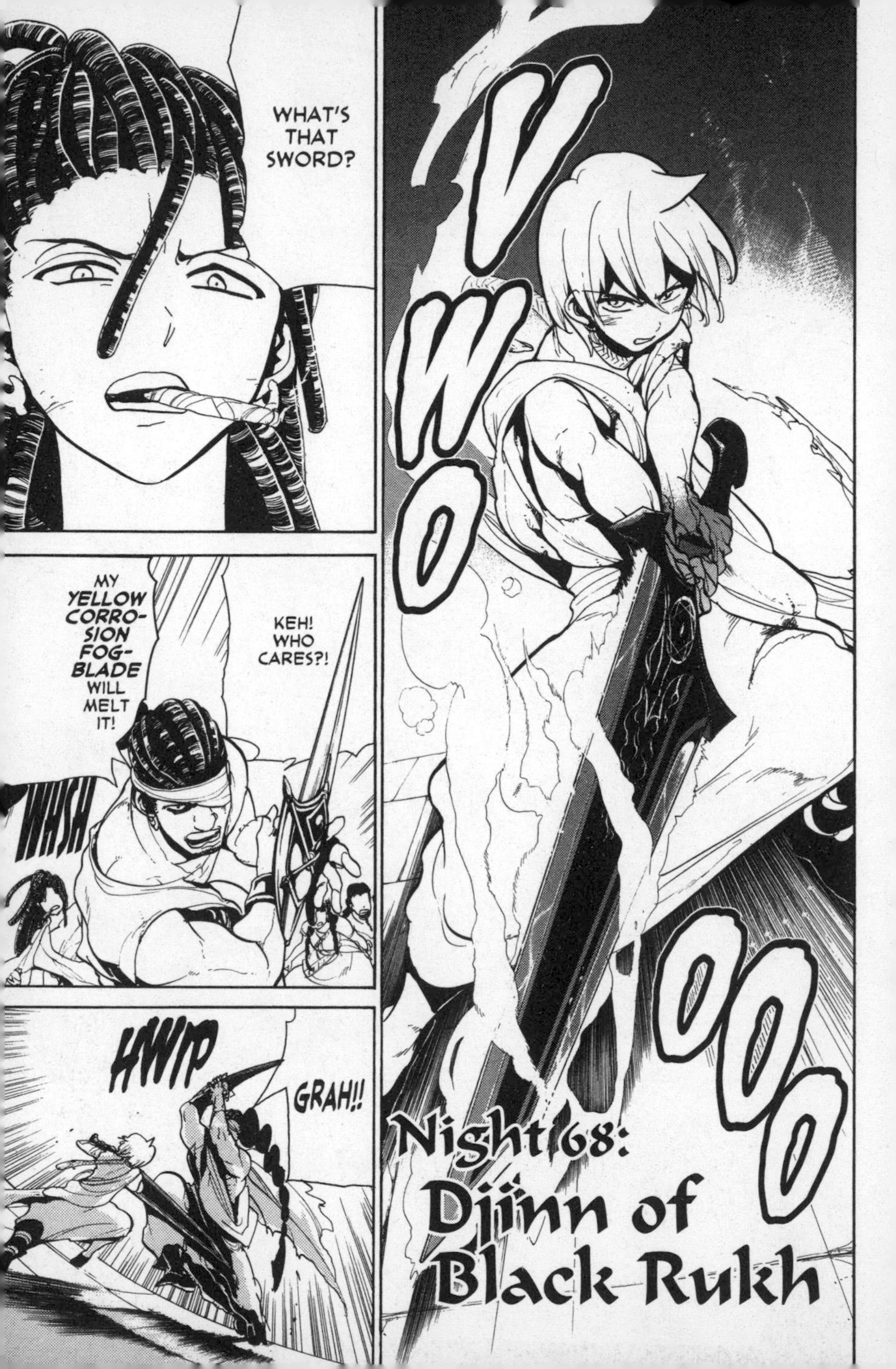
WOOOOOOO
WHAT'S THAT SWORD?
MY YELLOW CORROSION FOG-BLADE WILL MELT IT!
KEH! WHO CARES?!
WHSH
HWIP
GRAH!!

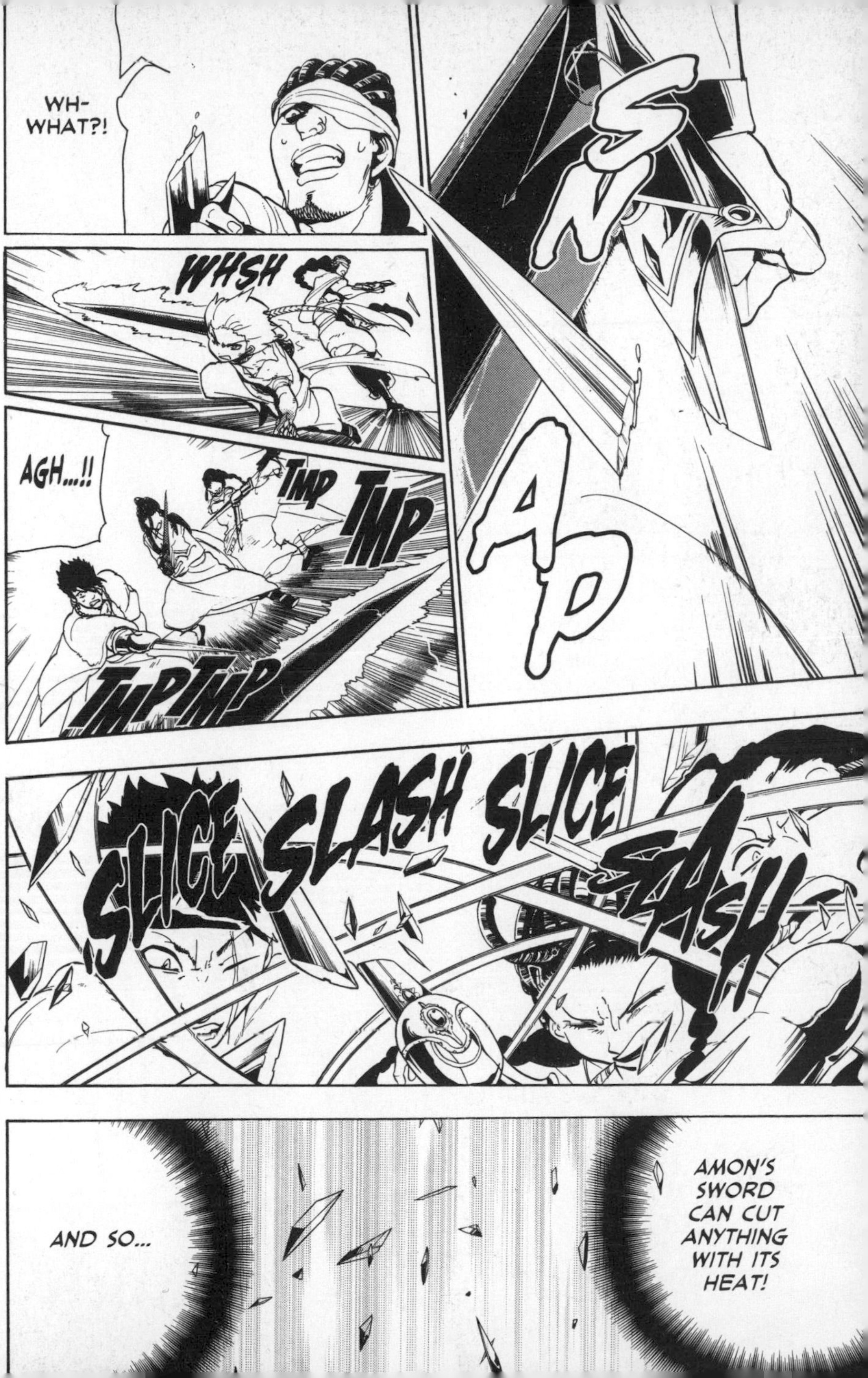
SNAP
WH-
WHAT?!
WHSH
TMP TMP
AGH...!!
TMPTMP
SLICE SLASH SLICE SLASH
AMON'S SWORD CAN CUT ANYTHING WITH ITS HEAT!
AND SO...

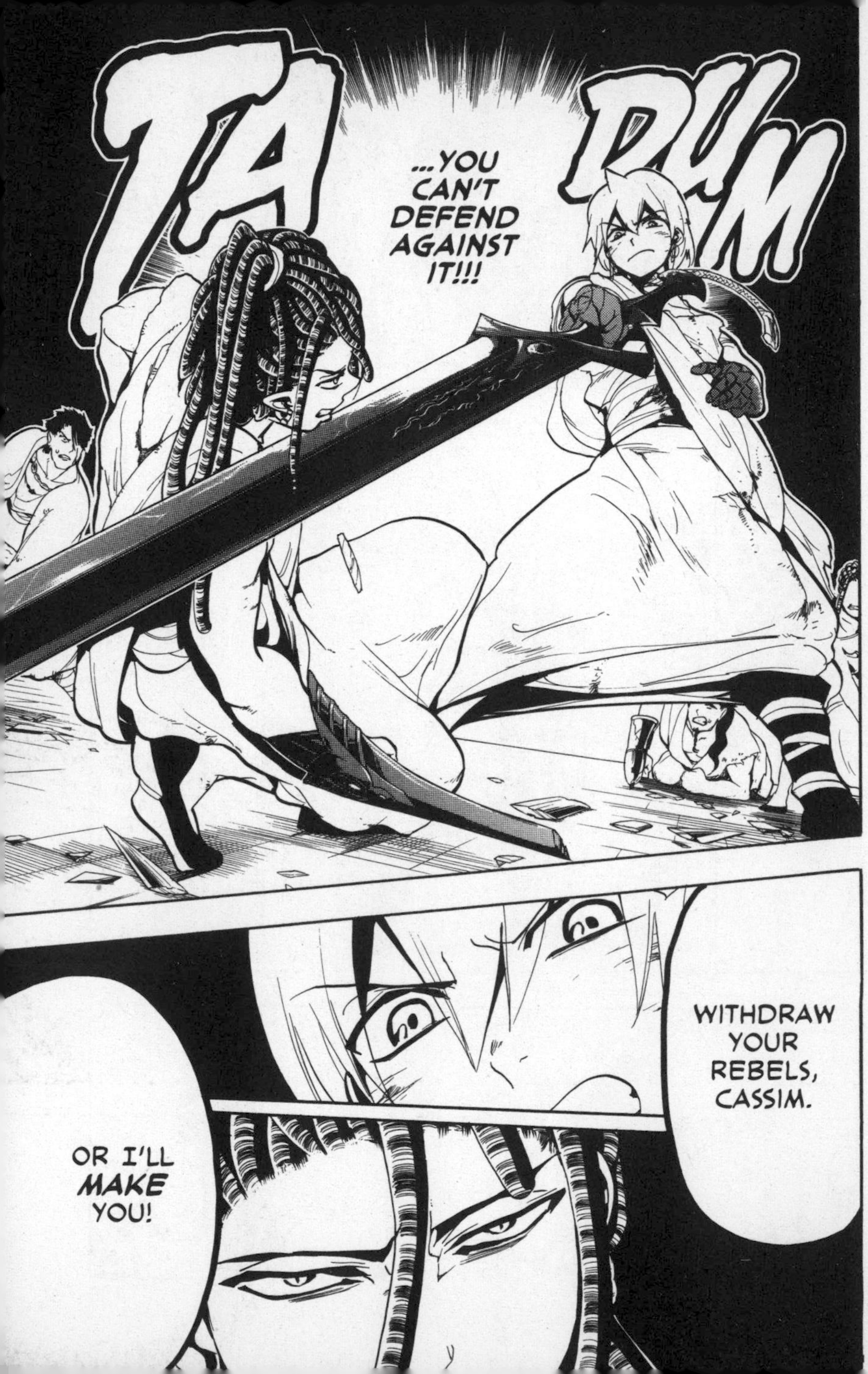
TA
DUM
...YOU CAN'T DEFEND AGAINST IT!!!
WITHDRAW YOUR REBELS, CASSIM.
OR I'LL *MAKE* YOU!

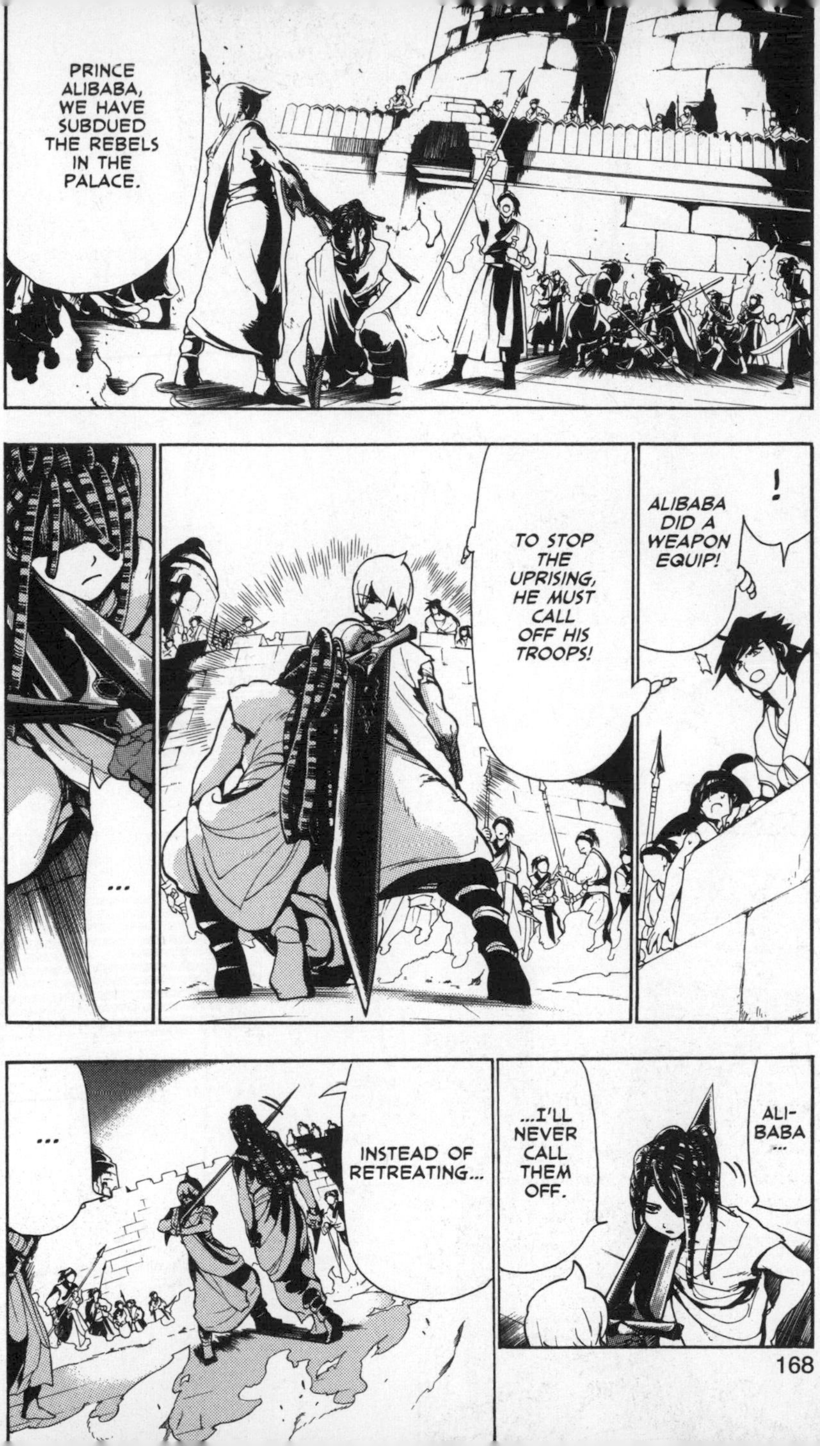
PRINCE ALIBABA, WE HAVE SUBDUED THE REBELS IN THE PALACE.
!
ALIBABA DID A WEAPON EQUIP!
TO STOP THE UPRISING, HE MUST CALL OFF HIS TROOPS!
...
ALI-BABA ...
...I'LL NEVER CALL THEM OFF.
INSTEAD OF RETREATING...
...

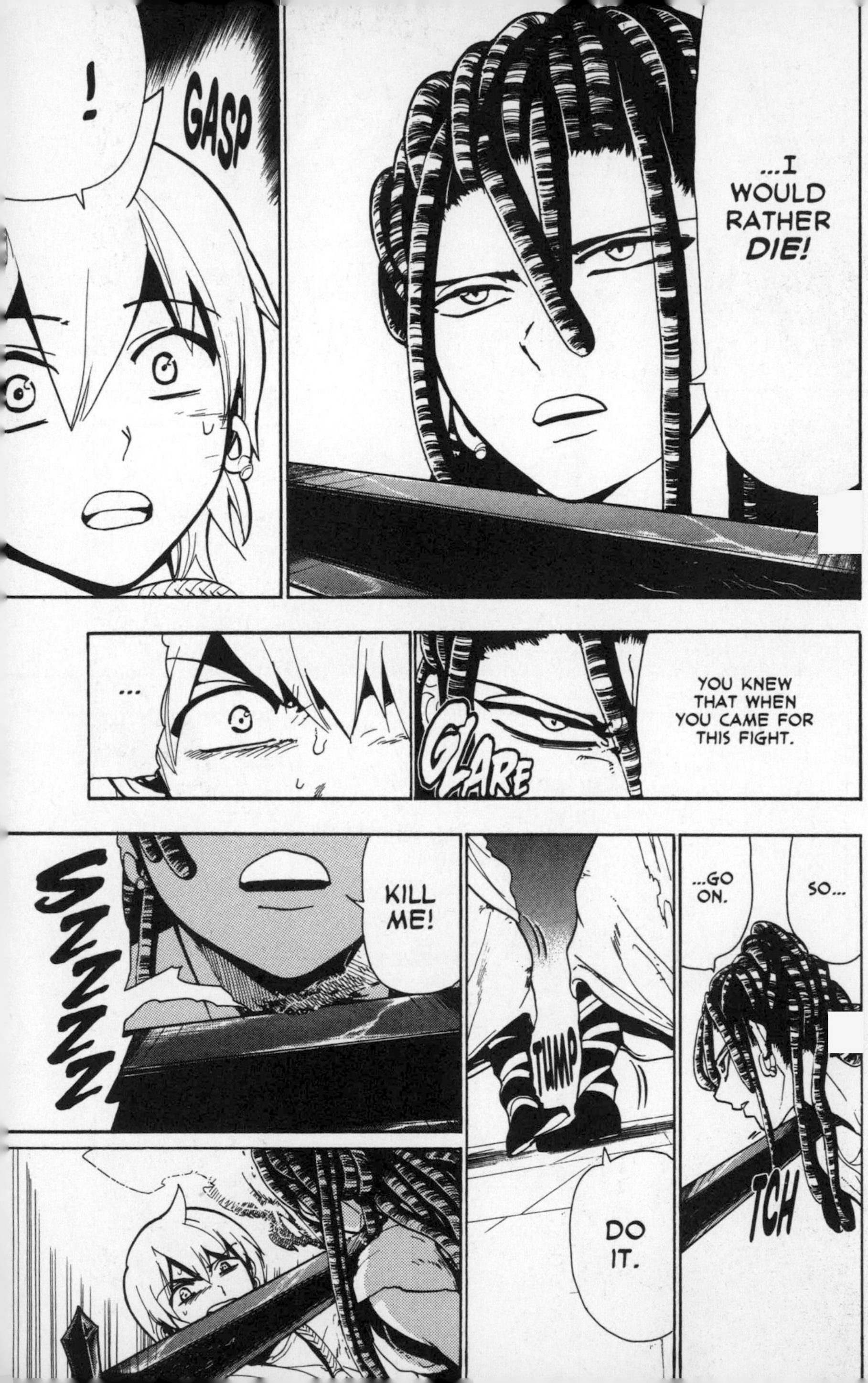
...I WOULD RATHER DIE!
!
GASP
YOU KNEW THAT WHEN YOU CAME FOR THIS FIGHT.
GLARE
...
SO...
...GO ON.
TCH
TUMP
DO IT.
KILL ME!
SZZZZZ

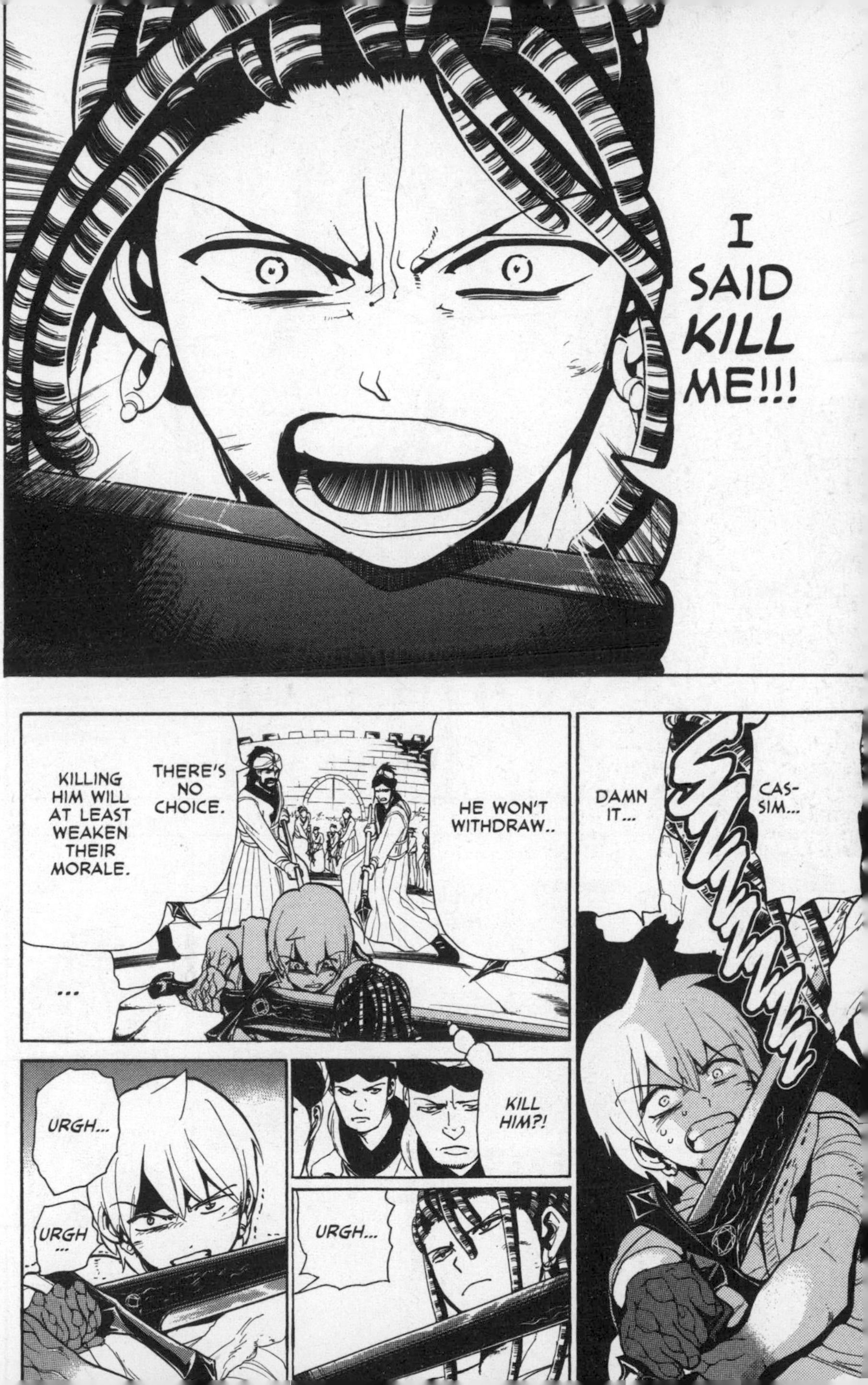
I SAID KILL ME!!!
CAS-SIM...
DAMN IT...
HE WON'T WITHDRAW..
THERE'S NO CHOICE.
KILLING HIM WILL AT LEAST WEAKEN THEIR MORALE.
...
KILL HIM?!
URGH...
URGH...
URGH ...

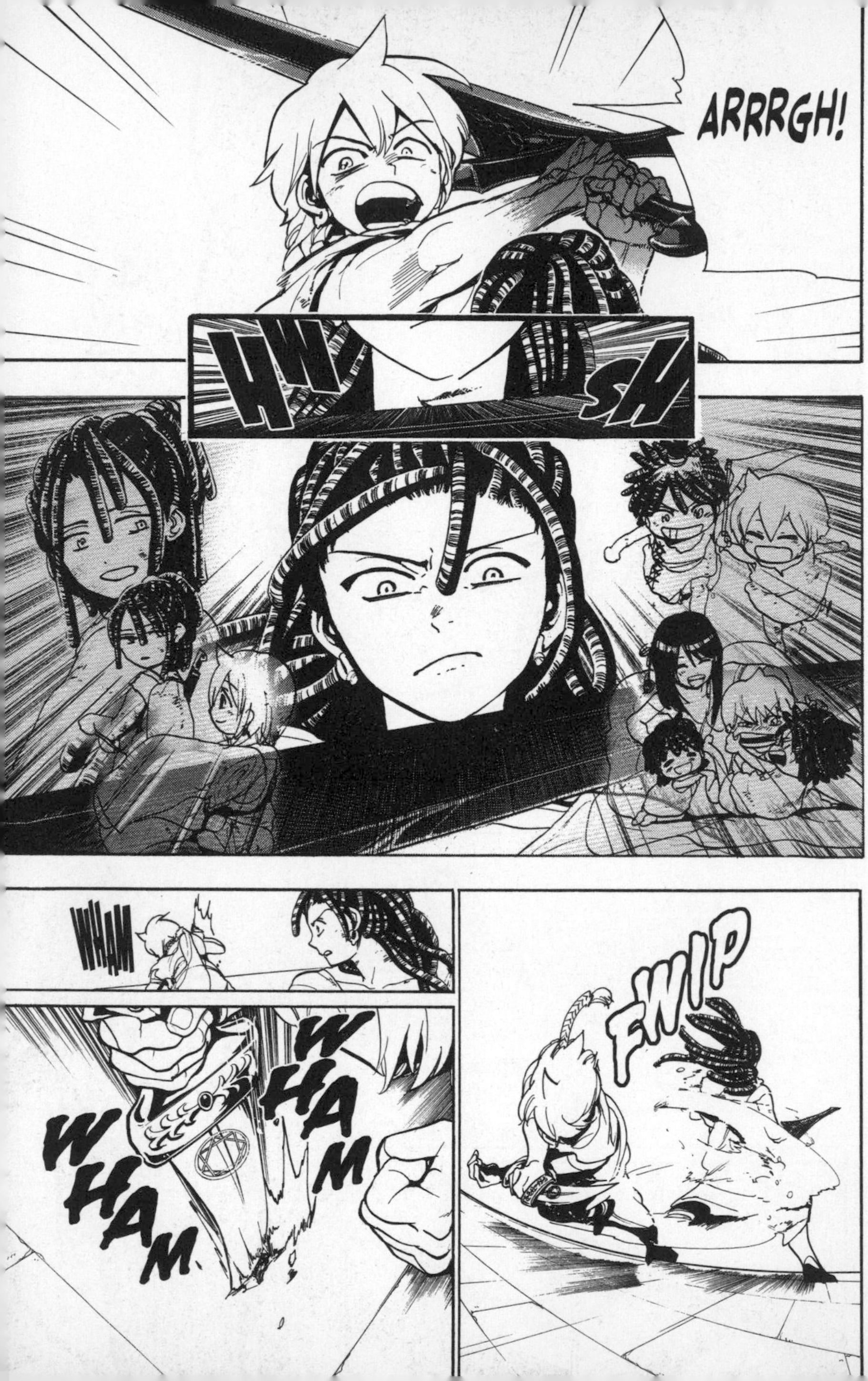
ARRRGH!
HWSH
FWIP
WHAM
WHAM
WHAM
WHAM.

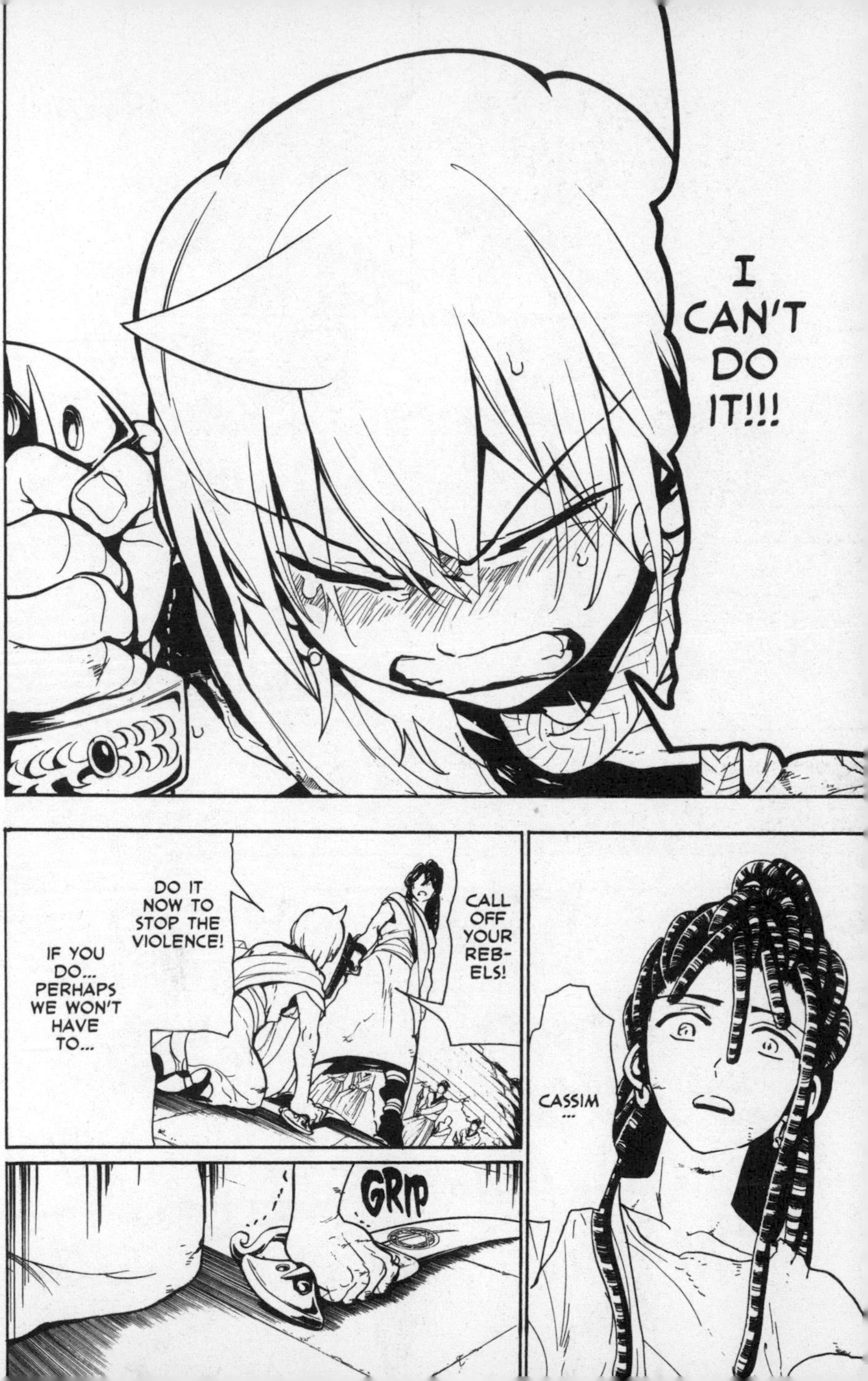
I CAN'T DO IT!!!
CASSIM...
CALL OFF YOUR REBELS!
DO IT NOW TO STOP THE VIOLENCE!
IF YOU DO... PERHAPS WE WON'T HAVE TO...
GRIP

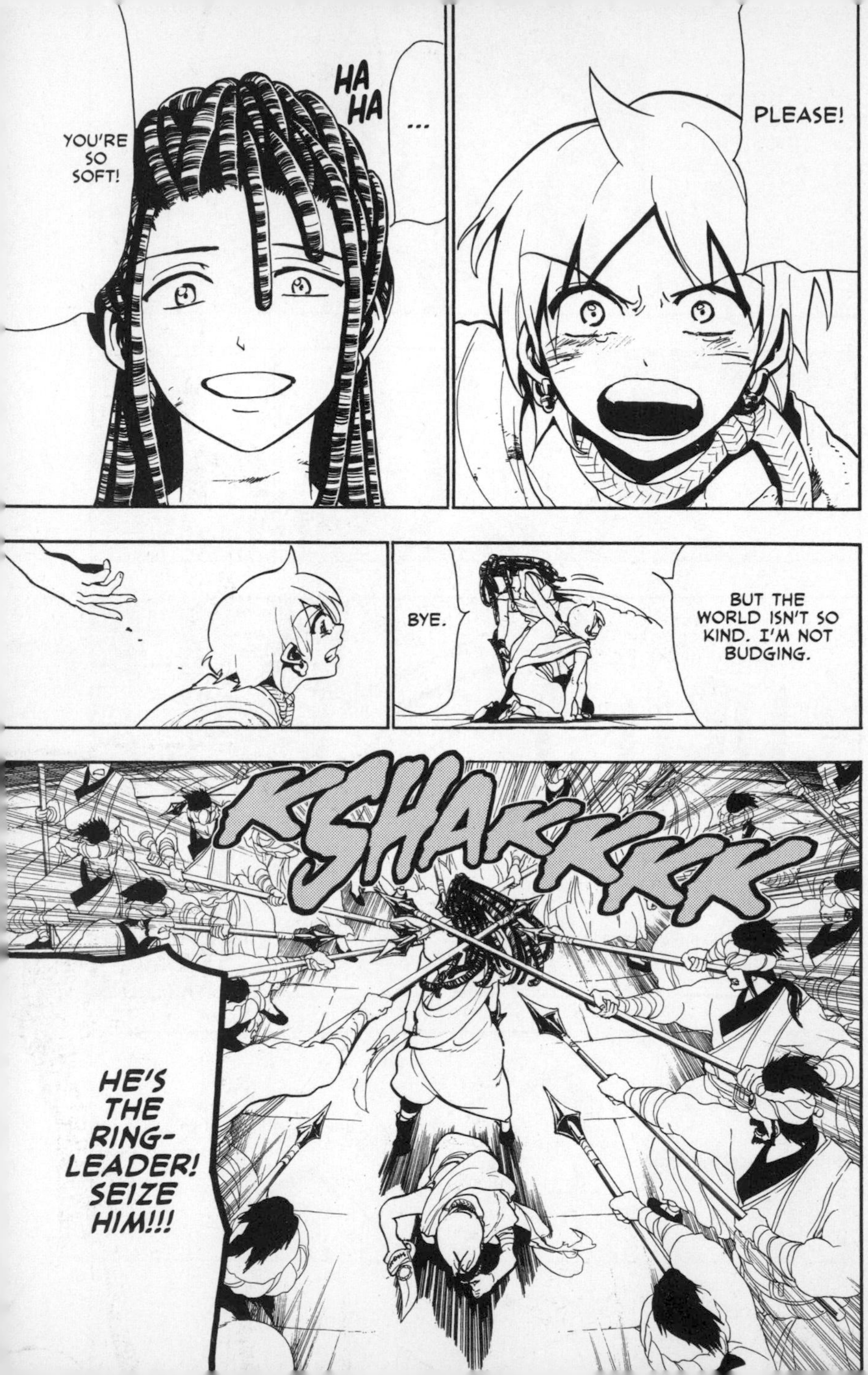
PLEASE!
...
HA HA
YOU'RE SO SOFT!
BUT THE WORLD ISN'T SO KIND. I'M NOT BUDGING.
BYE.
KSHAKKKK
HE'S THE RING-LEADER! SEIZE HIM!!!

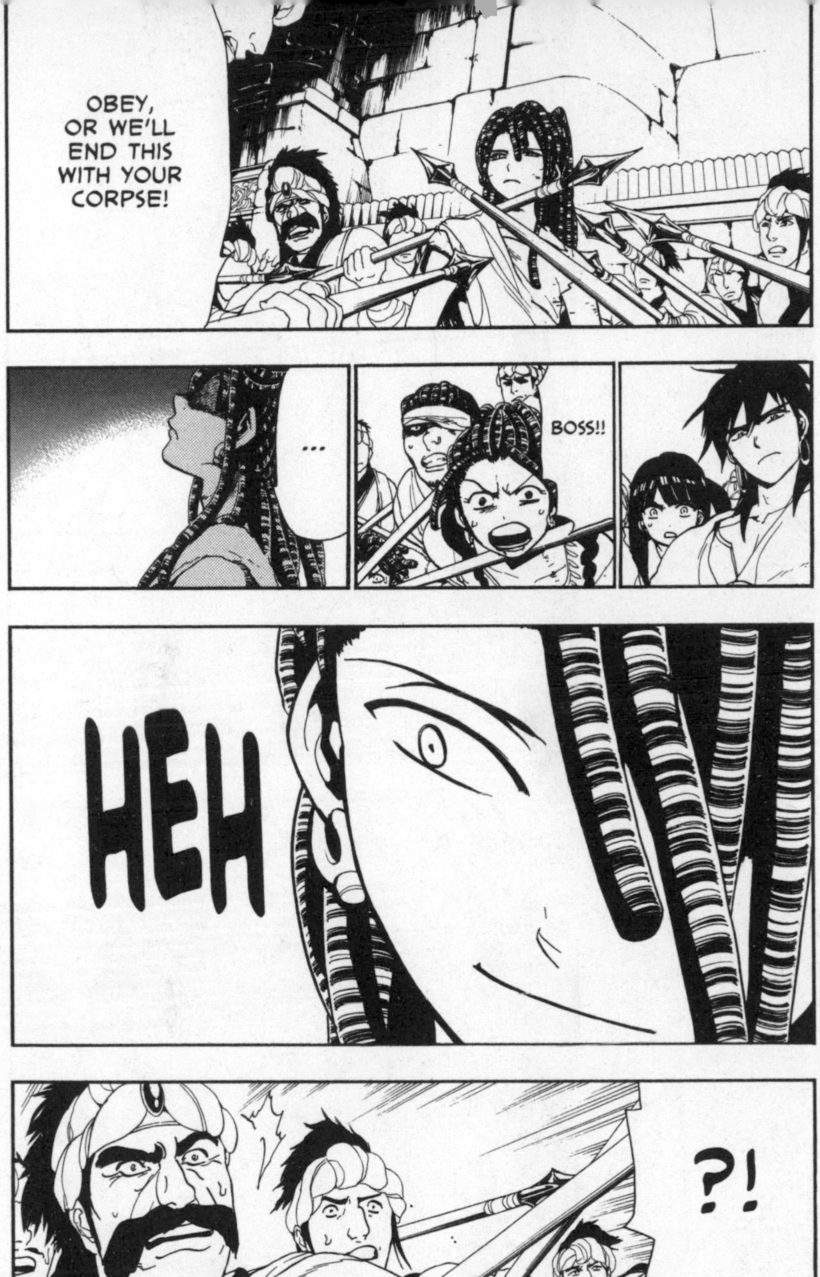
OBEY, OR WE'LL END THIS WITH YOUR CORPSE!
BOSS!!
...
HEH
?!

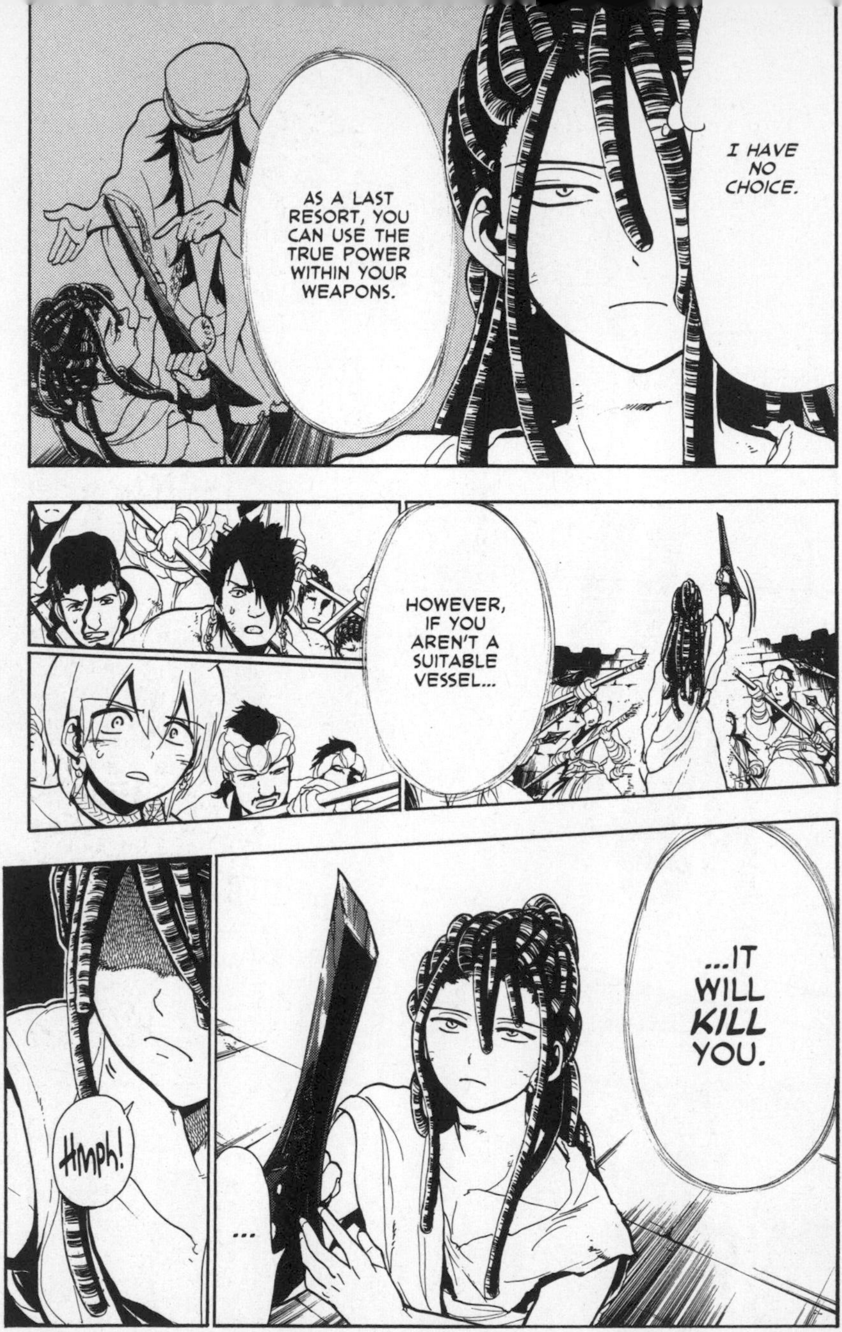
I HAVE NO CHOICE.
AS A LAST RESORT, YOU CAN USE THE TRUE POWER WITHIN YOUR WEAPONS.
HOWEVER, IF YOU AREN'T A SUITABLE VESSEL...
...IT WILL KILL YOU.
...
Hmph!

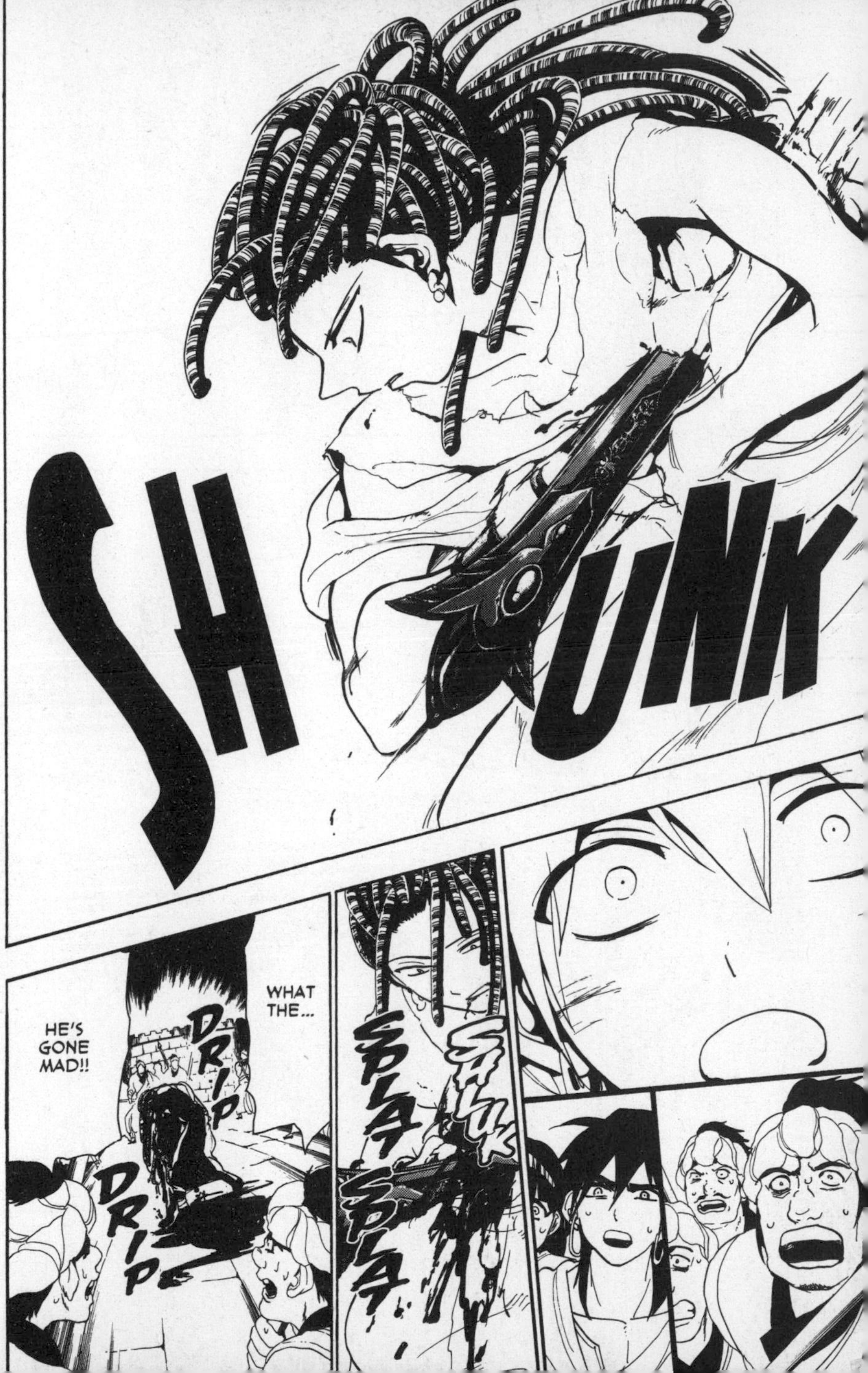
SHUNK
SHLUK
SPLAT SPLAT
WHAT THE...
DRIP DRIP
HE'S GONE MAD!!

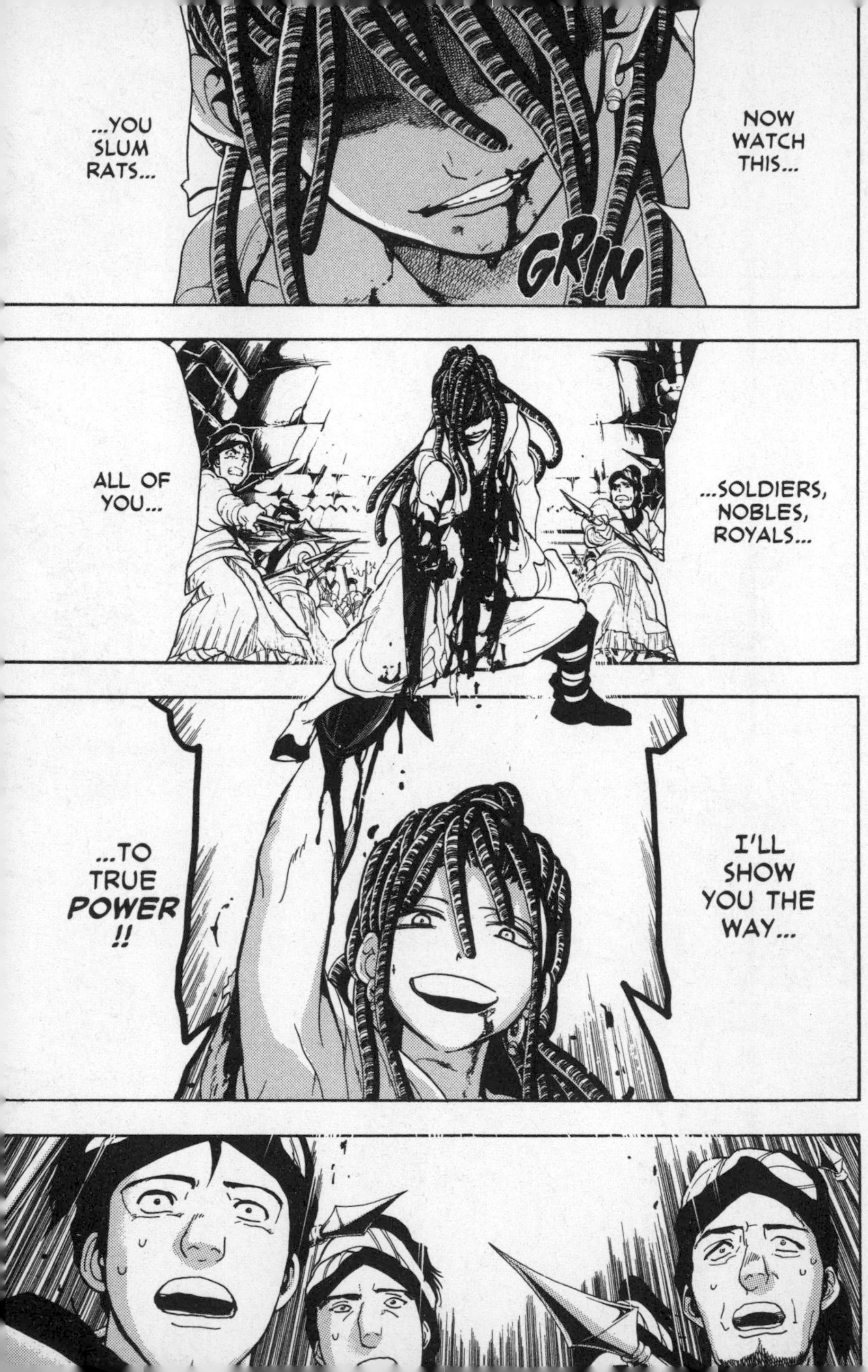
NOW WATCH THIS...
...YOU SLUM RATS...
GRIN
...SOLDIERS, NOBLES, ROYALS...
ALL OF YOU...
I'LL SHOW YOU THE WAY...
...TO TRUE POWER !!

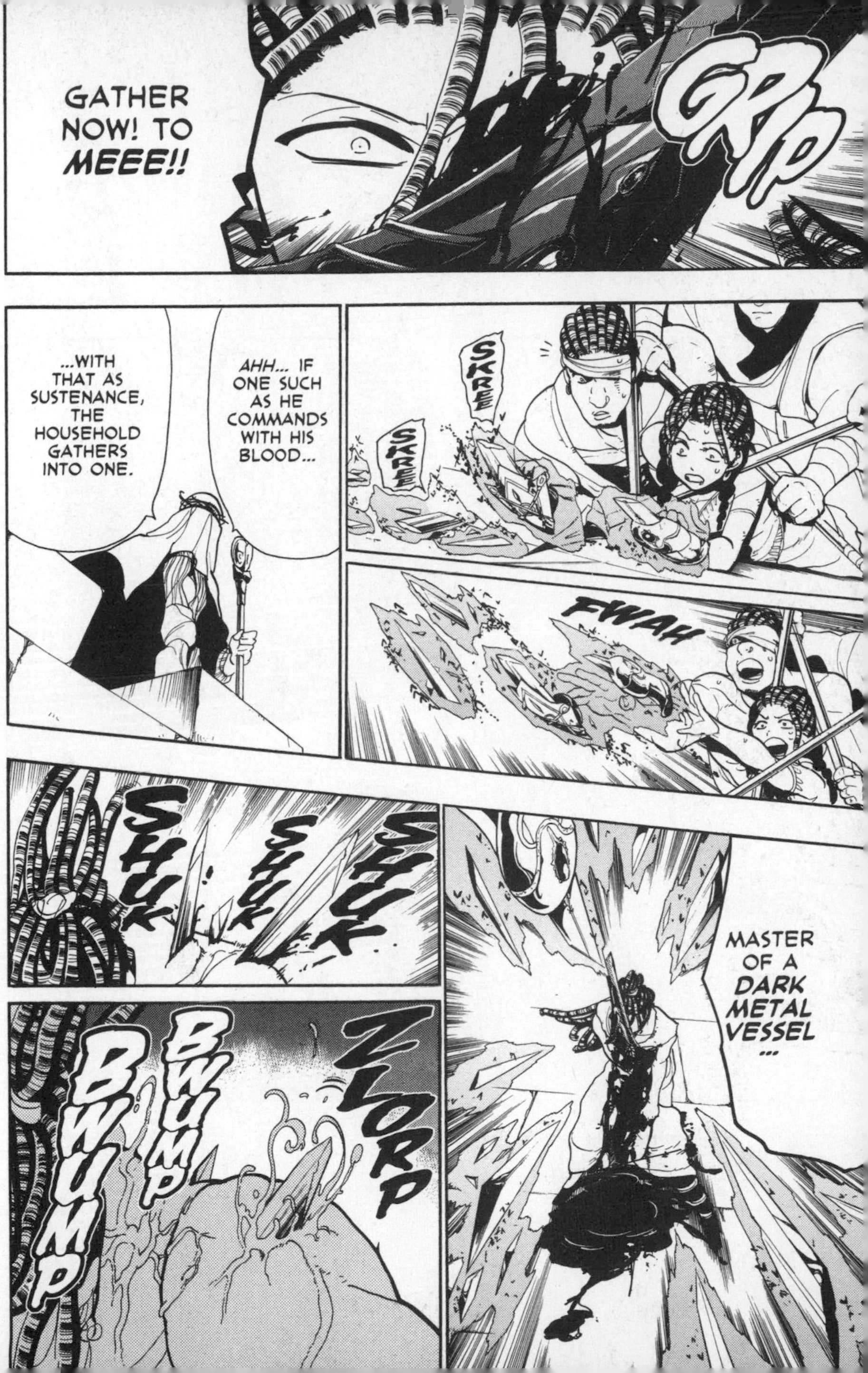
GRIP
GATHER NOW! TO MEEE!!
SKREE
SKREE
FWAH
AHH... IF ONE SUCH AS HE COMMANDS WITH HIS BLOOD...
...WITH THAT AS SUSTENANCE, THE HOUSEHOLD GATHERS INTO ONE.
MASTER OF A DARK METAL VESSEL...
SHUK
SHUK
SHUK
ZLORP
BWUMP
BWUMP

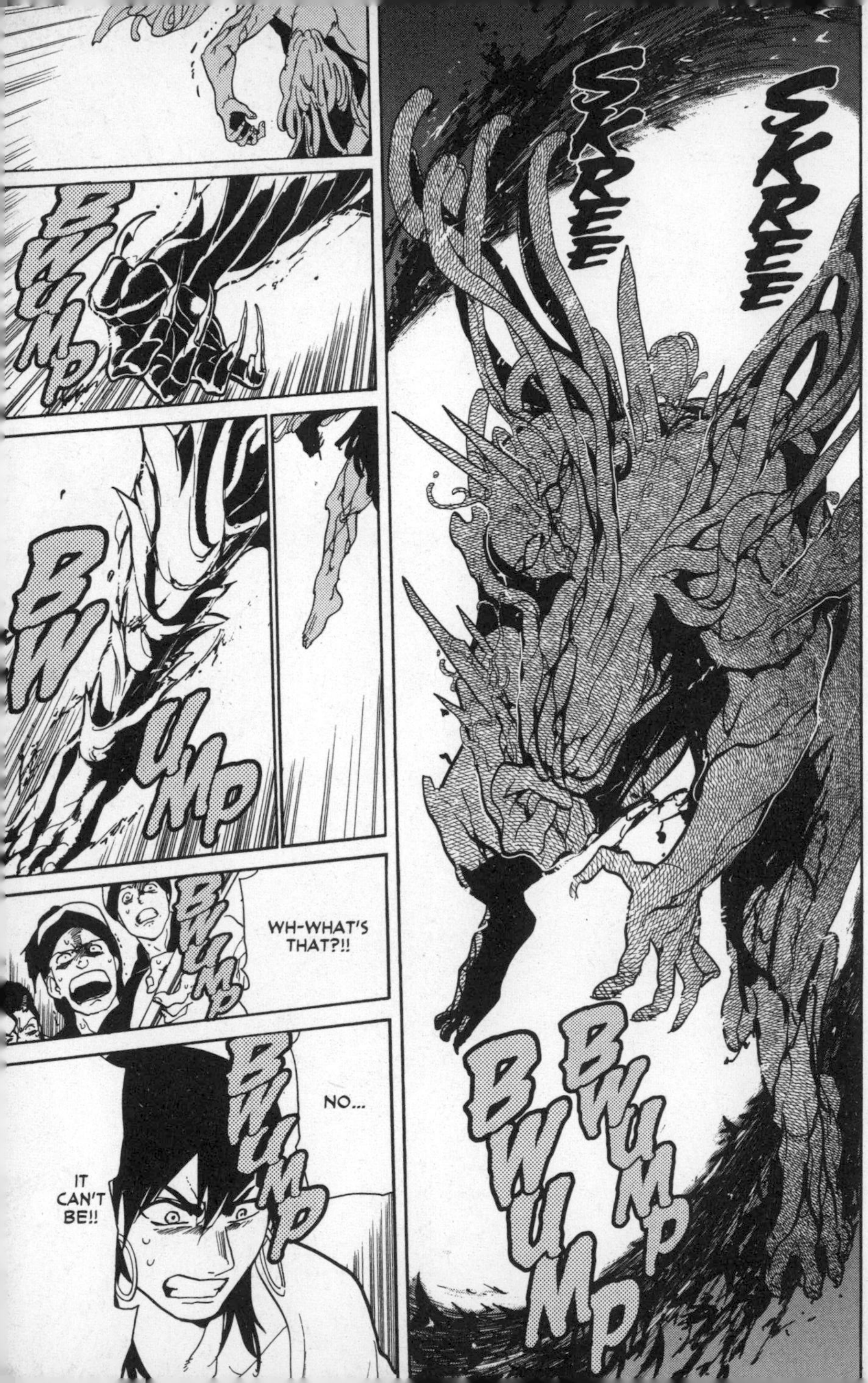
SKREE
SKREE
BWUMP
BWUMP
BWUMP
BWUMP
WH-WHAT'S THAT?!!
BWUMP
NO...
IT CAN'T BE!!
BWUMP

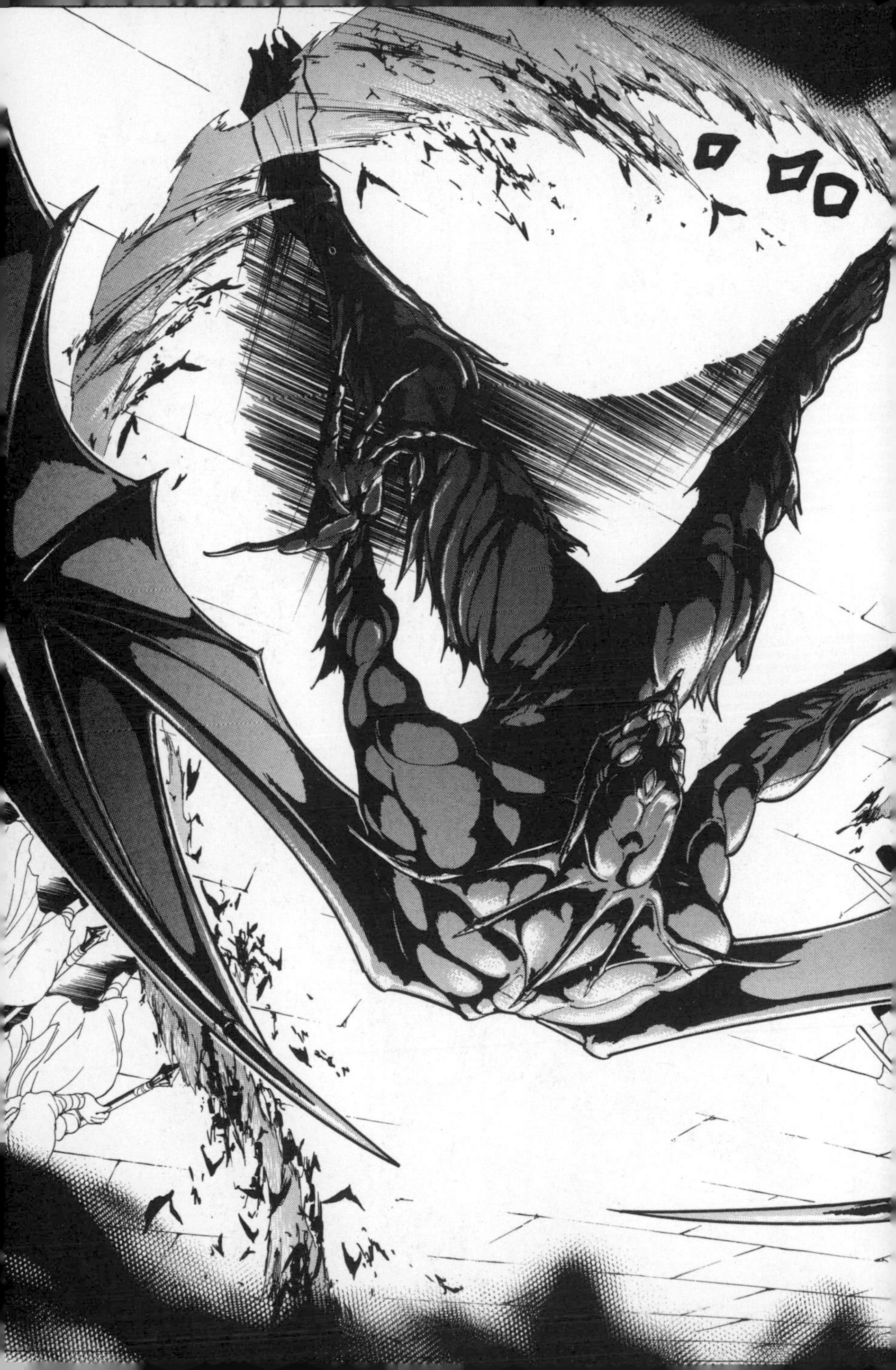

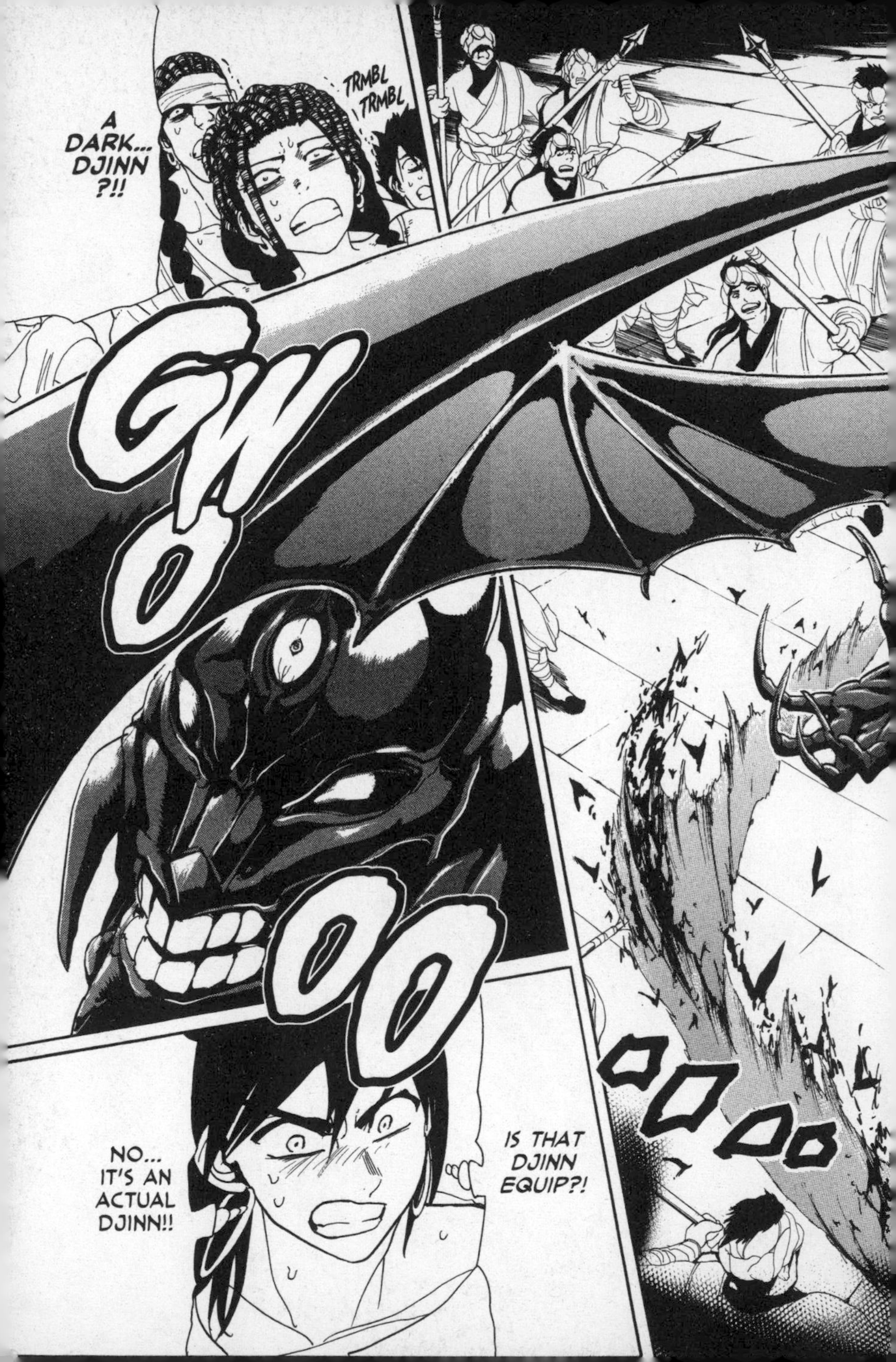
TRMBL TRMBL
A DARK... DJINN?!!
GWOOOO
OOOO
IS THAT DJINN EQUIP?!
NO... IT'S AN ACTUAL DJINN!!

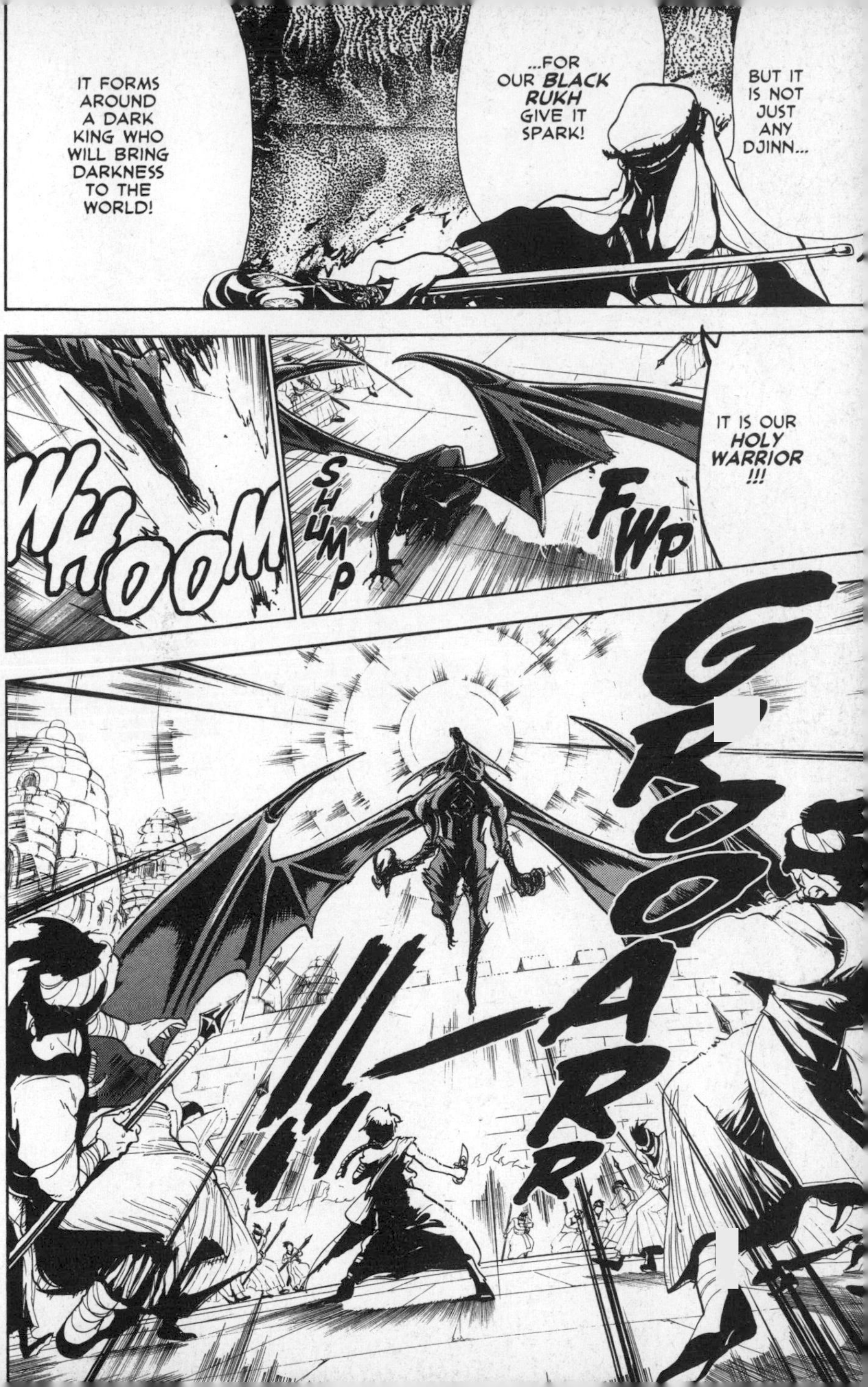
BUT IT IS NOT JUST ANY DJINN...
...FOR OUR BLACK RUKH GIVE IT SPARK!
IT FORMS AROUND A DARK KING WHO WILL BRING DARKNESS TO THE WORLD!
IT IS OUR HOLY WARRIOR!!!
FWP
SHUMP
WHOOM
GROOAARR

MAGI
The labyrinth of magic

7

Staff

■ Story & Art
Shinobu Ohtaka
Shinobu Ohtaka

■ Regular Assistants
Matsubara
Matsubara
Miho Isshiki
Miho Isshiki
Akira Sugito
Akira Sugito
Tanimoto
Tanimoto
Yamada
Yamada

■ Editor
Kazuaki Ishibashi
Kazuaki Ishibashi

■ Sales & Promotion
Shinichirou Todaka
Shinichirou Todaka
Tsunato Imamoto
Tsunato Imamoto

■ Designer
Yasuo Shimura + Bay Bridge Studio
Yasuo Shimura + Bay Bridge Studio

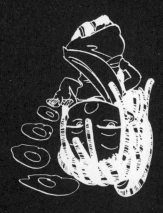

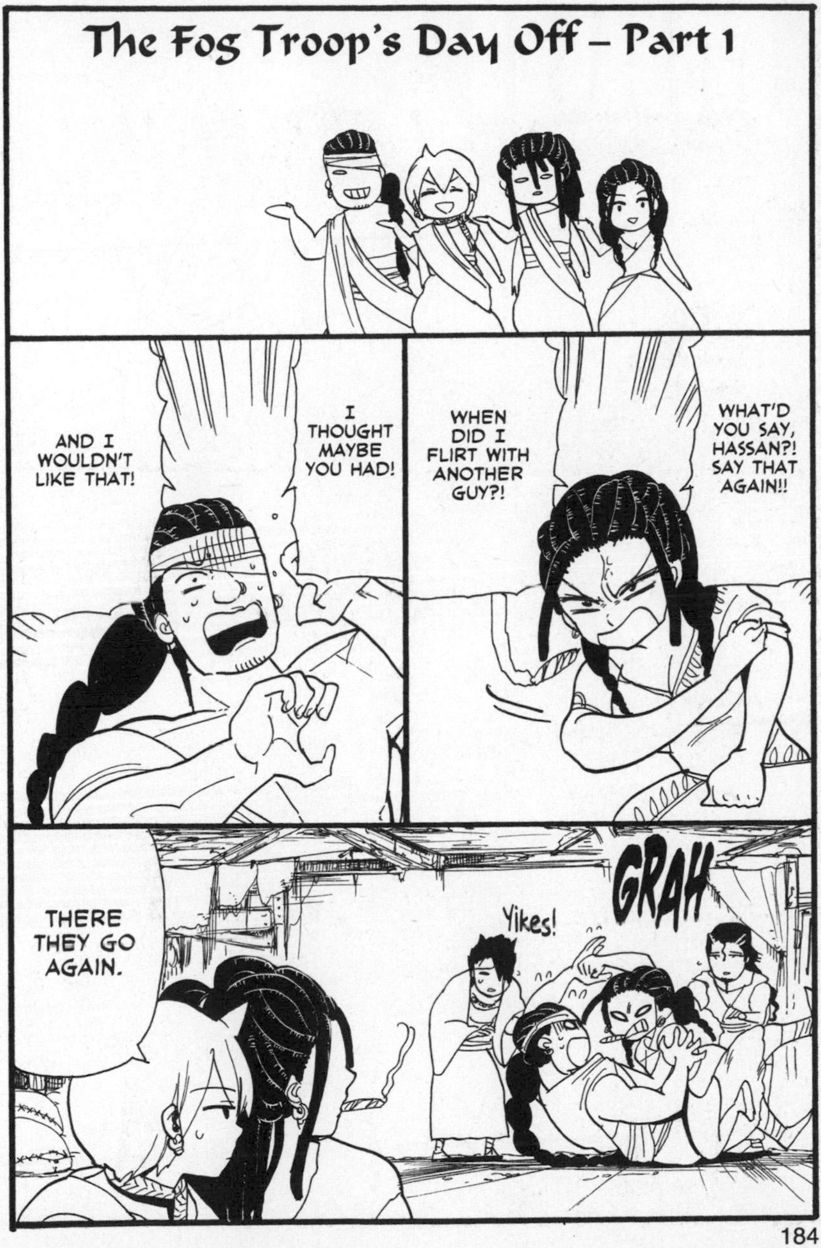
The Fog Troop's Day Off – Part 1
WHAT'D YOU SAY, HASSAN?! SAY THAT AGAIN!!
WHEN DID I FLIRT WITH ANOTHER GUY?!
I THOUGHT MAYBE YOU HAD!
AND I WOULDN'T LIKE THAT!
GRAH
Yikes!
THERE THEY GO AGAIN.

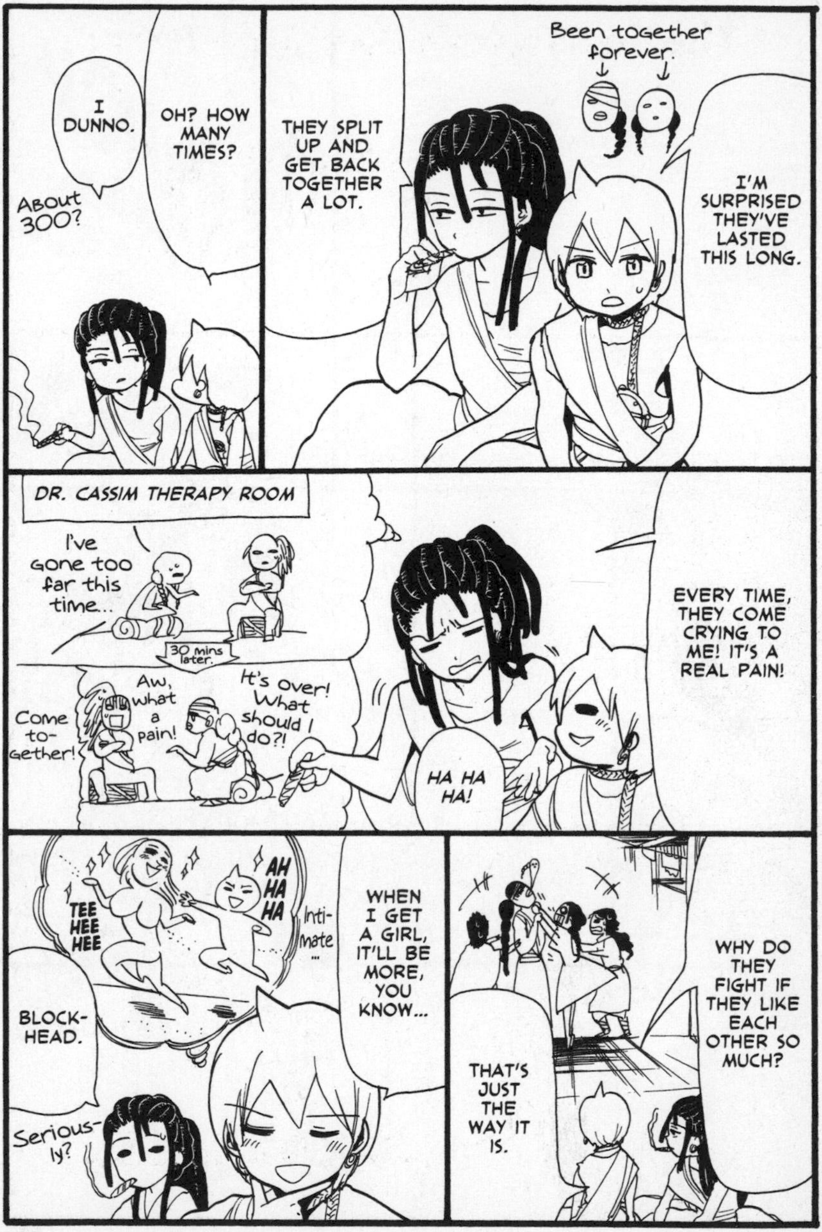
I'M SURPRISED THEY'VE LASTED THIS LONG.
Been together forever.
THEY SPLIT UP AND GET BACK TOGETHER A LOT.
OH? HOW MANY TIMES?
I DUNNO.
About 300?
EVERY TIME, THEY COME CRYING TO ME! IT'S A REAL PAIN!
HA HA HA!
DR. CASSIM THERAPY ROOM
I've gone too far this time...
30 mins later.
It's over! What should I do?!
Aw, what a pain!
Come to-gether!
WHY DO THEY FIGHT IF THEY LIKE EACH OTHER SO MUCH?
THAT'S JUST THE WAY IT IS.
WHEN I GET A GIRL, IT'LL BE MORE, YOU KNOW...
AH HA HA
Inti-mate...
TEE HEE HEE
BLOCK-HEAD.
Serious-ly?

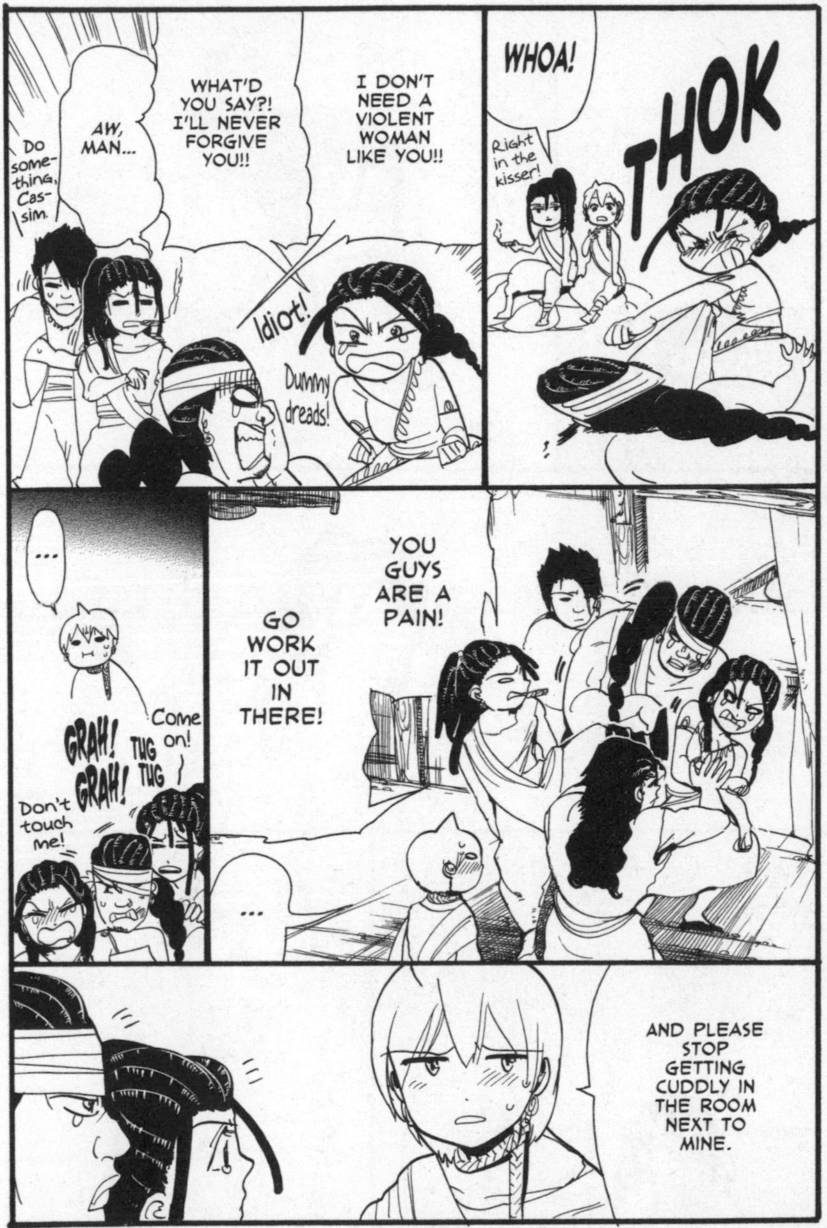
WHOA!
THOK
Right in the kisser!
I DON'T NEED A VIOLENT WOMAN LIKE YOU!!
Idiot!
Dummy dreads!
WHAT'D YOU SAY?! I'LL NEVER FORGIVE YOU!!
AW, MAN...
Do something, Cassim.
YOU GUYS ARE A PAIN!
GO WORK IT OUT IN THERE!
...
...
Come on!
TUG TUG
GRAH! GRAH!
Don't touch me!
AND PLEASE STOP GETTING CUDDLY IN THE ROOM NEXT TO MINE.

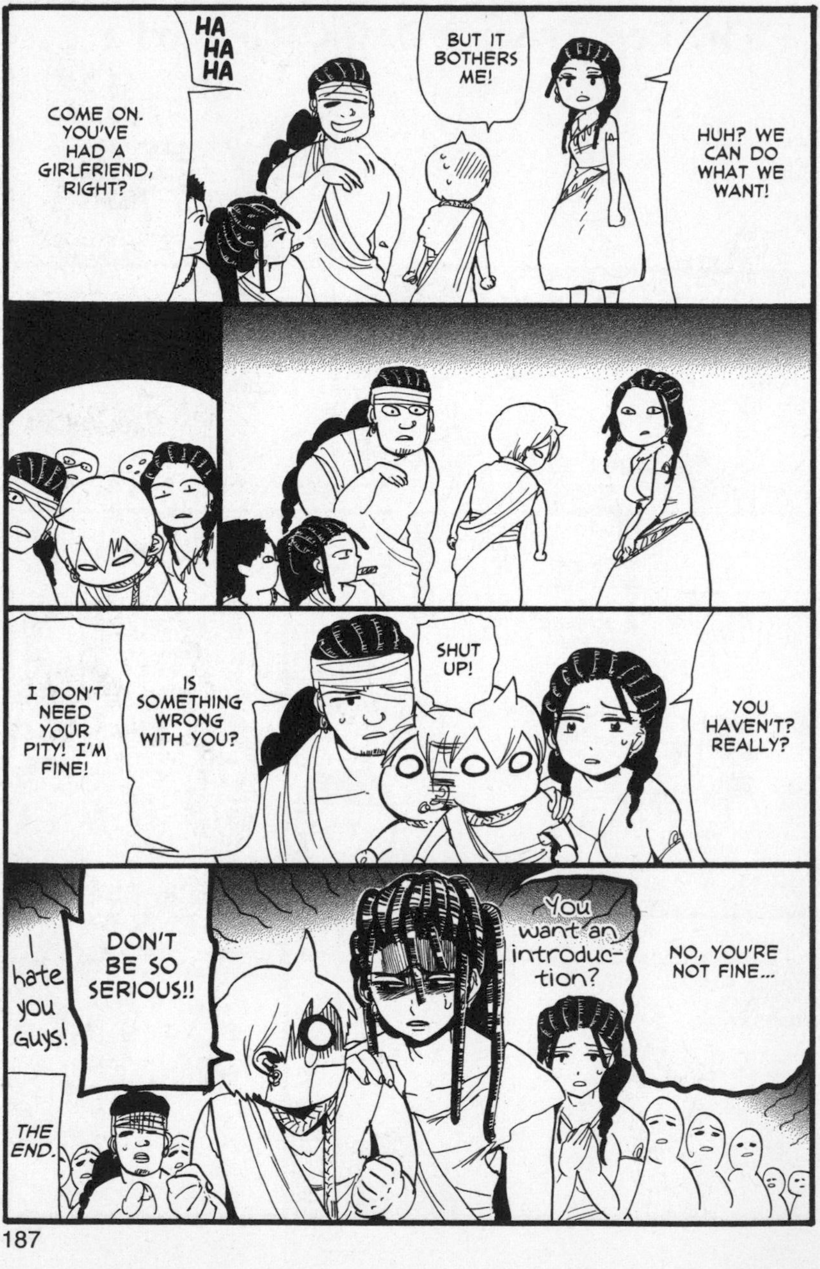
HUH? WE CAN DO WHAT WE WANT!
BUT IT BOTHERS ME!
HA HA HA
COME ON. YOU'VE HAD A GIRLFRIEND, RIGHT?
YOU HAVEN'T? REALLY?
SHUT UP!
IS SOMETHING WRONG WITH YOU?
I DON'T NEED YOUR PITY! I'M FINE!
NO, YOU'RE NOT FINE...
You want an introduc-tion?
DON'T BE SO SERIOUS!!
I hate you guys!
THE END.

The Fog Troop's Day Off – Part 2

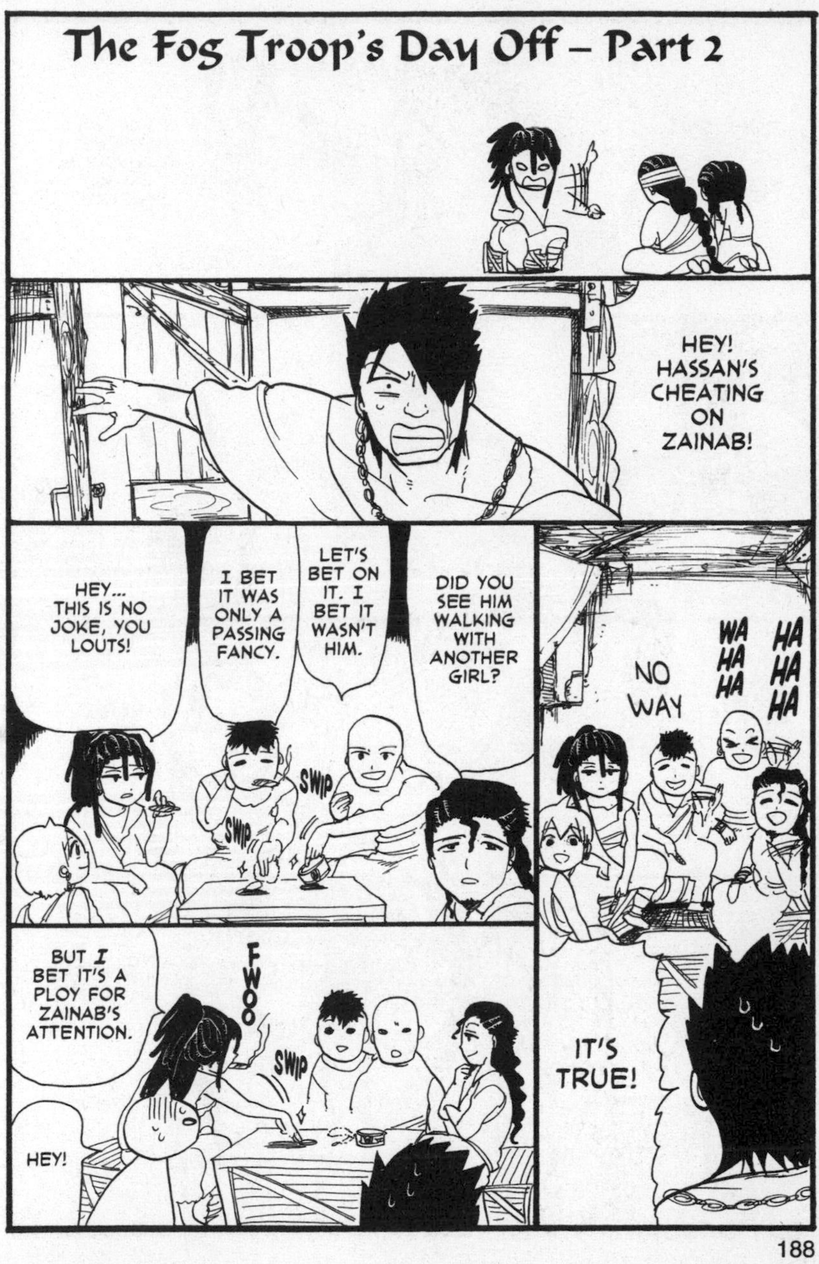
HEY! HASSAN'S CHEATING ON ZAINAB!
HA HA HA
WA HA HA
NO WAY
IT'S TRUE!
DID YOU SEE HIM WALKING WITH ANOTHER GIRL?
LET'S BET ON IT. I BET IT WASN'T HIM.
I BET IT WAS ONLY A PASSING FANCY.
SWIP
SWIP
HEY... THIS IS NO JOKE, YOU LOUTS!
SWIP
FWOO
BUT *I* BET IT'S A PLOY FOR ZAINAB'S ATTENTION.
HEY!

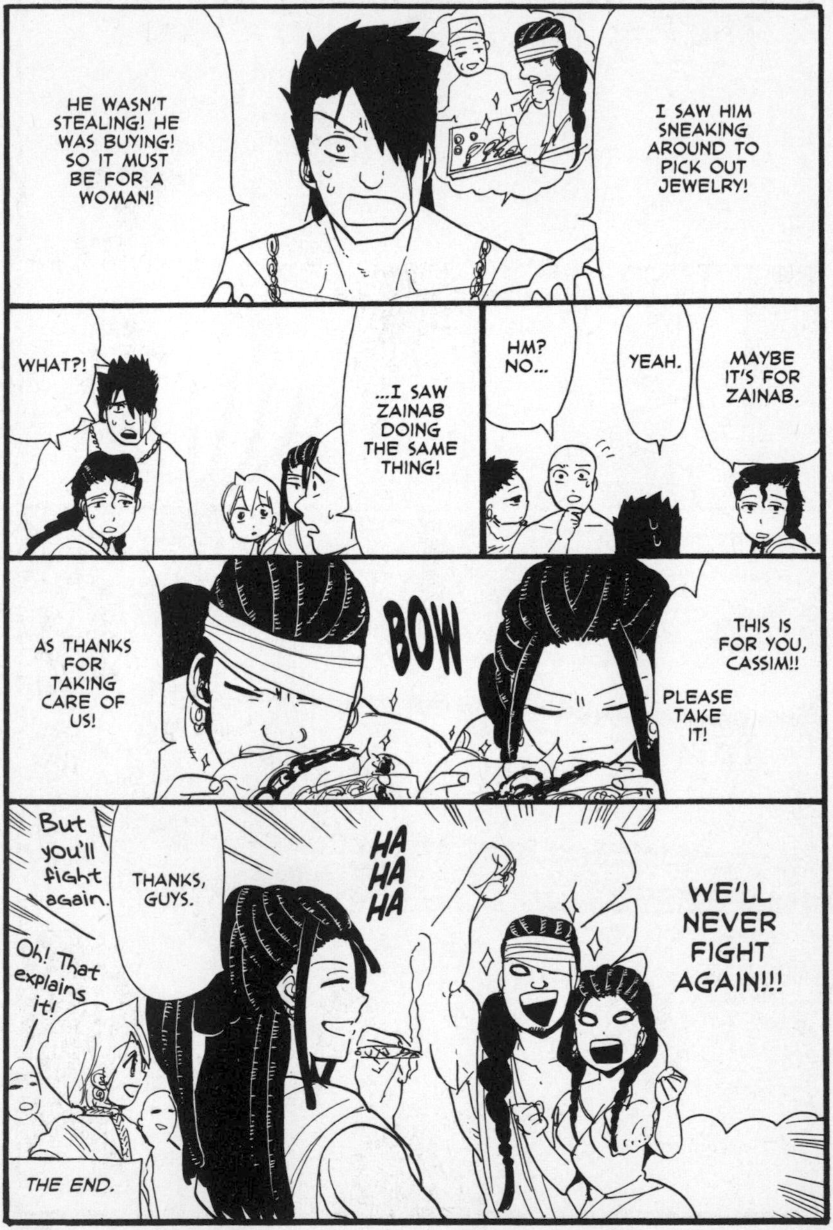
I SAW HIM SNEAKING AROUND TO PICK OUT JEWELRY!
HE WASN'T STEALING! HE WAS BUYING! SO IT MUST BE FOR A WOMAN!
MAYBE IT'S FOR ZAINAB.
YEAH.
HM? NO...
...I SAW ZAINAB DOING THE SAME THING!
WHAT?!
THIS IS FOR YOU, CASSIM!!
PLEASE TAKE IT!
BOW
AS THANKS FOR TAKING CARE OF US!
WE'LL NEVER FIGHT AGAIN!!!
HA HA HA
THANKS, GUYS.
But you'll fight again.
Oh! That explains it!
THE END.

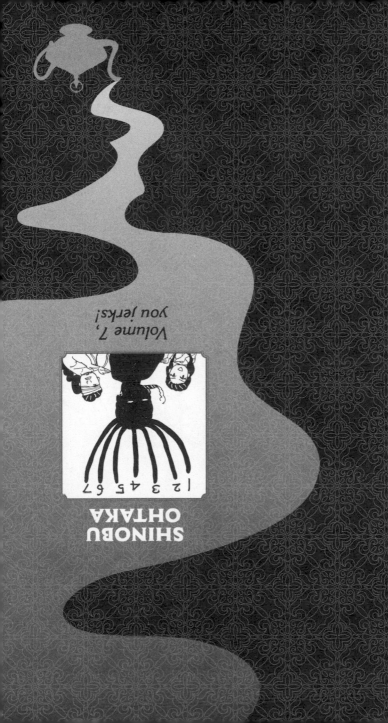

SHINOBU OHTAKA

*Volume 7,
you jerks!*

You're reading the
WRONG WAY

◇◇◇◇◇◇◇◇◇◇◇◇◇◇◇◇◇◇◇◇◇◇◇◇◇◇◇◇◇

MAGI reads from right to left, starting in the upper-right corner. Japanese is read from **right** to **left**, meaning that action, sound effects, and word-balloon order are completely reversed from English order.

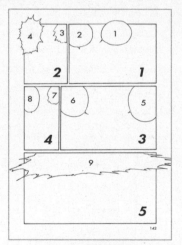

MAGI
Volume 7
Shonen Sunday Edition

Story and Art by
SHINOBU OHTAKA

MAGI Vol.7
by Shinobu OHTAKA
© 2009 Shinobu OHTAKA
All rights reserved.
Original Japanese edition published by SHOGAKUKAN.
English translation rights in the United States of America, Canada, the United Kingdom, Ireland, Australia and New Zealand arranged with SHOGAKUKAN.

Translation & English Adaptation   John Werry

Touch-up Art & Lettering   Stephen Dutro

Editor   Mike Montesa

Printed in the U.S.A.

Published by VIZ Media, LLC
P.O. Box 77010
San Francisco, CA 94107

10 9 8 7 6 5 4 3 2 1
First printing, August 2014

WWW.SHONENSUNDAY.COM

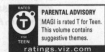

PARENTAL ADVISORY
MAGI is rated T for Teen. This volume contains suggestive themes.
ratings.viz.com

www.viz.com